PASSOVERS OF BLOOD

PASSOVERS OF BLOOD

EUROPEAN JEWS AND RITUAL MURDER

Ariel Toaff

Translated by
Gian Marco Lucchese and Pietro Gianetti

New York, London
CLEMENS & BLAIR, LLC

CLEMENS & BLAIR, LLC

Original Italian text: 2007

English translation: 2016

This edition, edited and copyright © 2020, by Thomas Dalton, PhD

All rights reserved. No part of this publication may be reproduced, stored in a retrieval system, or transmitted, in any form or by any means, electronic, mechanical, photocopying, recording, or otherwise.

Clemens & Blair, LLC, is a non-profit educational publisher.

Library of Congress Cataloging-in-Publication Data

Toaff, Ariel
Passovers of Blood (Pasque di sangue)

      p.   cm.
Includes bibliographical references.

ISBN 978-1-734-8042-18   (pbk.: alk. paper)

  1. Religion. 2. Judaism. 3. History of

Printing number: 9 8 7 6 5 4 3 2 1

Printed in the United States of America on acid-free paper.

CONTENTS

Foreword, by Thomas Dalton   9

Preface   15

Chapter 1: AT VENICE WITH HOLY ROMAN EMPEROR FRIEDRICH III   25
Chapter 2: S. DA PIOVE, PREDATORY FINANCIER   56
Chapter 3: ASHER, THE BEARDED JEW   73
Chapter 4: PORTOBUFFOLÈ, ETC.   102
Chapter 5: FROM ENDINGEN TO REGENSBURG   122
Chapter 6: MAGICAL AND THERAPEUTIC USES OF BLOOD   148
Chapter 7: CRUCIFIXION AND RITUAL CANNIBALISM   172
Chapter 8: DISTANT PRECEDENTS AND THE SAGA OF PURIM   191
Chapter 9: SACRIFICE AND CIRCUMCISION   209
Chapter 10: BLOOD, LEPROSY, AND CHILD MURDER IN THE HAGGADAH   229
Chapter 11: THE DINNER AND INVECTIVE   240
Chapter 12: THE MEMORIAL OF THE PASSION   253
Chapter 13: TO DIE AND KILL FOR THE LOVE OF GOD   278
Chapter 14: "DOING THE FIG"   291
Chapter 15: ISRAEL'S FINAL DEFIANCE   308

Bibliography   328

Passovers of Blood

FOREWORD
Thomas Dalton, PhD

To call the present book controversial is perhaps the understatement of the decade. These days, any book casting a negative light on Jews is in for trouble. But a well-researched and thoroughly-documented book that implicates Jews in the killing of Gentiles, especially children, and for reasons of religion, is sure to cause an uproar. And that's exactly what happened with *Passovers of Blood*.

The topic at hand is 'ritual murder'—that is, the Jewish killing of non-Jews, often youths, simply in order to use their blood in various bizarre religious ceremonies. For centuries, Jews have been accused of ritual murder; and for centuries, ritual murder has been dismissed as so much anti-Semitic clap-trap. The very accusation has routinely been condemned as lies and slander against European Jews, as a weapon used solely for the purpose of inciting hatred and violence against them. Given that much of the alleged killing occurred centuries ago, in the Middle Ages, when investigators had few tools at their disposal, and given the strange and secretive lives of European Jews, the situation was understandable: both that such accusations might occasionally appear, and that they might be believed by the populace. At the time, such charges were taken very seriously; trials were initiated, witnesses interrogated, suspects detained, and judgements pronounced—often fatally, for the Jews. But in more modern times—say, the past 50 years—researchers, mostly of Jewish origins, have almost uniformly denied the reality of such claims. 'Blood libel' is now officially an 'anti-Semitic canard' of the first order, and anyone asserting a factual basis for it is surely a maniacal Jew-hating fanatic.

Or so they said—until a Jewish-Italian researcher and historian, Ariel Toaff, decided to investigate the matter a bit more deeply in the early 2000s. Delving into primary sources in Hebrew, German, and Latin, and including transcripts of Medieval trials, Toaff came to a different conclusion: that certain extremist Ashkenazi Jews—those of Polish-Germanic background—might indeed have engaged in such ritual murder. At a minimum, it was certain that Jewish hatred of Christians and non-Jews was so intense in those communities that they may well have felt justified in such action. Human blood—sometimes liquid, often dried and powered—was seen as having magical powers, including of physical rejuvenation, and was viewed as giving tremendous potency to ritual curses against the Gentiles. That some Jews would thus engage in such practices is unsurprising, in retrospect.

But no matter how compelling the evidence, one cannot say so—at least, not in English, German, Italian, or Spanish—that is, in any language that might gain circulation in the contemporary West. In today's world, one in which the Jewish element has so much authority in media and politics, one cannot accuse "the Jews" of anything, let alone involvement in ritual killing of children. But that's precisely what a 65-year-old Toaff did in 2007, with his publication, in Italian, of *Pasque di Sangue*—"Passovers of Blood." The reaction was predictable and savage.

Even before its actual release in February of that year, the media was on the story. On 6 February, the pending book received a very positive review in the Italian paper *Corriere della Serra*. This prompted a short article the next day in the *Jerusalem Post*, which reprinted portions of the Italian story in English and cited one prominent Jewish critic, who denounced Toaff's "bizarre and devious historical theses" and who "expressed dismay at the sensationalism" in the Italian story. A few days later, on 12 February, the Israeli paper *Ha'aretz* managed to arrange a short interview with Toaff, who held firm to his principles; "I will not give up my devotion to the truth and academic freedom even if the world crucifies me," he said. "I do not claim that Judaism condones murder," he added. "But within Ashkenazi Judaism, there were extremist groups that could have committed such an act and justified it."

Sadly, Toaff's brave face quickly wilted, and just two days later, on 14 February, he literally stopped the presses. That day, the AP carried the story, "'Blood libel' author halts press"; apparently Toaff had directed his Italian publisher, Il Mulino, to stop distribution until he could "re-edit" certain key passages that had been the basis of "distortions and falsehoods." It seems that Toaff's employer, the Israeli university Bar-Ilan, had expressed "great anger" over the book and was highly perturbed that "its contents might have offended the sensitivities of Jews around the world." Toaff quickly issued an apology and then set to work revising the offensive passages. A sanitized version was released, by the same Italian publisher, in 2008. What follows below is an English translation of the original, 2007 edition.

And yet, even the withdrawal of the book did not pacify the critics. Experts like Ronnie Hsia of Penn State, and Kenneth Stow, formerly of Haifa University, were enlisted to write scathing critiques. Toaff, they said, engages in too much speculation, and seems too certain of his conclusions. He extrapolates from a few extreme cases and, by implication, impugns all

Jews. Perhaps worst of all, they said, he relies heavily on the truth of statements by Jewish suspects who were subject to torture. In many cases, Jews "admitted" to their crimes under duress, but at that time, in the Middle Ages, that was considered sufficient evidence to convict. Today, of course, such a thing is completely prohibited in legal proceedings, but it does continue to occur in the military and in the pursuit of "terrorists." The reason that the military continues this brutal practice is, of course, that *sometimes it works*—sometimes they do get valuable and accurate information from tortured captives.

This, in fact, is precisely Toaff's defense: that sometimes the tortured Jews admitted the truth—a truth that can be confirmed independently. Simply because they were tortured, it does not follow that everything they said is entirely false. Much may be, but much may be true. The challenge for the contemporary historian is to sift out the truth from the falsehood.

The Author Responds

At the close of the revised, 2008 edition of *Passovers*, Toaff included a new and lengthy Afterword which serves as an extended reply to his critics. His main points, in brief, include the following: (1) Some critics did not actually read the book, but based their judgments on promotional blurbs, interviews, and news stories. (2) He now admits that "so-called ritual homicides or infanticides pertain to the realm of myth," but he also adds that "nevertheless, one cannot exclude the possibility that certain criminal acts, disguised as crude rituals, were indeed committed by extremist groups or by individuals demented by religious mania." (3) Most usage of blood was in fact *paid for*, sold by willing (and often poor) Christian donors; few if any donors were killed in the process. (4) As mentioned above, it cannot be assumed that tortured Jews always lied; and indeed, the truths of Jewish hatred of Christians were often verified and well-known. (5) Other researchers—most notably, Israel Yuval in his book *Two Nations in Your Womb* (2000)—have documented the Jewish "ritual of curses" against Christians and Gentiles, which are very close in nature to the tortured confessions—suggesting some truth in them. (6) The hate-filled rituals "were not ordinary Passover ceremonies, but rather peculiar rites performed by fringe German-Jewish groups [Ashkenazi] characterized by a virulent anti-Christianism." (7) His use of allegedly "discredited" sources was careful and selective, not indiscriminate; again, even questionable sources contain some measure of truth. (8) Jewish authors have, for centuries, "practiced rigid self-censorship" regarding such hateful rituals, "erasing or omitting facts and events that might tarnish the image of the

Jewish people"—explaining why there are so few historical sources on this troublesome topic.

Continuing in his self-defense, Toaff then explains the widespread use of blood in the Middle Ages. Owing to the superstitions of the time, "Christians and Jews unhesitatingly consumed animal and human blood, cooked, dried, and reduced to powder, to which they attributed extraordinary magical powers." The Jews, though, had a problem: The Bible expressly prohibits drinking—and implicitly, using—blood. For example, already in Genesis we find: "You shall not eat flesh with its life, that is, its blood" (Gen 9:4). Then more explicitly in Leviticus, "Moreover you shall eat no blood whatever, whether of fowl or of animal" (Lev 7:26), and "If any man...eats any blood, I [God] will set my face against that person who eats blood... No person among you shall eat blood" (17:10-12). And yet again, "You shall not eat the blood of any animal..." (17:14). As well, we find this recurring later, in Deuteronomy: when hunting animals, "be sure that you do not eat the blood; for the blood is the life, and you shall not eat the life with the flesh" (Deut 12:23).

Toaff raises two points here. First, and granted that humans are animals, the Bible seems to place a greater prohibition on (non-human) animal blood than on that of humans—which is not apparently banned at all. If medieval Jews could be assured that they were using human blood, they could avoid God's condemnation. Toaff cites one Jewish sect "that went so far as to allow the consumption of human blood, if it was evident and verified that it was not animal blood." Such a practice, he says, is "entirely coherent" with Medieval confessions under torture. Second, it is not clear that *dried* blood is prohibited; and in fact, many rabbis made explicit exceptions for this. Thus, concludes Toaff, it is "not at all improbable" that "the use of Christian blood during the Passover supper" occurred—again, likely in the form of dried blood of a willing (and living) donor.

Looming over this whole discussion is the issue of Jewish hatred of Christians and Gentiles, which was widespread and deeply-rooted. Toaff gives a few examples of such 'ritual curses': "may our enemies be destroyed"; "the hanged man, Jesus the heretic"; "in contempt and shame of the hanged Jesus, and may this befall all our enemies." That similar testimony emerged from torture, and in error-ridden Hebrew, suggests to Toaff that they were "authentic" phrases, not added simply to please the inquisitors.

Toaff closes his Afterword by reiterating that "certain fringes of Ashkenazi Jews developed a virulent and unyielding anti-Christianism" and that "some...were prepared to take revenge," in the form of violence. He then cites an intriguing but unpublished—too controversial—essay by Philippe Ben Natan, which emphasized the medieval Jews' determination to wreak vengeance on the alien and oppressive society that surrounded them... Perhaps only still unclear, regarding the image of the Jews and their vengeance, was how ferocious their vengeance would be. ... Could the Christians have hoped that the Jewish vengeance would not be relentless and unbearably cruel, and would not be unleashed against innocent victims as well? Judging from testimonies drawn from Jewish sources originating among the pietists of Germany and northern France...one has serious doubts that these questions can be answered in the affirmative. And such doubts are strengthened by the evidence on lesser-known social and moral features of the Ashkenazi Jewish community which have been uncovered in recent years; evidence which reveals that a substantial number of Jews engaged in criminal activities.

Though worded in a typically academic, roundabout way, Ben Natan's point is clear: Jews felt aggrieved by their treatment in a majority white, Christian society, and they therefore were determined to take revenge on the white Christians—a revenge "relentless and unbearably cruel." (This, of course, is merely a continuation of 2,000 years of Jewish misanthropy, that is, hatred of the human race—see Dalton 2020.) Christians, in turn, could reasonably expect that these vengeful Jews might indeed kill, both in order to exact revenge and to acquire the much sought-after magical blood. It was this very "medieval Ashkenazi Judaism," says Toaff, "animated by a visceral anti-Christianism," and driven by "extremist groups... of crazed delinquents capable of savage killing rituals," that was the factual basis behind blood libel claims.

The Text

The translation here was originally done in 2007 by Lucchese and Gianetti, then modified in 2016. The editor of this edition is grateful for their diligent work. Further minor revisions to the text were made by the editor to improve readability. Also, in order to provide for a more compact presentation, the illustrations and lengthy Appendix (mostly in Latin) have been deleted.

For his part, Prof. Toaff seems to have gone into hiding. He has produced no new works since 2008, and apparently has made no public appearances. We can only hope that he has been hard at work, writing the next iconoclastic book on the Jews.

References and Further Reading

Dalton, T. 2020. *Eternal Strangers: Critical Views of Jews and Judaism through the Ages.* Castle Hill.
Luther, M. 2020. *On the Jews and Their Lies* (T. Dalton, ed.). Clemens & Blair.
Toaff, A. 2008. *Pasque di Sangue* (in Italian). Il Mulino.
Toaff, A. 2008. "Afterword: Trials and historical methodology." https://www.medievalists.net/files/ 08111401.pdf
Yuval, I. 2008. *Two Nations in Your Womb.* University of California Press.

PREFACE

Ritual homicide trials are a difficult knot to unravel. Most researchers simply set out in search of more or less convincing confirmation of previously developed theories of which the researcher himself appears firmly convinced. The significance of any information failing to fit the preconceived picture is often minimized, and sometimes passed over entirely in silence. Oddly, in this type of research, that which is to be proven is simply taken for granted to begin with. There is a clear perception that any other attitude would involve hazards and repercussions which are to be avoided at all costs.

There is no doubt that the uniformity of the defendant's confessions, contradicted only by variants and incongruities generally relating to details of secondary importance, was assumed by the judges and so-called "public opinion" to constitute "proof" that the Jews, characterized by their great mobility and widespread dispersion, practiced horrible, murderous rituals in hatred of the Christian religion. The stereotype of ritual murder, like that of profanation of the Host and cannibal sacrifice, was present in their minds from the outset, suggesting to both judges and inquisitors alike the possibility of extorting symmetrical, harmonious and significant confessions, triggering a chain reaction of denunciations, veritable and proper manhunts and indiscriminate massacres.

While attempts have been made, in certain cases, to reconstruct the ideological mechanisms and underlying theological and mythological beliefs, with their theological and mythological justifications, which rendered the persecution of the Jews possible as the practitioners of outrageous and blood-thirsty rituals, particularly in the German-speaking countries of Europe, little or nothing has been done to investigate the beliefs of the men and women accused – or who accused themselves – of ritual crucifixion, desecration of the host, haematophagy [eating of blood products] and cannibalism.

On the other hand – if an exception be made for the first sensational case of ritual crucifixion, which occurred in Norwich, England, in 1146, or the equally well-known "blood libel" case at Trent, Italy, in 1475 – the trial records and transcripts (usually referred to under the generic term "historical documentation") constitute, in actual fact, very poor and often purely circumstantial evidence, highly condensed in form and very sparse in detail, totally insufficient for research purposes. Perhaps for this very same reason, that which is missing is often artificially added, assumed or formulated as a hypothesis, in the absence of any explicit probative evidence one way or another (i.e., in the desired direction); in the meantime, the entire matter is immersed in a tinted bath, in which the emerging image is superficial at best, enveloped in a cloud of mystery, with all the related paraphernalia from a distant past, and must remain forever incomprehensible to researchers intent on examining these problems through the application of anachronistic interpretive categories. These efforts – obviously unreliable – are generally performed in good faith. Or, more exactly, *almost always* in good faith.

Thus, in Anglo-Saxon (British and American) historical-anthropological research on Jews and ritual murder (from Joshua Trachtenberg to Ronnie Po-Chia Hsia), magic and witchcraft traditionally feature among the favorite aspects under examination. This approach, for a variety of reasons, is enjoying an extraordinary rebirth at the present time.[1] But that which seems to obtain a high degree of popularity at the moment is not necessarily convincing to meticulous scholars, not content with superficial and impressionistic responses.

Nearly all the studies on Jews and the so-called "blood libel" accusation to date have concentrated almost exclusively on persecutions and persecutors; on the ideologies and presumed motives of those same persecutors: their hatred of Jews; their political and/or religious cynicism; their xenophobic and racist rancor; their contempt for minorities. Little or no attention has been paid to the attitudes of the persecuted Jews themselves and their underlying patterns of ideological behavior – even when they confessed themselves guilty of the specific accusations brought against them. Even less attention has been paid to the behavioral patterns and attitudes of these same Jews; nor have these matters been considered worthy even of interest, attention or serious investigation. On the contrary: these behavioral patterns and attitudes have simply been incontrovertibly dismissed as non-existent – as invented out of whole cloth by the sick minds of anti-Semites and fanatical, obtusely dogmatic Christians.

Nevertheless, although difficult to digest, these actions, once their authenticity is demonstrated or even supposed as possible, should be the object of serious study by reputable scholars. The condemnation, or, alternatively, the aberrant justification of these rituals cannot be imposed upon researchers as the sole, and banal, options. Scholars must be permitted the possibility of attempting serious research on the actual, or presumed, religious, theological and historical motivations of the

Jewish protagonists themselves. Blind excuses are just as worthless as blindly dogmatic condemnation: neither can demonstrate anything other than that which already existed in the mind of the observer to begin with. It is precisely the possibility of evading any clear, precise and unambiguous definition of the reality of ritual child murders rooted in religious faith which has facilitated the intentional or involuntary blindness of Christian and Jewish scholars alike, both pro- and anti-Jewish.

Any additional example of the two-dimensional "flattening" of Jewish history, viewed exclusively as the history of religious or political "anti-Semitism" at all times, must necessarily be regretted. When "one-way" questions presuppose "one-way" answers; when the stereotype of "anti-Semitism" hovers menacingly over any objective approach to the difficult problem of historical research in relation to Jews, any research ends up by losing a large part of its value.

All such research is thus transformed, by the very nature of things, into a "guided tour" conducted against a fictitious and unreal background, in a "virtual reality show" intended to produce the desired reaction, which has naturally been decided upon in advance.[2]

As stressed above, it is simply not permissible to ignore the mental attitudes of the Jews who were tried, tortured and executed for ritual murder, or persecuted on the same charge. At some point, we must ask ourselves whether the "confessions" of the defendants constitute exact records of actual events, or merely the reflection of beliefs forming part of a symbolic, mythical and magical context which must be reconstructed to be understood. In other words: do these "confessions" reflect merely the beliefs of Gentile judges, clergy and populace, with their private phobias and obsessions, or, on the contrary, of the defendants themselves? Untangling the knot is not an easy or pleasant task; but perhaps it is not entirely impossible.

In the first place, therefore, we must investigate the mental attitudes of the Jews themselves, in the tragic drama of ritual sacrifice, together with the accompanying religious beliefs and superstitious and magical elements. Due attention must be paid to the admissions which made historical and local context, identifiable within a succession of German-speaking territories on both sides of the Alps, throughout the long period from the First Crusade to the twilight of the Middle Ages. In substance, we should investigate the possible presence of Jewish beliefs relating to ritual child murders, linked to the feast of Passover, while attempting to reconstitute the significance of any such beliefs. The trial records, particularly the minutely detailed reports relating to the death of Little Simon of Trent, cannot be dismissed on the assumption that all such records represent simply the specific deformation of beliefs held by the judges, who are alleged to have collected detailed but manipulated confessions by means of force and violence to ensure that all such confessions conformed to the anti-Jewish theories already in circulation at the time.

A careful reading of the trial records, in both form and substance, recalls too many features of the conceptual realities, rituals, liturgical practices and mental attitudes typical of, and exclusive to, one distinct, particular Jewish world – features which can in no way be attributed to suggestion on the part of judges or prelates – to be ignored. Only a frank analysis of these elements can make any valid, new and original contribution to the reconstruction of beliefs relating to child sacrifice held by the alleged Jewish perpetrators themselves – whether real or imagined – in addition to attitudes based on the unshakeable faith in their redemption and ultimate vengeance against the Gentiles, emerging from blood and suffering, which can only be understood in this context.

In this Jewish-Germanic world, in continual movement, profound currents of popular magic had, over time, distorted the basic framework of Jewish religious law, changing its forms and meanings. It is in these "mutations" in the Jewish tradition – which are, so to speak, authoritative – that the theological justification of the commemoration [in mockery of the Passion of Christ] is to be sought, which, in addition to its celebration in the liturgical rite, was also intended to revive, in action, vengeance against a hated enemy, continually reincarnated throughout the long history of Israel (the Pharaoh, Amalek, Edom, Haman, Jesus). Paradoxically, in this process, which is complex and anything but uniform, elements typical of Christian culture may be observed to rebound – sometimes inverted, unconsciously but constantly – within Jewish beliefs, mutating in turn, and assuming new forms and meanings. These beliefs, in the end, became symbolically abnormal, distorted by a Judaism profoundly permeated by the underlying elements and characteristic features of an adversarial and detested religion, unintentionally imposed by the same implacable Christian persecutor.

We must therefore decide whether or not the alleged "confessions" relating to the crucifixion of children the evening before Passover; the testimonies relating to the utilization of Christian blood in the celebration of the feast of the Passover, represent, in actual fact, mere myths, i.e., beliefs and ideologies dating far back in time; or actual ritual practices, i.e., events which actually occurred, in reality, and were actually celebrated, in prescribed and consolidated forms, with their more or less fixed baggage of formulae and anathemas, accompanying the magical practices and superstitions which formed an integral part of the mentality of the Jews themselves.

In any case, I repeat, we should avoid the easy short-cut of considering these trials and testimonies only as projections – extorted from the accused by torture and other coercive methods, both psychological and physical – of the stereotypes, superstitions, fears and beliefs of the judges and populace. Such a method would trigger a process inevitably leading to the dismissal of these same testimonies as "valueless documents with little basis in reality", except as "indications of the obsessions of a Christian society" which saw, in the Jew, merely a "distorted mirror image" of its own defects. This task appears to have seemed absolutely prohibitive to many scholars, even famous ones, well-educated men of good will, having concerned themselves with this difficult topic.

First, Gavin Lanmuir, who, starting from the facts of Norwich, England, considers the crucifixion and ritual haemotophagia, which appear in two different phases of history, as simply the cultivated and interested inventions of ecclesiastical groups, denying the Jews any role at all except a merely passive one, devoid of responsibility.[3]

Lanmuir was later followed by Willehad Paul Eckert, Diego Quaglioni, Wolfgang Treue and Ronnie Po-Chia Hsia, who, although examining the phenomenon of ritual child murder from different points of view, intelligently and competently, starting with the late Middle Ages, paying particular attention to the Trent trial documentation, considered it all *tout court* and often *a priori* a baseless libel, an expression of hostility on the part of the Christian majority against the Jewish minority.[4]

According to the point of view adopted by these researchers, the inquisitor's interrogation methods and tortures served no purpose other than to orchestrate a completely harmonious confession of guilt, i.e., of adherence to a truth already existing in the minds of the inquisitors. The use of leading questions and a variety of stratagems, including, in particular, refined torture, were intended to force the defendants to admit that the victim had indeed been kidnapped and tortured according to Jewish ritual, and finally killed in hatred of the Christian faith. The confessions are said to be obviously unbelievable, since the murders were allegedly committed to permit the ritual use of Christian blood, in violation of the Biblical prohibition against the ingestion of blood, a prohibition scrupulously observed by all Jews. As to torture, it is best to recall that its use in the municipalities of northern Italy, at least from the beginning of the 13th century, was regulated, not only by tractate, but by statute as well. As an instrument for determining the truth, torture was permitted in the presence of serious and well-justified clues in cases in which it was considered truly necessary by the podestà [magistrate] and judges. All confessions extorted in this manner, to be considered valid, had to be corroborated by the inquisitor, later, under normal conditions, i.e., in the absence of physical pain or even the threat of renewed torture.[5] These procedures, while unacceptable in our eyes today, were therefore in fact normal, and seem to have been observed in the case of the Trent trials.

Israel Yuval, following in the footsteps of Cecil Roth's stimulating pioneering study,[6] is more critical and seems more open-minded. Yuval stresses the link between the "blood libel" accusation and the phenomenon of the mass suicides and child murders among the German Jewish communities during the First Crusade. The picture which emerges is one of Ashkenazi Jewry's hostile and virulent reaction against surrounding Christian society, a reaction finding expression, not only in liturgical invective, but above all, in the conviction that the Jews themselves were capable of compelling God to wreak bloody revenge against their Christian persecutors, thus bringing redemption closer.[7] More recently, Yuval very relevantly demonstrated that the Ashkenazi responses to ritual murder accusations were surprisingly weak.

These responses, whenever they were recorded, contained not the slightest rejection of the probative evidence; rather, they consisted of a mere *tu quoque* of the accusation against Christians: "Nor are you, yourselves, exempt from guilt of ritual cannibalism".[8] As Yuval wrote, David Malkiel had already noted the manner in which phenomenal prominence was given to the scene, described in a secondary *Midrash* even in the illustrations of the Passover *Haggadah* of the German Jewish communities, of the Pharaoh taking a health-giving bath in the blood of cruelly massacred Jewish children.[9] The message, which cast not the slightest doubt upon the magical, therapeutic effectiveness of children's blood, seemed intended to turn the accusation around. "It is not we Jews, or, if you wish, not just we Jews, who have committed such actions; the enemies of Israel in history have been guilty of these things as well, in which case it was Jewish children who were the innocent victims".

Any showing that these murders, celebrated in the Passover ritual, represented, not just myths, i.e., more or less consistently widespread, consistent religious beliefs, but, rather, actual rites, pertaining to organized groups and forms of worship which were actually practiced, requires a respect for due methodological prudence. The existence of this phenomenon, once it is unequivocally proven, must be viewed within its historical, religious and social context, not to mention the geographical environment in which it is presumably said to have found expression, with all the related and peculiar characteristics which cannot be replicated elsewhere. In other words, we must attempt to search for the heterogeneous elements and particular historical-religious experiences which are alleged to have made the killing of Christian children for ritualistic purposes appear plausible, during a certain period, within a certain geographical area (i.e., the German-speaking regions of trans-Alpine and Cisalpine Italy and Germany, or wherever there were strong ethnic elements of German Jewish origin, any time between the Middle Ages and the early modern era), as the expression of collective adjustment of Jewish groups and a presumed desire on the part of God in this sense, or as the irrational instrument of pressure to reinforce that desire [on the part of God], as well as in the mass suicides and child murders "for the love of God", during the First Crusade.

In this research, we should not be surprised to find customs and traditions linked to experiences which did not exist elsewhere: experiences which were to prove more deeply rooted than the standards of religious law itself, although diametrically opposed in practice, accompanied by all the appropriate and necessary formal and textual justifications. Action and reaction: instinctive, visceral, virulent, in which children, innocent and unaware, became the victims of God's love and vengeance. The blood of children, bathing the altars of a God considered to be in need of guidance, sometimes, of impatient compulsion, impelling Him to protect and to punish.

At the same time, we must keep in mind that, in the German-speaking Jewish communities, the phenomenon, where it took root, was generally limited to groups in which popular tradition, which had, over time, distorted, evaded or replaced the ritual standards of Jewish *halakhah*, in addition to deeply-rooted customs saturated with magical and alchemical elements, all combined to form a deadly cocktail when mixed with violent and aggressive religious fundamentalism. There can be no doubt, it seems to me, that, that, once the tradition became widespread, the stereotypical image of Jewish ritual child murder continued inevitably to take its own course, out of pure momentum. Thus, the Jews were accused of every child murder, much more often wrongly than rightly, especially if discovered in the springtime. In this sense, Cardinal Lorenzo Ganganelli, later Pope Clement XIV, was correct in his famous report, in both his justifications and his "distinctions".[10]

The records of the ritual murder trials should be examined with great care and with all due caution. In connection with the witchcraft trials, Carlo Ginzburg pointed out that the defendants (or victims), in a "show trial" of this type, "...ended up by losing all sense of their own cultural identity, as a result of the acceptance, in whole or in part, by violence or apparently out of spontaneous free choice, of the hostile stereotype imposed by their persecutors [i.e., a sort of Medieval "Stockholm Effect"]. Anyone who fails to conform by simply repeating the results of these findings of historical violence must seek to work upon the rare cases in which the documentation is not just formally set forth in question and answer form; in which, therefore, one may find fragments relatively immune from distortions of the culture which the persecution was intent upon blotting out".[11]

The Trent trials are a priceless document of this very kind. The trial records – especially, the cracks and rifts in the overall structure permitting the researcher to distinguish and differentiate, in substance, not just in form, between the information provided by the accused and the stereotypes imposed by the inquisitors – are dazzlingly clear. This fact cannot be glossed over or distorted by means of preliminary categorizations of an ideological or polemical nature, intended to invalidate those very distinctions. In many cases, everything the defendants said was incomprehensible to the judges – often, because their speech was full of Hebraic ritual and liturgical formulae pronounced with a heavy German accent, unique to the German Jewish community, which not even Italian Jews could understand;[12] in other cases, because their speech referred to mental concepts of an ideological nature totally alien to everything Christian. It is obvious that neither the formulae nor the language can be dismissed as merely the astute fabrications and artificial suggestions of the judges in these trials. Dismissing them as worthless, as invented out of whole cloth, as the spontaneous fantasies of defendants terrorized by torture and projected to satisfy the demands of their inquisitors, cannot be imposed as the compulsory starting point, the prerequisite, for valid research, least of all for the present paper. Any conclusion, of any nature whatsoever, must be duly demonstrated after a strict evaluation and verification of all the underlying evidence *sine ira et studio*, using all available sources capable of confirming or invalidating that evidence in a persuasive and cogent manner.

The present paper could not have been written without the advice, criticism, meetings and discussions with Dani Nissim, a long-time friend, who, in addition to his great experience as a bibliographer and bibliophile, made available to me his profound knowledge of the history of the Jewish community of the Veneto region, and of Padua in particular. The conclusions of this work are nevertheless mine alone, and I have no doubt that that the above named persons would very largely disagree with them. I have engaged in lengthy discussions of the chapters on the Jews of Venice with Reiny Mueller, over the course of which I was given highly useful suggestions and priceless advice. Thanks are also due to the following persons for their assistance in the retrieval of the archival and literary documentation; for their encouragement and criticism, to Diego Quaglioni; Gian Maria Varanini; Rachele Scuro; Miriam Davide; Elliot Horowitz; Judith Dishon; Boris Kotlerman and Ita Dreyfus.

Grateful thanks are also due to those of my students who participated actively in my seminars on the topic, held at the Department of Jewish History at Bar-Ilan University (2001-2002 and 2005-2006), during which I presented the provisional results of my research. First and foremost, however, I wish to thank Ugo Berti, who persuaded me to undertake this difficult task, giving me the courage to overcome the many foreseeable obstacles which stood in the way.

* * *

NOTES TO PREFACE

[1] J. Trachtenberg, *Jewish Magic and Superstition. A Study in Folk Religion*, Philadelphia (Pa.), 1939; Id., *The Devil and the Jews*, Philadelphia (Pa.), 1961; R. Po-Chia Hsia, *The Myth of Ritual Murder. Jews and Magic in Reformation Germany*, New Haven (Conn.) – London, 1988.

[2] For example, the recent volume by S. Buttaroni and S. Musial, *Ritual Murder. Legend in European History*, Krakow – Nuremberg – Frankfurt, 2003, opens with a preamble which is, in its way, conclusive: "It is important to state from the very beginning that Jewish ritual murder never took place. Today, proving such theories wrong is not the goal of scientific research" (p. 12).

[3] See, in particular, G.L. Langmuir, *Toward a Definition of Antisemitism*, Berkeley – Los Angeles (Calif.) – Oxford, 1990, containing his major contributions in this field, reached in the previous years.

[4] W.P. Eckert, *Il beato Simonino negli "Atti" del processo di Trento contro gli ebrei*, in "Studi Trentini di Scienze Storiche", XLIV (1965), pp. 193-221; Id., *Aus den Akten des Trienter Judenprozesses*, in P. Wilpert, *Judentum im Mittelalter*, Berlin, 1966, pp. 238-336; D. Quaglioni, *I processi contro gli ebrei di Trento (1475-1478)*, in

"Materiali di lavoro", 1988, nos. 1-4, pp. 131-142; Id. *Il processo di Trento nel 1475*, in M. Luzzati, *L'Inquisizione e gli ebrei in Italia*, Bari, 1994, pp. 19-34; W. Treue, *Ritualmord und Hostienschändung, Untersuchungen zur Judenfeindschaft in Deuschland im Mittelalter and in der frühen Neuzeit*, Berlin, 1989; R. Po-Chia Hsia, *Trent 1475. A Ritual Murder Trial*, New Haven (Conn.), 1992.

[5] In this regard, see E. Maffei's recent *Dal reato alla sentenza. Il processo criminale in età communale*, Rome, 2005, pp. 98-101.

[6] C. Roth, *Feast of Purim and the Origins of the Blood Accusations*, in "Speculum", VIII (1933), pp. 520-526.

[7] I.J. Yuval, *Vengeance and Damnation, Blood and Defamation. From Jewish Martyrdom to Blood Libel Accusations*, in "Zion", LVIII (1993), pp. 33-90 (in Hebrew); Id., *"Two Nations in Your Womb". Perceptions of Jews and Christians*, Tel Aviv, 2000 (in Hebrew).

[8] Id. *"They Tell Lies. You Ate the Man". Jewish Reactions to Ritual Murder Accusations*, in A. Sapir Abulafia, *Religious Violence Between Christians and Jews. Medieval Roots, Modern Perspectives*, Basingstoke, 2002, pp. 86-106.

[9] D.J. Malkiel, *Infanticide in Passover Iconography*, in "Journal of the Warburg and Courtauld Institutes", LVI (1993), pp. 85-99.

[10] C. Roth, *The Ritual Murder Libel and the Jews. The Report by Cardinal Lorenzo Ganganelli (Pope Clement XIV)*, London, 1935. The Ganganelli Report was recently republished by M. Introvigne, *Cattolici, antisemitismo e sangue. Il mito dell'omicidio rituale*, 2004.

[11] C. Ginzburg, *Storia notturna. Una decifrazione del sabba*, Turin, 1989, p. XXVII.

[12] The expressions in Hebrew (ritual and liturgical) appearing in these depositions can usually be reconstructed with precision, fitting easily into the context of the ideological and religious discourse of the world of Ashkenazi Jewry to which these Jews belonged. There is, therefore, no question of any Satanic language redolent of witchcraft, or "pseudo-language" invented by judges to demonize the Jews, as suggested by many writers (A. Esposito and D. Quaglioni, *Processi contro gli ebrei di Trento, 1475-1478*, I: *I processi di 1475*, Padua, 1990: "The introduction into the depositions of the Jews of curses against Christians and their religion, rendered into transliterated Hebrew, more often in pseudo-Hebrew, then translated into Italian, is thought to have had the function of stressing the ritual nature of the infanticide on the one hand, and of creating a thick fog of mystery on the religious practices of the Jews and conveying the impression of an obscure witchcraft-like and Satanic rite").

CHAPTER ONE

AT VENICE WITH HOLY ROMAN EMPEROR FRIEDRICH III (1469)

It was in February of 1469 that Holy Roman Emperor Friedrich III, traveling from Rome, made his solemn entrance at Venice with a long retinue for which that which was to be his third and last official visit to the city which he so loved and admired.[1] It was to be his first visit to the City of Venice since his triumphant reception immediately following his coronation as Holy Roman Emperor by the Pope in Rome in 1452.[2]

As was customary on these magnificent occasions, Friedrich spent entire days in diplomatic meetings and in receiving the official visits of ambassadors, and in conferring diplomas, stipends and privileges of all sorts upon beneficiaries selected from long lists of names prepared by his officials, as dictated by imperial interests and his own. In those days, intriguers, wheeler-dealers and adventurers attached to the monarch's court, or who thought they were, toiled with a calculated industriousness to intercede in favor of various persons seeking official ratification of their own professional and economic success; of priests, patricians and academics bent upon crowning their own *cursus honorum* through the attainment of some precious imperial investment, or those of a variety of ethnic and religious communities intent on achieving confirmation of their ancient or recent privileges, not to mention merchants and intriguers intent on covering up affairs of dubious honesty and scraping up advantages for themselves during the solemn visit.[3]

Friedrich was known as a fanatical and often naive collector of relics of all types. It is not therefore surprising that the objectives of his trip to Venice should have included a passionate and unrestrained hunt for relics, hawked about in abundance by wheeler-dealers and impertinent intermediaries at high prices, a fact noted with malicious humor by Michele Colli, a salt superintendent, in a report sent from Venice to the Duke of Milan, in which he cast doubt on Friedrich's alleged competence where relics were concerned. According to the Milanese official, the Emperor, in this type of business, which he presumed to carry out directly and without regard to price, was a sucker to be plucked assiduously, adding, to accentuate the ridicule, half-seriously half facetiously, that "certain Greeks sold him dead bones including the tail of the ass that brought Christ to Bethlehem".[4]

On this occasion, some supposed relics of Saint Vigilius found their way to Venice in the hands of a loving and faithful subject of Friedrich, Giovanni Hinderbach, a famous humanist and man of the Church who had traveled from Trent to the City of the Lagoons, not only to present the Emperor with the highly-valued relics, but above all as an act of gratitude, on the occasion of his receipt of his much sought-after investiture of the temporality of the episcopate of Trent. Again, it was Colli who informed the Duke of Milan that "His Illustrious Majesty invested the Bishop of Trent with a thousand temporal solemnities and celebrations".[5] But Hinderbach was not the only person to have undertaken the uncomfortable journey from Trent to Venice during the German Emperor's distinguished presence in the city.

Tobias da Magdeburg was an obscure Jewish herb alchemist who, after traveling down from his native Saxony and finding exile among the mountains of the region of Trent, practiced the art of medicine and surgery with some success, at least on the local market. A few years later, he was to meet Hinderbach under much unhappier circumstances, under indictment for participation in the cruel ritual murder of Little Simon, later sainted as Simon of Trent. Imprisoned in the castle of Buonconsiglio and admitting his guilt, he was to meet a cruel death at the stake, accompanied by the confiscation of all his goods.[6]

Maestro Tobias appears to have been acting in accordance with other motives during the Emperor's official visit to Venice, particularly, the possibility of meeting large groups of German Jews arriving from the other side of the Alps along with Friedrich's baggage train, many of whom Tobias looked forward to seeing again after years of involuntary separation. There was no shortage of German Jews at Venice in February of 1469: disciplined, humble, but totally self-absorbed and self-interested.

In his depositions before the judge of Trent in 1475, Tobias was not exaggerating when, after recalling his own presence in the city during "His Most Serene Highness's visit to Venice", he stressed that many Jewish merchants, in crossing the Alpine barrier, had actually traveled from the German territories to the City of the Lagoons for the purpose of acquiring a wide variety of high-priced goods without paying taxes or duty of any kind, passing them off as goods owned by the Emperor, in whose baggage train they were said to have found their way back to Germany. This astute and bold stratagem was well worth the physical and economic cost of the difficult trip to the city of the

Doges.⁷

But Tobias's presence in Venice was not due to any mere nostalgia for the people among whom he had been born and grew up. As a physician, and as a Jewish physician in particular, he knew that the Emperor, during his visit, would, as he was normally accustomed to do, grant doctoral degrees in medicine to a swarm of more or less highly recommended candidates, including a few Jews. In fact, it was during that same February of 1469 that Friedrich granted a license permitting the College of Physicians of San Luca, an institution of higher learning teaching students of various origins – not just Venetians – to confer the insignia of Imperial Authority upon eight medical graduates per year.⁸ Enea Silvio Piccolomini, later Pope Pius II, recalled the manner in which Friedrich graduated a swarm of medical students during his second visit to Italy.

The number of Jews on the Emperor's lists of candidates remains unknown. Nor do we know who filed the petitions to inscribe these Jewish candidates, or the methods used, or the reasons for doing so. We only know that many Jewish physicians, of various origins, in addition to Tobias, a resident of Trent, were in Venice during the Emperor's visit, attracted by an opportunity of obtaining some much sought-after title from Emperor Friedrich in person; nor do we know how many of them had already spent considerable periods of time in the City of the Lagoons in search of fame and fortune.⁹ Among them were the Jews Moschè Rapp, Lazzaro¹⁰ and the better-known Omobono (Simcha Bunem or Bunim), keeper of the pharmacy "*della Vecchia*" at San Cassian, with a house at San Stae, only a few steps from the Albergo dei Bresciani ("*magister Homobon*, Jewish physician, at the *Speziaria de la Vecchia* at San Cassian, with his house near San Stae, not far from the Casa de Bressani, at Venice").¹¹ Accompanying them was the physician Moisè da Rodi, whose presence is attested to with certainty in 1473,¹² but who probably arrived in Venice even earlier, and "Maestro Theodoro (Todros), Jewish physician", who reached Venice in 1469 with Friedrich.¹³

The best-known of all, however, was, without doubt, the rabbi and barber surgeon Jehudah messer Leon, certainly a product of Ashkenazi Jewish environment, if his origins at Montecchio in the Vicentino region are indeed a fact.¹⁴ This same Leon, who resided in Venice starting in 1469 at the earliest, where his son David was born, was officially granted his degree in medicine during the Emperor's visit, although formally the diploma was only signed a few days later by the imperial notary at Pordenone (but still in the month of February).¹⁵ Similarly, years later, in August of 1489, the Emperor, still at

Pordenone, is said to have granted a doctorate in medicine to two Jewish candidates, both of them from Sicily and belonging to the Azeni family at Palermo, David di Aronne and Salomone di Mosè.[16]

The petitions of the Jews to the Emperor, who had always been highly esteemed for his benevolent attitude, filed during his stay in Venice during the winter of 1469, were submitted by an ambassador admitted to Friedrich's presence for that particular occasion. The occasion was described as follows, early in the 16th Century, with some satisfaction although with undoubted exaggeration, by the chronicler Elia Capsalia, rabbi of Candia, who had studied medicine at the Talmudic academy of Padua:

"The Emperor (Friedrich III) was very favorable to the Jews. During his visit to Venice (in 1469), when his vassals and subjects presented him with (gastronomic) gifts, he never refused to eat them before his servants and functionaries had tasted them first, as is the custom among emperors. Whenever the Jews brought him gifts of this kind, Friedrich never hesitated to eat any of the dishes immediately, saying that he had complete faith in the loyalty and honesty of his Jewish subjects.

"Later, Frederic, traveling from Venice, went to Padua to gain an impression of that city. On that occasion, the Serenissima prepared a carriage for him and placed it on the city walls: the horses pulled the carriage from which the Emperor admired the entire city. This was done so that he might easily verify the thickness and solidity of the walls (of Padua). Friedrich signed a pact with Venice and remained its faithful ally for the entire time he lived".[17]

In all probability, the ambassadorship of the Jews conferring with Friedrich III as described by Capsali was headed by David Mavrogonato (in Italian, Maurogonato), an adventurer and not overly-scrupulous businessman in the service of the Republic of Venice, a person of enormous financial resources and great influence, a native of Candia who was often sent on hazardous missions to the lands of the Aegean and the Great Turk, where he was to run many risks and die a cruel death; on the other hand, he was certainly capable of procuring sumptuous stipends and profitable privileges for himself.[18]

Maestro Tobias da Magdeburg, the humble physician from Trent, had seen Mavrogonato at Venice during the days of the imperial visit, although he did not know Mavrogonato's name. He had observed Mavrogonato with respect and reverential fear; he knew approximately where he lived, although he did not know the exact address; but he was well aware that he would never have been able to approach Mavrogonato without undergoing the suspicious appraisal of

Mavrogonato's bodyguards. Perhaps Tobias thought that Mavrogonato's recommendation would help get him, Tobias, included in the list of people enjoying the Emperor's favor, or those about to receive a Doctorate, but he was unable, or did not dare, to ask for it. The personage and appearance of Mavrogonato nevertheless remained imprinted in his memory after many years; in 1475, in speaking to the judges at Trent, he envisioned Mavrogonato as follows, erroneously imagining that he might be still alive:

"He might have been forty four or forty five years old; he wore his hair long and wore a black beard, like the Greeks. He wore a black cloak that came down to his feet, and covered his head with a black cap. In substance, he dressed like the Greeks".[19]

But who was David Mavrogonato really? An ambiguous and mysterious character, Mavrogonato appeared in Venice in 1461 on his own initiative to reveal a conspiracy being hatched on the island of Candia against the Serenissima. The Council of Ten did not hesitate to take the Jewish merchant into its service and send him back to Candia on a secret mission to spy on the conspirators and report them to the Venetian authorities, after gathering the evidence required for their arrest.[20] Mavrogonato carried out the mission to perfection, although his tireless commitment finally ended by blowing his cover, rendering continued residence on his native island impossible, since, as he claimed, both Greeks and Jews "pointed him out with their fingers", considering him a vile informer, or *malshin* in Jewish juridical terminology, a term with lethal penal implications.[21] We also know that Mosè Capsali, rabbi at Constantinople, had threatened Mavrogonato with excommunication at the request of the Jews of Candia.[22]

The privileges requested early in his career by Mavrogonato in return for services rendered were granted without delay and with expressions of profound gratitude by the Council of Ten in December of 1463. These rights, which extended to his sons Jacob and Elia and his descendants in perpetuity, included, among other things, exemption from the wearing of the distinctive sign required of the Jews, and authorization to move about armed wherever he wished. He was not, however, granted the privilege, odd in appearance, but perfectly consistent with the type of persons with whom he had to deal, of striking two names off the list of banned persons wanted by the Serenissima for the crime of homicide.[23] Mavrogonato, *Judeus de Creta et mercator in Venetiis*, knew full well who might have benefited from such a clause, and had very definite ideas about certain people condemned *in absentia* who might thus have been permitted to return to the territories under Venetian domination. At this point, the entrepreneurial Jew from Candia, a permanent resident of Venice since the beginning of 1464, traveling frequently and easily, supervising his goods and entering and leaving the port en route for Candia and Constantinople, was officially a spy in the service of the Republic and at its disposal for other, more or less hazardous, secret missions.

In effect, Mavrogonato is thought to have been sent to Candia and Constantinople at least four times, in 1465, the next year, in 1468 and in 1470, during the first Venetian-Turkish War.[24] It is possible that, in 1468, on the eve of Friedrich's imperial visit to Venice, Mavrogonato may have accompanied a vessel, loaded with goods owned by himself, from Candia to the Venetian landing place. In June of 1465, a decree signed by the Council of Ten officially admitted that Mavrogonato had been sent to the capital of the Great Turk to spy on the enemy; in 1466, he was referred to the "Jew from Crete, called David", called upon by Venice to participate in the peace negotiations with the Sultan Mahomet II.[25]

David Mavrogonato died as mysteriously as he had lived, probably during his fourth mission. On 18 December 1470, the Doge of Venice, writing to the Duke of Crete, mentioned the death of his secret agent, but without providing any details as to the circumstances of his death.[26] Mavrogonato may have accepted the dangerous assignment of plotting the Great Turk's assassination in one way or another, and may for some reason have failed in the mission, meeting an unexpected death in the process. Other, later, clues are also thought to point in this direction.

Among the requests filed by Mavrogonato with the Council of Ten after his first secret mission to Candia in the years 1461-1462, was that of being permitted to avail himself of a bodyguard, assigned to his personal defense ("that you might deign to grant him the privilege [...] of keeping [...] some person near him for the safety of his person, so that no violence or ignominy may be done to him by some villain or other evil person").

Once his petition had been accepted by the Venetian legal authorities in February 1464, the merchant from Candia made haste to appoint a person originally described as a sort of bodyguard, but referred to in the document as Mavrogonato's "associate", a designation quite distinct in scope as well as quality. This bodyguard, or "associate", was to share in almost all the privileges granted by the city of Venice to Mavrogonato, including that of being authorized to engage in business of any kind, on a basis of equality with Venetian merchants, and being permitted to move about the city and territory wearing the black hat of a Christian gentlemen instead of the crocus-colored beret of the Jews (for this reason, Mavrogonato, in Venice and its domains, was known as "Maurobareti").[27] Mavrogonato was an experienced and rich businessman, but not a muscular street fighter or expert in the martial arts; these latter services were to be provided by a man bearing the name of Salomone da Piove di Sacco, known throughout Venice and the entire Veneto region as a banker, merchant and rough-and-ready financier, as bold as he was unscrupulous.[28] Starting in 1464 and continuing thereafter, Mavrogonato is thought to have entrusted his affairs to Salomone da Piove di Sacco during his enforced and prolonged absences from Venice, including the management of his lordly dwelling at San Cassian and his joint interest in commercial ventures undertaken on the maritime routes to the great markets of the Levant.

Finally, Mavrogonato is also believed to have entrusted Salomone da Piove with some of his own precious secrets as a diplomatic spy in the pay of Venice. On the eve of his first, risky trip to Constantinople in June 1465, David Mavrogonato informed the Council of Ten that he had indeed confirmed Salomone as his business agent at Venice "due to the complete faith which I have in him".[29]

Salomone's ancestors had arrived in Italy in the last part of the 14th century from the Rhine region in Germany, perhaps from the same important seat of the archbishop of Cologne. The family had gradually extended its offshoots from Cividale del Friuli, where Marcuccio (Mordekhai) and Fays – Salomone's father and grandfather respectively – had operated in the local money market, to Padua, where, in the mid-15th century, the same Salomone managed the bank of San Lorenzo in the city district of the same name.[30]

Salomone and his clan formed part of a migratory flow extending to all regions of northern Italy since the very late 14th century, involving the massive transalpine migration of entire German-speaking communities, both Christians and Jews, from the Rhineland, Bavaria and upper and lower Austria, Franconia and Alsace, the Kärnten, Styria and Thuringia, Slovenia, Bohemia and Moravia, Silesia, Swabia and Saxony, Westphalia, Württemburg in the Palatinate, Brandenburg, Baden, Worms, Regensburg and Spira. A heterogeneous German-speaking population, made up of rich and poor, entrepreneurs and artisans, financiers and scoundrels, men of religion, adventurers and rascals, traveling from the transalpine territories via the mountain crossings in a process of long duration, towards the lagoons of Venice, as well as the cities and lesser centers of the terra firma of the Veneto region.[31]

This was a large-scale phenomenon containing a large Jewish component which had already come to the fore in the regions of northern Italy, in consequence of the persecutions following the Black Death in the mid-14th century as well as sporadically during the century before.

Ashkenazi, i.e., German, Jewish communities of diverse numerical consistency, formed in a myriad of localities, large and small, from Pavia to Cremona, from Bassano to Treviso, from Cividale to Gorizia and Trieste, from Udine and Pordenone to Conegliano, from Feltre and Vicenza to Rovigo, from Lendinara to Badia Polesine, from Padua and Verona to Mestre.[32] Here they stayed, a stone's throw from Venice, an enterprising Jewish community of considerable economic weight, whose members came mostly from Nuremberg and the adjacent areas. In 1382, a few Jews from Mestre obtained authorization to move to Venice to practice money-lending, but were expelled a few years later, in 1397, for failing to comply with the conditions under which the government of Venice had admitted them to the city.[33]

The Serenissima thus returned to its traditional policy of refusing to grant permanent residence to Jews on the banks of the Great Canal, except under exceptional circumstances and for periods of short duration. This policy, frequently quite contrary to actual practice, witnessed Jews crowding the streets of certain city districts during the day and remaining there in great numbers even after dark, lodged in houses and inns, sometimes for long periods of time. There was no shortage of Jews in Venice: mostly physicians, influential merchants and bankers, having established themselves more or less permanently at Venice. The numerical consistency of this community, heterogeneous in professions but more or less homogenous in ethnic origin, originating from the transalpine German-speaking territories, has, until today, been considered from an unjustly simplistic point of view. Beginning in the second half of the 15th century, they tended to gather in one particular strategic area, a sheltered location in the international market at Rialto, the node of the great trading systems linking the city of Venice, by land and sea, to the centers of the plains of the Po River valley and the German-speaking regions which constituted a constant point of economic, social and religious reference, towards which the eyes of these Ashkenazi Jews continued to be directed.[34] These areas included the districts of San Cassian, where a kosher butcher's shop soon opened, preparing meat according to the Jewish custom, Sant Agostino, San Polo and Santa Maria Mater Domini. At San Polo, they probably also attended the German-rite synagogue, authorized by the Venetian government in 1464 to serve "the Jews who reside in the capital or who meet there to carry on their businesses", with a decree which nevertheless limited their liturgical collective meetings to the participation of ten adults of the male sex.[35]

Moreover, the Jewish community at Venice, like the others of more or less distant Ashkenazi origin to be seen in the more immediate and smaller centers of northern Italy, formed part of a German-Jewish *koinè*, consisting of German-speaking Jews on both sides of the Alps, linked by liturgical usages and similar customs, sharing the same history, often marked by events both tragic and invariably mythologized, as well as by the same attitude of harsh hostility to the arrogant Christianity of surrounding society, the same religious texts of reference, the same rabbinical hierarchies, produced by the Ashkenazi Talmudic academies to whose authority they intended to submit, and the same family structures.[36] These communities made up a homogenous entity from the social and religious point of view, which might be called supranational, in which the Jews of Pavia identified themselves with those from Regensburg, the Jews from Treviso with the Jews of Nuremberg, and the Jews of Trent with those from Cologne and Prague, but certainly not with those from Rome, Florence, or Bologna.

Relations with the Italian Jews who often lived alongside them, where such relations existed, were markedly fortuitous, based on contingent common needs of an economic nature, and the common perception of being viewed as identical by the surrounding Christian environment.

Many of these Ashkenazi Jews did not speak Italian, and if or when they did speak it, it was difficult to understand them due to the heavy German inflection of their pronunciation and the many Germanic and Yiddish terms with which their phrases were cram-packed. Not only the Hebrew language, but the common liturgical usage of German and Italian Jews, was pronounced in a radically different way, so that the two groups considered it impossible to pray together.[37] It is not therefore surprising that Italian Jews were not on terms of much familiarity with German Jews.

Despite their close proximity, the Italian Jews had little knowledge of the German ones, distrusted their aggressive economic audacity, which generally had little respect for the nation's laws, and dissented from their religious orthodoxy, which they considered exaggerated and depressing. Sometimes, rightly or wrongly, they feared them.

The Italian Jewish *koinè*, i.e., of distant Roman origin (Jews active in the money trade only moved from Rome to seek permanent residence in the municipalities of central and northern Italy starting in the second half of the 13th century), lived side by side with the German Jewish *koinè*, of more recent origin, but without assimilating, without merging and without being influenced, except to a minor and quite secondary degree. They were distant brothers, even if they were not "brothers who hate and fear each other".

The first group of "Roman" Jews, i.e., Jews of Italian origin, flowing into the centers of the plane of the Po from their preceding seats in the Patrimonio of San Pietro, in Umbria, in the Marca d'Ancona, in the Lazio and in Campagna to carry on the authorized money trade, i.e., regulated by permits, did not reach these regions simultaneously with the arrival in those regions of the German transalpine Jews, active in the same profession. They in fact preceded them by several decades. The first Jewish money lenders at Padua and Lonigo, in the Vicentino region, were Italians, and initially settled there between 1360 and 1370. Jews of German origin only reached the region in consistent numbers at a later time, at the end of the century, and, in particular, at the beginning of the 15th century.[38] A comparison of the clauses of the permits granted to the German Jews compared to those granted to the Italian Jews, often active in the same areas, reveals obvious traces of profound differences in religious usage and mentalities, sediments of particular and diverse historical experiences. The attitudes and ceremonial components, the fears and mistrust, the meaning and dimensions of life, the relations with the surrounding Christian society of these German Jews, immersed in the new Italian reality in which they felt profoundly foreign, remained influenced and marked by their experiences in the Germanic world from which they originated, and which they had only left physically.

The principal concern of these immigrants seemed to be, understandably, that of ensuring their physical safety and the protection of their property against the dangers represented by a surrounding society which considered them treacherous and potentially hostile. Almost obsessively, the chapters of the permits repeatedly mention the exemplary punishments to be threatened to anyone causing harm or injury to the Jews, or subjecting them to trouble or vexations. The permit granted by the municipality of Venzone to the money lender Benedetto da Regensburg in 1444 contained the condition that wet nurses and Christian personnel in the service of the Jews were not to be molested or offended, nor could they be made to work on Sunday or the feast days of the Christian calendar.[39] The transalpine Jews were particularly sensitive to the possibility of being falsely accused and, in consequence, of suffering from legal proceedings and expropriations, as shown by their preceding experience in the German territories, the scars of which they still bore. In 1414, Salomone da Nuremberg and his companions requested and obtained a concession from the government of Trieste stating that, if Jews were accused of any crime or offense before the judges of that city, they would not be subjected to torture to extort confessions without at least four citizen witnesses, trustworthy and of good reputation, against them.[40]

The permits signed by the municipalities of Lombardy and Triveneto with the Ashkenazi Jews were characterized by a constant concern that they be guaranteed the freedom to observe their religious ritual and ceremonial standards with zealous scrupulousness. The religious clauses inserted in the chapters were more detailed in this sense than those found in the contemporary permits granted to Jewish money lenders of Italian origin, undoubtedly an indication of greater adherence to the observation of religious precepts on the part of the Ashkenazi community than the Italian one. It was significant in this regard that the appearance of the clause relating to the undisturbed provision of kosher meat, i.e., meat butchered according to ritual law, appears for the first time in the permits granted to German Jews at the end of the 14th century (from Pavia in 1387 to Udine in 1389, from Pordenone in 1399 to Treviso in 1401), approximately twenty years before this made its initial appearance, certainly in imitation of, and under the influenced by, the Ashkenazi prototype, in the permits of the Italian Jews.[41]

The religious clauses inserted in the permits of the German Jews include, in addition to the right to supply themselves with kosher meat to observe their festivities freely, the right not to be compelled to violate the standards of Hebraic law in the exercise of their lending activities or having to appear in court on Saturday or the feast days of the Hebraic calendar. The same clauses furthermore permitted the safeguarding of the other Jewish alimentary norms, such as the supervised preparation of the wine, cheeses and bread (a clause usually missing from the permits granted to Italian Jews); the right to "attend synagogue" (Pavia 1387); to use a piece of land as a cemetery and to permit Jewish women to take regular baths of purification, after the end of their menstrual periods, in the city baths on particular days set aside for them (Pordenone, 1452).[42]

But the most characteristic clause, absolutely generalized in the permits of Jews of German origin, but significantly absent from the permits of the Italian Jews, was that referring to protection against forced conversions to Christianity. In particular, the Ashkenazi appeared obsessed with the possibility that their children might be kidnapped, subjected to violence or swindled with snares and tricks to drag them to the baptismal font. That this possibility was anything but remote seemed obvious to anyone having had this type of traumatic experience at first hand on the banks of the Rhine or the Main. Permits issued in Friulia, Lombardy and Veneto granted to German money lenders, as early as the end of the 14th century, explicitly prohibited friars and priests of any order from proselytizing among Jewish children not yet having reached their 13th birthday.[43] In 1403, Ulrich III, bishop of Bressanone, granted the Jews of the Tyrol protection from any possible ecclesiastical claims to a right of forced conversion of Jewish children. This protection could, and did, include the dangers represented by baptized Jews, zealous and implacable in plotting the ruin of the Jewish communities from which they originated.[44] In 1395, Mina da Aydelbach, representing the Jewish families of German origin residing in Gemona, first stopping place on the main road to the lagoons of Venice after the mountain crossing of Tarvisio, obtained, in the initial clauses of their permits, explicit provision for the immediate removal from the city of so-called "Jews turned Christian", who were said to constitute elements of scandal and disturbance.[45]

The die was already cast between the Italian and German Jews, settled in the lands beyond the River Po, by the mid-15th century. With a few exceptions, the piazza was henceforth solidly in the hands of Yiddish-speaking Jews who, in the best of cases, spoke badly mangled Italian.[46] In former times, they had crossed the Alps fearfully and almost on tip-toe, in search of sufficiently modest and desirable dwellings so as to live and survive comfortably, but they also, when need arose, proved themselves enterprising in financial matters, courageous and even bold in their commercial undertakings, nonchalant and often arrogant and impudent in their relations with the government, only obeying the law when it was strictly necessary or too dangerous to do otherwise. Victory was now theirs, and it was because of these same bankers and merchants that many of them had been able to accumulate huge sums of capital in a relatively short lapse of time, such as to bear no comparison with the fortunes possessed by Christian mercantile families and patricians who were both more distinguished and of higher rank.

The chronology is relatively precise. In 1455, all Italian Jews active in the money trade were expelled from Padua and compelled to shut down their banks, while the "Teutonic" Jews, divided from, and now entirely separate from, the Italian Jews, gained the upper hand in the local money market [Padua], the most important in the terra firma of the Veneto region, as early as ten years before. At Verona, all lending banks owned by Italian Jews had already been closed in 1447, while, in 1445, the permits of the Jewish bankers of Vicenza were not renewed.[47] With the Italian Jewish banks shut down in all the principal centers of the Veneto region, a few district lending banks, few in number but of great economic potential, particularly because of the higher interest rates charged by them in comparison to the rates formerly charged by banks controlled by Italian Jews, remained open to serve the needs of the clientele in the cities and in the countryside.[48] These were the banks of Soave and Villafranca in the district of Verona, Mestre for Venice, and Este, Composampiero and, above all, Piove di Sacco in the Padua district.[49]

The forced and almost simultaneous dismantling of the Jewish banks of Padua, Verona and Vicenza led, as an immediate consequence, to the almost total extinction of the Hebraic community of Roman origin, which was compelled, for the most part, to flow into the centers on the nearer side of the Po; on the other hand, however, it allowed other money lenders, from Treviso and the territories of Friulia, who took over the assets and management of the few remaining lending banks, to make extraordinary fortunes. As we have seen, these banks benefited from an extremely broad catchment area and could rely on a numerous and heterogeneous clientele. Their economic success was therefore guaranteed and proved to be exceptional in scope. The lucky few bankers remaining on the piazza were almost all Ashkenazi, the same Jews who had hastened or more or less directly procured the financial ruin of the Italian Jews. The most prominent among them was, in the end, Salomone di Marcuccio, owner of the Banco di Piove di Sacco and, after 1464, David Mavrogno da Candia's official business associate, with a more or less official residence at Venice.[50]

Rich and influential, Salomone, although not a man of great culture, was not averse to sponsorship ventures, in which field he established himself with flare and good taste. At Piove, where the local community was practically one of his fiefdoms, in 1465, he became associated with the German printer Meshullam Cusi, whose presence at Padua is attested to in the same year. Cusi undertook the initial printing of one of the first Hebraic cunabulae, certainly one of the most important and monumental, at Piove, towards the end of 1473. This was a classic ritualistic code, *Arba'a Turim*, a work of the German rabbi Ya'akov b. Asher (1270 circa 1340), whose family originated from Cologne but had carried on its activities for the most part at Barcelona in Catalonia, and later at Toledo in Castille.

The four volumes, printed on Cusi's presses with great care and heedless of cost, were completed in July 1475 and constituted one of the most splendid and elegant examples of Hebraic printing.[51] Certain copies of great beauty were printed on parchment and intended for a highly sophisticated readership, particularly from the economic point of view, one of the most important of whom was to be Salomone da Piove. The printing costs linked to the supplies of machinery, type, materials and labor, were to fluctuate between seven hundred and one thousand ducats, a large sum which Cusi might not have had available, without the direct or indirect joint involvement of the Jewish banker di Piove.

We believe that consideration should be given to the possibility that Salmone may have also undertaken another artistic-literary project of great importance, at proportional economic cost. The precious miniatures of the so-called "Rothschild Miscellany", one of the most sumptuous and famous of all Jewish legal codes, were executed in the decade between 1470 and 1480, probably in Leonardo Bellini's workshop at Venice. The artistic decoration of the manuscript cost almost one thousand ducats, a sum equivalent to half the taxes paid by the entire Jewish community of the Duchy of Milan during the same period.[52] Salomone may well have been the only Jewish sponsor living more or less permanently in the city of the lagoons able to make an investment of such magnitude without difficulty. For purposes of comparison, we know that in 1473, Salomone, still active on the piazza of Venice, together with one of his sons, Marcuccio, his first born, was able to pay a gigantic sum, equal to 300 ducats in cash and another 360 in credits, intended for the restoration of the perimeter wall of the old Arsenal.[53]

Between 1468 and 1469, in view of Emperor Friedrich's forthcoming visit to Venice, Salomone hosted a plenary meeting at Piove of the German rabbis of the Jewish community of northern Italy, presided over by their most authoritative exponent, the jurist Yoseph Colon, then active in the community of Mestre.[54] The petitions said to have been presented by the Jewish ambassadorship to the solemn and magnificent Emperor during the anticipated audience described by Rabbi Elia Capsali di Candia in his chronicles may have been drawn up on that occasion.

During the summer of 1470, David Mavrogonato set sail from Venice to return to Candia for what was to be his last mission. He had long since prudently avoided reappearing on his native island. He was probably accompanied on this voyage by Salomone da Piove himself, who, at the end of June, left his son Salamoncino with a power of attorney for the purpose of collecting a huge loan from the bank Soranzo at Venice, a transaction which he would normally have conducted directly.[55] As we know, this was a voyage from which Mavrogonato is thought never to have returned alive, meeting with his tragic demise a few weeks later, certainly before September of that year. From that time onwards, Mavrogonato's name and memory were to be systematically omitted from all documents signed by his former associate, Salomone da Piove, as well as by Salomone's sons, although reference to the privileges obtained by the influential merchant from Candia appears to have become an established custom. This is not surprising and cannot be merely accidental. Salomone certainly knew the truth about that last voyage to Constantinople in which Mavrogonato is believed to have met with unexpected death. Did Salomone know too much? Did he wish to forget, or rather, cause others to forget, that he had been with him on that tragic maritime voyage? What is certain is that Salomone da Piove was close to David Mavrogonato until the end. Perhaps too close.

It is not therefore surprising to learn that, at around this same time, Salomone personally took over a bold project, perhaps planned beforehand by his associate and collaborator from Candia, "to take the life of the Great Turk", thus doing the government of Venice a great favor.[56] To provide for the assassination of Mahomet II, the nonchalant financier informed the Council of Ten that he had sent a Jewish doctor named Valco, whose Italian name was probably derived from the well-known family of doctors, natives of Worms, called Wallach, Wallich or Welbush, to Constantinople, at his expense.[57]

"Salomon, as appears in the books of Your Majesties the Council of Ten, due to his wish to do a great ourselves and all of Christianity a great service by attempting to take the life of the Great Turk, chose, at his expense, to send for a Maestro Valco, a Jewish doctor, whom he sent with his own money".[58]

Even before that, we know that the Venetian authorities had been glad to avail themselves of the services of a Jewish barber-surgeon, Jacob da Gaeta, the Sultan's personal physician, an expert spy and double agent, greedy for gain and treacherous, with whom Mavrogonato had maintained frequent contacts.[59] It also appears that Maestro Jacob had reached Venice in secrecy, together with Gaeta, on the same vessel from Ragusa, in very late 1468, on the eve of the imperial visit and the Venetian congress of Jewish physicians, held on that occasion.[60]

Maestro Valco, paid by Salomone, moved to Constantinople, and went quickly to work, but apparently with little result. Mahomet II was still alive and kicking when the Jewish banker from Piove finally died, between the end of 1475 and the very early part of the following year. But Salomone was occupied with certain other matters, much more serious and more disagreeable then merely "taking the life of the Great Turk" during that period, which was to prove fraught with danger for all the Jewish communities of northern Italy. The Trent trials of the Jews accused of little Simon's martyrdom had ended with the condemnation and execution of the principal defendants, who were burnt at the stake or decapitated in June of 1475. Other defendants, including the women of the small community, were waiting to learn their final fate, after which the trial proceedings were suspended in April by order of Sigismundo IV, Count of Tyrol, and were then newly interrupted the following July by order of Pope Sixtus IV after a brief recommencement, requested by several parties for purposes of intervening in the affair. The Pope then personally sent a special commissioner to Trent, the Dominican, Battista de' Giudici, bishop of Ventimiglia, with the task of investigating and reporting on the facts. De' Giudici, who had initially taken up lodgings at Trent, later moved to the nearby, but more secure, seat of Rovereto, in territory belonging to Venice, where they met with the lawyers, all of top rate importance, whom the Jews of Padua had decided to make available to the defendants.[61] Salomone da Piove played a prominent role in the affair, requesting the Pope to appoint an apostolic inquisitor and probably meeting Battista de' Giudici at Padua, on de' Giudici's way to Trent.[62]

In accordance with de' Giudici, with whom he maintained intense epistolary relations, as well as through another Jew from Piove, belonging to the Cusi family of typographers, having strategically moved, to Rovereto, Salomone provided a safe conduct to a Paduan Jew, a native of Regensburg, and sent him to Innsbruck with the mission of pleading the cause of the Trent defendants still in prison, before Sigismundo, Count of Tyrol, and, if possible, of obtaining their release. Salomone Fürstungar, his agent on this delicate mission, was an unscrupulous intriguer who camouflaged himself by dressing, not as a Jew, but "in the German-style, with a short overcoat and a cap on his head", returned from Tyrol disappointed and empty-handed. His bitter failure was also an indication of the failure of the efforts of all the German-origin Jewish communities from the Veneto region to avoid the tragic consequences of the Trent affair for the defendants who were still alive.[63] Salomone da Piove is said to have died shortly afterwards.[64]

The leadership of this conspicuous group, committed, as always, to avoiding the political and financial effects and repercussions of the Trent trials on their Jewish brethren, thus passed into the hands of Manno di Aberlino (Mandele ben Abraham) of Vincenza, maximum exponent of the influential Ashkenazim community of Pavia.[65] A prestigious banker with vast financial resources, he had been appointed collector of Jewish taxes to the Lombard communities by the Duke of

Milan in 1469. Manno was related to Salomone da Piove, whose firstborn son Marcuccio had married one of his brother Angelo's daughters.[66] Manno was to meet Salomone da Piove at fairly frequent intervals at Venice, where he had more or less officially opened a money lending shop, of secondary importance compared to the great bank at Padua but still of strategic importance.[67]

Letter in Hebrew sent by the banker Manno (Mandele) of Pavia to the physician Omobono Bonim of Venice, March 1476 (State Archive of Trent, Archivio Principesco Vescovile, S.L., 69, 68).

When Salomone Fürstungar, just recovering from the setback at Innsbruck, thirsting for revenge or just to reshuffle the cards, took to considering murdering the captain of the guards of the podestà of Trent and even bishop Hinderbach himself, hiring an assassin for the task, a person above suspicion, a priest named Paolo da Novara, the industrious Manno offered to finance the bold initiative, without regard to cost.[68] Manno asked the priest, Paolo da Novara, who was probably contacted through his brother Bartolomeo, a druggist at Piove di Sacco,[69] to poison the persons responsible for the Trent trial and to obtain the arsenic required to do so from the Venetian physician Omobono (Bunim), owner of the "della Vecchia" pharmacy at San Cassian, who is also believed to have issued instructions on how to use the arsenic. As a reward, Paolo was to receive four hundred ducats, half of it immediately, and the other two hundred to be withdrawn over the counter at Manno's bank at Venice.[70] But the conspiracy, the most prominent members of which were all Jews from Pavia, Padua, Novara, Soncino, Parma, Piacenza, Modena, Brescia, Bassano, Rovereto, Riva and Venice, failed miserably, with the arrest and confession of the fanciful and avaricious priest.

***

NOTES TO CHAPTER ONE

[1] Cfr. P. Ghinzoni, *Federico III Imperatore a Venezia (dal 19 febbraio 1469)*, in "Archivio Veneto", n.s., XIX (1889), no. 37, pp. 133-144.

[2] On the Roman coronation of Friedrich III in 1452 see, recently, Ph. Braunstein, *L'événement et la mémoire: regards privés, rapports officiels sur le couronnement romain de Federic III*, in "La circulation de nouvelles au Moyen Age", Société des Historiens Médievistes de l'Enseignement Supérieur Public, Publications de la Sorbonne, Ecole Française, Roma, C. (1994), pp. 219-229. Friedrich had also been in Venice in 1436, returning from a pilgrimage. The imperial retinue in 1452 was particularly numerous, as shown by the Cronaca di Zorzi Dolfin, cited by Marin Sanudo ("[...] con bocche 1.500 a spexa della Signoria e a Trivixo erano cavalli 1.200 che lo aspettavono; la spexa era al giorno ducati 1000 per dodici giorni" ["with 1,500 mouths to feed at His Lordship's expense and 1,200 horses at Treviso waiting for him; the expenses amounted to 1,000 ducats per day"]. The dance in the hall of the Greater Council was held "cum infinite donne della terra, 250") ["with infinite numbers of ladies from the mainland, 250"]. For this passage from the Cronaca del Dolfin, see the Biblioteca Marciana, Venice, Italian manuscripts, cl. VII, cod. 794 (8503), c. 310r. See also Marin Sanudo, *Le vite dei dogi (1423-1474). I: 1423-1457*, by A. Caracciolo Aricò, Venice, 1999, pp. 471-473. During his visit to Venice in 1469, where "li fo fatti grandissimi apparati" ["where great displays of magnificence were prepared for him"], Friedrich's retinue was reduced and consisted of eight hundred dignitaries. Friedrich, on this third visit, was sumptuously received at the Palazzo Ducale "et, venendo a veder Rialto, errano sopra li banchi posti assaissimi ducati et do garzoni picholi in camixa con una palla per uno in mano, che l'uno et l'altro si butavono li ditti ducati, si come si butta formento" ["and, when he came to see the Rialto, large quantities of gold ducats had been placed on stands in a high place, where two little boys in shirt sleeves, each with a paddle in his hand, were tossing the ducats about, as if they were grain"]. (see Marin Sanudo, *Le vite dei dogi. II: 1457-1474*, Venice, 2004, pp. 109-111).

[3] On this visit, and probably on the preceding visit in 1452 as well, it seems that some Venetian patricians were awarded the rank of knight

by Friedrich (Sanudo, *Le vite dei dogi*, cit., vol. II, p. 109: "li fo fatto festa in sala del Gran Conseio [...] et sopra il soler lo Imperador fece alchuni zentilomeni cavalieri") ["The Emperor was greeted in the Greater Council with great pomp and ceremony [...] and on the terrace he dubbed several gentlemen knights"].

[4] On Michele Colli's report to the Duke of Milan cfr Ghinzoni, *Federico III imperatore a Venezia*, cit., p. 151. See also D. Rando, *Dai margini la memoria. Johannes Hinderbach (1418-1486)*, Bologna, 2003, pp. 345-346. Michele Colli was probably a member of the entourage of Andrea Colli, Milanese ambassador at Venice, of whom he was a relative.

[5] Cfr. Rando, *Dai margini la memoria*, cit., p. 346. In 1452, Hinderbach had taken advantage of Friedrich's stay at Padua, on the way to Rome, where he was to be crowned Emperor, to obtain his own doctorate in a solemn ceremony, held in the cathedral, in the presence of large numbers of prelates, noblemen and academics, "quo actu nullus numquam insignior habitus, cui tot et tanti principes et nobiles interfuissent" ["in which act there was never anything more magnificent, there were so many princes and noblemen there"] (cfr. V. von Hofmann-Wellenhof, *Leben und Schriften des Doctor Johannes Hinderbach, Bischofs von Trent, 1465-1486*, in "Zeitschrift des Ferdinandeums für Tirol und Vorarlberg", s. 3, XXXVII, 1893, pp. 259-262).

[6] For the text of the depositions of Tobias da Magdeburg before the Trent judges during the 1475 trials for the death of Simon, son of Andrea Lomferdorm, see A. Esposito and D. Quaglioni, *Processi contro gli ebrei di Trento, 1475-1478. I: I processi del 1475*, Padua, 1990, pp. 307-348. See also G. Divina's argument in *Storia del beato Simone da Trento*, Trent, 1902, vol. II, pp. 8-12; pp. 45-47. Quaglioni (*"Orta est disputatio super matheria promotionis inter doctores". L'ammissione degli ebrei al dottorato*, in "Micrologus. Natura, scienza e società medievali", IX, 2001 [Gli ebrei e le scienze], pp. 249-267) examines in detail the deposition of the physician Tobias at the Trent trial, whose confession was extorted "con torture raffinatissime che conducono l'inquisito in punto di morte" ["with exceedingly refined methods of torture which practically kill the person under investigation"], but he nonetheless considers it a document rich in details of indubitable truthfulness.

[7] "Tempore quo Serenissimus Imperator erat Venetiis, modo possunt esse VI vel VII anni, ipse Thobias reperit se Venetiis [...] et dicit quod tunc erat ibi magna multitudo Iudeorum, qui tunc venerant Venetiis post Serenissimum Imperatorem, causa emenda merces, ad

finem ut non haberent causam solvendi gabellas pro mercibus predictis, quia illas tales mercea postea mittebant cum preparamentis seu caribus prefati Serenissimi Imperatoris, dicendo quod erant bona prefati Domini Imperatoris" [Approximately: "During the Emperor's stay at Venice, perhaps about 6 or 7 years ago, this Tobias found himself at Venice, too [...] and he said that there were great multitudes of Jews there, who followed the Emperor to Venice to sell goods, since they didn't have to pay any duty on those goods, because they took the goods with them in the Emperor's baggage train, saying they belonged to the Emperor:"] (cfr. Esposito and Quaglioni, *Processi*, cit., vol. I, pp. 328-329).

[8] The privilege granted by Friedrich to the Board is dated 16 February 1469 (cfr. R. Palmer, *The "Studio" of Venice and its Graduates in the Sixteenth Century*, Triest-Padua, 1983, p. 58). With regards to the imperial visit to Italy in 1452, Enea Silvio Piccolomini, in his *Historia Australis* reported that "multos [doctores Federicus] in Italia promovit, quibus aurum pro scientia fuit" (cfr. M.J. Wenninger, *Zur Promotion jüdischer Ärzte duch Kaiser Friedrich III*, in "Aschkenas", no. 2, p. 419). The *Diario Ferrarese* reports that Friedrich III, visiting Ferrara in 1452 after the Roman coronation, was received in a solemn ceremony by the Marchese Borso d'Este and the bishop of Ferrara, "con tutta la chierexia et multi doctori ferraresi" ["with the whole hierarchy and many learned men from Ferrara"], cit., in R. Bonfil, *Rabbis and Jewish Communities in Renaissance Italy*, Oxford, 1990, p. 87.

[9] In this regard, see D. Nissim's recent publication, *Un "minian" di ebrei ashkenaziti a Venezia negli anni 1465-1480*, in "Italia", XIV (2004), pp. 41-47.

[10] On Mosè Rapa (Moshè Rapp), whose documentary evidence dates back to 1475, cfr. "Hebräische Bibliographie", VI (1863), footnote p. 67. On Raspe and the other physician "Lazzaro", recorded at Venice in December 1465, see also I. Munz, *Die Jüdischen Ärzte im Mittelalter*, Frankfurt A.M., 1922.

[11] On Maestro Omobono and his involvement in the Trent trials, see Divina, *Storia del beato Simone da Trento*, cit., vol. II, p. 169. For other information relating to him, cfr. D. Carpi, *L'individuo e la collettività. Saggi di storia degli ebrei a Padova e nel Veneto nell'età del Rinascimento*, Florence, 2002, pp. 221-224. Carpi reports that Leone, son of the "magistri Hominisboni medici ebrei de Veneciis" ["Omobono, the master Jewish doctor from Venice"], in 1471 had had a certain Marco di Salomone Ungar incarcerated at Padua for debt. Omobono lived "appresso la Casa dei Bresciani" and G. Tassini

(*Curiosità veneziane*, Venice, 1863, pp. 96-97), notes in this regard that "alcuni paesi della Repubblica, come Brescia, godevano il diritto di tenere in Venezia particolare alberghi coll'oggetto di alloggiare i propri nunzi, con l'andare del tempo transformate in communi osterie e taverne" ["a few regions of the Republic, such as Brescia, enjoyed the right to keep private inns in Venice for the purpose of lodging their own nuncios, and in time these inns became transformed into ordinary eating houses and taverns"]. For the correspondence of the name Omobono or Bonomo with Simcha Bunem or Bunim among the Ashkenazi Jews, see V. Colorni, *Judaica Minora, Saggi sulla storia dell'ebraismo italiano dall'antichita all'età moderna*, Milan, 1983, p. 787.

[12] Cfr.P.C. Ioly Zorattini, *Processi del S. Uffizio contro ebrei e giudaizzanti*. I: *1548-1560*, Florence, pp. 339-340.

[13] Cfr. R. Sege, *Cristiani novelli e medici ebrei a Venezia: storie di Inquisizione tra Quattro e Cinquecento*, in M. Perani, *Una manna buona per Mantova. Man tov le-Man Tovah. Studi in onore di Vittore Colorni per il suo 92° compleanno*, Florence, 2004, pp. 383-389.

[14] In the ample bibliography on Jehudah messer Leon, see, in particular, D. Carpi, *Notes on the Life of R. Judah Messer Leon*, in E. Toaff, *Studi sull'ebraismo italiano in memoria di C. Roth*, Rome, 1974, p. 37-62; V. Colorni, *Note per la biblografia de alcuni dotti ebrei vissuti a Mantova nel secolo XV*, in "Annuario di Studi Ebraici", I, (1935), pp. 169-182; M. Luzzati, *Dottorati in medicina conferiti a Firenze nel 1472 da Judah Messer Leon da Montecchio a Bonaventura da Terracina e ad Abramo da Montalcino*, in *Medicina e salute nelle Marche dal Rinascimento all'età napoleonica*, in "Atti e memorie", XCVII (1992), pp. 41-53. The hypothesis that Jehudah messer Leon was a native of Montecchio Maggiore in the Vicentino is advanced by I. Rabbinowitz, *The Book of the Honeycomb's Flow* by Judah Messer Leon, Ithaca (N.Y.)-London, 1983, p. XX, and recently made by H. Tirosh-Rothschild, *Between Worlds. The Life and Thought of R. David b. Judah Messer Leon*, Albany (N.Y.), 1991, p. 25, and by G. Busi, *Il succo dei favi. Studi sull'umanesimo ebraico*, Bologna, 1992, p. 19.

[15] The text of the imperial diploma granted to Jehudah messer Leon, dated 21 February 1469, and published in full by Carpi, *Notes on the Life of R. Judah Messer Leon*, cit., pp. 59-60.

[16] The imperial privileges granted to the two Jewish Sicilian physicians, dated 4 August 1489, the their text, has been published by Wenninger (*Zur Promotion jüdischer Ärtzte*, cit., pp. 413-424). Salomone Azeni was almost certainly identical with Salomone Siciliano, active at Padua in the last decade of the Fifteenth Century

(cfr. Carpi, *L'individuo e la collettività*, cit., pp. 222, 224).

[17] E. Capsali, *Seder Eliyahu Zuta*, by A. Schmuelevitz, Sh. Simonsohn and M. Benayahu, Jerusalem, 1977, vol. II, p. 260. On this matter, cfr Nissim, *Un "minian" di ebrei ashkenaziti a Venezia*, cit., pp. 42-43. On Capsali's work, see, recently, G. Corazzol, *Sulla Cronaca dei Sovrani di Venezia ("Divre' hayamim le-malke' Wenesty'ah") di Rabbi Elia Capsali da Candia*, in "Studi Veneziani", XLVII (2004), pp. 313-330.

[18] On David Magrogonato, "judeus de Creta et mercator in Venetiis" ["Jew from Crete and merchant at Venice"], see, in particular, D. Jacoby, *David Mavrogonato of Candia. Fifteenth Century Jewish Merchant, Intercessor and Spy*, in "Tarbiz", XXXII (1964), pp. 388-402 (in Hebrew); Id., *Un Agent juif au service de Venise. David Mavrogonato de Candie*, in "Thesaurismata. Bollettino dell'Istituto Ellenico di Studi Bizantini e Post-Bizantini", IX (1972), pp. 68-77, (republished in Id., *Recherches sur la Méditerannée orientale du XIIe au XVe siècle*, London, 1979, pp. 68-96); M. Manoussacas, *Le receuil de privilèges de la famille juive Mavroganto de Crète (1464-1642)*, in "Byzantinische Forschungen", XII (1987), pp. 345-366; Carpi, *L'individuo e la colletività*, cit., pp. 41-43.

[19] "Et erat etatis annorum XL quatuor vel quinquaginta, cum capillis et barba nigra prolixa, more Greco, et indutus clamide nigro usque ad pedes, cum caputio nigro in capite, dicens quod aliquando induebat se veste sicut portant Greci" ["He was about 44 or 45 years old, with black hair and a long black beard, in the Greek style, and wore a black cap on his head, saying that he preferred to dress like a Greek"], (cfr. Esposito e Quaglioni, *Processi*, cit., vol. I, p. 329). On the indubitable identification of the personage in question with David Mavrogonato, see D. Nissim, *Il legame tra I processi di Trento contro gli ebrei e la tipografia ebraica di Piova di Sacco del 1475*, in "Annali dell'Istituto Storico Italo-Germanico in Trento", XXV (1999), pp. 669-678.

[20] Cfr Jacoby, *Un agent juif*, cit., pp. 69-70; Manoussacas, *Le recueil de privilèges*, cit., p. 345.

[21] "Praedictus David [...] passus fuit et publicum odium, quod ipse in tota insula tam per Christianos quam per Judeos acquisisset, cum jam digito mostraretur ab omnibus." ["The aforementioned David [...] became an object of public hatred, known to both Jews and Christians all over the island, who pointed him out with their fingers"]. This document, dated 29 December 1463, together with other privileges granted Mavrogonato by Venice, is located in the Archivio di Stato di Venezia (henceforth: ASV), *Inquisitorato agli Ebrei*, envelope 19, doc

no. 3.

Late printed copies of these privileges, entitled *Per David Mavrogonato contro Senseri Ordinari di Rialto e Stampa dell'Università tutta degli Ebrei di Venezia* are located in the ASV, *Inquisitorato agli Ebrei* (envelopes 39 and 5 respectively). See also, in this regard, Manoussacas, *Le recueil de privilèges*, cit., p. 346.

²² Cfr. Jacoby, *Un agent juif*, cit., pp. 81-82.

²³ "Se degni concierderli ch'el porta segno del O. per sua salude ch'el possa portare Arme [...]. Item li sia concesso poder cavar de Bando per puro omicidio do Persone solamente." ["If he be deemed worthy to be granted the right to bear the insignia of the O. [O. = possibly "Uomo da bene", gentleman or Christian] for his health and to bear arms [...]; that he be granted the right to cause certain persons wanted for homicide to be stricken from the list of banned persons"]. This last clause appears in the printed document in the ASV, *Inquisitorato agli Ebrei*, envelope 39, while it is missing from the manuscript text of the privileges (ibidem, envelope 19, doc no. 4).

²⁴ Cfr. Jacoby, *Un agent juif*, cit., pp. 75-77.

²⁵ Cfr. Manoussacas, *Le recueuil de privilèges*, cit., p. 345. See also Sanudo's comments on the year 1466: "In questo mezo Vettor Capello, Capetanio Zeneral nostro, havendo hautto pr via di quel David (Mavrogonato) hebreo il salvoconducto dal Signor turcho di poter la Signoria mandarli uno ambassado [... per] veder i tratar qualche acordo" ["In this way, Vettor Capello, our Captain General, having obtained through David (Mavrogonato) a safeconduct from the Great Turk to send an ambassador [...to] attempt to reach some agreement"], (Sanudo, *Le vite dei dogi*, cit., vol. II, pp. 88-89.

²⁶ In a letter dated 18 December 1470 and addressed to the Duke of Crete, the Doge referred to Mavrogonato's death ("qui denique eundo in servitiis nostris admisit vitam") ["who was furthermore acting in our service at the risk of his life"], praising his loyalty to the Republic (cfr. Jacoby, *Un agent juif*, cit., pp. 76-77).

²⁷ Among the privileges granted on 2 July 1466 by the Consiglio dei Dieci to David Mavrogonato, his children and descendents, in addition to his bodyguards, Andrea Cornaro also reported that of "di non portar beretta giallo o altro segno, che portano li Hebrei nel capello, ma portino il capello negro come li Christiani, per la qual cosa d'alhora in qua detti Hebrei Mavrgonato si dicono Mauroberti (recte: Maurobereti) per sopranome, che vuol dire baretta negra" ["of not wearing a yellow cap or other sign usually worn by Jews on their hats, but to wear a black cap like the Christians, for which reason Mavrogonato was thereafter called by the last name of Mauroberti

(*recte*: Maurobareti), which means black cap"] (cfr. Jacoby, *Un agent juif*, cit., p. 79).

[28] "David praedictus dixit et declaravit quod socius suus, signi non portandi et arma [ferendi], est Salamon qn. Marcu, cuius auxilio et consilio usus fuit in praedictus et omnia (recte: circa) praedicta" ["the aforementioned David said and declared that Salomone, son of the late Marcuccio, was his assistant and advisor in all the aforementioned activities, being entitled to carry a weapon and go about without any insignia"] (ASV, *Inquisitorato agli Ebrei*, envelope 39, Per David Maurogonato contro Senseri Ordinarj di Rialto, dated 1 February 1464 [1463 *more veneto*].

[29] On 17 June 1465, David Mavrogonato announced to two representatives of the Consiglio dei Dieci "quod relinquit pro eo et agendis suis in Venetiis Salomonem de Plebisacci hebreum, quia de eo se confidet" ["that the Jew Salomone da Piove was acting on his behalf and as his agent, since he had complete confidence in him"]; (the document, published in the original by Manoussacas, is cited by Jacoby, *Un agent juif*, cit., p. 74 and by Carpi, *L'individuo e la collettività*, cit., p. 42). The privileges granted by the authorities at Venice to Salomone da Piove are indirectly confirmed in a *parte*, approved by the Consiglio del Comune di Padova on 22 January 1467. In this, the Paduan rulers claimed that they were applying the standards of the Statutes against Salomone ("casum querelle seu accuse contra Iudeum de Plebe") ["because of the quarrels caused by his accusations against Salomone da Piove"], notwithstanding the protection which he enjoyed in Venice (Archivio di Stato di Padova [henceforth: ASP], Consiglio del Commune, Atti, 7, c. 202v).

[30] On Salomone di Marcuccio da Piove di Sacco and his family, see D. Jacoby, *New Evidence on Jewish Bankers in Venice and the Venetian Terraferma (c. 1450-1550)*, in A. Toaff and Sh. Schwarzfuchs, *The Mediterranean and the Jews. Banking, Finance and International Trade (XVI-XVIII Centuries)*, Ramat Gan, 1989, pp. 151-178; Carpi, *L'individuo e la collettività*, cit., pp. 27-60; D. Nissim, *I primordi della stampa ebraica nell'Italia settentrionale. Piove di Sacco-Soncino (1469-1496)*, Soncino, 2004, pp. 9-13.

[31] In this regard, see, among others, Ph. Braunstein, *Le commerce du fer à Venise au Xve siècle*, in "Studi Veneziani", VIII (1966), pp. 267-302; *Le prêt sur gage à Padoue et dans le Padouan au milieu du XVe siècle*, in G. Cozzi, *Gli ebrei e Venezia (secoli XIV-XVIII)*, Milan, 1987, pp. 652-653; M. Toch, *The Formation of a Diaspora. The Settlement of Jews in the Medieval German Reich*, in "Aschkenas", VII (1997), no. 1, pp. 55-78. For an illustration of this phenomenon, see

also L. Boeninger, *La Regula bilingue della scuola dei calzolai tedeschi a Venezia del 1383*, Venice, 2002.

[32] Cfr. A. Toaff, *Migrazioni di ebrei tedeschi attraverso i territori triestini e friulani fra XIV e XV secolo*, in G. Todeschini and P.C. Ioly Zorattini, *Il mondo ebraico. Gli ebrei tra Italia-nord-orientale e Impero asburgico dal Medioevo all'Età contemporanea*, Pordenone, 1991, pp. 3-29; A. Toaff, *Gli insediamenti ashkenaziti nell'Italia settentrionale*, in *Storia d'Italia. Annali*. XI: *Gli ebrei in Italia*, tome I: *Dall'Alto Medioevo all'età dei ghetti*, by C. Vivanti, Turin, 1996, pp. 153-171.

[33] Cfr. R.C. Mueller, *Les prêteurs juifs de Venise au Moyen Age*, in "Annales ESC", XXX (1975), pp. 1277-1302; Id., *The Jewish Moneylenders of the Late Trecento Venise. A Revisitation*, in "Mediterranean Historical Review", X (1995), pp. 202-217.

[34] Cfr. E. Concina, *Parva Jerusalem*, in E. Concina, U. Camerino and D. Calabri, *La città degli ebrei. Il ghetto di Venezia: architettura e urbanistica*, Venice, 1991, pp. 24-25.

[35] Cfr. E. Ashtor, *Gli inizi della communita ebraica a Venezia*, in "La Rassegna Mensile di Israel", XLIV (1978), pp. 700-701 (the essay has been republished in U. Fortis, *Venezia ebraica*, Rome, 1982, 17-39). See also Nissim, *Un "minian" di ebrei ashkenaziti a Venezia*, cit., pp. 44-45.

[36] Cfr. Toaff, *Migrazioni di ebrei tedeschi*, cit., pp. 7-8, 15-21; Id., *Gli insediamenti ashkenaziti nell'Italia settentrionale*, cit., pp. 157-159, 165-171.

[37] Still at the beginnings of the Seventeenth century, Leon (Jehudah Arieh) da Modena, rabbi at Venice, observed, in this regard, that "nella pronuntia di essa lingua Hebrea sono talmente poi tra di loro differenti, che a pena sono intesi i Thedeschi da gl'Italiani" ["they pronounce the Hebrew language so differently that Italian Jews can hardly understand the German ones"]. (Leon da Modena, *Historia degli riti hebraici*, Paris, 1637, p. 36). An informative document in this regard is the inventory of goods transported by an Ashkenazi Jew, a native of one of the Jewish communities of northern Italy and traveling to Schwedt in the diocese of Brandenburg, not far from Frankfurt am Oder, in the last quarter of the 15th Century, on his travels. The interesting list appears drawn up in Hebrew and Yiddish, while the Italian terms are transcribed in Hebrew letters (cfr. A.K. Offenberg, *How to Define Printing in Hebrew. A Fifteenth-Century List of Goods of a Jewish Traveller and his Wife*, in "The Library", Oxford, VI s., XVI (1994), pp. 43-49).

[38] Cfr. A. Toaff, *Convergenze sul Veneto di banchieri ebrei romani e tedeschi nel tardo Medioevo*, in Cozzi, *Gli ebrei e Venezia*, cit., pp.

595-613. See also Ph. Braunstein (ibidem, p. 690), which accepts my own conclusions as stated above.

[39] Cfr. M. Lucchetta, *Benedetto Jew of Ratisbona de fu maestro Josef banchiero pubblico di Venzone*, Udine, 1971. See also M. Davide, *La communità ebraica nella Venzone del Quattrocento*, in "Ce fastu", LXXX (2004), pp. 167-186.

[40] Cfr. M de Szombathely, *Libro delle Riformazioni or Libro dei Consigli (1411-1429)*, Trieste, 1970, pp. 4-6.

[41] Cfr. Toaff, *Gli insediamenti ashkenaziti nell'Italia settentrionale*, cit., pp. 162-163.

[42] Cfr. Id., *Migrazioni di ebrei tedeschi*, cit., pp. 11-14.

[43] Cfr. Id., *Gli insediamenti ashkenaziti nell'Italia settentrionale*, cit., pp. 160-161.

[44] Cfr. A. Sinnacher, *Beyträge zur Geschichte der bischöflichen Kirche Säben und Brixen in Tyrol*, Brixen, 1826, pp. 3-21; R. Palme, *Sulla storia sociale e giuridica degli ebrei in Tirolo nel tardo Medievo e all'inizio dell'età moderna*, in "Materiali di Lavoro", 1988, nos. 1-4, 119-130.

[45] Cfr. L. Billiani, *Dei Toscani ed ebrei prestatori di denaro a Gemona*, Udine, 1895, pp. 123-126.

[46] The most important (and perhaps not the only) exception seems to be that of Vicenza, in which the Italian (Roman) element gained the upper hand over the Ashkenazi during the Fifteenth Century. See R. Scuro, *Alcune notizie sulla presenza ebraica a Vicenza nel XV secolo*, in G.M. Varanini and R.C. Mueller *Ebrei nella Terraferma veneta del Quattrocento*, Florence, 2005, p. 106.

[47] The processes and events which, in the mid-Fifteenth Century, led to the forced transfer of money lending in this zone from Italian Jews to German Jews have been studied in many precise research papers. See, among others, Braunstein, *Le prêt sur gage à Padoue*, cit., pp. 651-669; G.M. Varanini, *Appunti per la storia del prestito de dell'insediamento ebraico a Verona nel Quattrocento*, in Cozzi, *Gli ebrei e Venezia*, cit., pp. 615-628; G.M. Varanini, *Il commune di Verona, Venezia e gli ebrei nel Quattrocento. Problemi e linee di ricerca*, in Id., *Communi cittadini e stato regionale. Ricerche sulla Terraferma veneta nel Quattrocento*, Verona, 1992, pp. 279-293; M. Nardello, *Il prestito ad sua a Vinceza e la vicenda delgi ebrei nei secoli XIV e XIV*, in "Odeo Olimpico", XIII-XIV (1977-1978), pp. 123-125; Carpi, *L'individuo e la collettività*, cit., pp. 34, 130-132; Scuro, *Alcune notizie sulla presenza ebraica a Vicenza*, cit., pp. 103-121.

[48] See Braunstein's intelligent contributions in this regard, *Le prêt sur gage à Padoue*, cit., pp. 662-663.

⁴⁹ It is significant that, on 12 January 1461, the Consiglio del Commune di Padova lamented the fact that, with the formal coverage of the banks of Piove di Sacco, Monselice and Este, the Jewish money lenders continued to operate illegally on the market at Padua, charging interest at rates over 40% ("contra Statuta nonnulli Iudei per quamdam viam indirectam fenerari incipient in civitate Padue hoc modo, videlicit quod in Padua accipiunt pignora et mutuant pecunias et postea fieri faciunt bulletinem per Iudeos fenerantes in Montessellice vel Plebe aut in Este, fingendo quod Iudeus de Plebe aut de Montesselice vel de Este sit ille qui mutuet tales pecunias, cum quibus Iudeis de ei habitantes Padue ses intelligunt cum lucro quadraginta pro centenario ut ultra") ["notwithstanding the laws stipulating that no Jew may lend at usury in the city of Padua, either directly or indirectly, particularly, that they accept collateral in Padua and lend money at usury and then fabricate vouchers from Jewish money lenders at Piove or Montesselice or Este, pretending that it is those Jews who are actually lending the money in Padua, thus making a profit of forty percent or more"]. The rulers of Padua protested before the Doge of Venice, objecting to the fact that Jewish money lenders had been granted the right to operate in this manner thanks to letters patent issued in their favor by the authorities of Venice ("quod sua Excelsitudo dignetur revocare dictas litteras concessas prefatis Iudeis, quia, stantibus dictis litteris, dicti Iudei per hanc viam mutuabunt pecunias sub uxuris; nam si mutuarent publice et palam sicut facere soliti errant, non haberent nisi .XV pr centenario" ["may his Excellency deign to revoke the said letters granted to the above mentioned Jews, because, being in the possession of such letters, these Jews are enabled to lend money at usury; while if they did so publicly and openly as they usually do, they would not even earn 15 percent"]. ASP, Consiglio del Comune, Atti, 7., cc. Cv-6r).

⁵⁰ Salomone, in 1441, when he was still called "da Cividale" and not yet "da Piove di Sacco", had set up banks at Verona and Soave, transferring them to Padua in 1442 (cfr. A. Castaldini, *Mondi paralleli. Ebrei e Cristiani nell'Italia padana dal tardo Medioevo all'Età moderna*, Florence, 2004, p. 59).

⁵¹ This is attested to by numerous studies by D. Nissim. Among others, particular attention should be paid to D. Nissim, *Nel quinto centenario delle prime stampe ebraiche (1475-1975)*, in "Atti e Memorie dell'Academia Patavina di Scienze", Lettere ed Arte, LXXXVI (1975-1976), part III, pp. 43-52; Id., *Spigolature di bibliografia ebraica*, in A. Toaff, *Studi sull'ebraismo italiano presentati ad Elio Toaff*, Rome, 1984; pp: 129-155; Id., *I primordi della stampa ebraica nell'Italia Settentrionale*, cit.

⁵² The hypothesis, sustained by Nissim (*Famiglie Rapa e Rapaport nell'Italia settentrionale, sec. XV-XVI. Con un' appendice sull'origine della Miscellanea Rothschild*, in A. Piattelli and M. Silvera, *Minhat Yehuda. Saggi sull'ebraismo italiano in memoria di Yehuda Nello Pavoncello*, Rome, 2001, pp. 190-192), is based on the studies of U. Bauer-Eberhardt (*Die Rothschild Miscellanea in Jerusalem: Hauptwerke des Leonardo Bellini*, in "Pantheon", XLII, 1984, pp. 229-237), expressing the opinion that the miniatures in the *Rothschild Miscellany*, currently preserved at the Israel Museum of Jerusalem, were probably executed at Venice in Leonardo Bellini's workshop, and perhaps by the same master. But see L. Mortara Ottolenghi, *The Rothschild Miscellany MS 180/51 of the Israel Musem in Jerusalem. Jewish Patrons and Christian Artists*, in "Hebrew Studies", British Library Occasional Papers, 13, London, 1991, pp. 149-161. In contrast to Bauer-Eberhardt and Nissim, the illustrious Canadian scholar attributes the miniatures to the schools of two major Christian artists of Cremona, Bonifacio Bembo and Cristoforo de Predis (circa 1460-1480), identifying the client as the Jew Furlano da Cremona, i.e., the banker Mosè di Consiglio Sacerdoti. According to Nissim, who believes that he has succeeded in identifying the client as Salomone di Marcuccio da Piove, a resident of Venice; the reason why the latter's name does not appear in the manuscript, where the name of the rabbi Moshè b. Jekutiel Coen Rapa, his protégé, does appear, could be explained by Salomone's sudden and mysterious death, occurring in 1475, when the code was not yet completed (written communication from D. Nissim dated 11 November 2004).

⁵³ Cfr. Segre, *Cristiani novelli e medici ebrei a Venezia*, cit., pp. 388-389.

⁵⁴ Cfr. Carpi, *L'individuo e la collettività*, pp. 44-45.

⁵⁵ Cfr. ibidem, p. 39. It is important to note that on 25 March 1470, a few months before David Mavrogonato's last voyage, the Serenissima charged Salomone da Piove with effecting, for his account, a loan of 100 ducats to Mavrogonato ("David hebreo de Candia"). The money was to be used by the Candian government to pay the captain of the galleys of Alexandria (ASV, Collegio, Notatorio, reg. 11, 68r). Venice's intention was therefore that Mavrogonato should reach Candia, a location to which he never returned – probably for good reason – after the first mission.

⁵⁶ Salomone da Piove's plan emerges clearly from a petition sent by his son Salamoncino to the Consiglio dei Dieci of Venice dated 9 July 1477. On the Venetian conspiracy against Maometo II, see, F. Babinger, *Ja'acub-Pascha, ein Leibartzt Mehmeds II, Leben und*

Schicksale des Maestro Jacopo aus Gaeta, in "Rivista delgi Studi Orientali", XXVI (1951), pp. 87-113.

[57] The famous family of Wallach di Worms, the members of which were physicians by tradition, have left us numerous testimonies, which are particularly far-reaching starting with the early Cinquecento. Cfr. *Jewish Encyclopedia*, New York-London, 1901-1906, s.v. *Wallich (Wlk)*. The name *Valk, Volk, Valke* for *Falco, Falcone* is attested to in the Middle Ages among the Jews of Cologne, Nuremberg and Frankfurt (cfr. A. Beider, *A Dictionary of Ashkenazic Given Names*, Bergenfield, N.J., 2001, p. 306).

[58] Cfr. Babinger, *Ja'aqub-Pascha*, cit., pp. 106-107.

[59] Cfr. ibidem, pp. 90-106; B. Lewis, *The Privilege Granted by Mehmed II to his Physician*, in "Bulletin of the School of Oriental and African Studies", XIV (1952), pp. 550-563.

[60] Cfr. Jacoby, *Un agent juif*, cit., pp. 76-77.

[61] On these events, see Esposito and Quaglioni, *Processi*, cit., vol. I, pp. 1-51. Among the defense attorneys acting for the Trent defendants was Antonio Capodilista, one of the most illustrious jurists in Padua (cfr. ibidem, pp. 447-454).

[62] Cfr. Nissim, *I primordi della stampa ebraica nell'Italia Settentrionale*, cit., pp. 12-13.

[63] "Salomon [Fürstungar] ivert ad Illustriss. Principem Ducem Austriae [...] et Salomon dixit res male succebat, quia persuasum erat Illustriss. Principi quod deberet pati quod iustitia haberet suum locum et quod, si volebat quod justitia haberet suum locum, erat necesse quod procedatur contra Judeos incarceratos, et hoc ut sciretur an praedicti Judaei incarcerati essent culpabiles vel inculpabiles, et quod si reperirentur inculpabiles relaxarentur, et si culpabiles punirentur. Et quo ex ista ratione Illustriss. Princips noluerunt mandare quod praedicti Judaei incarcerati relaxarentur". ["Salomon [Fürstungar] turned to the Prince Duke of Austria [...] and Salomon said that things were going very badly, because the Illustrious Prince was convinced that justice should be done and that, if he wished justice to be done, it was necessary to proceed against the imprisoned Jews, and a determination should be made as to their guilt or innocence, and that if they were innocent, they should be released, and that if they were guilty they should be punished. And it was for this reason that the Illustrious Prince did not wish to release the aforementioned Jews from prison".] Cfr. [Benedetto Bonelli], *Dissertazione apologetica sul martirio del beato Simone da Trent nell'anno MCCCCLXXV dagli ebrei ucciso*, Trent, Gianbattista Parone, 1747, p. 145. Bonelli's research, although often invalidated by anti-Semitic prejudice in its conclusions, is always

documented and performed with scientific accuracy. See also Divina, *Storia del beato Simone da Trento*, cit., vol. II, pp. 77-94. "Salomone [Fürstungar] could not be recognized as a Jew because he wore a jacket cut in the German manner and a short cloak and had a German-style cap on his head" (cfr. ibidem, pp. 92-93).

[64] In 1476, in a document from Verona, Salamoncino's son is referred to as "Salamoncinus quondam Salamonis de Plebe" (cfr. Varanini, *Appunti per la storia del prestito*, cit., p. 627).

[65] On Manno di Aberlino (Mendele b. Abraham), banker at Pavia and one of the most important exponents of the Jewish community in the Duchy of Milan, see Sh. Simonsohn, *The Jews in the Duchy of Milan*, Jerusalem, 1982, vol. II, pp. 486, no. 1144, and p. 534, no. 1267. Manno da Pavia's geneology has been reconstructed by Carpi (*Notes on the Life of R. Judah Messer Leon*, cit., p. 62). The Jews in the Ashkenazi community of Northern Italy called Manno da Pavia "uno de' più ricchi hebrei" ["one of the richest Jews"].

[66] Cfr. Simonsohn, *The Jews in the Duchy of Milan*, cit., vol. II, pp. 864-865, no. 2078.

[67] In 1476, as shall see below, Manno offered to pay an assassin to kill the bishop of Trent, offering him a sum to be paid to him in part out of the bank in Venice. Cfr. Divina, *Storia del beato Simone da Trento*, cit., vol. II, p. 167.

[68] "Dum ipse Presbyter Paulus esset Papiae, Man Judaeus ibi habibator dedit sibi Presbytero Paulo certas litteras, quas deferre debebat Venetias et illas consignare cuidamn Omnibono Judaeo, quae litterae, prout Man dixit sibi Presbytero Paulo, continebant istud, videlicet quod Man mittebat ipsum Presbyterum Paulum ad Omnibonum ut idem Omnibonus instrueret ipsum [...] de modo venenandi praelibatum Reverendissimum D. Episcopum Tridentinum" [Approximately: "When Paolo the priest was in Padua, Manno the Jew, who lived there, gave Paolo, the priest, certain letters which he was to take to Venice and deliver to a certain Omobono, a Jew. The letters said that Manno was sending Paolo to Omobono and that Omobono was to instruct the priest [...] on how best to poison the Most Reverend Bishop of Trent"] (cfr. [Bonelli], *Dissertazione apologetica*, cit., pp. 146-147).

[69] Cfr. Divina, *Storia del beato Simone da Trento*, cit., vol. II, p. 147.

[70] The records of the Trent trials contain transcriptions, marred by many errors, of a letter in Hebrew, signed by Manno da Pavia and addressed to Omobono in the month of March 1476 ("all'esperto medico Simcha Bunim Sal di Venezia"). The letter had been confiscated from the priest Paolo da Novara, who intended to visit

Venice to meet the Jewish physician according to instructions received. The letter carried information relating to the forthcoming payment of 90 ducats "nelle mani della persona in oggetto" ["into the hands of the person in object"] (the beneficiary is a Christian), as part payment of an agreed sum. The message contains a covert allusion to the delicate mission which the priest from Novara intended to undertake, and to Omobono's involvement in the conspiracy against Hinderbach: "Se il latore della presente lettera (sc. Paolo da Novara) ti parlara, prestagli ascolto e poi decidi secondo la tua intelligenza" ["If the bearer of the present letter speaks to you, pay attention and then decide according to your intelligence"] (Archivio di Stato di Trento [henceforth: AST], Archivio Principesco Vescovile, s.l., 69, 68). Another letter, preserved in the same compendium, but written in Yiddish and dated 5 May 5236 (=1476) contains confirmation of the physician Omobono di Venezia's major role within Ashkenazi society of northern Italy and of the fear which he inspired among the Jews themselves: "Sappiate, miei cari che Bunim (Omobono) il medico ci ha portato un invito, che ci obbliga a recarci a Padova, perche e lui stesso a convocarsi tutti colà [...], ma qui, grazie a Dio, non abbiamo paura di lui" ["Know, my dear friend Bunim (Omobono), the doctor has brought us an invitation, which obliges us to go to Padua, because he's inviting us all there personally [...] but here, thank God, we are not afraid of him"].

[71] On these events, see Divina, *Storia del beato Simone da Trento*, cit., vol. II, pp. 146-177.

CHAPTER TWO

SALAMONCINO DA PIOVE DI SACCO, PREDATORY FINANCIER

Salamoncino da Piove had four sons and a daughter. His family, in addition to managing the Volto dei Negri lending banks of Piove di Sacco and Padua, had major joint interests in other banks operating in Verona, Ferrara, Montegnara, Soave, Monselice, Cittadela, Bassano and Badia Polesine and was active in the textiles and precious stone trade. A secret and elite clientele, ranging from the Sforza at Milan to the Soranzo of Venice,[1] came to them for huge sums. Marcuccio, Salomone's first-born son, when not operating in Piove si Sacco and Padua,[2] supported by his brothers, stayed at Venice to assist his father in the company set up with David Mavrogonato, and to take over their functions when they accompanied the merchant from Candia in his maritime missions, which were conducted more or less secretly. He was in the City of the Lagoons in the autumn of 1466, as well as in the first half of the following year; thus, he was there in 1468, at the beginning of 1469, during the imperial visit of Friedrich III, and in 1473.

While Salomone was considered a bold and nonchalant businessman, his first-born, Marcuccio, and above all his other son, Salamoncino, darkened his reputation, at least in this respect. Marcuccio was famous to all for his overbearing boastfulness. It was said that, in that of Padua, he used to brag of his strength, real or presumed, with resounding threats: "There is no Christian who would have had the temerity to touch me with one finger, and would not have gotten a good hiding from a couple of well-armed ruffians".[3]

Marcuccio, who lived at Padua "facing the Parenzo or Volto dei Negri" at least until the end of the winter of 1473, made his appearance as an officially approved money lender at Montagnana in 1475. He was still to be found in that financial center at the beginning of the summer of 1494, when Bernardino da Feltre arrived there to preach. On that occasion, Marcuccio did not hesitate to strut about on the piazza with a defiant air where the violent and fiery Friar da Feltre was expected to preach. As a result, Marcuccio was soon recognized by a Christian who insulted him, and the whole affair terminated in a sensational brawl, with a mutual exchange of fisticuffs, at the culmination of which the infuriated Marcuccio unsheathed his dagger threateningly. It is not surprising that he was to find himself imprisoned in the prisons of the Republic with relative frequency.[4]

Marcuccio could nevertheless still count on the influential protection of the city of Venice, which protection he had inherited, together with the privileges obtained by his father, Salomone da Piove. In April 1480, the Council of Ten declared him a *fidelis noster civis* [loyal citizen] of Venice, under the terms of a law approved by the Serenissima at the end of 1463 on the protection of Jewish money lenders. We know that his father chose to live in Venice during this same period, and it is not difficult to believe that this law was in some way the product of some self-interested initiative.[5]

But it was Salamoncino, his brother, who maintained uncontested primacy in this poorly regulated financial sector, where transactions took place with the underworld and the law was only obeyed in those rare cases in which its defenders refused large bribes. Salamoncino took over the management of the bank at Piove di Sacco after 1464, when his father took up a more or less stable residence at Venice for the purpose of looking after Mavrogonato's interests, although – as we shall see – he seems to have taken up provisional residence at Verona in the years 1470-1480.[6] In 1474, the Duke of Milan ordered an inquiry of Salamoncino and his suspected accomplices, all accused of illegally purchasing and selling pearls, despite the legal provisions prohibiting Jews from engaging in this trade.[7]

Salamoncino had already experienced serious legal problems. In 1472, two common criminals, Giovanni Antonio da Milano and Abbondio da Como, were arrested in Venice under the accusation of importing large quantities of counterfeit silver coin from Ferrara and selling it in Venice, earning large profits.[8] This fraudulent trade was operated through a front operation, a butcher shop owned by a certain Nicola Fugazzone, "butcher at Venice", at San Cassian, and a Jewish intermediary, Zaccaria di Isacco, who had his provisional residence in Venice, and was responsible to Salamoncino, money lender at Piove di Sacco.[9] The police authorities succeeded in laying their hands on all members of the gang, and they were tried before the judges of the Municipal Avogaria of Venice on 29 May 1472.

The two criminals, from Lombardy, Giovanni Antonio and Abbondio, were sentenced to the cruel amputation of the right hand, the loss of an eye, a fine of five hundred ducats in gold each, and were banned in perpetuity from Venice and all the territories of the Republic.[10] The sentence was carried out publicly on the same day, in the usual place, the Piazza San Marco, between the columns of San Marco and San Todaro, where the waters of the lagoon washed the pavement. The butcher, Nicola, and one accomplice, Lorenzo Paolo, were condemned to one year's imprisonment, and banned from Venice for eight years. Paolo was also fined one hundred ducats.[11] The intermediary, Zaccaria, considered Salamoncino's "enforcer", was sentenced to one year's imprisonment, in addition to the fine of two hundred gold ducats. After serving the sentence, he is said to have been banned from Venice and its territories for eight years.[12]

Salamoncino was obviously linked to the shady traffic at both ends: at Ferrara, where his family had a bank, and where the counterfeiters operated, sending the counterfeit coins to Venice, via their couriers; and at Piove di Sacco, where Salamoncino usually resided, and where the counterfeit coins were usually shipped before being distributed to retailers.[13] Arrested and subjected to torture, Salamoncino signed a confession and admitted that he had earned a profit of ten percent from the trade in counterfeit coin.[14] The Venetian judges sentenced him to six months imprisonment and the huge fine of three thousand gold ducats: two thousand payable to the Arsenal, and the remaining one thousand payable to the Avogaria di Comun. Furthermore, the banker from Piove was banned for ten years from Venice and the surrounding district, as well as from Padua and the territory of Padua. In the event of violation of the ban, the penalty of another year's imprisonment and a further fine of one thousand gold ducats was provided for.[15] While, on the one hand, Salamoncino may have more or less voluntarily submitted to the fine and perhaps to the imprisonment, at the same time, he is thought to have found a way – and it is not difficult to imagine how – to evade the ban, at least in part. At the end of the year, he was already active again at Soave and Verona; five years later – as we shall see – he firmly resumed management of the bank at Piove di Sacco and the Volto dei Negri bank at Padua.[16]

The wolf had lost a few tufts of fur, but not his teeth. According to records written by the Paduan orator, Giolamo Campagnola, in 1480, Salamoncino was then presumably resident at Verona, and once again found himself in prison, at the disposition of the Council of Ten, under the accusation of selling clipped and counterfeit coin, a charge which he was able to evade in part by shifting the blame onto an accomplice, a miserable brigand from Verona, who ended up at the stake.[17]

Salamoninco da Piove, Salamoncino's father, was dead by the beginning of 1477. Maestro Valco, the Jewish physician who had received the assignment – obviously for pay – of assassinating

Mahomet II at the behest of the Serenissima, had, in the meantime, returned to Venice, presumably to render account to his instigator of the progress of the plot. At Venice, or during the course of his voyage from Constantinople, the physician had been informed that Salamoncino was no longer alive. Understandably anxious about the continued existence of the mission, but, above all, because he feared for his pay, which had been promised by the now-deceased banker, Valco set out to track down Salamoncino, returning rapidly to Piove di Sasso.

At first, Salamoncino was thunderstruck; but, then, examining his father's records, he found clear evidence of the contract signed with the homicidal physician in the past. As a practical and alert person, Salamoncino was immediately aware that Valco possessed the necessary talents to carry out the hazardous mission of assassinating the Great Turk successfully. At the same time, he weighed all the potential benefits to be derived from future relations with the government of Venice. At this point, Salamoncino did not hesitate to assume responsibility for continuation of his father's commitment from both the strategic and financial points of view. On 9 July 1477, he officially informed the Council of Ten of his resolution to do so, making it to appear an act of disinterested devotion to the Republic. Obviously, in 1470, Salomone da Piove, perhaps inheriting a project initially dreamed up by Mavrogonato, suggested that Maestro Valco should carry out the plan "to take the life of the Great Turk", by 1480 – a period of ten years, believed sufficient for the task. Salamoncino, rejoining the ranks of the conspiracy, ensured the city of Venice that the task would indeed be carried out during the stipulated time period, and that Mahomet II would meet the death he deserved, at Valco's hands, in less than two and one half years.

"Maestro Valco, a Jewish physician [...] who returned and, finding the said Salomon (a Jew who kept the banco da Pieve) to be dead, turned to Salamoncin, son of the said Salomon, and, having informed him of the matter, and Salomon, examining the books, found this to be the case.

"Not wishing to be a lesser servant of your most Illustrious Lordship than he who was my father, and having learned from the said Maestro Valco, Jewish physician, of that which had happened to the person of the Great Turk [...], Salamonzin examined the said Maestro Valco, and having witnessed his courage and intelligence and being convinced of his determination, being the slave and servant of your Most Illustrious Lordship,[18] as was his father, without costing your Most Illustrious Lordship one penny, offers to send the said Maestro Valco, with all things requested by the said Valco, at Salamoncin's own expense [...] and is certain that the said Maestro Valco will kill the said Lord Turk by the end of 28 May, which matter will be to the glory of this Illustrious State and all Christianity."[19]

It goes without saying that Salamoncino was not entirely disinterested. In exchange for these services, "because, in so doing, he acts in danger of his life, which cannot be repaid with money", if the mission ended successfully, Salamoncino, following in Mavrogonato's footsteps, asked Venice for a few privileges, including an annual provision of two thousand florins, the beneficiaries of which are said to have included Salamoncino, Maestro Valco and their descendants in perpetuity, the entitlement of occupying themselves with some branch of trade ("request that the said Salamoncino and his brothers, with their descendants, be permitted to deal in trade in this terrain, as any gentleman may do"), a privilege generally prohibited to Jews, and to purchase real property at Venice and its dominions, up to a total value of twenty five thousand ducats.[20] Salamoncino, who was certainly not lacking in healthy doses of impudence, in addition to an uncommon dose of greed, furthermore requested that he be permitted to open lending banks modeled on the example of those operating at Mestre, and, in particular, one in the much-sought after piazza of the island of Murano ("intending that one of these locations be understood to refer to Murano"). He finally requested that he enjoy immunity from any possible future bans issued by the Venetian authorities against him personally or any member of his family.[21]

The Council of Ten officially accepted Salamoncino's petitions, but on the condition that the granting of the privileges be subject to the presentation of certain proof of the death of Mahomet II at the hands of Maestro Valco. But things turned out differently. In 1480, Mahomet II was still alive, despite the efforts of Valco and Simoncino to bring about a contrary state of affairs, while Venice, concerned with the pressure of the Turkish armies on its confines, had already signed a peace treaty with the Sublime Porte a year before. The Sultan then terminated his earthly existence in 1481 – in all probability, as the result of perfectly natural causes. Salamoncino's financial plans and those of his family, linked to the ambitious plot, which had failed miserably, therefore appeared definitely on the wane.

Either something or someone had moved the city of Venice to grant the benefits requested by Salamoncino, at least in part. In fact, we know that the government of Padua, in 1495, under pressure from the weavers' guild, had requested Venice to abrogate the privileges enjoyed by Salamoncino and his family at Piove di Sacco and Padua.[22] Even more interesting is the confirmation that, much later, in 1557, a certain "Salomon, a Jew, a certain Marcuzio, known as 'da Muran' ", was called upon to testify in a trial held before the Holy Office at Venice. This Salomon was certainly a descendant of Salomone da Piove – or, to be more exact, a nephew of his son Giacobbe. The fact that he was known as the "Jew of Muran" is an indication, not to be undervalued, in support of the hypothesis that the plan to open a lending bank on the island of Murano, strongly desired by Salamoncino, had in some way succeeded, for reasons unknown to us.[23]

During the second half of the 15th century, the family of Salomone da Piove and the Camposampiero was experiencing the ups and downs of the loan market sector at Padua, enjoying undisputed hegemony within the local Jewish community.[24] It was in 1453, precisely in the palace of Salomone di Marcuccio da Cividale (who is later believed to have become the famous Salomone da Piove), at Padua, in the Santo Stefano district, that Salomone Levi had taken over the ownership of the bank of Camposampiero, thus initiating his fortunate career as a high-ranking banker.[25]

But the unforeseen and disagreeable presence of a certain someone constituted grounds for disturbance and concern. After the Jewish banks of Padua were officially closed in 1455, a Swiss Jew appeared in the city in the early summer of 1464, not concealing his own intentions and, above all, without having asked and obtained the implicit and apparently indispensable authorization of the powerful bankers of Piove and Camposampiero. The Swiss Jew was Aronne di Jacob, a Jew from Wil, north of Zurich, a short distance from Schaffhausen, on the Rhine, a village located at the boundary between the Swiss Confederation and Germany. Aronne had decided to move to the strategic Venetian financial center in search of money and fortune, dragging his two brothers, Vita and Benedetto, along with him.[26] Furthermore, around 1471, just as other Jewish bankers had already done in the district, in 1468, Aronne obtained authorization to carry on activity as approved lender at Padua, three days in the week, ultimately freeing himself from this de facto restriction. He thus began to operate the bank "del Duomo" with undeniable success, despite the powerful cartel of his adversaries.[27]

It should not surprise us that in the spring of 1472, an anonymous denunciation, easily attributable to the entourage of bankers of Piove and Camposampiero, noted that Aronne's bank, against all the regulations, had kept its doors open on Sunday, in open violation of the Christian religion.[28] In the summer of 1473, Salomone da Piove, in a dispute with Mattia, lender of the Paduan bank of San Lorenzo, appointed as arbiter a friend of the family, i.e., Jacob, the son of

Salomone da Campsosampiero. Representing the adverse party was Aronne, who did not bother to conceal his own enmity towards the powerful bankers of Piove and Camposampiero.[29]

A few years later, in 1476, the Swiss Jew saw himself compelled to sell the two banks owned by him, the "del Duomo" bank at Padua and the bank at Monselice, to Abramo di Bonaventura, a Jew of Ashkenazi origin from Ulm, Germany.[30] Abramo hastened to fall in line with the Paduan cartel of Jewish bankers, particularly, Jacob, Salomone di Padova's son, and Simone, Salomone da Camposampiero's son, who already controlled the two most important banks in the town center of Padua – the Volto dei Negri bank and the bank of San Lorenzo – since 1472. Exactly who formed this powerful cartel emerges clearly from the negotiations between the Republic of Venice and the Paduan Jewish bankers in 1486, including Jacob da Piove, Simone da Composampiero, Abramo da Ulm and Isacchetto Finzi.[31]

Aronne appears not to have been very successful in the difficult business of lending money at interest, both at Padua and Monselice. Obstacles were placed in his way on many occasions, and it was a consolation to him that he had not been broken or killed. Aronne had already restricted his activity to that of "rag paper making" as early as 1473;[32] a few years later, he attempted to invest the modest sums he had been able to scrape together from the sale of his bank in a safe manner. Aronne, the Swiss Jew from Wil, had arrived at Padua as an outsider, bold and without resources, at least in the eyes of Piove and Camposampiero. Salomone da Piove's impatient and fiery sons had their pockets full and were waiting for Aronne to hit bottom.

In 1481, Salamoncino da Piove dreamed up a colossal swindle – this time to the detriment of other Jews – to rake in money by the wheelbarrow full. In cahoots with David di Anselmo, known as "David Schwab", he secretly decided to transfer the savings invested by Paduan Jews in the Bank at Soave, to the bank at Piove di Sacco, owned by David di Anselmo. These savings amounted to a huge sum, as much as 1,500 ducats in gold, belonging to Paduan Jews, from the lower middle classes, mostly small investors and savers. The victims of the inevitable, deliberate, collapse of the Banco di Soave included rabbis, students, widows and other poor people, among them the unfortunate Aronne da Wil, who had deposited the money collected from the sale of his banks there in 1476. Aronne, acting on behalf of the other victims of the fraud as well, had the Banco di Soave agent – Jacob di Lazzaro – arrested; this same agent was still in jail at the end of 1485, when he finally succeeded in obtaining his release, after withdrawing part of the money earlier stolen via Salamoncino's bank and returning it to Aronne.³³ But he was obviously the smallest fish of the lot.

"David Schwab" went bankrupt "with his pockets full", in an artful financial crash thought up in league with the negligent bankers of Piove, who had gotten their hands on a notable slice of the money embezzled from the tills of the Banco di Soave. But Schwab was pursued by a religious interdict (*cherem*), pregnant with consequences, handed down against him by Rabbi Anshel (Asher) Enschkin, who had lost more than a thousand ducats entrusted to him for investment by persons of modest wealth. Enschkin publicly unmasked Schwab, who had declared bankruptcy "notwithstanding the fact that he still had all the money". The religious condemnation handed down by Enschkin, was approved and subscribed by some of the most influential rabbis of Germany.³⁴

Nor did Aronne da Wil intend to stop attempting to bring an action directly against Salamoncino da Piove and his Paduan accomplices. In the spring of 1481, the two contending parties, by common accord, decided to submit to the arbitration of two Jews of German origin, residents of the region of Padua. The two arbitrators were the rabbis Isach Ingdam and Viviano da Vacheron, residents of the Duomo and San Cancian districts, at Padua, respectively.³⁵ Obviously the final award, expressed in accord with the legal system in use at Venice, was far from satisfactory to Salamoncino, who was, on several occasions during the following years, obliged to face his exasperating and implacable rival in court. In the end, the Piove di Sacco banker lost his patience – which he must not have possessed in excessive doses – and decided to take the law into his own hands, freeing himself from what he now considered an enemy to be eliminated.

In the winter of 1487, Salamoncino sent a hired killer to Venice, where Aronne was staying at that time, with the assignment of getting rid of Aronne without a trace. In a night in January Isaia Teutonico, known as Salamoncino's servant and bodyguard, attacked the impoverished Aronne from behind, just as Aronne was leaving the Jewish hospice at San Polo, before he could reach his son-in-law's home, a few islands away. Aronne was struck on the head with an edged weapon and left to die, on the ground, in a pool of blood.³⁶

Aronne, despite a serious head wound and skull fracture, survived the attack, and later denounced his unknown aggressor. A reward was immediately placed on the attacker's head, and his identity was quite soon discovered by the police authorities.³⁷ On 22 May 1488, the would-be killer, Isaia, who had, in the meantime, prudently taken flight, was tried *in absentia* and banned in perpetuity from Venice and its territories. If he was captured, he was to suffer a particularly cruel fate: dragged to the scene of the crime, he was to lose his right hand, after which, with his own hand appended to his neck, he was to be conducted to the Piazza San Marco and publicly beheaded between the two usual columns.[38]

Once the attacker was identified, it was child's play for the Venetian city authorities to identify the instigator, the unscrupulous businessman from Piove di Sacco, who had already served more than one term in the prisons of the Republic. Finding himself unmasked, Salamoncino spontaneously appeared at the Public Prosecutor's office, admitting to commissioning the crime and paying the killer to commit it. He then excused himself by saying that the victim had never ceased importuning him, dragging him through one long, exhausting judicial dispute after another until, driven to his wits' end, he had decided to free himself from the intolerable nuisance once and for all.[39] Salamoncino got off with a relatively mild sentence, which is not surprising in view of the type of relationship linking him, more or less obviously and officially, with the Venetian authorities. In the end, he was sentenced to six months in prison, in commutation of which he would be banned from Venice and its territories for four years, in addition to the payment of a fine of two hundred gold ducats, to be paid partly to the Hospital of Piety.[40]

But Salamoncino was back at work as early as one year later, in 1489, managing his network of banks, at Piove di Sacco and Padua.[41] In 1495, the municipality of Padua petitioned the Republic of Venice to revoke the chapters of the loan granted to Salamoncino as well as all related privileges.[42] But Venice refused. As mentioned by Marin Sanudo in his *Diaries*, in 1499, "Salamonsin de Piove de Sacho" was one of the Jewish bankers engaged in negotiations with Venice for the concession of the huge sum of fifteen thousand ducats, to be pledged by the Republic "in the Turkish matters", i.e., the war effort against the Sublime Porte.[43] Salamoncino – who had intended to remain at Piove di Sacco at least until 1504, according to Sanudo – was definitively expelled from the city of Venice one year later, allowing the city to breathe one last sigh of relief. Salamoncino's memory, ambiguous and disturbing, was then lost in the mists of the lagoons of Venice.

***

NOTES TO CHAPTER TWO

¹ Cfr. D. Carpi, *L'individuo e la collettività. Saggi di storia degli ebrei a Padova e nel Veneto nell'età del Rinascimento*, Florence, 2002, pp. 39, 48.

² On the activities of Marcuccio at Padova and Piove di Sacco, cfr ibidem, pp. 45-50.

³ Girolamo Campagnola da Padova, in an unpublished oration, written after 1480 in celebration of the martyrdom of Simone da Trento and of Sebastiano Novello at Portobuffolè, recalled Marcuccio's exasperating arrogance, at that time a money lender at Montagnana: "Quis Marcutio fratre (Salamoncini hebraeo), etiam carcere concluso, audacior et insolentior unquam fuit? Ille mihi ait: scias, velim, Christiani nominis esse neminem, qui mihi digiti, ut ajunt, offensiunculam faciat, quin alteram duorum sibi lacertorum non reddam" [Approximately: "Is there anybody more audacious and impudent than Marcuccio, the brother of Salmoncino the Jew, who spends half his time in jail? He told me, look, no Christian would dare do me any offense, without getting a good beating from two of his henchmen"] (cfr. [Benedetto Bonelli], *Dissertazione apologetica sul martirio del beato Simone da Trento nell'anno MCCCCLXXV dagli ebrei ucciso*, Trent, Grianbattista Parone, 1747, pp. 280-281).

⁴ On 27 February 1473 Marcuccio, at that time a resident of Padua, together with his brother Salomoninco and their father Salomone da Piove, were denounced for calumny and embezzlement by a law student at the Studio (ASP, Notarile, Luca Talmazzo, 253, cc. 252r-254r). On his long residence in Montagnara, documented since 1475, his activity as an approved money lender and the events linked to the visit of Bernardino da Feltre, see, in particular, V. Meneghin, *Bernardino da Feltre e i Monti di Pietà*, Vicenza, 1974, pp. 489-502.

⁵ ASV, Consiglio dei Dieci, Lettere, file 2 (1476-1483). The heads of the Consiglio called Marcuccio "fidelis noster civis Marcuonus (recte: Marcutius) ebreus quondam Salomonis de Plebesaccii" ["Marcuccio, loyal citizen of our city, (son of) the late Salomone di Plebe di Sacco"], then a resident of Montagnana. The privileges Marcuccio enjoyed, and his father as well, constituted an extension of those granted by Venice to David Mavrogonato and his family in the past. The Doge, in a letter to the rulers of Candia in 1532, referring to Meir Mavrogonato, a descendent of David, recommended the application in his regard of the privileges which he enjoyed, "essendo

trattato come li cittadini Venetiani nelle datiii et alter fattioni, et esento lui et figlioli dell'angarie che fanno l'Hebrei, secondo la forma delli soi privilegge" ["being treated like the citizens of Venice in all respects, and free of the annoyances suffered by Jews, according to the manner of their privileges"] (cfr. D. Jacoby, *On the Status of Jews in the Venetian Colonies in the Middle Ages*, in "Zion", XXVIII, 1963, pp. 57-69 [in Hebrew].

[6] On Salamoncino's mercantile and financial activity at Piove di Sacco, Padua and Verona, see D. Jacoby, *New Evidence on Jewish Bankers in Venice and the Venetian Terraferma (c. 1450-1550)*, in A. Toaff and Sh. Schwarzfuchs, *The Mediterranean and the Jews. Banking, Finance and International Trade (XVI-XVIII Centuries)*, Ramat Gan, 1989, pp. 155-156; Capri, *L'individuo e la collettività*, cit., pp. 54-58; G.M. Varanini, *Appunti per la storia del prestito e dell'insediamento ebraico a Verona nel Quattrocento*, in G. Cozzi, *Gli ebrei e Venezia (secoli XIV-XVIII)*, Milan, 1987, p. 621.

[7] Cfr. Sh. Simonsohn, *The Jews in the Duchy of Milan*, Jerusalem, 1982, vol. I, p. 633, no. 1538. The document is dated: Lonate, 30 October 1474.

[8] ASV, Avogaria di Comun, Raspe, 3653 (II), cc. 8v-9r (29 May 1472). I wish to express my sincere thanks to Dr. Rachele Scuro for her invaluable assistance in transcribing the documents and my friend Reiny Mueller of Venice for his archiving tips, which were always illuminating. "Joannes Antonius de Mediolano et Abundius de Cumis [...] confessi fuerunt se pluries conduxisse e Farraria Venetias multam quantitatem monetarum argenti falsarum verum grossestos et grossones ad similitudinem stampe Dominii Nostri, quas monetas scienter accipiebant a fabricatoribus illarum et illas, reductas Venetias, dispensabant diversis personis, a quibus habebant ad incontrum ducatos auri et argenti cum certa sua utilitate". On the crisis of May 1472 and the "monetary war" being waged between Venice and Milan, see, in particular, R.C. Mueller, *L'imperialismo monetario veneziano nel Quattrocento*, in "Società et Storia", VIII (1980), pp. 227-297 (292-294); Id., *Guerra monetaria fra Venezia e Milano nel Quattrocento*, in *La Zecca di Milano*, Records of the Congress, Milan, May 1983, pp. 341-355.

[9] ASV, Avogaria di Comun, Raspe, 3653 (II), c. 9rv (29 May 1472): "Nicolaus Fugaconus, becharius de Veneciis et socii quos processum fuit [...] pro eo quod etiam ipse habuit commertium cum Abundio infrascripto, conductore monetarum falsum, a quo recepit satis bonam quantitatem dictarum falsarum pecuniarium, cum utilitate .XIII pro centenario, et fuit medius ad faciendum quod Salamoncinus

supascriptus haberet de dictis monetis cum infrascripto Zacharia, etiam judeo [...] quod procedatur contra Nicolaus Fugaconus, Laurentium Paulo et Zachariam iudeum qui, spiritu avaritie ducti, scienter acceptaverunt, cum certa utilitate, monetas argenti falsas ex Ferraria Venetias conductas, illas dispensando pro bonis".

[10] ASV, Avogaria di Comun, Raspe, 3653 (II), cc. 8v-9r (29 May 1472): "[...] quod Johannes Antonius infrasciptus hodie postprandium hora solita conducatur in medio duarum colunnarum, ubi per ministrum iustitie sibi ascindatur manus dextera et eruatur unus oculus et solvat ducatos quingentos auri [...] et postea banniatur perpetuo de Venetiis et de omnibus terris et locis Dominii Nostrii, tam a parte terre quam maris [...] et quod iste Abondius hodie post prandium hora solita conducatur in medio duarum colunnarum, ubi per ministrum iustitie ascindatur manus dextera eruatur unus oculus et solvat ducatos. Vc. Auri [...] et postea banniatur perpetuo de Venetiis et de omnibus terris Dominii Nostri, tam a parte terre quam maris".

[11] ASV, Avogaria di Comun, Rapse, 3653 (II), c. 9v: "[...] quod iste Nicolaus Fugaconus compleat annum in carcere et deinde banniatur per annos octo de Venetiis et districtu [...] et quod banchum becharie reservetur, et Laurentius Paulo compleat annum unum in carcere et solvat ducatos centum Advocatoribus et deinde banniatur per annos octo de Venetiis et districtu".

[12] ASV, Avogaria di Comun, Raspe, 3653 (II), c. 9v: "Zacharias iudeus quondam Isahac, hospes in Venetiis, compleat annum unum in carcere et solvat ducatos ducentos auri [...] et deinde banniatur per annos octo de Venetiis et districtu".

[13] Salomone di Marcuccio da Piove and his children were the proprietors of the "Banco dei Carri" on the town square of Ferrara in 1473 (cfr. P. Norsa, *Una famiglia di banchieri: la famiglia Norsa, 1350-1950*, Napoli, 1953, p. 15).

[14] ASV, Avogaria di Comun, Raspe, 3653 (II), c. 9r (c. 114r of the modern pencil numeration at the bottom of the page, 29 May 1472): "Salamoncinus Salamonis, hebreus de Prebesacci, contra quem fuit et est processum [...] quod spiritu avaritie ductus, non contentus de usuris [...] scienter se inmiscuit in acceptando et dispensando de monetis falsis, cum utilitate ducatorum .x pro centenario, sicut ad torturam confessum est".

[15] The Trial "contra Salamoncinum filium Salomonis fenetoris in Plebesacci" concluded with the sentence "quod iste Salamoncinus stet menses sex in carceribus clausus, et solvat ducatis duomille nostro arsenatui et mille Advocatoribus nostris, qui dent quantum accusatori, et non incipiat tempus carceris nisi cum integritate persolverit et deinde

banniatur per annos decem de Venetiis et districtus et Padua et territorio paduano, et si tempore banni contrafecerit stet anno in carcere et solvat ducatos mille et iterum remittatur ad bannum et sic publicetur in schalis Rivoalti". Salomone, his father, being compelled to take over the management of the Banco di Piove di Sacco, on 16 July 1472 conferred the position upon Moisè di Elyakim de Alemannia for the duration of ten years (cfr Carpi, *L'individuo e la collettività*, cit., p. 40). Salomone, who is thought to have passed on to a better life before 1476, truly could not have imagined that five years later, in 1477, Salamoncino would already have returned to Piove.

[16] Cfr. Carpi, *L'individuo e la collettività*, cit., pp. 47, 55.

[17] "Fama est Salamoncinum hebreum, decem Virorum issu, in vinculis in presentarium detentum, cum adulterinae monetae majestatis crimine alias damnatus esset. Ut se ab exitio per Christiani hominis pernicem liberaret, pauperem quendam Veronensem ad cudendam monetam circumvenisse; ab eo postmodo accusatum flammarum subisse supplicium; utque alterum civem ab se furti crimine accusatum in exilium compelleret, quidquid fide dignis testibus ostendere non valuit, magicis artibus conjectari, indiciarique curasse; quibus corvum humanam emisse vocem, ipsumque furem nominasse fertur" ([Bonelli], *Dissertazione apologetica*, cit., pp. 280-281). This quotation, together with the fact that the manuscript oration of Girolamo Campagnola is preserved at Verona, seems to confirm the arguments put forth by Varanini (*Appunti per la storia del prestito*, cit., p. 621) that Salamoncino was residing in Verona more or less permanently around 1470-1480.

[18] The expression may refer to the role of "Hofsklaven", assigned to the Jews under the Germanic Empire.

[19] Salamoncino da Piove's petition to the Consiglio dei Dieci, dated 9 July 1477, has been published in its entirety in F. Babinger, *Ja'aqub-Pascha, ein Leibarzt Mehmeds II, Leben und Schicksale des Maestros Jacopo aus Gaeta*, in "Rivista degli Studi Orientali", XXVI (1951), pp. 196-197. Similar privileges are said to have been requested by Salamoncino's brother, Fays, from Francesco II Gonzaga in 1495 (cfr. E. Castelli, *I banchi feneratizi ebraici nel mantovano, 1386-1808*, Mantua, 1959, p. 215).

[20] This would have had to have been in obvious derogation from the law of 1423, otherwise rigid relating to the landed property of the Jews (cfr. R.C. Mueller, *Les prêteurs juifs de Venise au Moyen Age*, in "Annales ESC", XXX, 1975, p. 1302, no. 96).

[21] Cfr. Jacoby, *New Evidence on Jewish Bankers in Venice*, cit., pp. 156-157; Carpi, *L'individuo e la collettività*, cit., pp. 54-55.

[22] Cfr. Jacoby, *New Evidence of Jewish Bankers in Venice*, cit., pp. 156-157; Carpi, *L'individuo e la collettività*, cit., p. 55.

[23] Cfr. P.C. Ioly Zorattini, *Processi del S. Uffizio contro ebrei e giudaizzanti*. I: *1560-1560*, Florence, 1980, pp. 270-272.

[24] Cfr. Jacoby, *New Evidence on Jewish Bankers in Venice*, cit., pp. 151-178; Carpi, *L'individuo e la collettività*, cit., pp. 27-110.

[25] Cfr. Carpi, *L'individuo e la collettività*, cit., p. 61.

[26] On 27 March 1466, Aronne di Jacob signed a postal service agreement with a porter from Padua, who was to look after his epistolary relationships with his father-in-law and brother-in-law, both of them resident at Wil (Vil), in Switzerland (ASP, Notarile, Giacomo Bono, 216, c. 51r). As early in 1464 (14 June) Aronne was a resident of Padua, in the district of San Cancian, lending money at interest, benefiting from the banking services at Piove di Sacco (ASP, Notarile, Francesco Giusto senior, 1591, c. 384r).

[27] Cfr. D. Carpi, *The Jews of Padua During the Renaissance (1369-1509)*, a doctoral thesis written in Jerusalem in 1967, p. 193. For the money lending activity carried on by Aronne at Padua, probably without official approval, in the past years, see ASP, Notarile, Nicolo Brutto, 3117, c. 414r (10 June 1465); Notarile, Giannantonio da Mirano, 2681, c. 214v (30 June 1466). Alessandro di Jacob was associated with the three brothers, Aronne, Vita and Benedetto da Wil, in the affairs of the Banco del Duomo at Padua and the other bank at Monselice, also under his ownership.

[28] Cfr. Carip, *The Jews of Padua*, cit., p. 193.

[29] On this controversy, see Carpi, *L'individuo e la collettività*, cit., p. 48. Aronne had already had a dispute with Salomone "*hebreus fenerans in Plebe Sacci*", but had in some way reached a settlement ("dictus Aron et dictus Salomon, nolentes ire per litigia sed parcere litibus et expensis, devenerunt ad compositionem"). See ASP, Notarile, Francesco Giusti senior, 1591, c. 384r. (14 June 1464).

[30] "Abram qm magistri Bonaventure ab Ulmo, hebreus fenerator Padue in contrata Domi, habens loco Ixep Sacerdotis et Aronis qm Jacob hebreorum ad fenerandum in Padua et Montselice, ut constat ducalibus datis die XVI augusti MCCCCLXXVI" (ASP, Notarile, Francesco Fabrizio, 2917, c. 271r). Abramo da Ulm was the father-in-law of that Abba del Medigo di Candia of whom we will have occasion to speak at length in the next chapter.

[31] Cfr. Capri, *L'individuo e la collettività*, cit., p. 47, 53.

[32] As early as 23 February 1473 Aronne appears as a "strazzarolo in contra' San Cancian" ["rag-paper maker in the San Cancian district"] at Padua (ASP, Notarile, Luca Talmazzo, 253, c. 251r).

[33] On the fraudulent insolvency of the Banco di Soave and the arrest of Jacob, David Schwab's factor, see ASP, Notarile, Ambrogio da Rudena, 779, c. 460r (3 November 1485). Jacob delivered 155 gold ducats to Aronne "existentes penes Salabmonzium hebreum de Plebe [...] quos denarios dictus Jacob affirmavit fuisse et esse dictorum bonorum intromissum ad dictum banchum Suapsis". As early as 1470, Aronne da Wil, turning to the Paduan tax authorities, asserted that he had operated mostly for the accounts of other savers: "io non trafego del mio altro che liere octozente [= 800 lire], e de questo, piasendo ale spectabilità vostre, sempre me ne faro fede de questo, ma io trafego robe de diversi zodii" (ASP, Estimo 1418, 92, c. 14r).

[34] In this regard, see J. Hutner, *Quattro responsi rituali relativi ad un rabbino che aveva emesso un interdetto religioso che colpiva colui che lo aveva defraudato*, in *Memoriale Volume in Honor of Rabbi J.B. Zolti*, Jerusalem, 1987, pp. 256-263 (in Hebrew).

[35] "Haron ebreus qm Jacob, habitator in contrata Domi, parte una, et Jacob qm Salamonis de Plebe, suo nomine et Fais et Salamonis (i.e.: Salamoncini) fratrum, Isachetus qm Consilii de contrata Strate, Enselmus filius quibuscumque differentiis existentibus inter dictas partes se compromiserunt in magistrum Isach Ingdam hebreum, habitatorem in contrata Domi elledum pro parte dicti Haron, et in magistrum Vivianum de Vaischoron de contrata S. Canciani, electum per superscriptos Jacob et socios, secundum morem, leges et stillum alme civitas Veneciarum" (ASP, Notarile, Luca Talmazzo, 251, c. 58r. (10 May 1481).

[36] ASV, Avogaria di Comun, Raspe, 3656 (II), c. 72r. (22 May 1488). "Isaas iudeus theothonicus, solitus esse famulus Salamoncini iudei de Plebesacci, absens, contra quem processum fuit [...] coram officium suum in consilio prefatorum dominorum Advocatorum comunis cum gravissima querella comparuisse Aron quondam Jacob iudeus et exposuisset quod quodam siro, circa prima in secunda horam noctis, dum veniret ab hospitio iudeorum de contracta sanctii Pauli et iret ad domum Jacob iudei, generi sui, parum procul ab ipso hospitio, fuerit a quodam incognito proditorie a parte posteriori cum uno case percussus et vulneratus una percussione de taleo supra caput cum maxima effusione sanquinis et fracturam longa[m] per unum digitum, pro quo quidem delicto petebat iustitiam administrari".

[37] "[...] et tandem posita est et capita fuit pars de talea sub die xxi aprilis proxima et consequentis publicata in schalis Rivoalti, cuius vertute data noticia officio prefatorum dominorum Advocatorum quod dictus Isayas fuerit et est ille qui tale maleficium commisit gratia et ad instantiam infrascripti Salamoncini [...] et sic captum fuit quod ipse

Isayas retinetur [...] Fuit itaque proclamatus in schalis Rivoalti ad se defenderum cum termine dierum octo, qui dum non comparuisset, immo in sua contumacia perseverasset, fuit absens".

[38] "[...] quod procedatur contra Isayam teothonicum iudeum, alias solitum esse famulum Salamoncini iudei de Plebesacci, absentem sed legitime citatum super schalis Rivoalti, ex eo quod, ad instantium dicti Salamoncini, de mense januarii 1486 [= 1487] tempore noctis, percussit Aronem iudeum proditorie una percussione de taleo super capite, cum incisione et effusione sanguine ac offensione ossis [...] et captum fuit quod iste Isayas sit bannitus perpetuo de Venetiis et districtus et de aliis terris et locis Nostri Dominii ad confinia furum, et si quo tempore contrafecerit banno et captus fuerit, conducatur ad locum delicti commissi ubi sibi manus dextera amputetur et deinde, cum ea appensa ad collum, conducatur in medio duarum collunnarum ubi sibi caput a spatulis amputetur sic quod moriatur".

[39] ASV, Avogaria di Comun, Raspe, 3536 (II), c. 72rv (c. 179rv according to the modern numbering in pencil on a paper label (23 May 1488). "Salamoncinus quondam Salamonis, iudeus de Plebesacci, contra quem processum fuit [...] super casu infrascriptis insultis et vulneris, illatis in personam infrascripti Aronis [...] venit ad officium advocarie se ipsum manifestavit et quomodo ipse erat in societate euisdem Isaie supscrascripti, ut quod eius Salamoncini causa motus ipsum taliter vulneravetur [...] quia sepius et continue fuerat molestatus Salamoncinus ipse in litibus ab ipso Arone".

[40] "[...] quod dictus Salamoncinus, iam prope ea retentus, bene retentus remaneat [...] et quod procedatur contra Salamoncinum quondam Salamonis de Plebisacci iudei, qui fuit mandator et auctor dicte percussionis [...] captum fuit quod ipse Salamoncinus complere debeat menses sex in carceribus clausus, solvat ducatos ducentos auri, quorum centum sint hospitali Pictatis, alii verum centum sint Advocatorum comunis, sit postea bannitus per annos quatuor".

[41] In the summer of 1490, Salamoncino invested capital in the Banco dei Finzi at Rovigo (cfr. E. Traniello, *Gli ebrei e le piccole città. Economia e società nel Polesine del Quattrocento*, Rovigo, 2004, pp. 116-117).

[42] Cfr. Jacoby, *New Evidence on Jewish Bankers in Venice*, cit., pp. 156-157; Carpi, *L'individuo e la collettività*, cit., p. 58. On 11 February 1495, a legal dispute was recorded between the municipality of Piove di Sacco and "Salamoncinus, hebreus phoenerans in hoc loc Plebiscacci". The document summarizes the clauses of the items for the loan, granted in a timely fashion by the community to Salamoncino, including that of being able to accept any type of pledge as security for

loans, with the exception of objects of worship of the Christian religion ("[...] per formam capitulorum concessum est ipsi Salamoncino libere praestari super quocumque pignore indifferenter, exceptis crucibus et calcibus, sive rebus ecclesiasticus sacratis, tamquam phoenerator publicus"). Cfr. P. Plinton, *Codice Diplomatico Saccense*, Rome, 1894, no. 552.

[43] Marin Sanudo, *I diarii*, by R. Fulin et al., Venice, 1879-1903, II, column 42 (22 May 1499), III, column 803 (1500).

CHAPTER THREE

ASHER, THE BEARDED JEW (1475)

Master Tobias da Magdeburg, the physician from Trent, who reached Venice in February 1469 during Friedrich III's visit, had other information to be supplied to the judges investigating the death of little Simon. His news was disturbing, linking the German Jews, reaching Venice in the Emperor's train, with the personage of the Candian merchant, David Mavrogonato, and his mysterious dealings.

It seems that Mavrogonato, for the occasion of the imperial visit, had brought with him, perhaps from Cyprus, a large consignment of sugar and blood to be peddled on the Venetian piazza. These were expensive ingredients, indispensable to the preparation of medications and unguents considered of certain effectiveness and of great advantage by the pharmacopoeia of the time, and it is not to be marveled at that the shrewd merchant from Candia intended to offer them for sale at Venice, where all the Jewish physicians, surgeons, herb alchemists, and specialists, both Christians and Jews, had agreed to meet on that occasion, attracted by the prospect of a flattering and profitable imperial recognition. But, according to Maestro Tobias, those German Jews who turned to Mavrogonato in great numbers – known by them as the "Jew with the sugar" – to acquire the precious goods he had for sale, were, in fact, seeking to purchase Christian blood, and, in particular, the blood of Christian children, for use, not only in the preparation of costly and miraculous medications, but in obscure magical and religious rites as well.[1] David Mavrogonato had no intention of dirtying his hands directly in negotiations of this kind, but used, as a go-between, an unscrupulous local charlatan, a certain Hossar (or Osser, a rendering, in the Ashkenazi pronunciation, of the name Asher, corresponding to the Italian Anselmo). This Jew, from Cologne, was known all over Venice as "the Jew with the beard".[2]

The name of this Hossar, dedicated to shady dealings between Venice and the cities of the mainland and linked twofold to Mavrogonato, appears in the depositions of another important personality in the Trent trials. Israel, son of Mayer (Meir) of Brandenburg in Saxony, was a young man twenty three years old, itinerant artist by profession, earning his money as a miniaturist, and, in the case in question, as a binder of manuscripts and Hebraic and Latin codes. He, too, was arrested in 1475 in Trent under the accusation of complicity in the killing of little Simon. He was to prove a bold and shrewd double-dealer, agreeing in appearance to convert to Christianity and assume the new name of Wolfgang, not just to save himself from a certain and cruel condemnation to death, but above all, camouflaged by conversion, to assist the Jewish women accused and arrested for the crime, obtaining their release or facilitating their escape.[3] Once discovered and unmasked, he was publicly executed in January of 1476. His body, broken on the wheel, was left at the place of execution, a spectacle for public mockery and a feast for animals.

Israel Wolfgang had informed the judges at Trent that he had been Salomone da Piove di Sacco's guest in the spring of 1471, for the Passover dinner, with the participation of the banker's sons, David Mavrogonato's business associates, and their respective families. The patron of the house was said to have made use of dried and pulverized blood for ritual purposes, as was the custom among German Jews, dissolving it in the wine and kneading into the unleavened bread. Under these circumstances, Salomon's son, Salamoncino, in the presence of the brother Marcuccio, is said to have informed young Israel that the blood, probably extracted from the veins of a Christian child, had been supplied "by a Jewish merchant, who had brought it from overseas, perhaps from the island of Cyprus", alluding, by means of this periphrasis [circumlocution], to Mavrogonato.[4] What is more, Salamoncino confirmed that the go-between in those sales was, as usual, Hossar, or Asher, whose business it was to sell blood from Venice to the other centers of the Republic in which there were active Jewish communities.

The famous money lender Salomone di Lazzaro "from Germany", active at Crema and Cremona, was also an assiduous client of this itinerant wanderer.[5]

Wolfgang knew Hossar personally, and visited Hossar in prison near the Ponte di Paglia in Venice, where he was detained for attempting to sell "alchemical silver", i.e., counterfeit money. The reasons for this strange visit are not clear, nor did Wolfgang bother to explain. Perhaps it would not be too far from the truth to think that he intended to supply himself with powdered gold and silver at advantageous prices from the capable and expert dealer which Hossar was reputed to be, for use in miniatures of any codes which he might be commissioned to paint by rich and influential persons. This might explain the presence of the enterprising artist at Piove di Sacco, in Salomone's house, whose table would otherwise be inaccessible to a young man of low rank and without resources, like him.

Wolfgang had furthermore come into contact with Hossar before, and knew that that alchemist of dubious reputation lived near the Rialto, in the direction of Mestre, and might be about forty years old, dressed in black and wearing a beard of the same color. At Venice, Hossar was known by boys as "the Jew with the beard". Hossar had a brother, some years older than he, called Big Salamoncino, due to his stature, and perhaps to distinguish him from Salamoncino da Piove, whose presence in the heart of the Jewish community of Venice and at the official ceremonies in the synagogue must have been frequent. According to Wolfgang, who made his depositions before the judges of Trent in November 1475, Hossar-Anselmo, "the Jew with the beard", had died about six months before, perhaps in prison.[6]

The information supplied by Israel Wolfgang da Brandenburg in his testimony is exactly, and very many ways, surprisingly, confirmed by the archive documents. Hossar-Asher "with the beard" (*Anselmus judeus a barba*) was in fact tried at Venice on 3 September 1473 on an accusation of selling two bars of false gold, i.e., silver covered with a foil of gold powder, to an artisan in that city, after having extorted a fraudulent official registration from the essayer of Rialto, responsible for the stamping and weighing of gold.[7] Hossar "with the beard" was sentenced to six months in prison and stricken from the registry of bulk gold and silver dealers at Venice.[8] He was also said to have been compelled to compensate the victim of the swindle for the economic harm done, before serving his term of imprisonment.

Strangely, the clauses of the sentence hint at the eventuality of an escape from prison by the Cologne-born Jewish alchemist, or his death in prison.[9] In effect, as reported by Israel Wolfgang to the judges at Trent, Hossar died in the first few months of 1475, and it may be that he was still in prison. It is therefore surprising that the Venetian judges should provide in advance for such eventuality, almost as if they knew for a fact that David Mavrogonato's unscrupulous ex-right arm man – dedicated to mysterious illegal dealings at Venice, where he was known by all, both Jews and Christians – had powerful friends in the mainland financial centers capable of helping him break jail or of silencing him for good, to prevent him from revealing his embarrassing secrets. Salamoncino da Piove, who was perfectly well aware of the German alchemist's activities, may have known him personally during his stays in Venetian prisons, "near the Ponte di Paglia", of which he was an influential and assiduous inmate.

Just what the artful German herb alchemist [Hossar] was selling on all those frequent trips which took him to the cities of the Veneto region, apart from medicinal blood and quack remedies of miraculous effectiveness and bright and treacherous "silver of alchemy" – in the manufacture of which he was considered a specialist – remains unknown. It is, however, certain that, the merchandise to be found in Hossar's haversack – according to Salamoncino da Piove – included one particular item, purchased from an itinerant merchant named Abramo, stopping by Trent in 1471 on his way from Saxony to Feltre or Bassano, and that this particular item was considered particularly valuable. According to Wolfgang's later statements before the Trent judges, Abramo's clients included the physician, Tobias da Magdeburg.

Abramo's red leather pouch, with its waxed bottom, in fact, concealed a certain amount of blood, to be put up for sale – clotted blood – coagulated and reduced to curdles or powder, as was normal practice, to cause it to harden over time.[10]

According to Maestro Tobias da Magdeburg, many of the Jewish and German merchants who reached Venice in 1469 along with Friedrich III's baggage train intended to supply themselves with the blood of Christian children for the Passover rite – blood which Mavrogonato was said to have brought from Candia or Cyprus on that occasion. It does not appear that the Jews of that island had ever been accused of ritual murder at that time. Yet, Jewish Passovers at Candia in the mid-15th century were anything but tranquil affairs, and were often the source of scandal and clamorous indignation.

During Passover week, 1451, the Jews of the ghetto of Candia were accused of crucifying suckling lambs (perhaps due to the impossibility of procuring Christian children) [NOTE: This is not necessarily Prof. Toaff's opinion here; he is summarizing the Latin: *fortasse quia fideles pueros captare nequiverat*], in contempt of the Christian religion, with a grotesque and sacrilegious anti-ritual.[11] The symbolism of the suckling lamb placed on the cross seemed obviously linked, in an intolerable and obscenely blasphemous manner, to the passion of Christ, the Agnus Dei [Lamb of God]. The accusation does not appear to have completely groundless, in view of the ancient Hebraic custom of roasting the Passover lamb skewered on the spit in a vertical position, with the head upwards, to ridicule and deride the crucified Christ; just how widespread this custom was, is difficult to determine from either a chronological or geographical point of view.[12]

The Venetian criminal judiciary was immediately informed of the affair by the Duke of Candia, Bernardo Balbi, while the Doge, Francesco Foscari, hastened to appoint Gradenigo, "district mayor in the Levant", who was already on the island, with responsibility for investigating the matter ("to obtain the truth about the crucified lambs in any manner whatever"), identifying the guilty parties, and punishing them with the maximum strictness. Edicts were posted "in the Piazza and in the Giudaica di Candia", promising cash rewards for anyone supplying the inquisitor with information useful to the investigation and threatening severe punishment to "any persons with knowledge of the above mentioned case of the crucified lambs who conceal the same".

The well-known Venetian politician and humanist, Lodovico Foscarini, already podestà [magistrate] of Feltre in 1439, of Vicenza in 1445 and at the time, podestà of Verona, also occupied himself with the thorny mater. In a letter, presumably written between 1451 and the following year, and addressed to Antonio Gradenigo, Foscarini praised the Venetian inquisitor [Gradenigo] warmly for bringing his investigation into the "sacrilegious sacrifice" to a close, zealously and with undoubted success, and for his success in demonstrating the guilt of the Jews of Candia in the crucifixion of the lambs to a certainty.[13]

The outcome of the matter came to our attention through a Jewish source which has until now been misinterpreted on this point: the chronicle of Elia Capsali. The Candian rabbi, based on a report on the events written in Hebrew, reported that the investigation into the crucifixion of the lambs was concluded on 26 January 1452, when the Council of the Forty informed Bernardo Balbi, the Duke of Candia, that, as a result of inquisitor Gradenigo's denunciation, nine notables of the Jewish community had been placed in shackles for their participation in the crime.

After a brief period of detention in the prisons of Candia, the prisoners were transferred in chains to Venice, where they were interrogated in expectation of the trial before the Avogaria di Commun. Two of the prisoners died as a result of torture, while the survivor remained in custody awaiting the decisions of the Major Council, which met on 15 July 1452, on Saturday. To everyone's great surprise, the Jewish defendants were absolved, notwithstanding Gradenigo's indignant protests, with 220 votes in favor, 130 against and 80 "not convinced", i.e., abstaining; on 9 August following, the defendants were released and left Venice. They finally landed in Candia after a 13-day voyage and were joyfully and triumphantly received by the entire Jewish community on the island.[14]

[The report reads in part:]

"In 1423, Francesco Foscarini was elected Doge of Venice [...] Under his government, almost at the end of his term, in 1451, the Jews of the community of Candia were falsely accused of the so-called 'calumny of the lamb',[15] by a nun named Orsa. The matter took an ugly turn when Antonio Gradenigo, the inquisitor, visited Venice at the

Avogaria di Commun to cause the Jews to be tried, setting forth the particulars of the accusations made against them. On 26 January, Bernardo Balbi, the Duke of Candia, received an order from Venice to arrest nine notables of the Jewish community, after which they were held in prison for thirty five days. The Duke then ordered their transfer to Venice in a ship captained by Giacomo Aponal di Candia, which docked after a 49-day voyage, during which the prisoners remained in chains, suffering terribly. At Venice, the defendants were thrown into a dark, unwholesome prison, separated from each other, and subjected to cruel and insupportable tortures and torments, which caused the miserable death of two of them 'in the sanctification of the name of God', but they confessed nothing. As a result, the case was presented to the judge of the Great Council [...] and the Jews were therefore absolved, thanks to the Lord's assistance and His mercy towards them. This happened on Saturday [...] on 15 July 1452 [...] and on 9 August following, these same Jews left Venice, and reached here [Candia] thirteen days later, expressing their praise and gratitude to God the Blessed."

But the matter was anything but over. The implacable Antonio Gradenigo appealed against the sentence of absolution before the Avogaria di Commun. According to him, the Jews of Candia had bribed some of the magistrates, purchasing their favorable votes with money. Once again, Capsali reported that the allegation had been examined by the Avogaria di Commun in March 1453. The subsequent investigation led to the arrest of one of the counselors, Girolamo Lambardo, on a charge of corruption and Lambardo's subsequent condemnation to one year in prison; he was also struck off the role of the Members of the Great Council for five years. The fate of the Jews of Candia was again in the hands of the "Great Council", which met on 16 May 1454 without reaching a decision. The meeting was adjourned on 7 June following, when the charges were finally dropped after innumerable rounds of voting, on 13 July.[16]

"On a Saturday in the month of Tamuz of the year 5214 [=1454] in the afternoon [...] our Messer Antonio Giustinian's galley docked here in the port of Candia, bringing us the happy news of our acquittal. May He be Blessed who rewarded us with all well-being, rendering vain the machinations brought against us. The Lord has saved, not only our fathers, but ourselves as well, our children and descendents. In fact, salvation has not only been granted to the Jewish community of Venice, because the Lord has thus liberated our community of the Jews of Candia and the other communities under the dominion of the Serenissima, and under the government of the gentiles generally, from terrible danger [...] This sort of persecution is the work of the perfidious Haman, seeking to exterminate women and children, old persons and notables and sack our property in one single day (Esther 3:13)."[17]

Capsali's report, richly detailed, finds precise confirmation in the official Venetian documentation, supplementing and clarifying the picture.[18] As early as September 1451, several months prior to conclusion of district mayor Antonio Gradenigo's inquiry into the crucifixion of the lambs at Crete during the Passover period of that year, Gradenigro appealed to the Greater Counsel that the defendants be transferred to another, more pliable, level of the legal system, such as the Quarantia Criminal [Council of Forty Judges] to ensure a more expeditious conclusion of the matter.[19] Gradenigo's appeal upon acquittal of the Jews in the court of first instance was preceded by a decision of the Greater Counsel to the effect that, in the interests of expediting the case, the presence of three hundred magistrates should in this case suffice instead of the four hundred judges provided for by law.[20]

What is certain is that, at the end of June 1452, twelve Jews from Candia were being held in a cell of the "New Prison" of Venice. Capsali reports that nine (and not twelve) Jewish notables were arrested in Candia; the idea that Capsali was simply mistaken seems implausible.

Perhaps the other three Jews from Candia were arrested for other crimes, unrelated to the foul charge of the "crucified lambs". It would not even surprise us to learn that David Mavrogonato, whose adventures as an "intriguer" with limited scruples did not always end happily, was one of them. These Jews at Candia were lodged in the same cell with a Christian, probably in jail for another crime, a certain Antonio da Spilimbergo. Spilimbergo was rather unhappy about being the only believer in Jesus Christ and the Virgin Mary in the forced company of these vociferous and arrogant Jews, who were as loud-mouthed as they were uncouth, and who did nothing but mutter their incomprehensible prayers and chant from morning to night, in Hebrew, with an unpleasant Ashkenazi inflection. Their actions, which the poor Antonio, out of ardent Christian zeal, presumed were highly heretical, as well as their strange and repellent garb, drove him practically mad. He therefore filed an urgent appeal with the commanding authorities for transfer to the "Carcere Novissima" [new prison], a petition which the authorities immediately granted, in a full understanding of Spilimbergo's plight.[21]

The text of the defendants' final acquittal, on 7 June 1454, contains important details relating to the case as a whole. The principal defendants turned out to be the physician, Abba di Mosè del Medigo di Candia, who, according to the denunciation of a converted Jew, "crucified a lamb in mockery of Jesus Christ, at night, in his own room, together with other Jews, on the very holy day of Holy Friday (of the year 1451)". Gradenigo's inquiry shows that the Jews of Candia repeated this contemptuous ritual every year, in the days preceding Christian Easter.[22]

Abba del Medigo and the other defendants' attempts to bribe the judges were not in vain, as attested to by the relevant documents. As we have seen from Elia Capsali's report in March of 1453, one of the members of the Greater Counsel, the nobleman Girolamo Lambardo, was arrested and sentenced for selling his vote to the Jews. The minutes of the Greater Counsel confirm that an inquiry against Lambardo had in fact been brought and had concluded with the condemnation of the noble counselor for improperly attempting to extort money from Abba.[23]

As early as February 1452, the ineffable Candian physician [Abba del Medigo], already under indictment for vilification of the Christian religion, was further accused of attempting to bribe one of the "district mayors in the Levant", Antonio Priuli, one of Gradenigo's colleagues, perhaps correctly considered more pliable than the implacable inquisitor of the crucified lambs.

But in fact, in a certain sense, Abba, rather than the author of the design to bribe judges and other high-placed persons involved in the trial, had himself been the naïve victim of a clever swindle. Bonomo di Mosè, a Jewish money lender active at Mestre, owner of the bank of San Nicolà at Padua,[24] was, out of piety or self-interest, accustomed to visiting Abba frequently in the New Prison where the latter was incarcerated. During one of these visits, Bonomo, who bragged of high-placed friendships in wealthy Venice, is said to have confessed to the impatient and depressed Candiota [Abba del Medigo] that one of the "district mayors in the Levant", Priuli to be exact, would gladly sell his vote in exchange for a loan of fifty ducats without interest.

Having scraped up the sum, the good Abba promptly delivered it to Bonomo, who misappropriated it, obviously without turning it over to Priuli, who was completely ignorant of the whole scheme. But the whole scheme finally came unraveled and the swindle was discovered.

The money lender from Mestre, responsible for the swindle, was sentenced by the Avogadori to the payment of a fine of one hundred gold ducats and one year in prison, after which he would be banned from Venice and its territory for five years.[25] Abba del Medigo, for his part, was tried for trying to bribe a public official, but was ordered acquitted.[26]

The island physician was less fortunate, however, at the end of October of the same year, when his Christian fellow prisoners accused him of serious offenses and blasphemies against the Christian religion. According to the denunciation, Abba, in his cell, was alleged to have unhesitatingly placed his filthy piss-pot right below the crucifix. Soundly rebuked by the other prisoners, the intemperate Candiota was said to have replied with profanity, insulting them and shamelessly ridiculing Jesus the Messiah and the blessed Holy Virgin. His condemnation was inevitable and well-deserved: one year's additional prison time, in addition to the payment of a fine of one thousand lire to the Avogadori di Commun.[27]

But who was this Abba del Medigo – the protagonist, despite himself, in the affair of the crucified lambs? He certainly came from one of the most illustrious Jewish families in Candia, being the son of Mosè "the Old Man", rabbi and head of the community, and related to the famous philosopher Elia del Medigo, a physician like himself. He had married Ritte, otherwise known as Rivkah, with whom he had had three children, Elia, Diamante and Yehudah, called Giuliano in Italian and known as Yudlin among the Ashkenazim of the Veneto community.

The latter had married Sofia, called Shifra in Hebrew, the aunt of the chronicler Elia Capsali. The family lived at Padua, but after the death of Abba, which occurred rather early in 1485, he moved mostly to Soave, where Elia and Yudlin del Medigo had obtained a money lending permit, which was renewed in 1496.[28]

Elia Capsali remembered that he had stayed with his aunt Sofia at Padua in the winter of 1508, on his way from Venice, and that he had heard her say "that my relatives (del Medigo) were no longer at Padua, because they had moved to Soave".[29] We know that Elia, Abba's firstborn, was murdered in Venice under mysterious circumstances in 1505. Implicated in the murder, one as the instigator and the other as an accomplice, were two Jews, from Soncino and Feltre, the latter a resident of Monselice, who were condemned by the Avogadori di Commun to prison, the confiscation of their property and expulsion from the territories of Venice, Padua and the surrounding district.[30] It is probable that Capsali stumbled across a copy of the trial documents relating to the crucifixion of the lambs on the island of Candia, in Padua, among Yudlin's letters, who had died many years before, stating the grounds for the acquittal, and that he used it among his sources.

Out of prudence, or perhaps simply desiring to respect the privacy of the Medigo-Capsali family, although half a century had already passed since these events, Elia preferred to omit any mention of the names of the defendants in the trial for the crucified lambs – mainly, any mention of Abba del Medigo, father-in-law of his aunt, Sofia, as well as of the assassination of the son of the latter two, Elia, committed at Venice by other Jews only a few years earlier.

Lodovico Foscarini was a friend of Gradenigo, the inquisitor for the crucifixion of the Passover lambs, but he was no friend of the Jews, least of all to Jewish physicians, whom he hated, feared and suspected, and against whom he considered himself engaged in incessant warfare (*perpetuum bellum*).[31]

Foscarini, the patrician of the Veneto region, recalled the manner in which the Jews, in their Passover ceremonies, solemnly swore on the Torah scrolls to cause serious injury and harm to those faithful in Christ and placed the Christians on guard against eating unleavened bread prepared by Jews. He was also convinced that Jewish physicians were the servants of the Devil and were dedicated to the magical arts and to necromancy, poisoning their Christian patients in body and spirit. In a letter written in the summer of 1462, Foscarini considered it unacceptable that many governors, particularly, those from Venice, tolerated the cheeky and arrogant presence of Jewish physicians and surgeons, and thus facilitated their presence, and maintained that presence for reasons of dubious honesty.[32] Foscarini, then Lieutenant of Friulia, had a short time before suffered two years imprisonment, lamenting that, during this period, the Serenissima, profiting from his absence, had signed official agreements with Jewish physicians.[33]

One scandalous example of blasphemous shamelessness, according to Foscarini, was a "gowned physician", garnished in gold and adorned with jewels, who had had the boldness to turn to certain noblewomen in mourning, maliciously deriding their religious belief, and in particular, the sacrament of the Host. "I pity you, ladies, for your ignorance", the learned Jewish surgeon is alleged to have said on that occasion, in a tone of open mockery, "in believing that your God, the Creator of Heaven and Earth, would offer Himself to be consumed, and thus does not therefore disdain to offer himself up as food to the jaws of obscene ruffians and the filthiest of whores".[34] In view of the fact that the most famous "gowned Jewish physician" living in Venice in Foscarini's time was Jehudah messer Leon da Montecchio, who is said to have been granted the honor of the imperial doctoral privilege by Friedrich III during the latter's stay in Venice in February 1469, and that his quarrelsome nature, accompanied by frequent and intemperate verbal outbursts against both Jews and Christians, his true or presumed adversaries, was common knowledge, identifying the "gowned physician" does not seem very hard to do.

In confirmation of this, reference may perhaps be made to a news item from a Jewish chronicle, archived until a few years ago in manuscript form, and perhaps compiled at Venice by an Ashkenazi Jew around the middle of the Sixteenth century, which seems to be a compilation of local traditions of indubitable antiquity.[35] The presumable chronology of the events to which reference is made dates back beyond the middle of the 15th Century. In Venice, the Jews were prohibited from circumcising their sons in the city.[36] The Jews therefore had to go to nearby Mestre to perform this rite, which was fundamental to their family life. It was then that a Jew, "among the most illustrious among those living in Venice", wishing to circumcise his new-born son in the city of the lagoons, thought up an astute expedient which might lead to revocation of the discriminatory law. He turned to an influential Venetian patrician with whom he stood on terms of familiarity and friendship, a gentleman who was, in those days, confined to bed with gout, and requested the gentleman to act as godfather at his sons' circumcision ceremony. The Christian nobleman was not only pleased to accept the honorific charge which the honored Jew had thought fit to entrust him with, but, being unable to reach Mestre due to his illness, which kept him confined at home, he seems to have decided to cause the child to be circumcised in the main room of his own palace. This was the first case, the precedent-setter, thereafter permitting the Jews of Venice to circumcise their sons in the City of the Lagoons. If the report, as stated, contains a core of truth, it should not be very difficult, in this case as well, to identify the Jewish notable as Jehudah messer Leon, the influential imperial physician esteemed by Jews and Christians alike, particularly among the higher classes, to whom a son, David was born in Venice, in approximately 1459.[37]

The Jewish community at Trent had formed relatively recently, and its numbers were always limited. When Maestro Tobias da Magdeburg, physician, surgeon and expert in ophthalmology, decided to establish himself at Trent in 1462, he found that there was no organized Jewish community in the city. In the early years of the century, in 1403, bishop Ulrich III had granted a Jewish money lender named Isacco and his family the right to carry on the money trade at Bolzano and Trent. This may have been the same Isacco whose presence in the city is attested to later, in 1440.[38] It is nevertheless certain that other Jews came to join him in the first quarter of the century, staying at Trent for longer or shorter periods, such as the same Mosè di Samuele from Trent who, in the summer of 1423, made his last will and testament at Treviso, where had had in the meantime moved with his numerous family.[39] The

Jewish community of Trent seemed consolidated by mid-century.

In fact, in 1450, Sigismondo, Count of Tyrol, decided to grant Elia and the other Jewish residents of Trent equality of rights with those of the Christian citizens of Trent.[40]

Nevertheless, when Maestro Tobias took up residence in the city, he found only one Jewish family, that of the money lender Samuele (Zanwil) di Seligman, originating from Nuremberg in Bavaria, who had settled in Trent one year before. The privileges accorded to Samuele in the money-lending permit signed upon his entry into the city were renewed by Giovanni Hinderbach in 1469, the year in which Friedrich III officially invested him with the temporal office of the episcopate of Trent, at Venice, in 1469.[41] In the meantime, a third family had come to reinforce the Jewish community of Trent. Angelo da Verona, from Gavardo in the Bresciano region, who had passed his youth at Conegliano in Friuli,[42] also moved to Trent, dealing alongside Samuele of Nuremberg in the local money market.[43] Although he had lived in Italy from birth, Angelo, too, was an Ashkenazi Jew; perhaps he no longer spoke Yiddish as his native language, in contrast to Tobias and Samuele, who had arrived from the German territories only recently, but he certainly understood it and spoke it, although rather badly.

Angelo's parents, in fact, Salomone and Brünnlein (Brunetta), were natives of Bern in the Swiss Confederation. The three Jewish families of Trent were quite unrestrained and very definitely considered themselves a multiple of patriarchal nuclei. The married children lived together with the parents, and several generations lived their everyday lives under the same roof: grandfather and grandmother, uncles, aunts and cousins, married women, widows and unmarried girls, servants, scullery maids and teachers, travelers and persons of passage, more or less established and occasional guests, professional beggars and impoverished relatives.

The Jews, whose habitations were contiguous, lived near the commercial center, known as "the Canton", in the western zone of the city, which included the quarters of the Market and San Martino. Their lending banks, which formed one whole with their houses, operated in contact with the shops and taverns of the German immigrants, whose presence in Trent was rather large, amounting to several hundred people.[44] German was spoken along the small canal which traversed the district, carrying turbid and muddy water, originating in the Adige.

Alongside the evil-smelling workshops of the Germanic shoemakers and tanners were the banks and dwelling houses of the Jews. One of these, that of Samuele da Nuremberg, was the location of the synagogue.

In fact, Samuele's family was beyond doubt the most religious, and the most highly cultivated in terms of Hebrew culture. The scrupulous observance of the standards of the Torah had induced the head of the family, in addition to setting aside certain areas as places of worship for the entire community, to draw water from the canal, which passed by the basement of the house, for use in a sort of ritual bath, where the women could easily immerse themselves for their own ablutions of purification after their menstrual period, without having to have recourse to the public baths, where feminine modesty and shame could not always be duly protected.[45] Samuele himself, to great benefit, had studied in the famous Talmudic academies of Bamberg and Nuremberg in the years 1440-1450, and had been the disciple of famous rabbis.

The oldest and most respected among the German Jews of Trent, his uncle Mosè da Franconia, who had reached the respectable age of eighty and was known by everyone in the city as "the Old Man", also found lodgings under his roof. Learned and authoritative, even if poorly equipped with purely economic means, he had found stable hospitality, with his family, with the enterprising and wealthy nephew, after having lived previously at Würzburg and Spira, one of the most important centers of Jewish culture in all of Germany. Samuele's household were strict followers of the rules relating to kosher food, which, among other things, prescribed the complete separation of meat and dairy products, according to the dictates of the Bible, amplified and codified in the rabbinical interpretation of the *halakhah*. To the judges in the Simon of Trent murder trial, interested in knowing why he carried two knives in a sheath hanging from his side, both Samuele and Mosè "the Old Man" patiently explained that which, in their eyes, was perfectly obvious. One knife was to cut edible meat, while the other was to be used for dairy products.[46]

On 23 March, eve of Passover of 1475, year of the jubilee, the mutilated body of Simonino, a two-year old child, son of the tanner Andrea Lomferdorm, was found in the waters of the ravine by-passing Samuele's cellar. This tragic discovery triggered the inquest which was to lead to the accusation brought against the Jews of Trent as suspects in the child's abduction and murder, to their interrogation in the castle of Buonconsiglio and their condemnation, after confessing under torture to being responsible for this tragic wickedness. Finally, the condemned were publicly executed, burned at the stake or decapitated, while their property was to suffer bitter confiscation. The transcripts of the Trent trials for the murder of Simon, later beatified, are said, as a result, to constitute the most important and detailed document ever written on the ritual murder accusation, a precious document retaining the words of the Hebrew defendants, in which the words of the accusers and inquisitors did not always succeed in superimposing themselves over, or confusing themselves with, the words of the defendants.

These texts are a glimpse into a different world: the world of the Ashkenazi Judaism of the German territories and northern Italy, in all its sociological, historical and religious particularity. This was a Jewish world, enclosed upon itself, fearful and hostile towards outsiders, often incapable of accepting its own painful experiences and overcoming its own ideological contradictions. It was this world which, moving from the negative and often tragic reality in which they lived, sought an improbable anchorage in the sacred texts which might illuminate a hope of redemption, which for the moment appeared beyond credibility: a Hebraic world discharging its energies in religious rites and antique myths, now re-enlivened with renewed and different meanings and translated into an alienating, harsh and rigorous confessional language, in which internal tensions and unresolved frustrations lay hidden at all times. A world which, having survived the massacres and forced conversions of men, women and children, continued to experience those traumatic events in a sterile effort to reverse the meaning of that world, rebalancing it and correcting history. It was a profoundly religious world in which redemption could not possibly be far off; in which God was to be involved despite Himself, and compelled to keep His promises, sometimes by force. It was a world drenched with magical rites and exorcism, within whose mental horizons popular medicine and alchemy, occultism and necromancy were often mixed, finding a position of their own, influencing and reversing the meaning of ordinary religious standards.

The participants in this magical mental horizon included not only the Jews, accused of witchcraft and infanticide, ritual cannibalism and evil spells, but their accusers as well, obsessed with diabolical presences and the continual search for virtuous talismans and stupendous antidotes, capable of curing and preserving the body and soul from the wiles of men and demons. Giovanni Hinderbach, prince bishop of Trent, the true organizer of the 1475 trials, had grown up in Vienna in the years following the great massacre of the Jews, accused of backing the Hussites (1421) and exposed by that same Duke Albert II to bloody vengeance as partisans of the heretics.[47] Even before poor Simonino's child murder, when he had not yet risen to his official fame as "punisher of the Jewish murderers", Hinderbach had already found ways to show his lack of sympathy for them.[48] In one case, thus, he had not hesitated to express his self-satisfied approval of cannibalism, when the victims were Jews. During the military confrontation between

Venice and Trieste in 1465, during which Friedrich III intended to enforce his rights, Hinderbach, who was then acting as imperial ambassador before the government of the Serenissima, sang the praises of the Hapsburg militia, called upon to defend Trieste, for their courage and their demonstrated loyalty to the Emperor. By true right, observed the pious bishop, the German soldiers, in case of necessity, rather than lay down their arms, were to alleviate their hunger by eating the flesh of cats, rats and mice; and even that of local Jews, Jews resident in the city.[49]

Friedrich III was, as Burcardo di Andwil informs us, in addition to mathematical sciences, a passionate cultivator of astrology and necromancy, and for this reason is said to have remarked that he liked to surround himself with Jews and Chaldeans, people highly partial to superstitious practices.[50] But Friedrich's faithful servant, Hinderbach, was no less so. Magic and witchcraft in fact exercised an irresistible fascination over the humanist bishop, who was a friend of Enea Silvio Piccolomini. Hinderbach assimilated Jews outright with necromanticists, always ready to perform exorcisms and curses in the service of the devil. Demons love blood; and the necromancers who resuscitated cadavers used blood with little parsimony in their divination, mixing it with water taken from fountains and rivers. Hinderbach had no hesitation in maintaining that the Jews were enchanters and necromancers, "because they kill Christian children and drink and consume their blood, as they did last year at Trent, and in many other places it has been discovered and proven".[51] The practical Caballah, which these Jews followed more or less in secret, was to be assimilated in all respects to black magic and necromancy. It is to be noted that, during the first festival of the sainted child, held at Trent in 1589 with a great confluence of people, a celebrative pamphlet, later published in Rome, was compiled with the title of *Ristretto della vita e martirio di S. Simone fanciullo della città di Trento*. This work maintained, in the wake of Hinderbach, that the child had been killed by the Jews, "followers of the Caballah, vain science under which name magic and necromancy often hide".[52]

From the records of the trial, we know that Brunetta (Brünnlein), widow of Samuele da Nuremberg, who was, in the end, burnt at the stake as guilty of infanticide, persisted in her refusal to confess, notwithstanding the torments to which he was subjected. To Hinderbach, there appeared to be no doubt that the woman was ill and bewitched by Jewish necromancers. For this reason, every suggestive pressure, exercised on the woman to persuade her to speak, had proven useless; from shaving her head and removing her body hair, to ablutions in holy water.

But the remedy was finally found. The holy cure-all, according to the bishop of Trent, constantly in search of miraculous enchantments and narcotic unguents, had proven itself exceptionally effective in the precedent Santa Lucia case, in which the victim was also possessed by demons. Brünetta was placed in a bath of urine, laboriously produced by a "virgin young boy" of Trent, and suddenly, after the extraordinary, if rather evil-smelling ablution, the woman, without further ado, began to sign her confession.[53]

* * *

NOTES TO CHAPTER THREE

[1] "Et inter ipsos Iudeos fuit dictum [...] quod in civitate Venetarium tunc erat quidam magnus mercator Iudeus de insula Candie, qui portavit magnum quantitatem sanguinis pueri Christiani ad vendendum, et etiam portaverat magnam quantitatem zuccari. Et quod dici audivit a quodam Ioseph Forles, qui venerat post Serenissimum Imperatorem Venetias, quod volevat emere de sanquine a dicto mercatore Hebreo. Et similiter dici audivit a quibusdam aliis, de quidibus non recordatur, quod volebant emere de dicto sanguine, licet ipse non emerit. Dicit tamen quod, crede suo, omnes alii Iudei, qui ibi aderant, emerunt de dicto sanguine" (cfr. A. Esposito and D. Quaglioni, *Processi contro gli ebrei di Trento, 1475-1478*: I: *I processi del 1475*, Padua, 1990, pp. 328-329). The fact that the blood put up for sale, together with the sugar, by Mavrogonato was of *"pueri Cristiani"* [Christian boys] appears to be an allusion by Tobias da Magdeburg or German Jews having moved to Venice in the retinue of Friedrich III, with whom he had spoken. There is nothing to cause us to believe, however, that the information supplied by Tobias should, on the whole, be considered "exotic details" (cfr. R. Po-Chia Hsia, *Trent 1475. A Ritual Murder Trial*, New Haven, Conn., 1992, p. 46), like the erroneous description of the Jew from Candia as a "great merchant in the imperial entourage, who sold sugar and blood" (ibidem). On the sugar manufactures transplanted from Venice to Crete starting at the beginning of the XIV century and on the curative uses of sugar, particularly widespread in the Jewish medieval medical treatises, see, in particular, S.W. Mintz, *Sweetness and Power. The Place of Sugar in Modern History*, Baltimore (Md.), 1985.

[2] "Et cum eo (qui vocabatur 'el Judeo dal çuccaro') conversabatur Hossar Iudesu, qui habitat Venetiis et vocatur 'el Zudio de la barba',

qui est de Colonia et ab omnibus cognoscitur" (cfr. Esposito and Quaglioni, *Processi*, cit., vol. I, p. 329).

[3] The figure of Israel Wolfgang da Brandenburg is interpreted differently by Po-Chia Hsia (*Trent 1475*, cit., pp. 91-104: "Oscillating between the different roles demanded of him, Israel was alternatively the wandering Jew, the Christian convert, informant of the apostolic commissioner, and the cooperative prisoner". In my view, a less superficial reading of his depositions permits an understanding of the consistency among the apparent contradictions in his behavior.

[4] "Salamon parvus [= Salamoncinus] dixit sibi Wolfgango quadam die in Plebe Sacchi, in Curia Domus praedicti Salomonis (Martuii), quod Salomon, pater ipsius Salamon parvi, habuerunt dictum sanguinem a quodam Judeo, qui illum detulerat de ultra Mari et, ut credit, de insula Cypri" (cfr. [Benedetto Bonelli], *Dissertazione apologetica sul martirio del beato Simone da Trento nell'anno MCCCCLXXV dagli ebrei ucciso*, Trento, Gianbattista Parone, 1747, p. 64). The blood referred to was dried and reduced to powder, and it is therefore difficult to believe that it could have been confused with wine, and, in particular, with the Malvasia wine from Candia, in which Mavrogonato seems to have dealt on a large scale. For the hypothesis of the Malvasia wine of Candia exchanged for blood, see D. Nissim, *Il legame tra i processi di Trento contro gli ebrei e la tipografia ebraica di Piove di Sacco del 1475*, in "Annali dell'Istituto Storico Italo-Germanico in Trento", XXV (1999), pp. 672-673, promptly followed by D. Carpi, who presents it as obvious (*L'individuo e la collettività. Saggi di storia degli ebri a Padova e nel Veneto nell'età del Rinascimento*, Florence, 2002, pp. 29, 43).

[5] On Salomone di Lazzaro "de Alemannia" and his money lending activity, cfr. C. Bonetti, *Gli ebrei a Cremona*, Cremona, 1917, p. 9; G.A. Mantovani, *La communità ebraica di Crema nel secolo XV e le origini del Monte di Pietà*, in "Nuova Rivista Storica", LIX (1975), p. 378; Sh. Simonsohn, *The Jews in the Duchy of Milan*, Jerusalem, 1982, vol. I, pp. 36-37, 220-221, 246-247 (nos. 48, 464, 524).

[6] Wolfgang's deposition on Hossar-Anselmo "de la barba" is summarized by G. Divina, *Storia del beato Simone da Trento*, Trent, 1902, vol. II, pp. 18-19.

[7] ASV, Avogaria di Comun, Raspe, 3653 (II), cc. 44v-45r (cc. 149v-150r, according to the modern numbering in pencil at the bottom of the page (3 September 1473). "Anselmus, iudeus a Barba, contra quem processum fuit et est per antescriptos dominos advocatores in Consilio XIta, pro eo quod, ad finem defraudandi mercationis et maiorus sui lucri, ausus est in fundo denariorum fundellorum, ubi

sollitum est accipi sagium argenti, fundidit aliquantum limare aurri, ita quod videbatur argentum ipsum tenere aurum [...] Sicque cum ipsis fundelis accessit ad sagiatorum folee auri in Rialto, qui sagium fecit et fecit bulletinum ipsi iudeo, prout solitum est fieri, quem postea argentum dictus Anselmus vendidit Joanne Antonio partitori, in eiusdem danno et deceptione". Further along in the same document it states that that the judges had decided to proceed "contra Anselmum iudeum pro istis duobus fundellis argenti fundatis, demonstrantibus tenere aurium et non tenentibus, nisi in locis in quibus solit acceperi sagium per sagiatorem comunis, vinditis Joanni Antonio partitori in euisdem deceptionem et damnum maximum". The victim of the swindle appears with the qualification *partitor*, i.e., a refiner of precious metals, assigned to the separation of gold from silver. It should be noted that at Venice, metal assaying was executed by approved assayers in the Zecca. In the Fifteen Century, four officials, two for gold and two for silver, were assigned to their registration and weighing, and an additional three assayers, who were entitled to operate in Zecca, in the "statione comune" at Rialto (the location selected by Hossar for his fraud), or in their own shop. In this regard, see F.C. Lane and R.C. Mueller, *Money and Banking in Medieval and Renaissance Venice. Coins and Moneys of Account*, Baltimore (Md), 1985, index, s.v. *Assay office* and *Gold, assaying of*; A. Stahl, *The Mint of Venice in the Middle Ages*, Baltimore (Md), 2000, index, s.v. *Assay* and *Gold Estimator*.

[8] "Quod iste Anselmus menses sex in carceribus et perpetuo perivetur possendi exercendi mercaturam auri et argenti grezorum Venetiis".

[9] "[...] quod non incipiat tempus carceriorum, nisi prius cum integritate satisfacerit et restituerit denarios suos Joanni Antonio partitori descripto. Verum si casus mortis ipsius Anselmi occurreret, aut quod de carceribus aufugerit, et tot bona ipsius Anselmi non invenientur, tunc argentum predictum, ad manus Advocatorum perventum, obligatum sit integre satisfactioni infrascipti Joanni Antonio".

[10] Cfr. Esposito and Quaglioni, *Processi*, cit., vol. I, pp. 327-328. "Dictus Abraham habebat dictum sanguinem in quodam coramine rubeo et erat coagulatus et in frusticulis et erat in totum ad quantitatem unius ovi." Maestro Tobias had bought some of it "quantum est una nucella pro uno rainense". The fact (at any rate already known to anyone possessing a certain familiarity with this type of trade, which was more widespread than one might imagine among both Jews and Christians, in the cities and above all the countryside, where it

constituted an indispensable ingredient for the preparation of prodigious medications) emerges from the depositions of the other defendants in the Trent trial that the blood was placed on sale in the form of powder, coagulated or converted into lumps ("portabat illum sanguinem ad vendendum, et illum tenebat in sinode seu çendado rubeo, et erat ille sanguis coagulatus et pulverizatus"; "et dicit quod sanguis, quem dictus Ursus portabat ad vendendum erat in uno vase [...] quod vas erat instagnatum a parte interiori, in quo vase erat sanguis pulverizatus, et erat tantum de sanguine in dicto vase quantum esset quarta pars unius amphiale val mosse, et dictus vas erat coopertum de quodam coramine albo").

[11] The information is found in Flaminio Cornaro, *Creta sacra sive de epis de episcopis utriusque ritus graeci et latini in insula Cretae*, Venice, 1755, vol. II, pp. 382-383 ("Non satis quidem habuit perfida Judaeorum natio Creatiae degens Christianos iniquis adeo molestijs divexare, sed ut religioni etiam illuderent, teneros agnos [fortasse quia fideles pueros captare nequiverat] in Jesu-Christi contumeliam cruci affixerunt, cujus facinoris nuntium cum Venetias delatum esset, Consilium XL virorum ad Criminalia, Cretensi regimini mandavit, ut omni studio in impios, qui adhuc ignoti erant, inquieret"). In this regard, see also H. Noret, *Document inédits pour servir à l'histoire de la domination vénitienne en Crète de 1380 à 1485*, Paris, p. 425, no. 1. At any rate, the accusation relating to the passion of the lambs at Crete may only with difficulty be classified as an "accusation du meurtre rituel", as it is perhaps interpreted by Jacoby (cfr. D. Jacoby, *Les juifs à Venise du XIVe au milieu du XVI siècle*, in H.-G. Beck, M. Manoussacas and A. Pertusi, *Venezia centro di mediazione tra Oriente e Occidente, secoli XV-XVI. Aspetti e problemi*, Florence, 1977, vol. II, p. 172).

[12] On this custom and its anti-Christian significance, see Y. Tabori, *Pesach dorot*, Tel Aviv, 1996, pp. 92-105; I.J. Yuval, *"Two Nations in Your Womb". Perceptions of Jews and Christians*, Tel Aviv, 2000, p. 89 (in Hebrew). Again, at the beginning of the Seventeen Century, the Inquisition ordered the persecution of those Jews from the communities of the plains of the Po of northern Italy who still retained the wickedness to crucify Passover lambs. The Holy Office recorded that the Jews, although not subject to the jurisdiction of the Inquisition, could be tried by those tribunals in particularly serious cases. One of these was "se beffassero i Christiani, et per disprezzo della passione di Nostro Signore nella Settimana Santa, o in alto tempo crucifigessero agnello, pecora o altra cosa" ["if they ridiculed Christians, or showed contempt for the Passion of Our Lord during the Holy Week, or

crucified lambs, sheep or anything else, at any time"] (*Breve informazione del modo di trattare le cause del S. Officio per li molto Reverendi Vicarii della Santa Inquisitione*, Modena, Giuliano Cassiani, 1608, p. 15).

[13] " 'Ex delictis quae tu studiossime contra hebraeorum pernitosissimam crudelitatem inquisivisti', Foscarini wrote to Gradenigo, 'unum de sacrilega immolatione, ita universis patefacere decrevi, quod nemo posthac sic tam amens qui dubitet vel tam improbus qui neget nequissimos iudaeos agnos temporibus nostris passim crucifigere' ". And further along, he invited him to persist in his uncompromising struggle "contra iudeos agnum crucifigentes" ["against the lamb-crucifying Jews"] (cfr g. Gardenal, *Ludovico Foscarini e la Medicina, in Unamesimo e Rinascimento a Firenze*, Florence, 1983, pp. 251-263 [p. 262]. In this case as well, it seems incorrect to consider, as Gardenal does (perhaps in the belief that "agni", "agnello", was a metaphor referring to Christian children), "questi sacrifici compiuti dagli ebrei nell'isola di Candia" ["these sacrifices committed by the Jews on the island of Crete"] as true and proper ritual homicides. He is followed in this error by Esposito ("Antonio Gradenigo had investigated alleged human sacrifices committed by Jews on the island of Candia").

[14] E. Capsali, *Seder Eliyahu Zuta*, by A. Schmuellevitz, Sh. Simonsohm and M. Benayahu, Jersulem, 1977, vol. II, pp. 225-226.

[15] In Hebrew, *'alitat ha-taleh*, the slander of the lambs. In Biblical Hebrew, *Taleh* is the suckling lamb, and this is the original reading of the text, which at any rate appears in this form and with reference to this occurrence in another section of Capsali's chronicle (*Seder Eliyahu Zuta*, cit., vol. I, p. 246). Other, corrupted or incomprehensible readings appear in many manuscripts, such as *ha-'lah*, understood by M. Benayahu as *ha-'orlah*, the foreskin. But "the slander of the lambs", without further explanation, makes no sense. At an earlier date, N. Porges (*Elie Capsali et sa Chronique de Venise*, in "La Revue des Etudes Juives", LXXVII, 1923, pp. 20-40 [p. 24]) had explained the word, considering it a corruption of *ha-mazah*, leaven, understanding the term in the sense of Host. Therefore, at Candia, in 1452, the Jews are said to have been accused of profanation of the Host. The hypothesis of Porges, who was unaware of the inquiry for the crucifixion of the lambs, is, today, uncritically accepted by others, who arbitrarily add the Candia case in 1452 to the case record of the desecration of the host (cfr. Simonsohn, in Capsali, *Seder Eliyahu Zuta*, cit., vol, III, p. 77; M. Rubin, *Gentile Tales. The Narrative Assault on Late Medieval Jews*, New Haven, Conn., 1999, pp. 115-116). Still more

recently, there are those who refer to Capsali's text as the "resoconto del processo intentato in 1452 contro nove ebrei di Candia con l'accusa di omicidio rituale" ["report on the trial proceedings brought against nine Jews of Candia on a charge of ritual murder"] (Cfr. G. Corazzol, *Sulla Cronaca dei Sovrani di Venezia* [*"Divre' ha-yamim le-malke' Wenesiy'ah"*] di Rabbi Elia Capsali da Candia, in "Studi Veneziani", XLVII, 2004, p. 318).

[16] Capsali, *Seder Eliyahu Zuta*, cit., vol, II, pp. 226-227. In this regard, see also Porges, *Elie Capsali*, cit., pp. 24-26.

[17] Capsali, *Seder Eliyahu Zuta*, cit., vol., II, p. 227.

[18] In this case as well, we are in debt to our friend Reiny Mueller for the invaluable archive information supplied in this regard, and to Dr. Rachele Scuro for the transcription of the documents utilized by myself.

[19] "Cum se Antonius Grandonico et socii sindici intromisit pro suo officio certas causas quibus in isto Maiori Consilio datum est principium et pro non dando tedium isti Maiori Consilio et tenere totam civitatem impeditam pro simili re, vadit pars quod omnes dicte licet melius videbitur et placebit et in illis capre finem, sicut multis vicibus fuit servatum". The proposal was approved by a large majority (ASV, *Maggior Consiglio*, Deliberazioni, *Libro Ursa* [reg. 22] [1415-1454], c. 178v. [c. 184v according to the pencil numeration at the bottom], 5 November 1451). One piece of information, perhaps connected with the accusation of the crucifixion of the lambs, dates back to 1448. In March of that year, Antonio Gradenigo had thrown a Jew from Candia, Yospe [Yoseph] di Retimo, into prison, in Venice, under an unknown accusation. Eight months afterwards, the prisoner complained to the officials of the Quarantia, who were visiting the prisons, so that Gredenigo might transfer him from prison to prison to compel him to confess and had not concluded the preliminary investigation and hearing within eight moths, as required by the laws of Venice ("Capita de XL [... in carceribus] reppererint inter ceteros Yoste [recte: Yospe] ebreum de Rethimo, se gravantem ver virum nobilem Antonium Gradenico, sindicum partium Levantis, teneri carceratum iam 8 mensibus contra id quod de iure facere potest, cum sic disponentibus legibus et ordenibus nostris introducto casu suo ad consilium eum expedire teneretur infra tres menses, ultra quem terminum eum minime teneri poterat, subiugitique ipse Yospe quod idem ser Antonius hoc tempore eum multociens permutavit de carcere suo modo, et videns non posse ab eo habere nisi ut mera est rei veritas, non curat ipsum expedire"). In fact, Gradenigo has presented Yospe's case before the Senate a good four times without obtaining his condemnation, as he

desired. The Senate granted him another one-month postponement in which to conclude the inquiry and bring the Jew to trial, otherwise he would have to be released (ASV, Senato Mar, reg. 3, c. 83v. 27 October 1448). I wish to express my thanks to Dr. Stefano Piasentini for this information. It is however possible that Yospe's imprisonment, desired by Gradenigo, district mayor in the Levant, should be placed in relation with the prohibition against the ownership of real property by the Jews of Retimo outside the Jewish quarter, which was reiterated by the Counsel of Forty of Venice on 11 December 1448. On that occasion, the judiciaries of the Serenissima were investigating the case in which Jews from Retimo had made fictitious sales of their real property (Cfr. D. Jacoby, *An agent juif au service de Venise. David Mavrogonato de Candie*, in "Thesaurismata. Bolletino dell'Istituto Ellenico di Studi Bizantini et Post-Bizantimi", IX, 1972, pp. 86-87.

[20] "Cum advocatores notri comunis et etiam sindici aliquotiens introducatur ad Maius Consilium aliquos casus et negocia pro officiis suis, quod consilium pro maiori parte male congregatur et bonum sit quod dicta negocia iudicentur et terminentur in numero competenti propter importantium rerum, vadit pars quod quotienscumque advocatores comunis vel sindici habere voluerint Maisu Consilium pro casibus et agendis officiorum suorum debeat dictum consilium esse congregatum ad minimum ad numerum quadrigentorum et eum minori numero non intelligature esse in ordine nec aliquid fieri possit absque dicto numero IIIc vel ab inde supra". The proposal was approved (ASV, *Maggior Consiglio*, Deliberazioni, *Libro Ursi* [reg. 22] [1415-1454], c. 182r [c.188r according to the pencil numeration at bottom], 24 June 1452). In the specific case of the legal proceedings against the Jews of Candia (and in particular against Abba del Medigo, as we shall see below) the reduced attendance of three hundred voters was granted. "Quoniam per experientiam visum est quod istud consilium pluries locatum est ad petitionem advocatorum comunis et sindicorum pro facto Abbe medici iudei et numquam potuit congregari ad numerum ordinatum et per consequens ius et iustitia non potuit habere locum nec dari expeditio dicto, qui dudum fuit et est in carceribus, scilicet vadit pars quod factum dicti iudei entroduci et experiri in Maiori Consilio, cum numero trecentorum et inde supra" (ASV, *Maggior Consiglio*, Deliberazioni, *Libro Ursa* [reg. 22] 1415-1454], c. 189r. [c. 195r according to the pencil numeration at the bottom], 5 May 1454.

[21] Antonio da Spilimbergo maintained that those Jews of Candia had reduced him to despair "quia illorum voces et mores [...] patarini tamtum pati non potest" (ASV, Consiglio dei Dieci, mixed, reg. 14, c. 117v., 28 June 1452). I wish to thank my friend Reiny Mueller for this

curious information.

[22] "Abas quondam Moisi ebreu absolutus est sed tamen contra quem processum fuit [...] in eo et pro eo quod dum alias viris nobiles ser Laurentius Honorandi et ser Antonius Gradonico, olim sindici ad partes levantis, se reperissent in civitate Candidae et ad eorum aures, ex fama publica, pervenisset quod ebrei ibidem commorantes in vilipendium catolice fidei christianae omni anno crucifigebant unum agnum in sanctissimo die veneris sancti, ipsi sindici super fama publica examinaverunt multos testes. Postea, post recessum suum per regiment Crette, fuit examinata Marina Vergi olim ebrea et effecta tunc christiana, ex qua testificatione inter alios nominatus fuit ipse Abbas in propria domo quadam nocte crucifigisse unum agnum in ignominia Jesu Christi [...] quod procedatur contra Abbatem quondam Moise del Medigo ebreum qui postposito omni timore huius christianissme rei publice, in maximum opproprium fidei catolicae aurus fuit una cum aliquibus aliis perfidis ebreis in civatate nostra Candidae in die veneris sancti renovare misteria passionis domini Jesu Christi et crucifixerunt unum agnum quod etiam ipse Abbas in domo fecit ut est dictum" (ASV, Avogaria di Comun, Raspe, 3650 [II], cc. 9v-10r., 7 June 1454). The decision of the Maggior Consiglio lead to the definitive acquittal of the accused and in so doing reference was made to their release in first instance ("ex quibus scripturis ipse Abbas et ceteri nominati in infrascripta testificatione fuerunt per sindicos placiti, collegati et introducti ad Maius Consilio et in tertio consilio absoluti") and on Gradinego's second appeal, discussed above, on 21 May 1454, "in quo nihil captum fuit".

[23] In two different notes, contained in the decision of the Greater Council, mutilated and undated (but which must date back to March 1453), mention is made of the inquiry against Lambardo or Lombardo. The first opens with the words: "Ut veniri possit in lucem si [Hyeronimus Lambardus] habuit tot denarios ab Abbate hebreo". The second starts in a rather similar manner, but offers further information: "Ut haberi possit veritas istius promissionis facte per Abbatem [e]breum viro nobili ser Hyeronimo Lombardo et denariorum sibi datorum, ipse ser Hyeronimus retinetur ad pecticionem advocatorum comunis et examinetur" (ASV, *Maggior Consiglio*, Deliberazioni, *Libro Ursa* [reg. 22] [1415-1454], c. 193 [c. 199r according to the pencil numeration at bottom], March 1453). In a document in the Raspe dated June 1454, relating to the definitive acquittal of Abba del Medigo, mention is made of the *"condemnatione facta contra virum nobilem ser Hieronymum Lambardo"* (ASV, Avogaria di Comun, Raspe, 3650, [II], c. 10r).

[24] This is a reference to the "Bonhomo da Mestre", recorded at Padua in 1432 as the person "qui tenet banchum sancti Nicolae" (cfr. A. Ciscato, *Gli ebrei in Padova, 1300-1800*, Padua, pp. 242-243). In the Paduan documents, it is also stated that Bonomo di Mosè da Ancona, money lender at Mestre (cfr. D. Carpi, *The Jews of Padua During the Renaissance, 1369-1509*, doctoral thesis, Jerusalem, 1967, p. 49 [in Hebrew]. His father, who appears in the documents as Moisè Rab di Jacob and originated from Nuremberg, lived at Padu in 1460, in the Mastellerie district, in a palace owned by the Capodivacca family of patricians (ASP, Notarile, Paolo Carraro, 1943, c. 452r).

[25] "Bonomus ebreus filius Moisi contra quem processum fuit [...] pro eo quod dum ipse Bonomus aliquotiens iret visitatum Abbam ebreum cerceratum in carcere novo ad requisitionem dominorum auditorum novorum sententiarum veluti sindicorum levantis et quandoque intercessissit nomine dicti Abbe cum viro nobili ser Antonio de Priolis, uno dictorum auditorum quinquaginta ex quo ipse Abbas, repertis ipsis denariis, etiam ipse mutuo eos dedit ipsi Bonomo ebreo, credens ut ipsos mutuo daret ipsis ser Antonio de Priolis, qui Bonomus ipsos denarios pro se retinuit. Cumque post aliquos menses ipse Abba vellet denario suos et hoc diceret ipse ser Antino de Priolis, ipse ser Antonius turbatus ex hac gulositate predictum manifestavit dominis advocatoribus comunis". It was therefore decided "quod procedatur contra Bonumum ebreum filium Moisi qui, posposito omni timore Dei et dominii nobilem ser Antonium de Prioles sindicum levantis et eos pro se retinuit." The final decision was that "captum fuit quod ipse Bonomus stare debeat uno anno in carceribus et solvat ducatos centum auri et quod sit bannitus per quinque annos de Venetiis et districtu et si in dicto tempore se permiserit reperiri quod stare debeat uno anno in carceribus et solvat ducatos ducentos auri et iterum banniatur" (ASV, Avogaria di Comun, Raspe, 3650 [I], c. 28rv., 28 February 1452).

[26] "Abba ebreus cerceratus absolutus, sed tamen contra quem processum fuit per dominos asvocatores comunis et offitium suum et pro eo quod dum esset carceratus, ad instantium virorum nobilium ser Antonii Grandonico et ser Antonii de Priolis auditorum et uti sindicorum levantis, et Bonomus ebreus filius qui ipsum quandoque visitabat in carceribus falso et contra scientiam ipsius ser Antoni sibi dixisset quod prefatus ser Antonius de Priolis rogabat ipsum Abba ut ei mutuaret ducatos quinquaginta; ipse Abbas potius pro subornando quem ad aliud finem dedit ipsi Bonomo ducatos Lta aura, credens quod ipse Bonomo eo daret ipsi ser Antonio sed ipse oes retinuit pro se". The Avogadori requested "quod procedarur contra Abbam ebreum, carceratum ad instantiam sindicorum levantis, qui postposito omni

timore dominii nostri dedit Bonomo ebreo ducatos Lts Auri ut eos daret pro subornatione viro nobili ser Antonio de Priolis sindico". Abba was, however, absolved by order, "et sic captum fuit de non et remansit absolutus" (ASV, *Avogaria di Comun*, Raspe, 3650 [I], c. 29r, 1 March 1452).

[27] "Abba Moise del Medigo ebreus contra quem processum fuit per dominos advocatores comunis et offitium suum in eo et pro quod, dum esset carceratus per sindicos levantis, inculpatus de crucifixione agni, parvipendens Dominum nostrum et spirito diabolico ductus quodam die accepta zangula de loco suo eam in vilipendium crucifixi posuit sub ymagine Jesu Christi crucifix dumque carcerati redarguerentur eum, cepit dicere quod christiani adorabant picturas et tabulas et quod ibant ad macellum sicut porci; postea cepit dicere quod domina notra virgo Maria fuerat incantatrix et docuerat Jesum talia facere et quod habuerat tres viros et alios filios" [Approximately: "Abba Moses del Medigo the Jew, who was tried by the district prosecutors in the course of their duties, when incarcerated by the district mayors in the Levant, under indictment for crucifying lambs in contempt of Our Lord, and led onwards by the spirit of the Devil, on that day he moved his piss-pot from its proper place in contempt for the Crucifix and placed it beneath the image of Jesus Christ Crucified, and when the other jail-birds told him off about it, he started to say that Christians adore pictures and planks, and that they even slaughtered pigs, after which he started to say that our Holy Virgin was a witch and that she taught Jesus to take revenge and she had three husbands and other children"]. The Avogaria requested "quod procedatur contra Abbam ebreum Moisis de Creta qui existens carceratus proper fidem, dictus spiritu diabolico in maximam ignominiam fidei catolice multa turpissima verba dixit contra virginem Mariam et Jesus Christum accipiendo zangulam et eam ponendo ante crucifium". ["that Abba, the Jew from Crete, be tried who, being incarcerated for his faith, led onwards by the spirit of the Devil, and spoke with the greatest ignominy of the Catholic Faith against the Virgin mary and Jesus Christ, taking his piss-pot and placing it beneath the crucifix"] The sentence established that "captum fuit quod iste Abbas stare debeat uno anno in carceribus et solvat libras mille advocatoribus comunis" ["if he was captured the said Abba should spend one year in jail and pay one thousand pounds to the municipal prosecutor's office"] (ASV, Avogaria di Comun, Raspe, 3650 (I), c. 49rv., 30 October 1452). On the custom of desecrating crucifixes and other sacred images, placing them in the latrines or using them as eccentric coverings for piss-pots and chamber pots; see C. Cluse, *Stories of Breaking and Taking the Cross. A Possible Context for the*

Oxford Incident of 1268, in "Revue d'Histoire Ecclesiastique", XV (1995), p. 218.

[28] On the figure of Abbadi Mosè del Medigo and his family see, in particular, Carpi, *L'individuo e la collettività*, cit., pp. 230-233.

[29] Capsali, *Seder Eliyahu Zuta*, cit., vol. II, p. 253.

[30] ASV, Avogaria di Comun, reg. 3660, cc. 107r-108r.: the trial of Abramo di David da Soncino, the client, and Bonaventura di Abramo da Feltre, the accomplice, guilty of the murder of "Elia greco", son of Abba del Medigo, "prestatore a Soave", was held at Venice at the beginning of the month of December of 1505. It appears that in 1506, Abba's widow, Ritte, was occupied in matters related to the estate of the deceased son (cfr. Carpi, *L'individuo e la collettività*, cit., p. 232). The murder of Elia the Greek (but not the identification of Elia the Greek with Elia, son of Abba del Medigo) is mentioned in M. Melchiorre, *Gli ebrei a Feltre nel Quattrocento. Una storia rimossa*, in G.M. Varanni and R.C. Mueller, *Ebrei nella Terraferma veneta del Quattrocento*, Florence, 2005, p. 101, no. 73.

[31] Cfr. Jacoby, *Les juifs at Venice*, cit., p. 172.

[32] Cfr. Gardenal, *Ludovico Foscarini e la medicina*, cit., pp. 251-263. On the position of the Jewish physician in Renaissance Italy and the frequent disputes in his regard, see, among others, A. Toaff, *Il vino et la carne. Una communita ebraica nel Medievo*, Bologna, 1989, pp. 265-285; G. Cosmacini, *Medicina e mondo ebraico. Dalla Bibbia al secolo dei ghetti*, Bari, 2001, pp. 143-211.

[33] See, in this regard, M.J.C. Lowry, *Humanism and Anti-Semitism in Renaissance Venice. The Strange Story of "Décor Puellarum"*, in "La Bibliofilia", LXXXVII (1985), pp. 39-54 in view of the fact that Foscarini had been incarcerated during the two-year period of 1460-1461, the city business permits granted by Venice to the Jewish doctors (and first of all to Yehudah messer Leon) should have been signed during that period. Notwithstanding Foscarini's protest, on the request of the Doge Cristoforo Moro, the Cardinal Bessarione, Papal legate, dated 17 December 1463, confirmed that these agreements were respected.

[34] Cfr. *Gardenal Ludovico Foscarini e la medicina*, cit., p. 260. "Nuperrime quidam Iudeus togatus, auro circumdatus, demissis capillis, severa facie ausus est nobillissiumis matronis in generosa familia lacrimantibus oculis dicere: compatior ignorantiae vestae quia creditis Deum factorem coeli et terrae ses manducandum preabere et non dedignari lenonum impurissimorum et vulgatissimarum meretricium ora."

[35] Cfr. M.A. Shulvass, *Racconto delle tribolazioni passate in Italia*,

in "Hebrew Union College Annual", XXII (1949), pp. 1-21 (17) (in Hebrew). The anonymous chronicle has been republished by I. Sonne, *From Paul IV to Pius V*, Jerusalem, 1954, pp. 183-202 (pp. 200-201) (in Hebrew).

[36] Fra Francesco Suriano, writing before 1483, noted with ill-concealed pride that the Jewish women of Venice, when they gave birth, often did not hesitate to ask the Virgin Mary for help, in a paradoxical, self-interested cult with magical connotations (F. Suriano, *Il trattato di Terra Santa e dell'Oriente*, by G. Golubuvich, 1900, p. 94-95): "Li Iudei similiter sono constrecti de reverirla (la Vergine Maria); e secundo che ho udito da obstretricie digne de fede, ne l'alma cita de Venetia e christiane che se sono retrovate alquante volte arcoglier loro fioli nel parto de piu Hebree, le qual testificavono e dicevono che non partuire senza la sua invocazione e recommendazione; et vede che loro mariti spargeano per la camara alquante monede d'argento furlane, le qual hano la sua ymagine. Ricevuta la gratia, e liberata dal parto, scopano e bugliano fori de la fenestra quelle monede, e diceano: 'fora Maria, fora Maria!' " ["Similarly, the Jews are compelled to revere Her (the Virgin Mary); and according to what I have heard from trustworthy midwives who went to assist several Jewesses in childbirth in the Christian city of Venice, they testified and said that the Jewesses never give birth without Her invocation and recommendation; their husbands toss a few Friulian silver coins around the room, bearing Her image. When they have received Her blessing and are freed from childbirth, they sweep them up and throw them out the window, saying 'Get out, Mary, Mary get out!' "]. The quotation appears in D. Nissim, *Due viaggi in Palestina*, in "La Rassegna Mensile di Israel", XL (1974), pp. 256-259 (259). However one wishes to take Franciscan's picturesque account, it seems to be a fact that, towards the end of the Fifteenth century, Jewish women giving birth in Venice were very numerous. It should be noted, without surprise, that such a practice was still widespread among Jewish women two centuries later, as testified to by Giulio Morosini (Derekh Emunah, *Via delle fede mostrata agli ebrei*, Rome Propaganda Fide, 1683, pp. 1050-1051).

[37] Cfr. D. Nissim, *Un "minian" di ebrei ashkenaziti a Venezia negli anni 1465-1480*, in "Italia", XVI (2004), p. 43.

[38] The little information on the origins of the Jewish community in Trent, from the episcopal privilege of 1403 to the money lending agreements and legal disputes of the mid-Fifteen Century, are contained in G. Menestrina, *Gli ebrei a Trento*, in "Tridentum", VI (1903), pp. 304-316, 348-374, 384-411. This information has been utilized, without addition, by the following authors: C. Andreolli, *Una*

ricognizione delle communità ebraiche nel Trentinto tra XIV e XVII secolo, in "Materiali di lavoro", 1988, nn. 1-4, pp. 151-181; Po-Chia Hsia, *Trent 1475*, cit., pp. 14-25, as well as D. Rando's recent monograph, *Dai margini la memoria. Johannes Hinderbach (1418-1486)*, Bologna, 2003, pp. 457-491, and S. Luzzi, *Stranieri in città. Presenza tedesca e società urbana a Trento (secoli XV-XVIII)*, Bologna, 2003, pp. 180-194. In this regard, see also F. Ghetta, *Fra Bernardino Tomitano da Feltre e gli ebrei di Trento nel 1475*, in "Civis", suppl. 2 (1986), pp. 129-177.

[39] Mosè di Samuele da Trento and the wife of Dolce di Ezzelino (Anshel Asher) had five children, Samuele, Ezechia, Benedetto known as Barukh, Perentina and Osella (Feige). Mosè's testament was ratified at Trento on 10 June 1423 (cfr. M. Davide, *Il ruolo economico delle donne nelle communità ebraiche di Trieste e di Treviso nei secoli XIV e XV*, in "Zhakhor. Rivista di storia degli ebrei d'Italia", VII, 2004, pp. 193-212 [206-208].

[40] Cfr. Menestrina, *Ebrei a Trento*, cit., pp. 304-306.

[41] Cfr. ibidem, pp. 307-308

[42] Now Conegliano Veneto.

[43] Angelo da Verona reached Trent in 1407. On that occasion, Hinderbach seized from the money lender, whom he called "hebreum qui venit huc (sc. a Trento), de Brixia sive eius territorio", an illuminated manuscript of the Vitae sanctorum (cfr. *"Pro Bibliotheca erigenda". Mostra di manoscritti ed incunabili del vescovo di Trento Iohannes Hinderbach, 1465-1486*, Trent, 1989, p. 69.

[44] Cfr. Luzzi, *Stranieri in città*, pp. 180-185.

[45] "Sarra ivit in canipam ipsius et se lavit in fossato ibi existente [...] quia passa fuerat menstrua Sarra diebus precedentibus, quia est de more Iudeorum quod mulieres Iudee post menstruase lavent." Deposition of Samuele of Nuremberg of 7 June 1475. Sarah was the wife of Maestro Tobias da Magdeburg (cfr. Esposito and Quaglioni, *Processi*, cit., vol. I, p. 244).

[46] "Ipsi Iudei portant duos cultellos in una vagina, quorum uno utuntur ad incisionem carnium, altero ad lacticinia" ["This Jew carried two knives in a sheath, one to cut meat, the other to cut dairy products"]. Deposition of Samuele of Nuremberg dated 7 June 1475 (cfr. ibidem, p. 246). "Moris est [...] portare duos coltellos in una vagina, quorum uno utuntur ad lacticinia, altero vero ad carnes". Deposition di Mosè "the Old Man" of Würzburg, dated 4 April 1475 (cfr. ibidem, p. 354).

[47] On the extermination of the five hundred Jews of the community of Vienna in 1421, known in the Hebraic sources such as the *Gezerah*,

i.e., "the persecution", see S. Krauss, *Die Wiener Geserah vom Jahre 1421*, Vienna, 1920; O.H. Stowasser, *Zur Geschichte der Wiener Geserah*, in "Vierteljahresheft für Sozial- und Wirtschaftsgeschichte", XVI (1922), pp. 104-118; Sh. Spitzer, *Das Wiener Judentum bis zur Vertreibung im Jahre 1421*, in "Kairos", II (1977), pp. 134-145.

[48] On Hinderbach's attitude towards the Jews, before and after the events at Trent, see, in particular, I. Rogger and M. Bellabarbia, *Il principe vescovo Johannes Hinderbach (1465-1486) fra tardo Medioevo e Umanesmo*, Atti del Convegno promosso dalla Biblioteca Communale di Trento (2-6 October 1989), Bologna, 1992; Po-Chia Hsia, *Trent 1475*, cit., pp. 1-13, and above all, Rando, *Dai margini la memoria*, cit., pp. 457-491.

[49] "Hiis diebus apud Tergestum Italiae civitatem a Venetis obsessiam alias fuit, in qua milites ultamontanes equos, asinos, canes, gattos, et sorices comederunt [...] quorum tanta fuit constantia fidei ut, priusquam urbem ob inediam deserere aut dedere (vellent), ita apud se statuerunt humanam prius Iudeorum, qui intus erant, [...] carnem vesci" [Approximately: "In those days, Trent, a city in Italy, was besieged by Venice, and the ultramontane defenders ate horses, donkeys, dogs, cats, and mice [...]; such was their constancy in the faith that, that when they were about to have to give up the city, they decided to nourish themselves on flesh of the Jews who lived there"] (cfr. Rando, *Dai margini la memoria*, cit., pp. 168-169).

[50] Burcardo di Andwil, *Bellum Venetum, Bellum ducis Sigismundi contra Venetos (1487)*, in *Carmina varia* by M. Welber, Rovereto, 1987, p. 105.

[51] Cfr. Rando, *Dai margini la memoria*, cit., pp. 478-491.

[52] *Ristretto della vita e martirio di S. Simone fanciullo della città di Trento*, Rome Filipp Neri alle Muratte, 1594, p. 4.

[53] Cfr. Rando, *Dai margini la memoria*, cit., pp. 483-487.

CHAPTER FOUR

PORTOBUFFOLÈ, VOLPEDO, ARENA PO, MAROSTICA, RINN

On 6 July 1480, three Jews accused of ritual child murder, required for the performance of their Passover rites, during the Passover period of that year, were executed at Venice. Servadio da Colonia, money lender at Portobuffolè, Mosè da Treviso and Giacobbe of Cologne,[1] having confessed – sometimes spontaneously and sometimes under torture – were impaled and burned alive in public in the Piazza San Marco, between the two columns of San Marco and San Todaro. Another defendant, Giacobbe "with the beard", committed suicide in prison to avoid torture. Other Jews, from Portobuffolè and Treviso, were condemned to various punishments of imprisonment for complicity in the crime and thereafter banned from Venice and its territory. Tried and condemned before the podestà of Portobuffolè, the Venetian Andrea Dolfin, the defendants had appealed to the Avogaria di Commun, but, notwithstanding the fact that they were defended by some of the best lawyers in Padua, their sentence was upheld.[2]

According to the indictment, a small wandering beggar about six years of age, a native of Seriate in the Bergamo region, had been abducted from the market place at Treviso, where he had been begging, by two Jews, who were alleged to have taken him to nearby Portobuffolè, on the Livenza river, in an eventful journey, the stages of which did not pass entirely unobserved by travelers and boatmen. Here, in the dwelling of the local money lender, Servadio, who was also the instigator of the abduction, the cruel crime was said to have been committed for ritual purposes, in the presence and with the active participation of other local and foreign Jews. After draining off the blood, the perpetrators burnt the body in the oven of a house owned by Mosè da Treviso, another money lender at Portobuffolè. Denunciations and informer's reports, including Donato, Seradio's servant, then converted to Christianity, are said to have led to the indictment of the Jewish defendants and to their condemnation for the murder of the nameless little victim, immediately rebaptized under the name of Sebastiano Novello, of obvious significance.

Portobuffolè, like so many other small centers of the Marca of

Treviso and the territory of Venice, was, in the 15th century the seat of a community of Ashkenazi Jews, the traces of which have remained in Hebraic manuscript texts, copied in that small city in the years preceding the Sebastiano Novello murder.[3] The chronicle of this cruel execution, as described by the diarist apologists of the time, inform us that at least one of the defendants, Servadio, faced death in prayer, accompanied by contemptuous remarks about Christianity.[4] This detail may be related to the legendary story of a stone slab, walled in the Ashkenazim synagogue Scola Canton of the ghetto of Venice, containing a verse from the psalms (32:10: '*Many sorrows shall be to the wicked: but he that trusteth in the Lord, mercy shall encompass him*'). In the local Hebraic tradition, this phrase is said to have been pronounced by Servadio himself, among the flames of the stake in the Piazza San Marco. During these terrible moments, the condemned man is said to have taken the time to point out the unhappy informer, his servant Donato, baptized under the name of Sebastiano, to the Jews in the crowd, who were present at this terrifying ceremony. The spectators are said to have included Josef, cantor of the synagogue of Portobuffolè (who was perhaps the same Fays who acted as teacher in Servadio's dwelling), who is said to have interpreted the Psalm with a new meaning, imparted by the person reciting it: "The bitter pains which I suffer, will fall on the wicked".[5] Thus history and hagiography became confused, while the authenticity and memory of the child's true martyrdom ricocheted back and forth between Christians and Jews.

Milan, summer of 1482. A brother of the Order of the Serviti, Giovanni Guerra, and Simone, Jew of Tortona were publicly executed by order of the Duke. Guerra was said to have been accused of barbarously killing a child about nine years of age, near the farmhouse Scorticavacca di Volpedo, near Tortona, on Holy Tuesday of that year; the second defendant was accused of instigating the friar to commit the crime, so as to obtain the blood of a Christian child, as required for the Jewish Passover rites. Both defendants confessed. In the preceding May, a special commission had left the Court of the Sforzas with the assignment of investigating the cruel death of Giovannino Costa, a young shepherd, who was accustomed to coming down from the hills to Tortona to sell eggs and butter on market days.[6]

The diligent commissioner ordered the arrest of all the members of the little Jewish community of German origin, including Madio (Mohar, Meir), the local money lender, and the requisition of all pledges deposited in the bank. The persons under investigation were subsequently transferred to Milan. At the conclusion of the investigation, the culpability of the Jew Simone, the instigator, and the "scoundrel friar", the unnatural, cruel executioner, was clearly established. The other persons under investigation, including the banker, were released, following a finding that they had had nothing to do with the crime, and were permitted to leave Tortona.

From the official correspondence sent by the court of the Sforzas to the podestà and the bishop of Tortona, we learn that:

"A certain homicide being committed during the past Holy Days against the person of a boy, at the instance of certain Jews in the diocese of Derthona, the following persons are held in prison here: Fra Giovanni Guerra of the Order of the Servants, and one Simon, a Jew, who did not deny having committed the said excess, the horrible and detestable nature of which, in the eyes of any faithful Christian, we leave to you to judge [...]. The wicked friar, with many wounds, cruelly killed the innocent boy in the region of Derthona to sell his blood to the Jews".[7]

The death of the presumed guilty parties and the prompt release of the other suspected Jews were insufficient to restore equilibrium to their relations with the community of Tortona. Many Jews emigrated elsewhere, the others became Christian. Simon's widow, executed at Milan, was left with a daughter, who took the name of Michela. Simon's other four sons, two aged less than seven, and the other two ten and twelve respectively, were made to take refuge with the Jews of Piacenza, out of fear that they might be converted to Christianity. On 24 April 1483, the Duke of Milan, under pressure from the justly impatient bishop of Tortona, Giacomo Botta, requested the podestà of Piacenza to do everything possible to ensure that his two smaller sons were returned with speed to Donna Michela to receive the holy baptism.[8]

In the collective memory of the Ashkenazi Jews of Northern Italy, the crime of Volpedo was to appear rather similar to that of Trent; it is true that Yoseph Ha-Cohen (Giuseppe Sacerdoti), one of the most famous Jewish chroniclers of the 16th century, after sadly reporting the events linked to the martyrdom of Simonino, observed that "in those years, the Jews in the territory of Tortona were slandered because of a Jew of the place, as had happened at Trent, and here, as well, the boy, named Giovannino, was called a saint; and the people went fornicating after him, and for us, it was only harm and disgrace".[9]

The Volpedo case, involving a criminal wearing the cassock of a brother in the Holy Orders, was not an isolated one. In the summer of 1481, a Minorite Franciscan friar was arrested at Cortemaggiore on a charge of accepting a commission from local Jews to commit a child murder intended to provide them with Christian blood for their

Passover, the generous commission amounting to four hundred gold ducats. Placed in a cage and appended from the bell tower at Cremona, the friar was left to die slowly of starvation, after which his body became a feast for birds of prey.[10] The documents say nothing of the fate of the Jews, the presumed instigators of this holy homicide.

Arena, April 1479. In this village on the banks of the Po river, a child disappeared along the road from Padua to Piacenza during the Passover period of that year, while suspicion immediately fell on the local money lenders Bellomo di Madio (Simha Bunim b. Meir), and his entourage. Finally, David, employed by Bellomo, decided to spill the beans and reveal the particulars of this obscure crime. His patron had commissioned Donato, a Jew from Padua, to abduct a Christian child "to prepare for the Jewish ceremonies". Conveyed in secrecy to Bellomo's dwelling, the child, known only by the nickname "Turlulu", was said to have been cruelly crucified in a holy ceremony with the participation of all the local Jews and others from other neighboring villages. The little victim's body is finally said to have been thrown by night into the muddy waters of the Po.[11]

This was considered sufficient to proceed with the arrest of the parties guilty of this brutal crime, as well as that of their accomplices, both men and women, including Bellomo's wife, who uselessly but vehemently protested her husband's innocence. Sacle (Izchak), a money lender from the Borgo San Giovanni, in the Piacenza region, who had, years before, been mentioned in the defendant's depositions at the Trent trial as an habitual consumer of Christian blood, and had for this reason been exposed to more than a few minor risks, was also arrested and taken to Pavia, where he was to be tried.[12]

In the meantime, Donato, the supposed author of the abduction and one of the principal perpetrators of the child's crucifixion, at the conclusion of a difficult interrogation confessed everything and pointed an accusing finger at Belomo and his family. The podestà of Pavia lost no time and proceeded with the seizure and confiscation of all the goods of the Jews of Arena.

But then a sensation occurred. Turlulu, the crucified child, turned up perfectly safe and sound. His body, examined by physicians and experts with all due diligence, didn't even have a scratch on it. At this point, Gian Galeazzo Maria Sforza and his mother, the duchess Bona, imperiously requested that Bellomo and Donato, the principal defendants, accused of a ritual infanticide that never happened, were transferred, without further delay, to Milan, together with the resurrected boy.

The protests of the Pavian authorities, who desired unperturbedly to proceed with preparations for the trial, as if nothing had happened, produced no effect. The guileless Turlulu was presented on a seat in the Senate, in Milan, unaware of the reasons for all the hullabaloo, having himself become the principal personage in a sort of "virtual" ritual homicide. His interrogation helped disperse the fog of mystery which still envelopes this grotesque tale. Finally, as might have been anticipated, Bellomo and Donato were acquitted of all charges in the indictment for a crime which was never committed, were released from jail and permitted to return to Arena.

The Duke of Milan and his mother did not fail to voice their own profound disappointment to the rulers of Pavia in a missive, sent after the release of the Jews, written without any moderation of discourse: "We are amazed, not without annoyance, by this scandalous invention, of which have just caused such great inconvenience to both people and subjects". He concluded the letter, celebrating his own sense of justice and equanimity, "that we have caused the truth to be known about such a scandalous imputation". The Duke then demanded that the property illegally seized at Bellomo and other Jews of Arena be immediately returned.[13]

One month later, there was still no change in the situation, and, as a result of the protests from the Jews, the Duke of Milan repeated, with renewed vigor, his request that the goods seized from them at the time should be returned. The response, from the podestà of Pavia, is an inimitable example of both impudence and insensitivity. He would release the Jews' property, and sign it back over to them, but the heavy burden of procedural costs, plus the salaries of all judges, notaries and functionaries having concerned themselves with the case, would have to be paid by the acquitted defendants. The ineffable podestà said that he was fully convinced that the Jews would be open-minded and well disposed to accede to the paradoxical statement that, "for so little money, I am certain the Jews will not prove themselves too unwilling".[14]

The facts of the Arena case led the representatives of the Jewish communities of Lombardy to appeal to Gian Galeazzo Maria Sforza, so that he might defend them from the ritual murder accusations which were spreading dangerously, like a spot of oil on water, throughout all the territories at that time, threatening to conclude in the same tragic manner as the Trent affair. Nor could the confessions, often extorted with torture and violence, constitute valid proof linking the Jews to such horrendous crimes, as indicated by the outcome of the affair at Arena Po ("the accused, at the said locality of Arena, as a result of the tremendous torments inflicted upon them in various parts of the body, confessed to committing a crime of which they were innocent, and confined in the Castello, and in the Casa del Capitanio di Giustizia, for acknowledging that what they had said was actually true, and if God, in his grace, had not sent word that the boy had been found, they would have fared worse than the defendants at Trent, which only God knows whether it was true or not, and let us just hope that God makes a demonstration of the truth in due time"). The Arena case was not an isolated one. The Jews, in their appeal of 19 May 1479, informed Sforza that other, repeated, accusations of ritual infanticide, all proving false and inconsistent, had been made over the last few months in various cities of the Dukedom, from Pavia to Valenza, from Stradella to Bormio.[15]

"The following case occurred two months ago: in Valenza, finding that a boy was missing, suspicion being aroused against the Jews of that region, the Jews were badly threatened, and if, by the grace of God, the boy had not been found drowned in a ditch, they would certainly have suffered worse. Similarly, a boy from Monte Castillo being lost, the Jews of that region were accused, but the boy was later found [...].

"The same thing happened at Bormio, as well as at Pavia: a boy remained outside the bridge of Ticino after nightfall and was taken in by a gentleman, to stay at his house, so as to return him to his own home; and as the boy was not immediately found, suspicion fell upon the Jews, with much murmuring against the Jews; a house was searched with many threats, in such a way that the patron of the house fled in fear and has still not returned. And if the boy had not then been found, the Jews would not have been without danger and serious trouble, as happened to the Jews of Stradella, as well as at Pavia, which were sacked, causing the people to grumble, at the risk of raising a great scandal and disorder to the detriment and danger of the State of Your Illustrious Lordship".[16]

After stating the classical motives, which should have deprived the ritual murder accusation of all credibility, particularly, in light of the Biblical prohibition against killing and against the consumption of blood, the representatives of the Jewish communities of Lombardy added another motive, which to our minds seems odd. In the lands of the Great Turk, where powerful and wealthy Jews lived and prospered, owning large numbers of Christian slaves, both adults and children, it was said to be an easy matter for Jews to procure the blood of Christian children without running any risk to their persons and property at all.

But this did not occur, and there was no news from those regions of child murders committed by Jews for ritual purposes.

"There are, it is said there, innumerable rich Jews in the lands of the Turks, Moors and other infidels, who hold slaves and servants, and are able to have the [Christian] boys at their pleasure, to do what they liked with them without respect or danger, which does not prevent them from doing such things in the lands of the Christians, at the price of great danger, not only to their property but also to their person".[17]

The argument could just as easily have been turned around. Even the most inveterate anti-Semites knew in fact that the accusations of ritual murder and profanation of the Host were confined to relatively small geographical areas, which included all Jewish communities of the German-language regions, as well as all the Ashkenazi regions in Italy, at the foot of the Alps.[18] Giovanni Hinderbach himself, in the autographic preamble to the trials, explained the manner in which the child murder committed by the Jews of Trent was in no way a novelty.

"In fact", he added, "the impiety of the Jews has come cruelly to light over the past few years in many cities and localities of Germany, as well as in regions such as Swabia and Bavaria, Austria and Styria, the Rhineland and Saxony, as well as in Poland and Hungary".[19] The lands of the Great Turk were obviously excluded.

Not many years had passed since the incidents at Arena, Portobuffolè and Volpedo, when a new ritual murder case came to light, upsetting the lives of the Jewish communities of northern Italy. During Holy Week, April of 1485, in Valrovina, in the territories of the Marostica region, a five-year old child, Lorenzino Sossio, was found murdered, his body horribly mutilated.[20] The macabre discovery, at the feet of an oak tree in a pasture on the upland plain, was made by a local goatherd, while a hermit ("a devout hermit, who had long been a spectator and had diligently observed everything") informed the authorities and populace that the killers had committed the horrendous crime by mutilating poor Lorenzino in the foreskin,[21] "inflicting upon him by force of repeated punctures and wounds in the blood vessels", finally stoning the body and covering it with stones. The news was immediately disseminated that the persons responsible for the ritual murder were Jews, from Bassano, "having come to the Vicentino for business or pleasure, but perhaps principally to commit the crime". Thus the chronicles reported the tragic fate of Lorenzino Sossio da Valrovina, later beatified as Simoncino of Trent, *de quo adest traditio cum fuisse ab hebreis occisum* [of whom tradition has it that he was killed by the Jews].

"In 1485, 5 April in the Villa di Valrovina under Marostica in the territory of the Vicentino region, the Jews stoned the Sainted Lorenzino, 5 years old, and buried him several times under rocks; but one of his arms always extended from the grave. Once discovered, the delinquents were punished, and all the Jews were expelled by the above mentioned residents of the Vicentino from their City and District; and the Serenissima Prince of Venice confirmed the sentence by Ducal order in 1486".[22]

Five years later, in the spring of 1500, the podestà of Vicenza, Alvise Moro, informed the Venetian authorities that the "devote hermit", sole eyewitness to the crime, after being incarcerated and duly tortured, had revealed the name of the person guilty of Lorenzino's murder. The murderer was alleged to be Marcuccio, money lender at Bassano ("which hermit is in prison here, and would like permission to speak, wishing to know the truth: that if they took one Marcuzzo, a Jew, they would find out something [...] take the Jew, accused of killing the boy, and take Marcuzzo da Bassan, and you will learn the truth, is what the hermit said, in those very words").[23]

Marcuccio was the son of Lazzaro Sacerdote of Treviso, who worked at Cittadella and was a nephew of Salomone da Piove di Sacco.[24]

Active at Bassano although highly unpopular locally, he had until then enjoyed the protection of Venice, constant over time, the City having renewed his ten-year money lending permit in April 1499.[25] We do not know whether the tardy revelations of the "devote hermit" induced Marcuccio to leave Bassano and turn over the management of the local money lending bank. But that was precisely what happened: after the nephew of Salomone da Piove had become, it seems, the principal protagonist of a tardy trial, brought at Vicenza for the murder of the boy Marostica. However that may be, even in that region, the mystery of the crime was not solved, nor were the guilty ever identified with certainty.

In the light of what we have just observed, it seems obvious that the expulsion of the Jews from Vicenza in 1486 and the cessation of their money-lending activities were not related to the presumed martyrdom of the Saint Lorenzino.[26] Of course, none of this will discourage historians, scholars and local priests constantly on the lookout for more or less imaginary holy personages by means of whom their own poverty-stricken, obscure village or locality may be exalted, causing it to perform an otherwise inconceivable quantum leap of fame.

Twenty three years before, at Rinn, diocese of Bressanone, on the road to Innsbruck, a company of Jewish merchants, returning from the fair at Merano, were traversing a small village in the Tyrol and bumped into a three-year old child, Andrea Oxner. Having informed themselves as to his family, the Jews knew that the mother was far from home, in the fields at Ambras reaping wheat, and that little Andrea had been entrusted to the care of his godfather, the "Weisselbauer" of Rinn, Hannes Mayr. Employing every possible stratagem and pretext, the Jews induced this dishonest peasant to hand the child over to them, promising that they would take him away with them to live a life of ease and comfort. But they had no intention of traveling very far with him. Stopping in a birch tree thicket, a little ways above Rinn, "the innocent victim's veins were barbarously and cruelly severed by those inhuman creatures, who then hung the bloodless cadaver from a tree". Having obtained the Christian blood which they needed, the Jewish merchants hurried to leave the scene, crossing the northern confines of the Tyrol on the road to Ellbogen.[27]

The martyred child's body was discovered by the desperate mother. The godfather, under intense interrogation, admitted entrusting Andrea to the Jews on the promise that they would educate the child in luxury and riches. He then confessed that he had been persuaded by innumerable glasses of wine, drunk in the company of those foreigners, and a hatful of gold coins which had been placed in his hand. The impious Mayr's fate was signed, more by God than by men. "The perfidious peasant who sold the child was condemned to perpetual imprisonment in his own house, linked with chains, where he lived imprisoned and mad for a good two whole years".[28] Thus recites the implausible hagiography of Andrea of Rinn, which is full of gaps and for which there is no convincing contemporary documentation. The report remains inextricably linked to local traditions whose relationship to reality can only leave one perplexed and dubious.

Nevertheless, the cardinal Lorenzo Ganganelli, later Pope Clement XIV, in his famous report of 19 January 1760, presented to the Congregation of the Holy Office, with which he intended in general to absolve the Jews from the accusation of ritual infanticide, made an exception in the case of Andreas of Rinn, as well as in the case of the martyrdom of Simon of Trent. The two cases were to be considered exceptional events, not to be generalized, but were nevertheless concrete and real:[29]

"I therefore admit as true the fact of the sainted Simon, the boy of three years of age killed by Jews in hatred of the faith of Jesus Christ in Trent in the year 1475 [...] I accept as true another crime, committed in the village of Rinn, diocese of Bressanone, in 1462, against the sainted Andrea, a boy barbarously killed by the Jews in hatred of the faith of Jesus Christ [...] I do not, however, believe, even admitting as true the true facts of Bressanone and Trent, that one can justifiably deduce that this is a maxim, either theoretical or practical, of the Hebrew nation, since two events alone are insufficient to establish a certain and common axiom".[30]

The accused in the Trent trial in 1475, under torture, supplied ample testimony of ritual homicides committed, according to them, in the preceding years in the German-speaking lands from which they came, and in the centers of northern Italy where communities of Ashkenazi Jews had formed more or less recently. The defendants were alleged to have assisted or participated in these murders directly; in some cases, they had only heard about them from others. Sometimes they were able to remember the names of the other Jews who had taken part.

Isacco da Gridel, near Vedera, immigrated from Voitsberg, a village near Cleburg, was employed as a cook by Angelo of Verona, one of the principal defendants in the trial for the death of Simonino. In 1460, Isacco attended the lower courses of a Talmudic school at Worms, in the territory of the Rhineland, and it was there that he participated in a ritual murder, a little before Passover. A Jew by the name of Hozelpocher is said to have purchased a two-year old child from a Christian beggar at a very high price and to have taken the child to his dwelling in the Jewish quarter. The murder is said to have been committed here, in the spacious "stufa" [parlor] of the house, in a collective ritual, with the participation of about forty local Jews. The blood is said to have been gathered in a glass receptacle, but is not said to have reached the quantity of liquid contained in two egg shells.[31]

Joav of Ansbach in Franconia was a domestic servant in the house of the Maestro Tobias da Magdeburg, the oculist physician of Trent. Joav had recently immigrated from the city of Prince Bishop Hinderbach, and had previously rendered service in the house of a Jew named Mohar (Meir) at Würzburg for over fifteen years. During this period, Joav testified to having seen the Christian servant, Elisabeth Baumgartner, assigned to housework, which was forbidden to Jews on Sabbath days, introduce Christian children into the dwelling, in secrecy and during the night, on at least three occasions. The murders were said to have been committed in the wood-shed, in a collective ritual which then concluded in the chapel-synagogue, in a ceremony with the participation of numerous local Jews. The blood was gathered in a silver chalice, while the children's bodies were buried at night in a terrain owned by Mohar, outside the city.[32] Mosè of Ansbach, the young teacher of Maestro Tobias's children, for his part, informed the judges that, in 1472, while he was working at Nuremberg, he had learned that a ritual murder had been committed approximately eight years beforehand, in the dwelling of a certain Mayer Pilmon, in the presence of and with the participation of all the males of the family.[33]

Mosè da Bamberg was a poor traveler who, having left Bayreuth with his son on his way to Pavia, had stopped for a brief stay in the city of Trent, as a guest in money lender Samuele da Nuremberg's house, and had, to his disgrace, been present during the tragic days of the murder, confessing his knowledge of the murders to the judges. In 1466, on the road from Frankfurt on the Oder, in the Mark of Brandenburg, while transporting some goods to be sold in that city, he had stumbled across some professional child hunters. While traveling through a thick forest, Mosè had, in fact, encountered two Jews, remembering only their first names, Salomone and Giacobbe, in the act of preparing to hurl into a nearby river the bodies of two boys, massacred by them previously. Their prey had been captured in a small peasant village at the foot of the forest.[34] The two hunters showed the appalled Mosè their tin-plated iron bottles, filled with red liquid, and were satisfied at the thought that they were going to rake in a tidy sum through the sale of that liquid. But they needed the money to live.[35]

Whether or not this was all simply a Grimm Brothers fairy tale, which might well be told at the right time and place to frighten children and give them sleepless nights, we don't know. It is certain that the poor Mosè da Bamberg could not precisely remember the identity of the two hunters and was unable to locate the forest in which the crimes had been committed; nor did he know the names of the two victims or the village from which they had been abducted, or the name of the river into which they were said to have been thrown. He recited this fantastic confession before his attentive inquisitors, oscillating, suspended by a rope tied around his feet and his head downwards.[36]

Israel da Brandenburg, the strange young painter, later baptized under the name of Wolfgang, knew how to be loquacious when he had to be, and had heaps of picturesque ritual murder tales to tell, tales which had reached his ears more or less directly, with which to regale his avid and powerful interlocutors. He had allegedly gathered this information for several months, moving from the Rhineland to the Tyrol, then down to Venice, traveling through the cities of the Veneto. He claimed to possess first hand information on the ritual murders of Christian children committed at Güzenhausen in 1461 and Wending ten years afterwards. At Piove di Sacco and Feltre, Jews from his native country had told him of the ritual murders recently committed at Padua and at Mestre.[37]

The women in the trial were no less prominent and their report of the child murders committed by their men, husbands, parents, friends and friends, were precise and detailed. Bona, Angelo da Verona's sister, was a survivor of family and marital problems. She had lived with her stepfather, Chaim, from the time she was a little girl, first at Conegliano del Friuli and then at Mestre. When she was little over fourteen years old, she had been married off, against her will, to Madio (Meir), a Jew from Borgomanero in the Novara region. Madio had a reputation as a madman and a thoroughly bad egg, who, after wasting the already scanty family fortune in gambling, had abandoned her, moving elsewhere. As a result, Bona had returned to her mother's house at Conegliano del Friuli, and was then taken to Trent with her mother Brunetta (Brünnlein), also an unhappy and frustrated woman, as the more or less welcome guests of her brother, Angelo da Verona, who had, in recent years, been able to scrape together a small fortune in the money trade. Before the judges, Bona admitted to using Christian blood during the Passover period, beginning as early as her brief matrimonial journey to Borgomanero. Her husband Madio had obtained it from a carpenter friend, guilty of killing a boy for this purpose from Masserano in Piedmont.

"(Bona) [said that], during the entire time that she stayed with the said husband (Madio), her husband used the blood of a Christian child [...] and she did the same during the three year period of her stay at the Castello di Borgomanero, adding, when asked, that her husband had obtained the blood he used from a certain Mosè, a Jewish carpenter and resident of Masserano in Piedmont; that Mosè had conveyed the blood to her husband through a servant of the said Mosè, whose name Bona said she did not know, and that the servant, in bringing the blood, in Bona's presence, had told Madio that Mosè had obtained the blood in this manner; and that one day, as Mosè was on his way home from someplace, he had met a Christian child whom he abducted and brought in secrecy to his dwelling, killing him and draining the blood".[38]

On the other hand, Bona, in perfect accord with Sara, Maestro Tobias's second wife, who came from Swabia and had lived in Marburg and the Tyrol, with Bella, Mosè da Würzburg's daughter-in-law, who had married Mosè's son Mayer (Meir) and knew how to write Yiddish, and Anna, Samuele da Nuremberg's young daughter-in-law, remembered another child murder committed a few years before, in 1472 or 1473, also at Trent, committed by more or less the same people guilty in the Simon of Trent affair. The victim of this murder was a three-year old child, sold to Maestro Tobias by a beggar in the German-speaking region and brought to Trent. The child was killed during a collective ceremony in the antechamber of the synagogue, with the participation of the majority of the Jews living in the city; the blood being collected in a silver vase. At night, this same Tobias took charge of throwing the body of the child into the Adige.[39] Sara, Maestro Tobias's wife, also remembered hearing talk, in the house, of another homicide, committed at Trent in 1451 by Isacco and other Jews from Trent; however, she knew nothing of the details.[40] Isacco was Maestro Tobias's father-in-law, being the father of Tobias's first wife, Anna, who had died, leaving Tobias a widower; Isacco is almost certainly identical with the money lender of the same name active at Trent in the first half of the 14th century.[41]

There are, of course, no objective records of these ritual murder stories, eventful and cruel, with their horrible and repulsive connotations.

The defendants were capable of inventing accusations out of whole cloth to placate their jailers; to make them more believable, these stories might have caused the names of relatives or even distant acquaintances to emerge jumbled up from the mists of the past, from the localities of the defendants' childhood or youth, or from localities in which they had lived for a while. It is impossible to believe that the ritual murders over the same period and within the same geographical confines as those we have discussed so far are any more reliable.

* * *

NOTES TO CHAPTER FOUR

[1] Giacobbe da Colonia was arrested under the accusation of having abducted the child while he was in Treviso, where he had stayed on his way from Piove di Sacco to Portobuffolè. He is almost certainly identical with the Yaakov b. Shimon Levi, who appears in Hebrew documents of the period (cfr. D. Nissim, *Famiglie Rapa e Rapaport nell'Italia settentrionale, sec. XV-XVI. With an appendix on the origins of the Rothschild Miscellany*, in A. Piattelli and M. Silvera, authors, *Minhat Yehuda. Saggi sul ebraismo italiano in memoria de Yehuda Nello Pavoncello*, Rome, 2001, p. 188).

[2] On the ritual murder at Portobuffolè, see, in particular, S.G. Radzik's documented monograph, *Portobuffolè*, Florence, 1984. In this regard, see the important compendium of texts in [Benedetto Bonelli], *Dissertazione apologetica sul martirio del beato Simone da Trento nell'anno MCCCCLXXV dagli ebrei ucciso*, Trent, Gianbattista Parone, 1747, pp. 272-282, and furthermore A. Ciscato, *Gli ebrei a Padova (1300-1800)*, Padua, 1901, pp. 136-137; B. Pullan, *Rich and Poor in Renaissance Venice*, Oxford, 1971, pp. 458-460; A. Esposito and D. Quaglioni, *Processi contro gli ebrei di Trento, 1475-1478. I: I Processi*

del 1475; Padua, 1990, pp. 86-89.

[3] At Portobuffolè in 1464, Chaim Israel Stein copied one manuscript of a text by Abraham Ibn Ezra (cfr. A. Freimann, *Jewish Scribes in Medieval Italy*, in M. Marx, *Alexander Marx Jubilee Volume*, New York, 1950, p. 262, no. 129j). See also Nissim's arguments in *Famiglia Rape e Rapaport*, cit., pp. 178-181.

[4] "In Piazza di San Marco in ognimano / piena di d'innumerabile persone / per veder arder quel ternario insano / che confirmando la sua confessione / brusaron vivi nell'Ebraico errore / del battesimo sprezzando l'oblazione" ["In the Piazza di San Marco, packed with innumerable people, they watched that maddened lunatic being burnt alive in the Jewish error, despising the offertory of baptism"] (Giorgio Sommariva da Verona, *Martyrium Sebastiani Novelli trucidati a perfidis Judaeis*, Treviso, Bernardinmo Celario de Luere, 12 May 1480, reported in [Bonelli], *Dissertazione apologetica*, cit., pp. 278); "[...] ligati sunt et circum circa ignis est accensus, quem sentientes, et se circum circa volventes, ab igne coquebantur et adurebantur, se lamentes et ululantes, quorum senior induratus alios socios ad martyrdom exhortabatur, legem suam enarrans" ["they were tied up and wood was piled up all around them. The wood was set light, which they perceived, and looked all around them while the wood cooked them and hardened them, with their laments and screams. The oldest one of them, tougher than his associates in martyrdom, exhorted them by reciting Jewish law"] in the *Diarium parmense*, in *Rerum Italicarum Scriptores*, vol. XXII Milan, Tipografia della Società Palatina, 1733, p. 345.

[5] Cfr. A. Ottolenghi, *Per il IV centenario della Scuola Canton. Notizie storiche sui templi veneziani di rito tedesco e su alcuni e su alcuni templi privati con cenni della vista ebraica nei secoli XVI-XIX*, Venice, 1932, pp. 18-19.

[6] In this regard, see F. Cogo, *Vita e martirio del Beato Giovannino da Volpedo*, Tortona, 1920; V. Legè, *Il Borgo di Volpedo e il Beato Giovannino Costa*, Venice, 1921, and, recently, I. Cammarata U. Rozzo, *Il beato Giovannino patrono di Volpedo. Un fanciullo "martyr" alla fine del secolo XV*, Volpedo, 1997.

[7] Cfr. Cammarata and Rozzo, *Il beato Giovannino patrono di Volpedo*, cit., pp. 19-24.

[8] Cfr. Sh. Simonsohn, *The Jews in the Duchy of Milan*, Jerusalem, 1982, vol. II, p. 873, no. 2103.

[9] Y. Ha-Cohen, *Sefer 'Emeq-Bakha (The Vale of Tears), with the Chronicle of the Anonymous Collector*, by K. Almbladh, 1981, p. 59 (in Hebrew). It is important to note that, as observed by Isai Sonne,

"Yoseph Ha-Cohen generally attributes the deterioration of relations between the Jewish communities in Italy with the surrounding Christian society to the deplorable conduct of the Ashkenazi Jews and their unscrupulousness. The attitude of Italian Jews towards Ashkenazi Jews was exactly similar to that of cultured and refined Italians towards barbarous and uncouth Germans [...]. The events and circumstances in which the responsibility of the Ashkenazi was ascertained, leading to the saddest consequences for the entire Jewish community, were covered up by Jewish historians in fear of encouraging anti-Semitism. At the most, they could be handed down to a small elect in whom one could trust" (cfr. I. Sonne, *From Paul IV to Pius V, Jerusalem*, 1954, pp. 185-186 [in Hebrew]. These observations had already been published in "Hebrew Union College Annual", XXII (1949), pp. 23-44.

[10] *Chronica Gestorum in partibus Lombardie et reliquis Italie*, by G. Bonazzi, in *Rerum Italicarum Scriptores*, vol. XXII, tome III, Città del Castello, 1904, p. 106. In this regard, see also Cammarata and Rozzo, *Il beato Giovannino patrono di Volpedo*, cit., p. 18. The few Jews in Cortemaggiore were linked with the larger community in Piacenza, *Dal Monte di Pietà alla Cassa di Risparmio: l'esempio piacentino*, in G. Boschiero and B. Molina, authors, *Politiche del credito. Investimento consumo solidarietà*, Asti, 2004, p. 348).

[11] On the facts of Arena del Po in 1479, see in particular C. Guidetti, *Pro Judaeis. Riflessioni e documenti*, Turin, 1884, pp. 280-294, and above all Simonson, *The Jews in the Duchy of Milan*, cit., vol. I, p. XXII, and vol. II, pp. 738-789, nos. 1794, 1868, 1877-1880, 1882-1884, 1888-1889, 1891-1892, 1895-1897.

[12] Mosè da Bamberg, a German traveller staying in Angelo da Verona's dwelling, told the Trent judges that he had been in the service of the Sacle, a money lender at Borgo San Giovanni, near Piacenza, and his wife, Potina. According to him, the Ashkenazi Jew had been accustomed to dissolve powdered blood, presumably that of a Christian child, in wine, during the Passover meal, pouring it from his silver chalice into the glasses of the guests. His wife Potina was said to have mixed the blood into the dough of the unleavened bread (cfr. G. Divina, *Storia del beato Simone da Trento*, Trent, 1902, vol. II, pp. 28-29). It should be noted that the name Sacle or Secle (Seckle), a rendering of the Hebrew Izchak (Isaac) was widespread among Jews from Frankfurt and Hessen (cfr. A. Beider, *A Dictionary of Ashkenazi Given Names*, Bergenfeld, N.J., 2001, p. 342).

[13] Cfr. Simonsohn, *The Jews in the Duchy of Milan*, cit., vol. II, p. 784, no. 1888.

[14] Cfr., Ibidem, vol. II, pp. 784-785, no. 1891.

[15] The petition of the Jews to the Duke of Milan (19 May 1479), the original of which is still preserved in the archives of the Jewish community of Verona, was apparently published for the first time by the famous Marrano apologist Isac Cardoso at the end of the Seventeenth Century (D. De Castro Tartas, 1679), who occupies himself at length with the question of the ritual murders. In this regard, see the important analysis, although sometimes accompanied by inexact references, of Y.H. Yerushalmi, *Dalla Corte di Spagna al Ghetto italiano*, Milan, 1991. The document was published *in extenso* by Guidetti, *Pro Judaeis*, cit., pp. 289-294, and later by G.A. Zaviziano, *Un raggio di luce. La Persecuzione degli ebrei nella storia. Riflessioni*, Corfu, 1891, pp. 173-180 (doc. XVIIIbis). In this regard, as well as with regard to the identification of Corrado Guidetti with the Paduan Jew Giacomo Treves, believed to be a pseudonym used by Guidetti, cfr. D. Nissim, *La risposta di Isacco Vita Cantarini all'accusa di omicidio rituale di Trento (Padova 1670-1685)*, in "Studi Trentini di Scienze Storiche", LXXIX (2000), pp. 829-835. References to the Jewish petition of the Duchy of Milan in 1479 are also found in V. Manzini, *La superstizione omicida e i sacrifici umani*, Padua, 1930, pp. 237-239, and in Simonsohn, *The Jews in the Duchy of Milan*, cit., vol. II, pp. 788-789.

[16] Cfr. Guidetti, *Pro Judaeis*, cit., pp. 289-290; Zaviziano, *Un raggio di luce*, cit., p. 174.

[17] Cfr. Guidetti, *Pro Judaeis*, p. 291; Zaviziano, *Un raggio di luce*, cit., p. 176.

[18] Cfr. R. Po-Chia Hsia, *Trent 1475. A Ritual Murder Trial*, New Haven (Conn.), 1992, pp. 92-93; "If we construct a cultural geography of blood libel in the region, the location of ritual murder trials coincided with the boundary of German settlements in the Alpine Highlands". Concerning himself with the geography of trials for desecration of the host, Rubin (Gentile Tales. *The Narrative Assault on the Late Medieval Jews*, New Haven, Conn., 1999, pp. 190-195) reaches the same conclusions, stating that "our story deals with German-speaking regions".

[19] "Nec novum videatur hanc pessimam rem ac nefarium scelus in civitate nostra (sc. Tridenti) hoc anno per impios Judeos esse perpetratum; cum longe crudeliora et atrociora retroactis temporibus in plerisque civitatibus et locis Germaniae et aliarum regionum, utpote Sveviae, Bavariae, Austriae, Stiriae, Rhenique ac Saxoniae, nec non Poloniae et Hungariae" (cfr. [Bonnelli], *Dissertazione apologetica*, cit., pp. 65-66).

[20] On the child murder of Lorenzino Sossio, later beatified,

attributed to the Jews on the grounds of ritual murder, see, among others, Francesco Barbarano, *Historia ecclestica della città, territori e diocesei di Vicenza*, Cristoforo Rosio, 1652, pp. 172-177; I. Scotton, *Compendio della vita, martirio e miracoli del Beato Lorenzino da Valrovina*, Venice, 1863; G. Chiuppani, *Gli ebrei a Bassano*, Bassano, 1907, pp. 73-76; G. Volli, *Il beato Lorenzino da Marostica, presunta vittima d'un omicidio rituale*, in "La Rassegna Mensile di Israel", XXXIV (1968), pp. 513-526, 564-569; M. Nardello, *Il presunto martirio del beato Lorenzino da Marostica*, in "Archivio Veneto", CIII (1972), pp. 25-45; T. Caliò, *Un omicidio rituale tra storia e leggenda. Il caso del beato Lorenzino da Marostica*, in "Studi e Materiali di Storia delle Religione", n.s., I (1995), no. 19, pp. 55-82.

[21] "Pueri cadaver, cuius abscisum fuisse videtur praeputium, quia a Judaeis occisu fuerit" ["The boy's body was seen to have had the foreskin cut off, as if he had been killed by the Jews"].

[22] Cfr. [Bonnelli], *Dissertazioni apologetica*, cit., pp. 246-255.

[23] The information is derived from Sanudo, (*I diarii*, by R. Fulin et al, Venice, 1879-1903, columns 250-266, 283). In this regard, see also T. Calio, *Il "puer a Judaeis necatus". Il ruolo del racconto agiografico nella diffusione dello stereotipo dell'omicidio rituale*, in *Le inquisizioni cristiane e gli ebrei*, "Atti dei Convegni Lincei", CXCI (2003), p. 475.

[24] Marcuccio moved to the Cittadella in Bassano after 1467 (cfr. Carpi, *L'individuo e la collettività*, cit., p. 38).

[25] We know that in April 1492, the Consiglio di Bassano had unsuccessfully asked Venice for authorization to expel Marcuccio from the City, revoking his permit. On these events, see Chiuppani, *Gli ebrei a Bassano*, cit., pp. 100-104.

[26] For a serious investigation into the real motives for the expulsion of the Jews from Vicenza in 1486, see Scuro, *Alcune notizie sulla presenza ebraica a Vicenza*, cit.

[27] In the ample, although tardy, bibliography on the martyrdom of Andrea of Rinn, see Ippolito Guarinoni, *Triumph Cron Marter und Grabschaft des Heilig-Unschuldigen*, Innsbruck, Michael Wagner, 1642; G.R. Schroubeck, *Zur Frage der Historizität des Andreas von Rinn*, in "Fenster", XXXVIII (1988), pp. 3766-3774; XXXIX (1986), pp. 3845-3855; G. Kofler, *La leggenda dell'omicidio rituale di Andrea Oxner di Rinn*, in "Materiali di lavori", 1988, nn. 1-4, pp. 143-149; B. Freschacher, *Anderl von Rinn: Ritualmordkult und Neuorientierung in Judenstein 1945-1995*; Innsbruck, 1996; G.R. Schroubek, *The Question of the Historicity of Andreas of Rinn*, in Buttaroni e Musial, *Ritual Murder*, cit., pp. 159-180.

[28] Cfr. [Bonelli], *Dissertazione apologetica*, cit., pp. 235-242.

[29] Cfr. Zaviziano, *Un raggio di luce*, cit., pp. 115-157 (doc. XIV); C. Roth, *The Ritual Murder Libel and the Jews. The Report by Cardinal Lorenzo Gangarelli on Ritual Murder*, in S. Buttaroni and S. Musial, *Ritual Murder Legend in European History*, Cracow-Nuremberg-Frankfurt, 2003, pp. 211-223. Cardinal Ganganelli's report has now been republished by M. Introvigne, *Cattolici, antisemitismo e sangue. Il mito dell'omicidio rituale*, Milan, 2004, pp. 83-123. Otherwise, Introvigne's work is nothing other than an encyclopaedia of the problem, accompanied by a bibliography which has been only partially updated.

[30] Cfr. Zaviziano, *Un raggio di luce*, pp. 144-147.

[31] "Dum ipse Isaac staret in dicta Civitate Burmi [...] quadam die ante festum Paschae ipsorum Judaeorum, in quadam stuba magna, in qua aderant circa quadraginta Judaei, dicti Judaei omnes adjuverunt ad interficiendum Puerum Christianum" ["When Isaac was in the said city of Worms [...] a few days before the Jewish feast of Passover, in a large parlor, in the presence of about forty Jews, who helped kill the boy"] (cfr. [Bonelli], *Dissertazione apologetica*, cit., p. 144). See also Divina, *Storia del beato Simone da Trento*, cit., vol. II, pp. 94-96; Po-Chia Hsia, *Trent 1475*, cit., p. 91. It should be noted that in the *halakhah*, Hebraic ritual law, the minimum units of measurement for foods, both solid and liquid, are the olive (*zait*), and the egg (*bezah*). Isacco's reference to the egg to quantify the amount of blood taken, which seemed so strange to Divina, should not surprise us.

[32] "Quaedam mulier Christiana, nomine Elisabth dicta Paumghartnerin et quae multum praticabat in Domo Mohar praedicti, clandestine portavit tres Pueros Christianos dicto Mohar Judaeo, et quos tres Pueros sic portavit in tribus vicibus et diversis annis, quibus istc Joff stetit famulus Mohar sexdecim annis [...] et dictos Pueros sic portavit de nocte et illos tradebat dictor Mohar". The ritual of the murder and meal of blood was committed "in quadam Camera, qua tenebantur ligna, et quae apud stabulum dictae domus" (cfr. Bonelli], *Dissertazione apologetica*, cit., pp. 142-143). On this case, see also Po-Chia Hsia, *Trent 1475*, cit., pp. 90-91.

[33] Cfr. Divina, *Storia del beato Simone da Trento*, cit., vol. II, p. 91; Po-Chia Hsia, *Trent 1475*, cit., p. 91.

[34] "Dum ipse Moyses iret [..] ad quendam terram vocatam Franchfort, quae est terra sub dominio Domini Marchionis de Brandenburg, una cum Salomon Hebraeo, cum applicuissent ad quoddam magnum nemus, ibi reperunt Salomonem et Jacob Hebraeos, et aliter nescit cognomina illorum [...] qui habebant quendam puerum, quem jam interfecerant et jugulaverant [...] etiam habebant unum alium

puerum, qui videbatur mortuus et jugulatus, et quod dicta duo corpora fuerunt projecta in preadictum flumen. Et qui etiam dixerant [...] quod ipse acceperant ipsos pueros in quadam Villa parva, in qua poterant esse quinque vel sex domus [...] et aliter nescit nomen dictae Villae" (cfr. Bonnelli], *Dissertazione apologetica*, cit., pp. 143-144). See also Po-Chia Hsia, *Trent 1475*, cit., pp. 89-90. It should be noted that Bonelli confuses Mosè da Bamberg, the author of the deposition, with Mosè da Ansbach, preceptor to Maestro Tobias' children. Po-Chia Hsia, for this part, erroneously stresses that the two "cacciatori di bambini" [child hunters] Salomone and Giacobbe, were both travel and destination companions of Mosè.

[35] "Qui Salomon et Jacob dixerunt ipsi Moysi et Salomon, socius ipsius Moysi, quod ipsi Jacob et Salomon interfecerant dictos pueros causa habendi sanguinem et causa portandi illum sanguinem ad vendendum et quod oportebat ita ipsos lucrari et ita vivere [...] et quod colligerunt sanguinem hoc modo: unuisquisque habebat suum flascum de ferro stagnato, qui habebat foramen, seu buchetum, multum latum ad magnitudinem unius pomi mediocritus grossitudinis [...] et Jacob et Salomon cum dictis flaschis colligebant sanguinem defluentem ex iugulatura per ipso facta in gutture dictorum Puerorum".

[36] "Et cum fuisset elevatus et staret appensus, Moyses fuit interrogatus ut supra".

[37] "In Paschate proxime praeterito fuit unus annus, dum ipse Wolfgangus esset Feltri, in Domo Abrahami Judaei, et loquetur cum Lazaro, fratre dicti Abrahame; idem Lazarus dixit sibi Wolfgango, quod Hebraei interfecerant quendam Puerum Christianum in loco Mestri, apud Venetias" (cfr. [Bonelli], *Disssertazione apologetica*, cit., pp. 141-142. See also Divina, *Storia del beato Simone da Trento*, cit., vol. II, p. 45; Po-Chia Hsia, *Trent 1475*, cit., p. 97.

[38] Deposition of Bona dated 11 March 1476, Vienna, Österr. Nationalbibl., MS 5360, c. 189v (doc. in of D. Quaglioni, in D. Nissim, D. Quaglioni and O. Stock, author, *Simonino 1475, Trento e gli ebrei*, cit., vol. II, 2001, CD ROM). See also Divina, *Storia del beato Simone da Trento*, cit., vol. II, p. 46. The first news having reached us on the Jews of Masserano, apart from the Trent trials, dates back to approximately one century afterwards (cfr. R. Segre, *The Jews in Piedmont Jerusalem, 1986*, vol. I, p. 475, no. 1052). It should be noted that in January of 1459, a Jewish woman from Borgomanero, named Bona, had expressed the desire to convert to Christianity with her children (cfr. Simonsohn, *The Jews in the Duchy of Milan*, cit., vol. I, p. 270, no 579).

[39] On this ritual murder, which is said to have been committed at

Trent two or three years before that of Simon, see, in particular, Divina, *Storia del beato Simone da Trento*, cit., vol. II, pp. 47-53. Cfr. moreover Po-Chia Hsia, *Trent 1475*, cit., p. 112.

[40] "Tobias dixit sibi Sarrae, quod ipse Isaac Hebreus habitor Tridenti et socer ipsius Tobiae, dixerat sibi Tobiae quod ipse Isaac, una cum certis aliis Judaeis interfecerant quendam puerum Christianu, jam tunc annis 24" (cfr. [Bonelli], *Dissertazione apologetica*, cit., p. 144). See moreover Divina, *Storia del beato Simone da Trento*, cit., vol. II, p. 46.

[41] Cfr. Menestrina, *Ebrei a Trento*, cit., pp. 304-306.

CHAPTER FIVE

FROM ENDINGEN TO REGENSBURG: RITUAL MURDERS OR GRIMM BROTHERS' FAIRY TALES?

Alfonso de Espina was confessor to King Henry IV of Castille and in 1460 was completing a treatise against the Jews, Moslems and heretics, entitled *Fortalitium fidei*.[1] To reach his objective, he presented his readers with reports of the crimes committed by the Jews to the detriment of Christians of which he had more or less directly become aware. Naturally, ritual child murders were the main course of his narration.

The Castillan Franciscan recorded that in 1456 a Jewish notable named Maestro Salomone, originating from the territories of the Republic of Genoa and belonging to the illustrious family of physicians, had come to see him in the Minorite Convent at Valladolid, expressing the desire to be baptized. To convince Alfonso of the repugnance which Judaism now aroused in him, the Jew pointed precisely to the horrible custom of the ritual murders, of which he had heard speak or in which he had directly participated.[2] According to him, he had learned from his parents that a famous Jewish physician from Padua, named Simon, had obtained a four-year old child from an unscrupulous Christian mercenary soldier and had sacrificed him in his own dwelling, laying the child across a table and cruelly decapitating him.[3]

Maestro Salomone then reported that he had participated, with his father, in a secret rite, performed at Savonne, with the participation of numerous Jews in the city at that time, culminating in the crucifixion of a two-year old Christian child. The victim's blood was poured into a recipient, the same recipient normally used to collect the blood during the circumcision of their own children.[4] Subsequently, he personally, together with other participants in this horrendous rite, claimed to have consumed the blood as the ingredient in their traditional foods during the Jewish Passover. The body of the sacrificed child was said to have then been thrown into a filthy latrine.

Logically, it is permissible to express serious doubt as to the truthfulness of this Maestro Salomone da Savona's testimonies; nor is it impossible that the entire report might have been invented out of whole cloth by the Spanish friar, whose violent hostility towards the whole world of Judaism was no secret to anyone. On the other hand, we cannot help but note the manner in which the supposed scene of these ritual murders was, once again, the Jewish communities of German origin (in this case, those of northern Italy, like Pavia and Savona),[5] instead of the numerous and flourishing Hebraic nuclei of Castille, Aragon and Catalonia, as one might logically have expected from a report originating from the imagination of a friar having lived and worked exclusively within the reality of the Iberian peninsula. If, therefore, we wish to speak of a stereotype, in reference to the phenomenon of ritual child murder, we must necessarily admit that, even from the point of view of a person openly professing his own anti-Jewishness in a general sense, and with no direct knowledge of events in distant lands, the phenomenon seemed exclusively confined to the Ashkenazi Jewish world.

There are no objective records of this long series of ritual homicides, in which the supposed protagonists accused themselves and each other in their confessions, whether voluntarily or under compulsion. We are speaking of the sensational cases at Endingen, in Alsace, where the first ritual child murder trial was held, which has left an ample and detailed documentation, echoes of which, not surprisingly, might be heard in the halls in which the Trent defendants were under investigation.[6]

At Endingen, a small village of some several hundred people, under the directorship of Breisach at Riegel in the Breisgau, workers found the remains of a man and woman, together with those of two decapitated children, during excavation and repair work to the ossuary of the parochial church of San Pietro, during the Passover period of 1470. In the local region, it was suddenly remembered that, eight years before, a couple of poor people, with a packhorse and two children of young age, a boy and girl, had taken shelter in the house of the brothers Elia, Aberlino (Avraham) and Mercklin (Mordekahai). These were the days of *Pesach*, the Jewish Passover. Many people had noticed them when they entered the dwelling of the Jews, but no one had ever seen them leave. All trace of them seemed to have vanished into thin air.

Karl, margrave of Baden, on a mission from Archduke Sigismondo, opened an inquiry and immediately ordered the arrest of the Jews suspected of having committed the crime. Even before being subjected to torture, Elia, the older of the brothers, confessed and implicated other local Jews as perpetrators or accomplices in the crime, which was said to have been committed that same evening, soon after the Christian family entered their house. To discharge her own responsibility and save her own life, Elia sustained that she had not participated directly in the murder and therefore had been warned, with threats and curses, against reporting what happened to the elders of the Jewish community of Endingen, out of fear that they would denounce the persons responsible to the authorities.

Aberlino, Elia's brother, hastened to explain to the judges the dynamics of the facts, and thereby avoid torture. The parents were allegedly the first to be killed, but their blood was not drained off because it was useless for ritual purposes. Then it was the children's turn to suffer the same fate, being decapitated, while their blood was gathered in suitable recipients. To cover up the victims' cries, the Jews involved in the macabre ceremony started to shriek their litanies in loud voices, as if they were in the middle of a religious ceremony. Finally, to throw police authorities off the track if the bodies were found, it was decided to bury them at night in the ossuary of the church of San Pietro.

Aberlino concluded his deposition by expressing his own intention to become a Christian, to expiate his guilt. Mercklin also confirmed the particulars of the confession of his brothers, adding other details.[7] And so did the other accused.

One of these, Smolle (Samuele), was not content simply to confess his participation in the massacre of Endingen, but added other repugnant details. He recalled that, ten years before, in 1460, he had purchased the little son of a beggar woman of Spira for money, and had then resold him to a rich Jew from Worms, named Lazzaro. The latter, together with other members of his community, were said to have sacrificed the child to drain off his blood. The victim's body was said to have been buried in the Jewish cemetery of the city. But that was not all. In 1465, Smolle was said to have kidnapped a five-year old shepherd boy at Worde to take him to Nuremberg, where he is said to have sold him in exchange for a large sum of money. A wealthy local Jew, Mosè of Freyberg, who was thereafter said to have charged the same ineffable Smolle with killing the boy for his own account, is said to have benefited from this precious acquisition.[8]

That was enough to convince the judges, if there had been any need, of the guilt of the accused, and to condemn them to capital punishment.

On 4 April 1470, the three brothers, Elia, Aberlino and Mercklin, were dragged by horses' tails to the place of execution, to be broken on the wheel and their bodies burnt. When the Emperor Friedrich III, at the request of the Jews, decided to intervene in favor of the condemned men, it was then too late and it only remained for him to rebuke the margrave of Baden, in a letter written one month later, for hastening to have "those accused of the supposed crime" put to death, without awaiting Imperial approval.[9]

In the meantime, there then opened the inevitable sequel to the Endingen trials, concerning the recipients of the blood collected during the two child murders. From the depositions of the accused, it appeared that the much-esteemed fluid had been sold at very high prices to the richest and most influential German Jews, including Leone da Pforzheim, who had, from 1463, enjoyed the protection of Friedrich, elector of the Palatinate.[10] By order of Karl of Baden, Leo was arrested in his lordly habitation at Pforzheim, together with three other Jews, his guests, who appeared involved in the child murders of Endingen as well as in the affair of the blood. In this case as well, the persons under investigation, with Leo leading the way, hastened to confess, adding significant details relating to the religious ceremonies in which they had intended to use the blood procured by them. The judges saw no solution but to decree the penalty of death for the four Jews of Pforzheim as well.

The accused at Trent were only dimly and indirectly aware of the recent events at Endingen and Pforzheim. Mosè da Ansbach, teacher to Maestro Tobias's children, reported to the judges that he had heard talk about a ritual murder committed by Jews a few years before in a city in Alsace; that some of the accused had been burnt at the stake, while others had taken refuge in flight.[11] On the same grounds, Lazzaro, servant to money lender Angelo da Verona, recalled how, while staying at his father's house, at Serravalle del Friuli, a stranger had told them of a ritual murder committed by a few Jews of Pforzheim against a Christian boy three years before. The guilty parties had been incarcerated, and, so that God might save them from certain death and from the hands of the Christians, the Hebraic community of the German lands had announced a general fast.[12] But the eccentric miniaturist, Israel Wolfgang da Brandenburg, was, as usual, the best informed of all. The young Saxon related to the judges everything he knew in this regard, stating that the child murder had indeed been committed at Endingen and that the guilty had been burnt alive at the stake for that act of wickedness, committed to obtain the blood for ritual purposes.

Israel had obtained this information in 1470 from Mosè of Ulm, the special envoy to whom the Germanic Jewish community had entrusted with the task of traveling to Emperor Friedrich III's palace by horseback to obtain the release from prison of the Jews involved in the affair.[13] As we know, the imperial intervention failed because it was received too late, after the public executions had already occurred. This same Hinderbach, in a missive sent to Friar Michele Carcano of Milan, remembered that numerous Jews from Endingen and Pforzheim, both men and women, had been found guilty of ritual murder and had been put to death on the order of the Count of Baden a few years before.[14]

One might be tempted to draw a clear line of demarcation between the evidence given by the Trent defendants, for which exact records exist, and the others, for which no historical documentation for these accusations and denunciations has thus far been found. The latter could be dismissed as fantasies and delirium, produced by atrocious suffering, under torture, by persons devastated by suffering and incapable of reacting, or as the nightmare projections of beliefs held by the judges and suggested by the inquisitors. But such an attempt does not seem logical or convincing, and would, in the last analysis, appear to be completely counterproductive if an attempt be made to confront the problem of ritual child murders and place these crimes in their historical context, establishing their geographical extent and limits. Thus, precisely those exact records which have come to light, at least where some of the testimonies are concerned, should teach us not to dismiss their reality out of hand, or without persuasive justification, even if they are in fact exaggerations or distortions of events for which the historical documentation has not yet been found.[15]

Moreover, at least one other case places us in the same dilemma; we find it difficult to dismiss detailed testimony confirmed by clear documentary fact. At the beginning of the trial, the Trent inquisitors decided to interrogate a convert – a "Jew turned Christian", as such converts were then called – who, in the days of Simon's tragic death, was being held prisoner at Trent for another crime which had nothing to do with ritual child murder. But as to the child murders, which the Jews were accustomed to commit on Passover eve, Giovanni da Feltre – that being the name of the convert, the son of Sacheto (Shochat), a Jew from Landshut in Bavaria – seems to have much to tell. Around 1440, at Landshut, to be exact, when he was a child and still a Jew, the recent convert had heard that the Jews of the local community, including his own father, had killed a Christian child to collect the child's blood for ritual purposes.

The police authorities arrested forty five Jews, as the result of a raid effected in their district, and later burnt them publicly at the stake. Other Jews, including Shochat, had taken refuge in flight, seeking shelter with their families in the Cisalpine regions of Italy.[16] Both the child murder at Landshut and the subsequent massacre of the Jews are precisely confirmed by the extant contemporary historical documentation.[17] So it is not easy to dismiss Giovanni da Feltre's familiar testimony, although it is considered automatically unreliable on all the particulars not confirmed by the historical documentation or in relation to which we lack sufficient means of verification.

According to his own statement, Israel Wolfgang had directly participated in a spectacular, sensational, and equally horrible, ritual child murder committed at Regensburg in 1467. In the second half of the 15th century, that which was considered the commercial port of the Holy Roman Empire towards south-eastern Europe, located on the banks of the Danube, was the home of a flourishing Jewish community of over five hundred people.[18] And the young Saxon, according to his own detailed deposition before the Trent judges, had been at Regensburg that year, during the feast days of the Jewish Passover. Wolfgang's report was lucid and precise down to the smallest particulars.

In those days, Rabbi Jossel di Kelheim had taken advantage of an opportunity and had purchased a Christian child from a beggar for the price of ten ducats. He took the child to his house, in the Jewish quarter, where he concealed him for two days, in anticipation of the solemn event of the *Pesach*, the feast of the unleavened bread, when the annual celebrations begin in remembrance of the miraculous escape of the people of Israel from captivity in Egypt would begin. In the early morning of the first day of the holiday period, Rabbi Jossel very carefully transferred the boy into the narrow confines of the "stiebel" [parlor] of Sayer Straubinger, the small and rustic synagogue located a short distance from his house, where he was accustomed to preside over the collective rites of the community and its daily and festive liturgical meetings. Awaiting him were at least twenty five Jews, previously informed of the extraordinary event. Israel Wolfgang was one of them, and he remembered the exact names of all the participants in the rite, both those from Regensburg and those from other regions. The transfer of the child from Rabbi Jossel's house to the synagogue, although performed at night, involved some danger, since it might have been noticed by prying eyes. But in view of the fact that the district was inhabited by Jews who locked their doors every night, with the keys entrusted to them by the city authorities, the margin of safety was considered sufficiently broad.[19]

The boy was undressed in the *stiebel* and placed on a chest containing the sacred parchments of the synagogue, and was then crucified, circumcised and finally suffocated over the course of a horrifying collective ritual, following a script accurately planned and perfectly well known by all the participants, by Jessel, the rabbi; by

Mayr Baumann, the *mohel*; by Sayer Straubinger, the owner of the chapel; by Samuel Flieshaker, one of Wolfgang's friends; by Mayr Heller; by the above mentioned Jew referred to as "bonus puer" (*Tov 'Elem*); by Johoshua, the cantor; and by Isacco, the water-bearer. Wolfgang himself had taken an active part in the crucifixion of the child, while the blood was collected in a bowl, to be distributed among the Jews participating in the rite or sent to the rich of the community.[20] The day after, rumor of the ritual infanticide spread in the district and many people rushed to Sayer's *stiebel* to see the body of the sacrificed boy, which was placed quite visibly inside the chest. The evening after, at the beginning of the ceremonies of the second day of *Pesach*, in the central room of the small synagogue, in the confined space of which about thirty of the faithful now crammed themselves, excited and curious, while the little victim was publicly exhibited, and the grisly ritual, which had now become merely commemorative, began afresh.[21] Finally, the child's body was buried in the courtyard of the chapel, in a remote corner, surrounded by a wall, accessed through a small door which was usually kept locked.[22]

Israel Wolfgang's report was too precise in its particulars and accurate in its descriptions to avoid awakening the interest of inquisitors in places other than Trent. His report contained exact names, dates, places, and facts requiring cogent verification. Perhaps the closest and most significant precedent to Simonino's martyrdom at Trent was to be sought at Regensburg: in the spectacular story of an unknown synagogue ceremony according to ritual standards following a pre-established order with a mysterious symbolism. The first night of *Pesach* at Regensburg in 1467, in Sayer's *stiebel*, from which the noisy flow of the waters of the Danube was quite audible, might provide a clue to the mystery of what really happened eight years later, during the *Pesach* period of 1475, at Samuele da Nuremberg's house, in the small synagogue of the Jews of Trent, located along a small murky canal used by tanners in the German-speaking district. Perhaps they were only fantasies, fearful fables, nourished by ancestral suspicions, settled stereotypes crystallized from years back; but the authorities had to be certain that the tale had no basis in truth.

In early 1476, Heinrich, the bishop of Regensburg was passing through Trent on his way back from Rome, when, suddenly, someone handed him a copy of Wolfgang's deposition before the Trent judges. Notwithstanding circumstances of this kind, it would hardly have been unprecedented, in the 15th century panorama of this city on the Danube, for the Jews of Regensburg to be accused of a good four cases of desecration of the Host and ritual murder in barely six years, from

1470 to 1476;[23] the good prelate was forcefully impressed and justifiably scandalized when he read the document. Returning to Germany, Heinrich hastened to advise the authorities of Regensburg to open an immediate inquiry intended to determine whether or not a ritual murder had really occurred in the Jewish quarter during the Passover feast of 1467.[24]

At the end of March of that year, the authorities of Regensburg proceeded with the arrest of the rabbi Jossel di Kelheim and another five influential leaders of the Jewish communities, including Sayer Straubinger, the owner of the *stiebel*, and Samuele Fleischaker, Wolfgang's friend. A few days after, seventeen Jews, all accused of participation or complicity in the ritual child murder were placed in irons. The interrogations were carried out under torture, and at least six of the accused issued a complete confession mentioning the names of other persons involved in the wickedness. Rabbi Jossel was the first to admit to the judges that he had purchased the child from a beggar woman at Regensburg eight years before, and had brought it to the synagogue as a sacrifice during the days of the Jewish Passover; he then withdrew his confession, accusing his inquisitors of extorting it through indescribable torture. Before him, Samuel Fleischaker had also confessed that the Jews had made use of children's blood, mixing it into the dough of the unleavened bread.[25]

The admissions, obtained from the accused by force, appeared overly general and insufficiently detailed to be convincing; the confessions were deemed insufficient as the factual basis for a ritual murder trial. Thus, on 15 April 1476, Friedrich III personally ordered the city counsel of Regensburg to free the prisoners immediately and hand them over to the Imperial authorities. But one week later, a dramatic sensation occurred.

A few workers, engaged in repairs on Rabbi Jossel's dwelling, found a skeleton while excavating and cleaning up the cellars. The skeleton, examined by a commission of physicians and surgeons in the presence of the bishop and other civil authorities, proved to be that of a child, presumably aged between three and six years.[26] The Jews replied to the accusations by claiming that the bones had been deliberately planted in the rabbi's cellar by those interested in his condemnation. Notwithstanding the discovery of the new evidence, Friedrich did nothing, and continued unperturbedly to demand the release of the incarcerated Jews, despite the claims of bishop Heinrich, who sustained the validity and plausibility of the defendant's confessions to the crime; Ludwig, Duke of Regensburg, petitioned the Emperor not to interfere in the internal affairs of the city.[27]

On 8 May 1478, two years after they began, the trials might be said to have concluded with the absolution of the Jews, imposed by the inflexible Imperial will. But the defendant's release was not obtained cheaply. Friedrich demanded ten thousand florins from the Jews as payment for his intervention in their favor, while the judiciary of Regensburg declared itself prepared to release them only following payment of all procedural expenses, amounting to five thousand florins, plus a fine of eight thousand florins, imposed on the city by the Emperor for holding the trial. In a plenary meeting announced by the rabbis of the German lands at Nuremberg, presumably in early 1478, an obligatory collection of funds began among the Jewish communities of Germany, accompanied by the creation of suitable committees responsible for coordinating the efforts made to save prisoners. In Italy, Yoseph Colon, formerly a rabbi at Mantua (until 1475) and now at Pavia, intervened with all his related authority; Colon is said to have died at Pavia a few years later, in 1480, after recommending that the appeal of the spiritual heads of German Judaism receive a rapid, positive and generous response.[28] From the very outset, the affair of the Jews of Regensburg made a profound impression on the Jews of the Ashkenazi communities of northern Italy. In a letter written in Hebrew dated 11 May 1476, the daughter and son-in-law of Crassino (Gherhon) da Novara, one of the richest and most influential Ashkenazi bankers of the Duchy of Milan, both wrote to him, probably from Brescia, making explicit reference to the "sensational affair in which, as a result of our sins, members of the holy community of Regensburg have been arrested and confined to prison, where God the pitiful and merciful caused them to exit the darkness and enter the intense light".[29]

In another missive, written in Yiddish by the same Ashkenazi Jews, the son-in-law again complained of the sad fate of the Jews of Regensburg, victims of the blood accusation.

"Alas! We have heard sad news, caused by our innumerable sins, originating from Regensburg. They have arrested all the Jews of the city and slandered them, turning against them the blood accusation of Trent. That God should have pity and not cause us to hear lying accusations of this type anywhere. We wish Him to render us assistance with His love. Amen."

Another message, also in Yiddish, sent by the young Geilin (Gaylein) to his father, the same Crassino of Novara mentioned above, dated mid-May 1476, once again made explicit reference to facts of Regensburg.

"The sad news reached me from Pavia. May God be merciful and help His people and the Jews of Regensburg who have suffered, for our sins, for this infamous slander. Ever since I heard this bad news, I have been unable to sleep. How much you must suffer for certain [...] May God give you strength and health; that is, how I wish your daughter Geilin, unhappy for having heard this unhappy news".[30]

The courier of this letter was Paolo of Novara, the shady priest who, according to him, had been paid by the Jews of the Dukedom of Milan to poison the bishop of Trent. The Jews alluded to him calling him *gallech*, the cleric, the man with the tonsure.[31]

Another two years went by before the Jews of the Ashkenazi communities on both sides of the Alps succeeded in scraping together the huge sums required to liberate the prisoners at Regensburg. But the seventeen defendants, still incarcerated, were finally removed from their shackles on 4 September 1480, four and a half years after their arrest.[32] Thus concluded a matter which perhaps began at Regensburg, rebounded to Trent, and new returned to Regensburg, leaving many unanswered questions and unresolved doubts, which the payment of another twenty thousand florins in gold by the German-speaking Jewish communities was certainly insufficient to dissipate. If the ritual child murder at Regensburg was really a fact, it should be possible to track down the blood, distributed free of charge among the participants, or put up for sale by them immediately afterwards, assuming that it might have reached the Jewish communities of northern Italy. The interrogation of the accused, more or less based on leading questions as to this point, seemed to vindicate the accusation.

The most important clue appeared to point to a certain Rizzardo (Reichard), a Jew from Regensburg who had moved to Brescia with his family in 1464.[33] The latter, with their two brothers Enselino (Anselmo) and Jacob, were engaged in lending money at interest through a bank they owned at Barvardo, deriving a large proportion of their clientele from the city of Brescia, where Rizzardo lived. Rizzardo of Regensburg had top connections, and enjoyed protection as a member of the influential entourage of Bartolomeo Calleone, Captain of the Serenissima.[34] In Angelo da Verona's house, Rizzardo was often mentioned, partly because Lazzaro, who rendered services for the banker, was his nephew, and did not hesitate to spend his holidays and vacations in his uncle's company. On one of these occasions, a few years before, when Lazzaro found himself at Brescia to be cured of an illness of the eyes, Rizzardo confessed to him that he had bought a certain quantity of blood originating from the Regensburg child murder. In addition, the Brescian Jew allegedly made use of it during the Jewish Passover period, administering it to his wife Osella (Feige), his sons Jossele and Mezla (Mazal), and his servant, Jacobo da

Germania.[35] Angelo da Verona also knew that Rizzardo trafficked in the blood of Regensburg, among other things, and had sent a letter to his brother Enselino, at Gavarda, promising him to supply him with some of the blood.[36] Isacco, Angelo's cook, confirmed that he had often heard the patron of the house and the young servant, Lazzaro, mention Rizzardo as the person who had received the precious blood of the infant boy sacrificed at Regensburg.[37]

But once again, it was the ineffable Israel Wolfgang who cast light on the entire affair. In the summer of 1474, he had been sent to Brescia as Rizzardo's guest, who had commissioned him with the execution of the miniatures for a precious Hebraic code owned by Rizzardo.[38] On one occasion, Rizzardo bragged to the young painter that he, Rizzardo, had come into possession of the blood of the child killed at Regensburg. He had been given it by his step-father, precisely the same Rabbi Jossel who had been one of the principal defendants in this sensational child murder. It was at this point that the young Wolfgang's vainglorious nature exploded in all its variegated intensity. Perhaps Rizzardo was unaware that he, Israel Wolfgang, had personally participated in the child murder in Sayer's *stiebel* at Regensburg? The Brescian Jew, even if he had been unwilling to believe it, now had to listen to Wolfgang blabbing out the whole story, down to the slightest detail, and congratulate himself upon receiving one of the lucky and fearless perpetrators in his own house.[39]

Confidence by confidence, Rizzardo, too, not to be outdone, reported that he had participated in a ritual homicide organized at Padua in the German synagogue together with the other Jews of the city and the district, four or five years before.[40]

Since the plague was raging at Brescia, Israel Wolfgang was compelled to cut short his stay at Rizzardo's house and move to nearby Gavardo, as Enselino's guest, with whom Angelo da Verona had long been in contact during his stay in Brescia. To earn some pocket money, he agreed to bind a breviary owned by the archpriest. In the six months spent in Padua, Wolfgang found further confirmation of the Padua child murder, the murder in which Rizzardo had participated. He was informed of this by Enselino, who had allegedly obtained the same blood, marketed in the Brescia region, by a certain Liebmann of Castelfranco da Treviso.[41]

This was too much, even for the inquisitors of Trent, no matter how eager they might have been for confirmation – real or imagined – of their suspicions. The eccentric painter from Brandenburg seemed to be teasing his inquisitors, churning out a continual stream of stories, new at all times, picturesque and astonishing, largely invented or exaggerated, calculated to make an impression on an audience whom he imagined to be highly naive. Instruments of torture may have been, and were, used on the other defendants to loosen their tongues; in the case of the wily Wolfgang, perhaps they might have been of more use in damming up the torrent of incredible revelations which he seemed unable to control. Hurt to the quick, and stung in his vanity, the young painter completely flew off the handle, raised his voice and shouted defiantly at anyone who would listen:

"By God! I have reported what Rizzardo told me, word for word, and thus I will repeat it, before any Lord or Prince: just take me to the place of execution and decapitate me, or kill me in any other way, but I will not speak otherwise than I have done".[42]

Rizzardo, the Brescian resident from Regensburg, Lazzaro's uncle, servant of Angelo of Verona, had been telling the truth. Or at least, his truth. The truth that Wolfgang claimed to have learned during the hot days of the preceding summer, while the plague raged at Brescia.

For his part, Rizzardo da Brescia had a no less famous namesake. The Jew Rizzardo (Reichard) of Mospach was a swindler and good-for nothing, arrested for theft at Regensburg in 1475. To his inquisitors, the latter Rizzardo confessed that he had been baptized several times to obtain money and other benefits from ingenuous Christians to whom he turned, both city people and peasants. But even the Jews, according to him, had proven the gullible victims of his tricks. The Jews Krautheim, Bamberg and Regensburg had purchased fake Hosts, which he claimed to have purloined from various churches in the area, to be "tortured" by the Jews during their anti-Christian rites. Rizzardo-Reichard – who lived alternately as a Jew and alternately as a Christian – was married to three women simultaneously, each one of them unaware of the existence of the others. Starting in 1476, he had spent years wandering back and forth between the villages and cities of Bohemia and Moravia, of the Rhineland and Brandenburg, of Alsace and Württemberg. He had been in Bern, Bamberg and Nuremberg. He admitted to having lived in Italy for a while, in various cities whose names he could no longer remember (was Brescia one of them?). But he clearly recalled having stayed at Trent, where he was in contact with the Jewish families then accused of the ritual murder of little Simon.[43]

If, as we have seen, one clue seemed to point to Rizzardo and the city of Brescia, a second clue pointed back to Regensburg, leading the authorities to a certain Hoberle (Kobele, Jacob or perhaps Hoverle, Haver), who earned his living selling powdered blood, wandering from one locality to another in the German-speaking lands in search of clients. According to Wolfgang, Hoberle had not participated in the ritual homicide in the *stiebel* at Regensburg, but certain persons had later proceeded to supply Hoberle with the blood which he [Hoberle] needed.[44] Mosè da Bamberg, the traveler who happened to be at Trent the night before Simon's killing, knew Hoberle personally and had followed his movements. He [Mosè da Bamberg] also recalled Hoberle's features perfectly. He might have been about sixty years old, low in stature, bald, with a white beard. He had an ugly stain on the skin of his head, as if he had had leprosy; for this reason, he wore a type of cloth cap beneath his beret. He usually wore a long loose gray overcoat.[45]

Before the judges at Trent, Mosè da Bamberg stated that he had met Hoberle for the first time in 1471, in the imperial city of Ulm. A few weeks later, he had seen him again at Padua, in the house of the Jews, and later at Piacenza, where he had stayed as the guest of Abramo, active in the city as money lender.[46] At Pavia, he lodged in the tavern of Falcone, the "Inn of the Jews", a place of dubious reputation where gambling was practiced and there were frequent brawls.[47] Falcone (Haqim), son of Yoseph Cohen, had opened the place around 1470, and is said to have managed it for about ten years.[48] The wife, unsatisfied with her husband's activity, had sought to induce him to abandon that rather uncouth undertaking, but without success. Annoyed and out of spite, she had abandoned him and had taken refuge in a convent, threatening to become a Christian. Then, due to a sudden change of mind, she had asked to be reconciled with him and to be permitted to return to the conjugal domicile. The rabbi Yoseph Colon, questioned on this matter, had authorized Falcone to take her back with him.[49]

In the summer of 1477, when a boy, son of a Christian shoemaker of Pavia, disappeared from his home, Falcone had some serious problems, accused of being the abductor and the executioner during a ritual homicide. A great crowd had gathered around the tavern, seeking to take justice into their own hands, while the guards had had a hard time controlling them and dispersing them. Luckily for him, the child then reappeared, alive and healthy, and the Jewish innkeeper was able to draw a breath of relief.[50]

Mosè da Bamberg knew that the merchant Hoberle, visiting the cities of the Veneto and Lombardy, wherever there were Jews, had sold a certain quantity of blood to Manno da Pavia, the richest Jewish banker in the dominions of the Sforzas.[51] As we have already seen, this same Manno is said to have been accused, together with other important exponents of the Jewish community of the Duchy of Milan, of hiring the priest Paolo of Trent to poison the Prince Bishop of Trent in 1476, for condemning to death and executing the presumed murderers of the sainted Simon. According to Mosè da Bamberg's deposition, Manno da Pavia, in turn, sold part of the blood obtained from Hoberle – for money – to the family of Madio (Mohar, Meir), a money lender at Tortona; the blood is then supposed to have been used during the Passover celebration. As we have seen, Madio is said to have been implicated in the supposed ritual murder of the sainted Giovannino da Volpedo in 1482, but, to his good fortune, is said to have been acquitted. Mosè of Bamberg, according to his own statement, had, for almost a year, been in the service of Leone, Madio's son, and his [Madio's] sister Sara, who lived in the nearby castle of Serravalle with her son, Mosè, and, with them, had consumed the same powdered blood, obtained at Regensburg, dissolved in wine during the Passover dinner of 1472.[52]

According to Leone, it was said that, during his sumptuous marriage to Sara, held in February of 1470 at Tortona, attended by over one hundred guests from the Ashkenazi communities of northern Italy, some local nobles, displeased at their exclusion from those princely festivities, had, perhaps with excessive enthusiasm, attempted to force open the host's doors. Unluckily for them, they were ill-received by the Jews who, with weapons in their hands, threw them out of the palace, pursuing them as far as the local the piazza. A case of ill-breeding and poor hospitality which cried out for vengeance. Obviously, Madio da Tortona's version of the facts and that of the guests differed radically. Taking advantage of the nuptial celebrations, general noise and confusion, the nobles of Tortona reportedly attempted, rather clumsily, if not downright stupidly, to break into the premises of the local bank, for the purpose of stealing money, collateral and other valuables, but were said to have been ingloriously routed.[53]

Jews in the Duchy of Milan were tried and sentenced for the possession of books, liturgical and study texts containing offensive and insulting expressions about Jesus, the Messiah, the Virgin Mary, the dogmas of the Christian religion and anyone practicing Christianity. On at least four occasions during the second half of the 15th century. In 1459, they were convicted, and fined sixteen thousand ducats.[54] In 1474 and 1480, the fines were increased to thirty two thousand ducats, promptly paid by the Jewish communities of the Duchy. As early as 1476, a large group of rich and influential Lombard Jews, active at Alessandria, Broni, Piacenza, Monza and Piove di Sacco, headed, as usual, by Manno da Pavia, were officially pardoned by Gian Galeazzo Sforza, presumably after paying a conspicuous fine, for insubordination, bad manners, and defaming and offending the Duke's illustrious father.⁵⁵ The mysteries of this trial – if any trial was held – remain to be revealed in full.

At any rate an undoubted echo of these events may be found in the predication of the Minorite Friar Antonio da Cremona at Chivasso in December 1471, in which the pious friar invoked the expulsion of the "perfidious and wicked Jewish race", guilty of continuous blasphemy against the Holy Faith in Christ in their books and prayers.⁵⁶

But a trial held at Milan in the spring of 1488 was more serious and dangerous than ever. Denounced by a converted Jew, forty of the most influential exponents of the Ashkenazim community in the Dukedom were arrested and transferred to the provincial capital in chains, accused of possessing texts – particularly, liturgical breviaries – suspected of containing prayers attacking Jesus as well as anti-Christian invective. The trial began on 16 March, in the presence of a commission of inquisitors, deputized by Ludovico the Moor, made up of Franciscan and Dominican friars in addition to Ducal officials, and presided over by the vicar of the curia of the archbishop of Milan. The accused, in the long and detailed interrogations, were requested to supply due explanations for the apparently contemptuous phrases found in their texts regarding Christians and the Christian religion, the Pope and baptized Jews, as well as Christ and Mary. The sentence, a severe one, was handed down the following 31 May. Nine of the accused were condemned to death; the rest were expelled from the territory of the Duchy, all property owned by all the accused was declared confiscated. Luckily for them, the Jews succeeded in commuting the cruel sentence into a heavy fine of nineteen thousand ducats, to be paid by January 1490.⁵⁷

When the due date rolled around, the full sum had not yet been collected, and only part of the sum had found its way to the coffers of the Sforzas. A few months later, the disillusioned Ludovico the Moor ordered a public bonfire of the seized books. Mendele (Menachem) Oldendorf, a young German Jew and son of a bankrupt merchant, a certain Herz (Naftali), also known as "Golden", perhaps in remembrance of when he had been rich, no doubt possessed a lively and versatile wit, in addition to an unusual degree of Hebraic culture; he was known for holding brilliant homilies in the synagogue and functioned as a ritual butcher. He was an able writer in the Yiddish language and was a respected copier of Hebraic codes. In 1474, he traveled from Regensburg to Venice, where he stayed until at least 1483, when he was present at the famous bonfire at the Ducal Palace. In his autobiography, the young Oldendorf described the manner in which he had been informed by trust-worthy persons of bonfires of

Jewish texts at Milan and other places in the Duchy of Milan in 1490, regretting that the burnt manuscripts included some which he had copied personally.[58]

"I learned from one of the wise men of Israel [...] that in the year 5248 (=1488) Lord Ludovico the Moor ordering the burning of a great number of Jewish books at Milan, the capital city, as well as in other localities in his territories. I, personally, a copier of codes, saw some of my own texts among the books consigned to the flames. Blessed be God who enabled me to witness the revenge of God's Law against that same nobleman (Ludovico the Moor), who has been captured and taken into France, where he died [...] Menachem Oldendorf, the German. 5274 (=1514)".

One of the most important defendants in the Milan trial of 1488 was – and this is not surprising – Jacob, son of Manno of Pavia, who had died in the meantime.[59] Before the inquisitors, Jacob was requested, among other things, to deny the rumor that the Jews were accustomed to "making images in the form of Jesus Christ and the Virgin Mary, and then throwing them in the fire, trampling them under foot or covering them with excrement".[60] The accusation was not a new one. During Passover in 1493, Joav (Dattilo) and the other Jews, living at Savigliano in Piedmonte, were condemned to the payment of a fine of five hundred gold ducats for a serious act of wickedness.

"[These Jews] kneaded the unleavened bread or *mazzot*, according to their rite and in outrage to the glorious crucifix [...] and prepared four images of dough in the form of our Lord, Jesus Christ, in mockery of God and the Catholic faith, then burnt these dough dolls in the oven".[61]

At a distance of only a few years from the Trent trials, it is not surprising that the judges should turn to one of the inquisitors, Lazzaro da San Colombano to ask: whether or not the Jews were actually accustomed to abduct Christians for the purpose of committing reprehensible acts against them in contempt for the Christian faith.[62]

* * *

NOTES TO CHAPTER FIVE

[1] On the personality of Alfonso de Espina and his virulently hostile attitude towards Jews and Marranos on the eve of the institution of the court of the Inquisition in Castille, see, in particular, Y. Baer, *A History of the Jews in Christian Spain*, Philadelphia (Pa.), 1966, vol. II, pp. 283-299).

[2] Alphonsus de Spina, *Fortalitum fidei*, Nuremberg, Anton Koberger, 10 October 1485, cc. 188-192.

[3] "Magister Symon [...] Medicus non modicum corde gavisus cepit Infantem (Christianum aetatis quattor annorum) et cum eo rediit in Civitatem Papiae, ubi domicilium suum habebat. Et cum ingrederetur domum suam, videns horam qua posset desiderium suae feritatis explere, capto Infante super mensam extendit, et evaginato gladio caput Infantis Christiani crudeliter abscidit".

[4] "Cum etiam essem in Civitate quadam subjecta Januae, quae dicitur Savona, ut viderem sacrificari quemdam Infantem Christianum, Pater meus deduxit me ad domum cujusdam Judaei, ubi fuerant septem vel octo Judeai congregati secretissime et clausus januis diligentissime juramentum fortissimum omnes fecerunt de celando id, quod facere volebant [...] quo peracto, ecce deducitur in medium Infantulus quidam Christianus aetatis fere duorum annorum, et deducto vase illo, in quo consuerverunt recipere sanguinem Infantium circumcisorum, posuerunt predictum Infantem nudum supra praedictum vas, et quatuor Judaei illorum intendebant occisioni sub tali forma et ordine".

[5] Savona, like other centers belonging to the territory of the Republic of Genoa, was the home of small nuclei of Jews in the Fifteenth Century, made up of merchants and money lenders from Germany, the Duchy of Milan and the Republic of Venice. Among these, we stumble upon (even at Savona, the names Manno da Pavia, who, as we have seen, was the most illustrious of the Jewish communities of the Duchy of Milan, and was also active at Venice (cfr. R. Urbani and G.N. Zazzu, *The Jews in Genoa*, Leyden, 1999, vol. I, pp. 34-37, 43, 47, nos. 71, 73-74, 99, 109).

[6] There is an ample bibliography on the ritual murders and trials of Endingen in 1470. We refer, in particular, to H. Schreiber, *Urkundbuch der Stadt Freiburg im Breisgau*, Freiburg, 1829, vol. II, pp. 520-525; K. von Amira, *Das Endinger Judenspiel*, Halle, 1883; I. Kracauer, *L'affaire des Juifs d'Endingen de 1470. Prétendu meurtre de Chrétiens par des Juifs*, in "La Revue des Etudes Juives", XVII (1888), pp. 236-245, and more recently R. Po-Chia Hsia, *The Myth of Ritual Murder. Jews and Magic in Reformation Germany*, New Haven (Conn.) – London, 1988, pp. 14-41.

[7] For the text of the confession of the three brothers, see Amira, *Das Endinger Judenspiel*, cit., pp. 94-97; Po-Chia Hsia, *The Myth of Ritual Murder*, cit., pp. 18-22.

[8] Cfr. Kracauer, *L'affaire des Juifs d'Endingen de 1470*, cit., pp. 237-238; Po-Chia Hsia, *The Myth of Ritual Murder*, cit., pp. 18-22.

[9] Cfr. Kracauer, *L'affaire des Juifs d'Endingen de 1470*, cit., pp.

236-245; Po-Chia Hsia, *The Myth of Ritual Murder*, cit., pp. 34.

[10] The accusation was that "Judei (urbis Endingen) transmiserunt sanguinem ad civitates et loca ubi divites morantur Judei" ["the Jews (of the city of Endingen) distributed the blood as gifts to Jews in the cities and locations where rich Jews lived"]. In this regard and on the confession of Leo da Pforzheim, see, in particular, Kracauer, *L'affaire des Juifs d'Endingen de 1470*, cit., pp. 237, 241-242.

[11] "Pauci anni sunt, quod puer quidam Christianus fuit interfectus a Judaeis in Helsas (= Alsace), de quo homicidio fuerunt combusti aliqui Judaei et aliqui eorum aufugerunt, prout dici audivit" ["It was only a few years ago, that a Christian boy was killed by the Jews of Alsace, a few Jews being burnt for the murder and others escaped, as he heard say"] (cfr. [Bonelli], *Dissertazione apologetica sul martirio del beato Simone da Trento nell'anno MCCCCLXXV dagli ebrei ucciso*, Trent, Gianbattista Parone, 1747, p. 143).

[12] "Dum ipse Lazarus staret cum ejus Patre in Seravalle, quidam Hebreus advena [...] dixit quod puer Christianus fuerat interfectus in Civitate seu terra Fortiae [= Pforzheim], quae est terra Alemaniae, et quod Judaei, qui illum puerum interfecerant, fuerunt capti, et propter hoc fuerat ordinatum inter Judaeos, quod deberent jejunare, ut Deus liberaret eos" (cfr. ibidem). In this regard, see moreover G. Divina, *Storia del beato Simone da Trento*, Trent, 1902, vol. II, p. 38.

[13] "(Israel Wolfgangus) modo possunt esse quinque vel sex anni, dici audivit, quod quidam puer Christianus interfectus a Judaeis causa habendi sanguinem, et quod sic fit interfectus in quodam loco nominato Hendinga [= Endingen] Alemaniae, qui Judaie fuerant combusti. Et dicit, quod hoc dici audivit primo a quodam Moyse Judaeo de Ulma, qui Mosès pro liberatione dictorum Judaeorum equitavit ad Serenissium Imperatorum pro dictis Judaeis liberandis" (cfr. [Bonelli], *Dissertazione apologetica*, cit., p. 140).

[14] "Ac novissime infra paucos annos in oppido Endingen et Pforzheim sub Marchione Carolo Badan quam plures Judae utriusque sexus, pro simile necatione duorum conjugam christianorum ac duorum filiorum, ultimo supplicio puniti fuerunt". The text of the letter from Hinderbach to Fra Michele is found in [Bonelli], *Dissertazione apologetica*, cit., pp. 65-66.

[15] The following persons have made excellent, even if not entirely convincing, contributions in this regard: Po-Chia Hsia, who, referring to the testimonies of the Trent defendants on the facts of Endingen and Pforzheim, considers it all a clumsy inquisitorial manipulation intended to confer plausibility on slanderous reports, invented out of whole cloth, using unnatural juxtapositions of evens, known and real. "And

so, the real and the imaginary fused into a seamless whole, the lies [...] told under duress only confirmed the veracity of the historical Endingen trial, which became, in turn, the fulcrum of the fictive universe of Jewish violence" (R. Po-Chia Hsia, *Trent 1475, A Ritual Murder Trial*, New Haven, Conn., 1992, p. 90). Elsewhere, the same author, referring to the detailed deposition of Maestro Tobias on Friedrich's visit to Venice in 1469, and on the presence in the city of the "merchant of Candia" (who, as we have seen, should be identified as David Mavrogonato), speaks of a fable with an exotic flavor, imagined by the Jewish physician to placate his tormenters and to put an end to the tortures to which he was being subjected (ibidem, pp. 46-47). But, as may easily be demonstrated, Tobias' testimony was precise in all its particulars and corresponded to that which he had actually seen and that which had really happened on that occasion. Miri Rubin, who has examined the German trials for desecration of the Host, although he considers them a slander, cannot help but note that the testimonies often contained elements the acceptability of which was beyond doubt ("the testimony contains true and imagined aspects of Jewish communal life"). Cfr. M. Rubin, *Gentile Tales. The Narrative Assault on Late Medieval Jews*, New Haven (Conn.), 1999, p. 123.

[16] "Quod modo possunt esse .xv anni vel circa, quod Sachetus de Alemania, pater ipsius testis, tempore eius vite dixit testi quod tunc poterant esse circa quadraginti anni, quod dictus Sachetus existens in civitate Lançhut de Alemania Bassa, et ibi cum familia sua habitaret, aliqui Judei existentes in dicta civitate, circum festa Pasce eorum, interfecerunt quendam puerum (Christianum) masculum, causa habendi sanguinem et utendi illo; et quod fuit manifestum domino illius civitatis qui dominus fecit detinere omnes Judeos qui ibi aderant; exceptis aliquibus qui affugerunt, inter quos fuit pater ipsius testis, qui aufugit et qui vix potuit evadere. Et pro morte cuius pueri sic interfecti dicebat idem pater ipsius testis quadragintaquique Judeos fuisse combustos" (cfr. A. Esposito and D. Quaglioni, *Processi contro gli ebrei di Trento; 1475-1478*; I: *I processi del 1475*, Padua, 1990, pp. 124-125). For a careful examination of the deposition of Giovanni da Feltre, see Quaglioni (ibidem, pp. 35-36).

[17] In this regard, see Po-Chia Hsia, *Trent 1475*, cit., pp. 31-32, 93.

[18] Cfr. M. Toch, *The Formation of a Diaspora. The Settlement of Jews in the Medieval German Reich*, in "Aschkenas", VII (1997), no. 1, pp. 55-78.

[19] "Dum ipse Wolfgangus staret in Civitate de Ratibona, cum Samuele Hebraeo, quidam Jossele Hebraeus emit quendam Puerum Christianum a quodam paupere mendicante Christiano, quem sic emit

per decem ducatis et quem Puerum idem Jossele emit per dies octo ante Pascha Judaeorum, et illus tenuit in ejus Domo usque ad diem Paschae ipsorum Judaeorum, in qua die Paschae de sero, circa duas vel tres horas noctis, idem Jossele portavit dictum Puerum in quandam Synagogam parvam, in qua erat ipse Wolfgang una cum 25, vel 26 Judaeis, quo Puero sic portato, quidam Mohar Hebraeus accept dictum Puerum et eum spoliavit, deinde illum posuit super quendam capsam" ([Bonelli), *Dissertazione apologetica*, cit., p. 140). See also Divina, *Storia del beato Simone da Trent*, cit., vol. II, pp. 38-39, 41-42.

[20] "Et dum Puer sic staret, quatuor vel six ex Judaeis ibi astantibus pupugerunt cum acubus Puerum et ipse Wolfgangus fuit unus ex illis qui pupugit [...] dum sanguis exiret, Heberle Judaeis cum quadam scutela stagni vel argenti, colligebat sanguinem" ([Bonelli], *Dissertazione apologetica*, cit., p. 141). See also Divina, *Storia del beato Simone da Trento*, cit., pp. 39-40.

[21] "Mane sequenti venerunt plures alii Judaei ad videndum dictum corpus et in quo die sequenti de sero idem corpus fuit sublatum de capsa et portatum in Synagogam praedictam, in quam tunc venerunt circa triginta Judaei" (cfr. [Bonelli], *Dissertazione apologetica*, cit., p. 141). See also Divina, *Storia del beato Simone da Trento*, cit., vol. II, pp. 30-40.

[22] "Jossele et Sayer praedicti mandaverunt Jacob et Isac, quod debere auferre corpus de dicta Synagoga et illud portare ad sepeliendum in quandam curiam contiguam dictae Synagogae, quae curia est versus Orientum, et quod illud corpus deberent sepelire in dicta Curia in quodam angulo a meridie, quae curia est circumdata muro et in eam intratur per quoddam ostium, quod tenetur clausum" ([Bonelli], *Dissertazione Apologetica*, cit., p. 141). See also Divina, *Storia del beato Simone da Trento*, cit., vol. II, p. 40.

[23] Cfr. Po-Chia Hsia, *The Myth of Ritual Murder*, cit., pp. 66-72; Rubin, *Gentile Tales*, cit., pp. 123-128.

[24] Cfr. Divina, *Storia del beato Simone da Trento*, cit., vol. II, pp. 38-39; Po-Chia Hsia, *The Myth of Ritual Murder*, cit., pp. 72; Id., *Trent 1475*, cit., pp. 97-98.

[25] In the vast bibliography on the Regensburg trials of the years 1476-1480, see R. Strauss, *Urkunden und Aktenstücke zur Geschichte der Juden in Regensburg, 1453-1738*, Munich, 1960, pp. 68-168; Id., *Regensburg und Augsburg*, Philadelphia (Pa.), 1939; Po-Chia Hsia, *The Myth of Ritual Murder*, cit., pp. 72-85; W. Treue, *Ritualmord und Hostienschändung, Untersuchungen zur Judenfeindschaft in Deutschland im Mittelalter und in der fruhen Neuzeit*, Berlin, 1989, pp. 52-58. See also the notes in this regard by W.P. Eckert, *Motivi*

superstiziosi nel processi agli ebrei di Trent, in I.Rogger and M. Bellabarba, *Il principe vescovo Johannes Hinderbach (1465-1486) fra tardo Medioevo e Umanesimo*, Atti del Convegno promosso della Biblioteca Comunale di Trento (2-6 October 1989), Bologna, 1992, pp. 383-394.

[26] Cfr. Strauss, *Urkunden und Aktenstücke zur Geschichte der Juden in Regensburg*, cit., pp. 73-80.

[27] Cfr. ibidem, pp 82-83, 144-148.

[28] Yoseph Colon, *Sheelot w-teshuot, Responsa*, Venice, Daniel Bomberg, 1519, resp. no. 5; Id., *Responsa and Decisions*, by E. Pines, Jerusalem, 1970, p. 282, response no. 104 (in Hebrew).

[29] In Hebrew, *Ha-ghedolah ha'awonotenu ha-rabbim ekh she-bene', KK. Re'genshpurkh (= Regensburg) hem tefusim*. The letter bears the date 8 Iyyar 5238 (=1478), but this is a transcription error for 5236 (= 1476). The Hebrew document is transcribed with many errors from a lost original and inserted in the records of the trial of the priest Paolo da Novara, in an authenticated copy by the notary Giovanni da Fondo, in the dossier of the Trent trial records, signed and sealed by the podestà Alessandro da Bassano, dated 11 March 1478 (ibidem).

[30] The letters in Yiddish are also preserved in the Trent trial records (AST Archivio Principesco Vescovile, s.l., 69, 68). These will be soon be published in full, with an introduction by myself from the Yiddish language point of view, in one of the coming editions of "Zakhor". The letters, which are the most ancient remaining documents in Yiddish, have been partially indicated with many inxactitudes (cfr. W. Treue, *Trienter Judeprozess. Voraussetzungen-Ablaufe-Auswirkungen, 1475-1588*, Hannover Forschungen zur Geschichte der Juden, 1977; pp. 114 ss.; Ch. Turniansky and E. Trimm, *Yiddish in Italia. Manuscripts and Printed Books from the 15th to the 17th Century*, Milan, 2003, p. 158). The missives, dated the first of May 1476, are drawn up partly in rhymed prose. The recipients are Ellan (Ellin, Ella), and her husband, the banker Crassino (Ghershom) of Novara, while the senders are his/her daughter Geilin, Geilin's husband, Mordekhai Gumprecht, and his brother Yoel.

[31] "Il prete [*gallech*] mi ha visto quando ho ricevuto le lettere che gli ho portato" ["the priest [*gallech*] saw me when I received the letter which I brought him"] (letter in Yiddish dated 5 May 5236 [= 1476].

[32] Po-Chia Hsia, *The Myth of Ritual Murder*, cit., pp. 77-82, Eckert, *Motivi superstiziosi*, cit., pp. 388-389.

[33] The name Rikhard (Reichard), which also appears in the form Reisshart (Rizzardo), is found solely among the Jews of Regensburg in the second half of the Fifteenth Century (cfr. M. Stern, *Regensburg im*

Mittelalter. The israelitische Bevölkerung der deutschen Städte, Berlin, 1934, pp. 48, 55; A. Beider, *A Dictionary of Aschkanezic Given Names*, Bergenfield, N.J., 2001, p. 406).

[34] Like Rizzardo da Regensburg, who lived at Brescia but had a bank in the district, at Gavardo, where he lived with his two brothers, Enselino and Jacob, another Jewish money lender, Leone di Maestro Seligman, had a dwelling at Brescia, carrying on the money lending activity in the district, at Iseo (cfr. F. Glissenti, *Gli ebrei nel Bresciano al tempo delle Dominazione Veneta. Nuove ricerche e studi*, Brescia, 1891, pp. 8-14; F. Chiappa, *Una colonia ebraica in Palazzolo a metà a del 1400*, Brescia, 1964, p. 37).

[35] "Modo possunt essi anni sex vel circa in loco Seravalli, cum Arone eius Patre staret, idem Aron dixit sibi Lazaro, quod fuerat interfectus quidam puer in dicta Civitate Ratisbonae et quod Rizardus frater Aron dixerat sibi Aron, quod habuerat de sanguine illius pueri interfecti Ratisbonae" ["Perhaps about six years ago or thereabouts, in a place called Serravalle, when Aaron was there with his father, Aaron told Lazzarus that a boy had been killed in that city of Regensburg and that Rizzardo's brother Aaron told him that he had some blood from the boy killed at Regensburg"] [Bonelli], *Dissertazione apologetica*, cit., p. 143.). See also Divina, *Storia del beato Simone da Trento*, cit., vol. II, pp. 15, 24-25, 37-38; Po-Chia Hsia, *Trent 1475*, cit., pp. 91-92.

[36] "Primo anno quo ipse Angelus habitavit in castro Gavardi territorii Brixiae cum Enselino, Rizardus Hebreus, qui habitavit Brixiae, scripsit unas litteras Enselino, in quibus significabat quod ipse Ricardus emeret de sanguine et quod inserviret sibi de eo" ["The first year that Angelo lived in the city of Gavrdo in the territories of Brescia with Enselino, Rizzardo the Jew, who lived at Brescia, wrote Enselino a few letters, in which he said that Ricardo sold blood and that he had used some of it"] (cfr. Esposito and Quaglioni, *Processi*, cit., vol. I, pp. 294-295.

[37] "Isac dici audivit ab Angelo quod Rizzardus de Brixia habuerit de sanguine cuiusdam puerii alias interfecit in Civitate Ratisbonae" ["Isacco heard Angelo say that Rizzardo had some blood from the other boys killed at Regensburg"] ([Bonelli], *Dissertazione apologetica*, cit., p. 144). See also Divina, *Storia del beato Simone da Trento*, cit., vol. II, pp. 36-37.

[38] Cfr. Po-Chia Hsia, *Trent 1475*, cit., pp. 97-98.

[39] "Rizzardus Hebraeus habuerat de sanguine cujusdam Pueri Christiani interfecti Ratisbonae, jam ab alisquibus annis et quod illum habuerat a Jossele, vitrico ipsius Rizardo; quem sanguinem sibi detulerat Salomon filius cuiusdam sororis Rizardi et quod ipse

Wolfgangus dixit eidem Rizardo, quod ipse Wolfgangus interfuerat, quando ille puer fuit interfectus Ratisbonae" ["Rizzardo the Jew had already possesed blood from that Christian boy killed at Regensburg for several years, and that he had received it from Jossele, Rizzardo's step-father, and that this Wolfgang told Rizzardo, that he, Wolfgang, had been present at Regensburg when the boy was killed"] ([Bonelli], *Dissertazione apologetica*, cit., p. 141). See also Divina, *Storia del beato Simone da Trent*, cit., vol. II, 43-45.

[40] "Et tunc Rizardus esset in Civitate Paduae, adjuverat ad interficiendum quendam Puerum Christianum, quem Puerum interfecerat ipse Rizardus, una cum certis aliis Judaeis habitantibus Paduae et in loca circumvicinia [...] et illum interfecerant in eorum scholis, sive Synagogae") ["And when Rizzardo was in the city of Padua, he helped kill the Christian boy, and that the person who killed the boy was this same Rizzardo, with certain other Jews living at Padua or other adjacent localities [...] and that they killed the boy in their school, or synagogue"] ([Bonelli], *Dissertazione apologetica*, cit., p. 141). It should be noted that at Padua in 1472, a "hostaria da judei" [Jewish inn] located at Sant' Urbano, was kept by a certain Rizzardo di Michele, who must not, however, be confused with Rizzardo di Brescia. In fact, the latter was the son of Lazzaro, and practiced medicine and money lending, not tavern-keeping (ASP, Estimo 1418, vol. 92, c. 43, ss: "Rizardus hebreus qm Michele sta a Santo Urban, non a altro nisi la persona e soa mogliere e tri fioli. Et dice far hosteria da zudei in la ditta contra: et paga de fitto da le hostaria a missier Archoan Buzacharin ducati XI" ["Rizzardo the Jew, son of the late Michele, at Santo Urbano has only himself and his wife and three children. And he said that he kept a Jew inn in the same district; and that he rented the inn from a certain Messer Archoan Buzachazin for eleven ducats"]; in this regard, see also C. De Benedetti, author, *Hativiwa: il cammino della speranza. Gli ebrei a Padova*, 1998, vol. I, p. 16). In 1472, Rizzardo received a certain sum due to him from the bank owned by Salomon da Piove, represented by the son Marcuccio (ASP, Notarile, vol. 249, c. 59v. 11 March 1472). A son of Rizzardo, Abramo, lived at Padua in 1485 in the Volto dei Negri district (ASP, Notarile, Agostino delle Conchelle, vol. 2056c, c. 23r 4 August 1485).

[41] Cfr. Divina, *Storia del beato Simone da Trento*, cit., vol. II, pp. 43-45.

[42] "Interrogatus quod dicat veritatem et non mentiatur, (Wolfgangus) audicissime loquendo dixit quod quae supradictum Rixardum dixisse, ipse Wolfgangus narrabit coram quocumque Domino et Principe; dicens etiam, quod per Deum, quando ipse

Wolfgangus ducetur ad justitiam, ut decapitetur, vel aliter interficiatur, affirmavit hoc quod supradixit" [quoted in text], ([Bonelli], *Dissertazione apologetica*, cit., p. 141).

[43] Cfr. Straus, *Urkunden und Aktestücke zur Geschichte der Juden in Regensburg*, cit., pp. 64-66.

[44] Cfr. ([Bonelli], *Disssertazione apologetica*, cit., p. 141; Divina, *Storia del beato Simone da Trento*, cit., vol. II, p. 42.

[45] Cfr. Divina, *Storia del beato Simone da Trento*, cit., vol. II, pp. 29-30.

[46] This Abramo, a banker at Piacenza, seems to have been active from 1455 until the end of Feburary 1476. Cfr. Sh. Simonsohn, *The Jews in the Duchy of Milan*, Jerusalem, 1982, vol. I, pp. 183, 653, nn. 391, 1585).

[47] On 7 August 1479, Falcone, "hostero de li hebrei in la città de Pavia" ["inkeeper for the Jews in the city of Pavia"], asked the Duke of Milan for authorization "de tenere zoghi [...] in la casa de la sua habitatione, et che cadauno hebreo gli possa zugare tam de nocte quam de die a suo piacere, libere et impune" ["to run gambling games [...] in his dwelling, and that each Jew may gamble there by night or day, at his pleasure, without punishment"]. The Duke consented, on the condition that gambling with Christians in the tavern would be prohibited (cfr. C. Invernizzi, *Gli ebrei a Pavia*, in "Bollettino della Societa Pavese di Storia Patria", V (1905), p. 211; Simonsohn, *The Jews in the Duchy of Milan*, cit., vol. II, pp. 773, 789-799, nn. 1870, 1917).

[48] Cfr. Simonsohn, *The Jews in the Duchy of Milan*, cit., vol. I, pp. 506-507, no. 1200; vol. II, pp. 798-799, no. 1917.

[49] Colon, *Sheelot w-teshuvot*, cit., resp. no. 160. In support of Colon's authoritative opinion came two other well-known rabbis, Yehuda Minz da Padova and Jacob Mestre di Cremona. On the matter as a whole, see J.R. Marcus, *The Jew in the Medieval World. A Source Book (315-1791)*, New York, 1974, pp. 389-393.

[50] Cfr. Simonsohn, *The Jews in the Duchy of Milan*, cit., vol. II, p. 702, no. 1701. Our Falcone is not identical with the Jew of the same name who had taken part in the conspiracy hatched in 1476 by the banker Manno da Pavia and other influential Jews from the Duchy of Milan to poison the bishop of Trent in revenge, as the priest Divina seems to believe (*Storia del beato Simone da Trento*, cit., vol. II, p. 30, no. 1). The personage in question was, in fact, explicitly called Falcone da Monza and had a house in that city (ibidem, pp. 161-165). In the spring of 1470, Falcone da Monza was arrested, on the denunciation of a converted Jew, with the accusation, later revealed to be unfounded, of

disfiguring an image of the Virgin Mary and throwing it in the flames (cfr. L. Fumi, *L'Inquisizione romana e lo Stato di Milano*, in "Archivio Storico Lombardo", XXX (1903), p. 307; Simonsohn, *The Jews in the Duchy of Milan*, cit., vol. I, pp. 518-519, 526, nn 1266, 1244). A native of Udine, Falcone was active in the money trade at Monza from 1472, while his money lending permit was renewed in 1479. In 1473, he was appointed tax collector for the Jews in the Duchy and on 4 December 1480 he appears among the representatives of the Milanese state, who paid into the ducal strongboxes the huge fine of thirty two thousand ducats, to which he had been sentenced for having kept Hebrew books containing injurious expressions with regards to Jesus and Christianity (cfr. Simonsohn, *The Jews of the Duchy of Milan*, cit., vol. I, pp. 599, 619, nn. 1440, 1494; vol. II, pp. 781, 849, nn. 1881, 2035).

[51] Cfr. Divina, *Storia del beato Simone da Trento*, cit., vol. II, p. 29. Manno, who, in 1441, had a stable residence at Padua, where he managed the main bank owned by him, and also had a house at Mestre starting in 1462, probably in concomitance with the opening of the Venice branch of the Paduan bank (cfr. R. Segre, *The Jews in Piedmont*, Jerusalem, 1986; vol. I, p. 289, no. 630; Simonsohn, *The Jews in the Duchy*, cit., vol. I, p. 342, no. 768).

[52] Cfr. Divina, *Storia del beato Simone da Trento*, cit., vol. II, pp. 27-29.

[53] Cfr. Simonsohn, *The Jews in the Duchy of Milan*, cit., vol. I, p. 515, no. 1217.

[54] In this regard, see A. Antoniazzi Villa, *Fonti notarili per la storia degli ebrei nei domini sforzeschi*, in "Libri e documenti", VII (1981), no. 3, p. 1-11; Ead., *Appunti sulla polemica antiebraica nel Ducato Sforzesco*, in "Studi di Storia Medioevale e Diplomatica", VII (1983), pp. 119-128; Ead., *Gli ebrei nel milanese dal Medioevo all'espulsione*, in F. Della Peruta, *Storia illustrata di Milano*, Milan, 1989, pp. 941-959.

[55] Cfr. Simonsohn, *The Jews in the Duchy of Milan*, cit., vol. I, pp. 436-437, no. 1019.

[56] Fra Antonio da Cremona claimed that he put an end to the "toleratam habitationem perfide et scellerate progenei ebrayce, que ultra id quod semper pertinax fuit et est in opbrobrium christiane, legis, semper etiam in suis officiis et orationibus in hoc perfide est obiecta christiane legi, quam ipsam cum operibus eius quotidie et incessantur blasfemat" (cfr. Segre, *The Jews in Piedmont*, cit., vol. I, p. 330-331).

[57] The trial testimonies have been studied and published by A. Antoniazzi Villa, *Un processo contro gli ebrei nella Milano del 1488*, Milan, 1986.

[58] Fragments of Mendele Oldendorf of Regensburg's autobiography have been published by E. Kupfer, in "Di goldene keyt. Periodical for Literature and Social Problems", 58 (1967) pp. 212-223 (in Yiddish). He has stressed its importance as a source for the history of the Jews at Venice and in the Ashkenazi communities of northern Italy in the last part of the Fifteenth century, D. Nissim, *Un "minian" de ebrei ashkenaziti a Venezia negli anni 1465-1480*, in "Italia", XVI, 2004, p. 45.

[59] In the trial documents, Jacob is referred to as "Jacob ebreus de Papia, filius quondam Manni, habitator in civitate Papie". (Cfr. Antoniazzi Villa, *Un processo contro gli ebrei nella Milan del 1488*, cit., pp. 90-92.

[60] "Si faciunt aliquam ymaginem ad symilitudinem Iesus Christi et Virginis Marie et ipsam ymaginam proyciunt in igne vel in aliquo, vel ponunt sub pedibus, vel alidquid faceunt in contemptum" (cfr. ibidem, p. 86; "[...] et ipsam ymaginem proyciunt in igne, vel stercore vel sub pedibus" ["Whether they make images in the likeness of Jesus Christ and the Virgin Mary and throw those images in the fire or in excrement, or stamp them underfoot, or otherwise hold them in contempt"] (cfr. ibidem, p. 88).

[61] "(Judaei} panes azymos seu mazoctos secundum ritum eorum legis confecisse ad instar tamen gloriossimi cruxifficii et eius vilipendium [...] quia fecerunt quatuor imagines de pasta ad imaginem domini nostri Jehesus Christi in obproprium Christi et fidei catholice, comburendo ipsas imagines infra quendam furnam" (cfr. Segre, *The Jews in Piedmont*, cit., vol. I, pp. 146-147, nos. 326-327). For documentation on other cases in which, in the Middle Ages, the Jews were accused of making, on the eve of the Passover, leavened bread with the image of the crucified Christ, and then causing them to be consumed in the heat of the furnace, see D. Nirenberg, *Communities of Violence. Persecution of Minorities in the Middle Ages*, Princeton (N.J.), 1996, p. 220.

[62] "Si (hebrei) capiunt aliquem christianum et aliquid de ipso in contemptum fidei christiane faciunt" (cfr. Antoniazzi Villa, *Un processo contro gli ebrei nella Milano del 1488*, cit., p. 86).

CHAPTER SIX

MAGICAL AND THERAPEUTIC USES OF BLOOD

Reading the depositions of defendants accused of ritual child murder with relation to the utilization of blood, one is left with the clear impression that, rather than explain the need for the blood of a Christian child, the defendants were attempting to provide a description of the wonderful therapeutic and magical properties of blood generally, and of blood extracted from children and young persons in particular. The principle emphasis was placed upon scorched, dried blood which had been reduced to powder; such blood is said to have been used as a haemostatic [coagulant] of extraordinary effectiveness when applied to the wound caused by circumcision. Angelo da Verona had no doubt in this regard and explained to the judges at Trent that, once the blood had been reduced to powder, Jews normally saved it for later re-use when their sons were circumcised, to heal the wound in the foreskin. If available, they were said to have used other haemostatic powders as an alternative, such as *bolo di Armenia* and the so-called "dragon's blood", a sort of dark red colored resin, known in pharmaceutics as *Calamus Draco* or *Pterocarpus Draco*.[1] The physician Giuseppe di Riva del Garda, known as the "hunchbacked Jew", who had circumcised Angelo's sons, normally used it during the course of the holy operation.[2]

Obviously, Maestro Tobias, who rightly considered himself a medical expert, also knew how to prepare the magic haemostatic: "You take the blood, allowing it to coagulate; then you dry it and make a powder out of it, which can be used in so many different ways".[3] Giovanni Hinderbach seemed scandalized by these revelations and censured the wickedness of the Jews in healing the circumcision wounds of their sons with the blood of Christian children in his opening address at the Trent trial. "As with other things Tobias confessed", explained the prince bishop, "they medicate their circumcisions with the powder of that coagulated blood and then, in the second or third day after the operation, recovering their health".[4]

Elias and Mercklin (Mordekhai), as well, two of the brothers accused of the terrible multiple homicide of Endingen in Alsace, during their trial in 1470, attempted uselessly to beat around the bush before the inquisitors' demands relating to the use of the blood of Christian children by Jews. This blood was then utilized for the marvelous balsamic qualities which it possessed, beneficial in curing epilepsy and eliminating the disgusting body odor of Jews [il disgustoso fetore giudaico]. But in the end, they both admitted to making use of the magical healing liquid to cure the circumcision wounds of their sons.[5] Leo da Pforzheim, the most illustrious among the defendants accused of acquiring blood from the children killed at Endingen, confessed that he had procured it because it was required for the circumcision procedure. Leo had known that the powdered blood of children was used as a coagulant of proven efficacy on those occasions for more than twenty years, ever since the first time he had been present at a circumcision ceremony with his father, twenty years before.[6] The Jews accused of ritual child murder at Tyrnau in Hungary in 1494 also declared, among other things, that they had used powdered blood as a circumcision haemostatic.[7] The widespread use of blood as a powerful haemostatic among the Jews is probably the reason for the widespread notion that Jewish males – all directly or indirectly guilty of Deicide – suffered painful and abundant monthly menstruation periods [presumably anally].

Perhaps first advanced by Cecco d'Ascoli in his commentary *De Sphaera* by Sacrobosco in 1324, this eccentric opinion is said to have received enthusiastic support from the Dominican friar Rodolfo de Selestat in Alsace.[8] The Jews, the killers of Christ, and their progeny, were said to been inflicted with an abnormal escape of blood, menstruations, bleeding hemorrhoids, hematuriae [blood in the urine] and exhausting fits of dysentery, which they were alleged to attempt to cure through the application of Christian blood as a haemostatic.

"I heard from the Jews [...] that all the Jews, descendants of those guilty of Deicide, have escapes of blood every month and often suffer from dysentery, from which they frequently perish. But they recover their health by virtue of Christian blood, baptized in the name of Christ".[9]

Circumcision hemorrhages, epistaxis [nosebleed], overly abundant menstruation, open hemorrhoids, abnormal abdominal flow. The most effective cure to control and heal them always seemed to be recourse to the powerful and magical powdered blood of children. But in this, the Jews were acting no differently from the Christians of surrounding society, despite Hindenbach's feigned and artificial stupefaction. In popular medicine, blood, whether human or animal, was alleged to be an indispensable component in the preparation of electuaries [powder-based medications mixed with honey or syrup to form a paste] and astringent powders of extraordinary effectiveness.[10] As Pier Camporesi wrote, "a sacred and alchemistic haemostatic, blood (and not incorrectly, in epochs in which hemorrhages represented a terrible tragedy, was considered a powerful healant".[11] According to the prescriptions of the *Theatrum Chemicum*, marvelous unguents and powders were derived from human blood, capable of arresting even the most resistant flow of blood and of expelling dangerous infirmities.[12] The most expert specialists knew that human blood possessed great therapeutic powers and was therefore to be prepared and treated with the greatest care. They therefore recommended that "it being ascertained that it is perfectly dry, it should be immediately placed in a bronze mortar, which must be quite hot, and should be ground with a pestle and made to pass through the finest sieve, and after all of it has passed, it shall be sealed in a small glass pot and must be renewed every year in the springtime".[13]

Be that as it may, the Jews, when they described the operation of circumcision addressing the Christian public, preferred to omit the use of children's blood among the "restrictive powders" and limited themselves to listing others, such as the classical Dragon's Blood and coral powder. Leon da Modena, the noted rabbi of Venice, in his classic *Historia de' Riti Hebraici* described the ceremony of circumcision (*berith milah*) briefly as follows:

"The *mohel* comes with a plate, upon which are the instruments and things necessary, such as razor, astringent powders, pieces of bandage with rose oil, and some similarly use a bowl of sand in which to place the foreskin, which is cut [...]. The *mohel* continues, and, with the mouth, sucks the blood flowing from the wound two or three times and spits it into a glass of wine, after which he places Dragon's blood, coral powder, or things which staunch, and piece of bandage soaked in of rose oil on the cut, and binds and bandages it tightly. He then takes a glass of wine [...] and bathes the infant's mouth with the wine in which he spat out the sucked blood".[14]

The omission of powdered blood from among the haemostatic powders could not be accidental. Confirmation of this point could easily be obtained from "Jews turned Christians". They would naturally never have concealed such a scandalous practice, assuming that they actually considered it scandalous. Shemuel Nahmias, a Venetian and disciple of Leon da Modena, later baptized under the name of Giulio Morosini, discussing the topic of circumcision, did not conceal his severe censure of the custom of placing blood mixed with wine on the child's mouth. This practice seemed to him in implacable conflict with the Biblical prohibition against the consumption of blood ("Tell me, moreover, is it not against the Divine Law, expressed in several places, that the blood is not to be eaten or drunk? And then in the rite of circumcision, you place the circumcised boy's own blood, issuing from the foreskin, mixed in wine, in his own mouth, adding, to your greater transgression, and repeating that in that blood he will live, almost is if he were to be nourished by that blood").

But of the utilization of the blood of the Christian child as a haemostatic applied to the wound caused by circumcision, the convert Morosini made no mention at all, almost as if the practice were unknown to him or did not merit considerable attention.

"At this point the *mohel* arrives, and, behind him, another person, with a basin or cup in his hand, containing all the instruments necessary to the ceremony, some silver tongs, which are placed as a sign of how much foreskin is to be cut, a container full of Dragons Blood and other astringent powders to clot the blood, and two cups or small soup plates, one containing an absorbent material cut up for the purpose, greased with oil of Balsam or rose oil to medicate the cut, and one filled with earth or sand in which to place the foreskin, burying the portion of the foreskin which had been cut off [...] having completed the above, the *mohel* squeezes the little member of the circumcised boy, and sucking in the blood several times, spits it into a glass of wine, prepared for this purpose, and finishes by treating the cut with the above mentioned oil and powder".[15]

Another converted Jew, Raffael Aquilino, baptized in 1545, and later appointed by the Holy Office with responsibility for confiscating the Talmud and burning it in the territories in the Duchy of Urbino and the Mark, never dwelt in the slightest upon the presumed Jewish custom of using powdered Christian blood to heal the circumcision wound, instead, concerning himself with the analogies between the Holy Trinity and the three recurrent elements in the ceremony, applied to the burying of the foreskin in the earth of the cemetery, the egg and wine, which, after washing the wound, is given to the infant to drink.

"Similarly, they take three things for the said circumcision, i.e., the earth from their sepulchers, and they put it in a basin in which they place the flesh which they cut off the foreskin, the wine with which they render thanks to God [...] and three eggs, while in the basin, into which they pour the wine used to wash the foreskin [...] and they wash the circumcision wound with the wine three times".[16]

The famous Tuscan convert Paolo Medici describes the ceremony of circumcision in detail, with obvious hostility, but seems unaware of the use of coagulated blood as a haemostatic powder. In fact, he restricted himself to observing, without further detail, that "the *mohel* [...] places astringent powders, rose oil and similar things on the cut, as a sort of dressing, ties it up, bandages it and delivers it to the Godmother".[17]

One could at this point conclude that the use of the powdered blood of children, and especially Christian blood, as a haemostatic during circumcision, in view of the disinterest in its regard shown even by converted Jews, on other points inclined to defame Judaism, is a chimera and a tendentious invention, either of the inquisitors, obsessed with blood, or of Jews themselves, terrorized by torture and slavishly eager to placate their tormenters. But this would be erroneous and misleading.

The texts of the practical Cabbalah, the handbooks of stupendous medications (*segullot*), compendia of portentous electuaries, recipe books of secret cures, mostly composed in the German-speaking territories, even very recently, stress the haemostatic and astringent powers of young blood, above all, on the circumcision wound. These are ancient prescriptions, handed down for generations, put together, with variants of little importance, by cabbalistic herb alchemists of various origins, and repeatedly reprinted right down to the present day, in testimony to the extraordinary empirical effectiveness of these remedies.

Elia ben Mosè Loan, rabbi of Worms, known as the *Baal Shem* (literally: the patron of the name), in his *Sefer Telodot Adam* ("Book of the Story of Man"), in Hebrew and Yiddish, prescribed that "to arrest the flow of blood from the circumcision and that which flows from the nose, one must take the blood, boil it over the fire until it is desiccated, reduce it to powder, and place it successively on the cut of the circumcision or on the nostrils, so that the blood coagulates".[18] We find a similar recipe in the *Derekh ha-chaim ha-nikra Segullot Israel* ("Way of the Life, also called the Book of Portentous Remedies of Israel") by Chaim Lipschütz, which adds another magical medication, this time intended to arrest the menstrual flow. "Take the menstrual blood and a chicken feather, which thou shalt immerse in the menstrual blood of the patient; when the blood with the feather has been well shaken, cause it to be dried before the fire, making a powder of it, which thou shalt administer to the woman in wine".[19]

Sacharja Plongiany Simoner, in his classic *Sefer Zechirah* ("Book of Medical Briefs"), was also rather precise as regards the Biblical references to the extraordinary curative and restrictive powers of blood.

"To stop the flow of blood from circumcision or nasal hemorrhage using the coagulated blood of the child or the patient: the blood is placed before the fire until it hardens, and then it is crushed with a pestle, making a fine powder to be placed on the wound. And that is what we find written in the book of Jeremiah (30:17): 'For I shall restore health unto thee, and I shall heal thee of thy wounds'. It is to be understood in fact that it shall be precisely from your wound, i.e., from your blood, that your health shall be restored to you".[20]

It does not, therefore, appear that there can be any doubt as to the fact that, through an antique tradition, never interrupted, empirical healers, cabbalists and herb alchemists prescribed powdered blood as a healant of proven effectiveness during circumcision or hemorrhage. The fact that this practice was probably anything but generalized should not lead us to suppose that it was not actually in use, particularly in the Ashkenazi Jewish communities, where stupendous "secrets", first transmitted orally, then printed in suitable compendiums, are said to have enjoyed extraordinary success over time. On the other hand, empirical knowledge of an analogous kind, even if obviously applied to contingencies other than circumcision, were a heritage of surrounding Christian society, proving themselves profoundly rooted, particularly on the popular level.[21]

Two other Jewish customs relating to circumcision, which do not appear to have been uniformly widespread from the geographical and chronological point of view, are also of particular interest. Here as well, popular beliefs, based on magical and superstitious elements, seem to possess a vigor and vitality capable of circumventing the precise norms of ritualistic Judaism (*halakhah*), or of seriously distorting them.

The ritual responses of the *Gheonim*, the heads of the rabbinical academies of Babylon, active between the VII and XI centuries, refer to the local custom of boiling perfumes and spices in water, thus rendering them fragrant and odorous, and of circumcising children, making their blood gush into that liquid until the colors were mixed. "It is at this point", the rabbinical response continues, "that all the young males wash themselves in that water, in memory of the blood of the pact, which has united God to our patriarch Abraham".[22] In this rite, of a propitiatory nature, the blood from the circumcision wound, united with the sweet-smelling potion, is said to have possessed the ability to transform itself into a potent aphrodisiac, used in curative electuaries, beneficial in lending vigor to amorous desires and to the procreative abilities of initiated males.

One form of magical cannibalism, related to circumcision, may be found in a custom highly widespread among both the Ashkenazi Jewish communities and [Jewish?] communities of the Mediterranean region. The women present at the circumcision ceremony but not yet blessed with progeny of the male sex, anxiously awaited the cutting of the foreskin of the child. At this point, throwing inhibition to the winds, as if at a pre-established signal, the women hurled themselves upon that piece of bloody flesh. The luckiest woman is alleged to have snatched it up and gulped it down immediately, before she could be mobbed by the competing females, who must have been no less hardened and highly motivated. The triumphant winner was in no doubt whatever that the proud tit-bit would be infallibly useful in causing the much-coveted virile member to germinate inside the impregnated abdomen through sympathetic medicine. The struggle for the foreskin among women without male progeny appears in some ways similar to today's competition among spinsters and nubile young girls for the conquest of the bride's bouquet after the wedding ceremony.

Giulio Morosini, alias Shemuel Nahmias, remembered with much annoyance this repellent custom, which he had seen rather in vogue among the young Jewish women of Venice.

"The superstition of the women is remarkable in this regard. If sterile women wishing to become pregnant happened, as they frequently did, to be present [at the circumcision ceremony], not a single one of them would hesitate to fight off the others and steal the foreskin; and the first one to grab it never hesitates to fling it in her mouth and swallow it as a sympathetic remedy of extremely great effectiveness in causing her to be fruitful".[23]

Rabbi Shabbatai Lipschütz confirmed this extraordinary custom "of the struggle amongst the women to swallow the foreskin immediately after circumcision, as a wonderful secret (*segullah*) in the production of male children". He added that there were rabbis who permitted it, such as the famous North African cabbalist Chaim Yosef David Azulay, known as the *Chidah* (the Enigma), and the rabbi from Salonica, Chaim Abraham Miranda, while others energetically prohibited it, considering it a scandalous and impermissible practice.[24] But the cabbalistic herb alchemist (Rafael Ohana), expert in the secrets of procreation, although he possessed little skill in gynecological sciences, referred with satisfaction to the results obtained from women having swallowed the foreskin of a circumcised boy, even in recent times. In his guide, intended for women wishing to have children and entitled *Mar'eh ha-yaladim* ("He Who Shows the Children"), the expert North African rabbi advised that, to make it more appetizing, the unusual dish be covered with honey, like a home-made sweet.[25] The magical and empirical tradition linked to the foreskin of circumcision as a fecundating element was not lost over the course of the centuries, but was protected by the secrets of the practical Cabbalah despite the disdainful opposition of rationalistic rabbis.

It was a common belief that the Jews used blood in powders, dried or diluted in wine or water, applying it to the eyes of the new-born, to facilitate their opening, and to bathe the bodies of the dying, to facilitate their entry into the Garden of Eden.[26] Samuel Fleischaker, Israel Wolfgang's friend, indicted for the ritual murder at Regensburg in 1467, attributed infallible magical properties to young blood, which, spread on the eyes, was said to have served to protect from the evil eye (*ayn ha-ra*).[27]

All the cases examined above, and in a great number of those present in the compendiums of the *segullot*, remedies and secret medications, drawn up and disseminated by the masters of the practical Cabballah, constitute the exterior use, so to speak, of blood, whether human or animal, dried or diluted, for therapeutic and exorcistic purposes. But the accusation leveled against Jews of ingesting blood, or of using it for ritual or curative purposes, in transfusions taken orally, appears at first glance destitute of any basis, being in clear violation of Biblical norms and later ritual practices, which permitted no derogation whatever from the prohibition.

It is not, therefore, surprising that the Jews of the Duchy of Milan, in their petition to Gian Galeazzo Maria Sforza in May dated 1479, intended to defend themselves from the ritual murder accusations spreading like oil on water after the Trent murder, by recalling the Biblical prohibition in stressing that these accusations had no basis in fact: "That they are not guilty is easily proven by very effective evidence and arguments, both legal and natural, from very trustworthy authorities, first for the Jewish Law *Moysaycha* which prohibits murder, and in several places, the eating of blood, not only human but of any animal whatever".[28]

Also the most authoritative among the accused in the Trent trial, Mosè da Würzburg, known as "the Old Man", in the initial phases of his interrogation, did not hesitate to mention the rigid Biblical prohibition against consuming any type of blood to demonstrate the absurdity of the accusation. "Ten Commandments given by God to Moses", the learned Hebrew leveled at his accusers, "commands us to refrain from killing and eating blood; it is for this reason that Jews cut the throat of the beasts which they intend to eat and, what is more, later salt the meat to eliminate any trace of blood".[29] Mosè "the Old Man" was very obviously perfectly well aware of the norms of slaughter (*shechitah*) and of the salting of meat (*melikhah*), prescribed by Jewish rituals (*halakhah*) and which apply the Mosaic prohibition against eating blood with the maximum severity. But his arguments, as we shall see, although apparently convincing, were to some degree misleading.

In fact, if we turn once again to the compendia of *segullot* in use among Jews of German origin, we will find a broad range of recipes providing for the oral ingestion of blood, both human and animal. These recipes are stupendous electuaries, sometimes complex in preparation, intended to alleviate ailments, act as a remedy, and protect and cure. For Shabbatai Lipschütz, to arrest the excessive flow of menstrual blood, it was advisable to dry before the fire and reduce into power a chicken feather soaked with the menstrual blood. The morning afterwards, a spoonful of that powder, diluted in wine and served up to the woman, on an empty stomach, was said to have infallibly produced the desired effect. Another secret medication, collected by Lipschütz and considered of extraordinary effectiveness on the basis of long tradition, was prescribed for women who wished to get pregnant. The recipe provided that a pinch of dried rabbit's blood be dissolved in wine and administered to the patient. As an alternative, a composite of worms and menstrual blood could be of great utility.[30]

Also Elia Loans, the Baal Shem of Worms, celebrated the extraordinary properties of rabbit's blood in impregnating sterile women. The expert Caballist moreover prescribed, for the cure of epilepsy, the dilution in wine of dried blood from a virgin having her first menstrual period.[31] In this regard, it should be noted that Mercklin (Mordekhai), one of those condemned for the plural ritual murder at Endingen in 1470, stressed the effectiveness of using young human blood in curing epilepsy.[32]

The compendia of *segullot* furthermore stressed the prodigious properties of human blood, naturally, always dried and prepared in the form of curdles or powder, as the main ingredient of aphrodisiacal elixirs inciting to love and copulation, in addition to their ability to bring about the fulfillment of the most audacious and consuming of erotic dreams. It is not surprising that blood was sometimes featured in relation to matrimony – another fundamental rite of passage – in addition to its uses in circumcision and in the preparation for death.

In the popular tradition, included, for example, by the Jews of Damascus, "a man who wishes to win the love of a woman should extract a bit of his own blood, and after drying it before the fire, cause it to be drunk, dissolved in wine, by the woman who is the object of his passion".[33] This electuary is said to have been of proven effectiveness in such cases. Other compendia of *segullot* state that the recipe was to be considered valid for both men and women and that, to be of greater effectiveness, the blood should be taken from the little finger of the right hand of the person suffering from an unrequited passion.[34] The defendants accused of the ritual child murder at Tyrnau in 1494 and at Posing, both in Hungary, in 1592, also mention the use of blood as an aphrodisiac and in inciting love, including, and most particularly, in the celebration of matrimony.[35] In the famous case of the supposed profanation of the Host stolen from the Knoblauch church in Brandenburg in 1510, the rich Jew Mayer of Ostenburg was accused of having purchased the Host at a high price to extract its essence, and then of using it on the occasion of his son Isaac's wedding to prepare an aphrodisiac elixir intended for the bride and groom.[36]

In the Trent trial, the women, particularly those linked to the authoritative Samuele da Nuremberg, the acknowledged head of the Jewish community, made no secret of their great faith in the effectiveness of the blood of children as an ingredient in sublime potions, both curative and protective, of which the popular medicine and the practical Caballah were extraordinarily rich, based on long tradition. Bella, Mosè da Würzburg's daughter-in-law, declared, without hesitation, in her statement in February 1476, that "that the blood of a child was beneficial in a manner wonderful to women, incapable of birth at term". The women recalled that, when young Anna of Montagana, daughter-in-law of Samuele da Nuremberg, was pregnant and suffering from the threat of miscarriage, her mother-in-law, Brunetta, as a woman and an expert in these things, as she was, visited her in her bedroom, making her take a spoonful of a medicament consisting of dried and powdered blood dissolved in wine.[37] On another occasion, Bella had seen Anna, pregnant and suffering, sustain herself with a bit of blood mixed with the yoke of a soft-boiled egg.[38]

For their part, Bona and Dolcetta, respectively the sister and wife of Angelo da Verona, recalled with nostalgic stupefaction their meeting with an herb alchemist of great fame and experience, a few years previously. According to them, this Cabballistic quack, known as Maestro Jacob, possessed a book full of "secrets" of exorbitant and extraordinary effectiveness, including that of causing pelting rain and hailstorms.

To do this, it was necessary to mix young blood with the clear water of a fountain while pronouncing formulae and exorcisms, incomprehensible to the uninitiated.[39] As we have already stressed several times, it is not difficult to arrive at the conclusion that, when the Jews were accused of ritual murder, rather than justify the necessity of the – so to speak – religious uses of blood, they preferred to expatiate at length upon the magical and therapeutic functions of blood generally, both human and animal, known and widespread among the people and, in particular, among German-speaking persons, both Jewish and Christian.

This does not yet explain how the Jews, and the Ashkenazi Jews in particular, could reconcile the Biblical prohibition against the oral consumption of blood – which was rigid and without exceptions – with the custom, apparently well-rooted, of using it, nonetheless, in medications and elixirs of various kinds, proven and tested over time. Since these elixirs are often true and proper medications, even if not contemplated by official medicine, the Jewish ritual law (*halakhah*) only permitted them when the patient was considered in danger of his life, in which case the complete and temporary abolition of all the norms of the Torah – Jewish law – was permitted in order to save the patient. But, as we have noted, in popular practice, blood, both human or animal, appeared even in preparations to be administered to patients suffering from minor complaints, or complaints of only relative seriousness, or even as a curative in the toils of love. Confronted by these obvious contradictions, even the defendants in the Trent trial found it necessary to take a position, and to explain and justify such things. And this was not an easy task at all, partly because many of them lacked the necessary culture to do so.

Lazzaro da Serravalle, servant in Angelo da Verona's house, attempted to do so instinctively, without entering into any over-complicated reasoning. In his view, the dictates of the Torah referred to animal blood only – which was always prohibited – while it was permitted to ingest the blood of a human being, particularly if it was the blood of a Christian, the declared enemy of the Jews and Judaism.[40] As usual, Israel Wolfgang, who must have possessed rather more culture than Lazzaro, although not strictly rabbinical, attempted to supply a more elaborate response, ingenious and less crude. To the young artist from Brandenburg, it was clear that the Torah and later rabbinical regulations presupposed two different moral codes, one applying to the Jewish world, and the other applicable to the surrounding Christian world, which was different and often hostile and menacing. Therefore, that which was prohibited between Jews was not necessarily prohibited in relations between Jews and Christians. For example, the Biblical norm which prohibited usury between two brothers (Deut. 23:21) ("unto a stranger thou may'st lend upon usury; but unto thy brother thou shalt not lend upon usury"), was interpreted as concerning exclusively relations between Jews, while usurious lending to Christians was automatically permitted – so much so as to be universally practiced.[41] With a bold analogy, which we decline to believe was extorted by judges exceptionally erudite in Jewish matters by means of ingenious verbal and psychological trickery, Israel Wolfgang maintained that even the Biblical prohibition against human blood was absolute for Jews, and rigid when it involved blood extracted from the veins of Jews, but was permitted and even recommended when originating from the body of Christians, or Christian children in particular.[42]

In this regard, it is worth recalling that, in that which Camporesi calls as "the dark tunnel of necromantic medicine", specialty shops offered alchemists and herb alchemists oils and balsams extracted from fetid mummies, miraculous electuaries containing the powder of craniums, often from persons condemned to death, fat from human flesh, distilled from the bodies of murdered persons and suicides.[43] It is not surprising that popular medicine should also have permitted them as legitimate medications, prescribing them not only in the cure of serious and dangerous complaints. The sole recommendation in these cases remains the explanation that oils, fats and bones in powder, mummies and human flesh in poultices – as Israel Wolfgang explained to the judges of Trent with reference to human blood – were not to be extracted from the corpses of Jews. The rabbinical responses were rather clear in this regard, when they hastened to stress that "there is no prohibition against usefully benefiting from the dead bodies of Gentiles".[44]

Perhaps the solution to the Biblical and rabbinical contradiction between the consumption of blood and the custom – established among the Ashkenazi Jews – of consuming it on the most varied occasions, may be identified in a late response of Jacob Reischer of Prague (1670-1734), head of the *yeshivah* of Ansbach in Bavaria and later active at Worms and Metz.[45] The ritualistic text contains testimonies to a practice widespread over time immemorial among the Jews of the German community, and considered de facto permissible, notwithstanding the fact that it obviously contradicted the dictates of the Talmud. Being a custom now generalized among the Jews (*minhagh Israel*), it came, over time, to assume the same strictness as a ritual standard. The inquiry and Reischer's response referred to the consumption of the blood of the *stambecco* (*Bocksblut*), for medicinal use, even in cases in which the patient was not in danger of his life.

"INQUIRY: What is the basis for the fact that most Jews traditionally permit the consumption and drinking of the coagulated and dried blood of the ibex [a long-horned Alpine mountain goat], known as *Bocksblut* and dried in the sun, even in the event that it may be consumed by patients whose lives are not in peril, such as people suffering from epilepsy, when it is one of the internal organs of the body which causes pain?

"RESPONSE: The legality of this custom must be upheld because it is long-established. This medication is obviously permissible, because clearly, when a custom becomes widespread among the Jews (*minhagh Israel*), it must be considered to be on the level of the Torah itself. The ritual motive of the permission is based, in my view, on the fact that (the blood) is dried to the point that it is transformed into a piece of wood and contains no moisture. It is not, therefore, prohibited in any way."

The authoritative German rabbi sought to uphold the ritual lawfulness of dried blood totally without any liquid component, stating that, in this manner, the blood must be considered to have lost any alimentary connotations. But obviously, the central justification of his argument remained the notion that a custom established over time in the community of Israel, even if in contrast with the norms, was to be considered perfectly authorized and permissible.

It has been accurately observed in this regard (but the reasoning may be opportunely repeated in other cases as well, as we shall see), that "the Ashkenazi Jewish community, in the eyes of its rabbis, represented the community of health, zealous in the application of the Law of the Lord; to those rabbis, it was impossible to conceive of the fact that thousands of Jews, devote, God-fearing and solicitous in sanctifying the name of the Lord, may His name be blessed, might be violating the names of his Law day after day. If therefore the community of Israel practiced a certain custom, even in conflict with the norms of the Torah, that meant that this was permitted. The consequence of this bold assumption did not alarm that generation [...] The German rabbis recognized in the actions of their people a sort of translation into reality of the Law of God, thus as it was transmitted for generations from father to son".[46]

If this reasoning was to be considered valid with reference to the standards of ritualistic law (*halakhah*), it was even more valid if applied to widespread and profoundly rooted customs, on the ritual lawfulness of which the Ashkenazi Jews, despite appearances, appeared to have no doubt.[47] Their rabbis did not therefore hesitate to approve practices and customs, such as that of the consumption of blood, even when they appeared in obvious violation of the prohibitions of Jewish law.

The persistence of the custom of ingesting dried blood in medicinal electuaries, widespread among the Ashkenazi Jews until modern times, is testified to in the response of Hayym Ozer Grodzinski (1863-1940), a respected rabbi of Vilna (Vilnius). Responding to a question (dated 1930!), relating to the lawfulness of medications based on dried animal blood to be administered to sick people who were not in peril of their lives, the Lithuanian rabbi recalled the tradition, rooted for generations among Ashkenazi Jews. "As to the problem of the lawfulness of administering animal blood to a patient who is not in danger, since the blood has lost part of its elements and has been dried, this is my response". Therefore, Grodzinski went on to explain:

"If the blood is completely dried, it must certainly be permitted [...] and, even in the case of true and proper blood, as long as it was watered down, permission may be granted, in an emergency. And yet, since it is easy to use dried blood, which is considered by all to be perfectly lawful, it is impossible to imagine a state of emergency which would permit the oral ingestion of blood dissolved in water".[48]

In conclusion, the Jewish custom in the Germanic territories, throughout history, of consuming potions and medications based on animal blood, without regard to the ritual prohibition of the Torah, appears to be incontrovertibly confirmed by authoritative and significant Hebraic texts. As we have seen, the compendiums of *segullot* in many cases expanded the lawfulness of using human blood, to be administered dried and dissolved in another liquid, which was to be recommended, not only for therapeutic purposes, but in conjurations and exorcisms of all kinds.[49] The Trent defendants were perfectly well aware of this, and listed a long case history of it based on personal experience, even if, during the first moments of the trial, they may have considered it expedient to mention the Biblical prohibition against the ingestion of blood, which is well known to everyone, as if it were applied by them scrupulously in everyday reality. The records of the Trent trial were also to reveal, not only the generalized use of blood by German Jews for curative and magic purposes, but the necessity which the accused, according to their inquisitors, are alleged to have felt to supply themselves with Christian blood (and that of a baptized child, in particular), above all, in the celebration of the rites of *Pesach*, the Jewish Passover. In this case, all they had to do was turn to specialized, acknowledged retailers of blood, or itinerant alchemists and herb alchemists, to obtain the required goods; but it was necessary to ascertain that the object of purchase was actually that precious and much sought-after commodity, young Christian blood, despite the facility of falsification and adulteration. And this was not an easy thing to do, or something to be taken for granted.

During the trial for ritual child murder brought against the Jews of Waldkirch, a village a short distance from Freiburg, in 1504, the victim's father, Philip Bader, was later found to be the murderer of the victim, little Matthew, and therefore executed publicly, thus illustrating the perpetrator's relations with Jews. In his deposition rendered to the Judge, Bader admitted obtaining a certain amount of blood from the child's neck, without intending to kill him, to sell the blood to the Jews, who, according to him, paid high prices for that type of merchandise. In this case, the Jews are said to have refused to buy it, saying that Bader intended to swindle them, offering them animal blood instead of the blood of a Christian child. For their part, the Jews of Waldkirch advanced the theory that the unnatural father had killed the child, probably during a clumsy attempt to take blood from the carotid artery and profit from the sale.[50] In any case, it seems certain that, in the reality of the German territories, blood was frequently purchased and sold, at high prices, for the most diverse purposes, and that young human blood was certainly preferable to animal blood. It was, therefore, foreseeable that the ambiguous and equivocal sector of selling and purchasing human blood was rife with fraud and counterfeiting for the purpose of increasing one's profits with the minimum of effort.

According to the Trent defendants, their more alert clients had demanded that the resellers provide certificates of ritual suitability, signed by serious and acknowledged rabbinical authorities, as was customarily done for food products prepared according to the religious rules of the *kashrut*. No matter how paradoxical and improbable this fact may appear to our eyes – so much so as to make one believe that it was invented out of whole cloth by the judicial authorities of Trent – we believe that this matter deserves a certain amount of attention and precise verification, where possible, of the underlying facts and particulars upon which it appears to be built.

Both Maestro Tobias and Samuele da Nuremberg, Angelo da Verona, Mosè "the Old Man" of Würzburg, and his son Mohar (Meir), all recalled having come into contact with these retailers of blood, often, according to them, equipped with written rabbinical authorizations.

Sometimes they even recalled their names and origins; in some cases, they described their physical appearance with numerous details.

Abramo (Maestro Tobias's supplier), Isacco of Neuss, from the bishopric of Cologne, Orso of Saxony, Jacob Chierlitz, also of Saxony, are not names which mean a lot to us. These are the names attributed to these itinerant merchants, originating in Germany and traveling, with their leather purses with waxed and tin-plated bottoms, to the Ashkenazim communities of Lombardy and the Triveneto region.[51]

"Old Man" Mosè da Würzburg assured the judges that, in his long career, he had always acquired the blood of Christian boys from trustworthy persons and retailers bearing the required written rabbinical guarantees, which he called "testimonial letters".[52] So as not to be too vague about it, Isacco da Gridel, cook in Angelo da Verona's house, recalled the manner in which the wealthier Jews of Cleburg, a city under the domination of Filippo de Rossa, acquired the blood of Christian children from a rabbi named Simone, who lived in Frankfurt, then a free city.[53] This "Simone of Frankfurt" is certainly identical with Shimon Katz, rabbi of the Jewish community of Frankfurt am Main from 1462 to 1478, the year of his death: Shimon Katz was also the chairman of the local rabbinical tribunal. Rabbi Shimon Katz maintained close relations with the spiritual leaders of the Ashkenazim communities of Northern Italy and enjoyed close relations and friendship with Yoseph Colon, almost undisputed religious head of the Italian Jews of German origin.[54] To consider him a common trafficker in Christian blood, as Isacco the cook claimed, frankly impresses me as an oversimplification and not very believable, in the absence of other information in support of such a singular thesis.

Undoubtedly more serious and worthy of consideration, even if extorted by means of cruel coercive methods, was the related testimony of Samuele da Nuremberg, undisputed head of the Jews of Trent. Samuele confessed to his inquisitors that the itinerant peddler Orso (Dov) from Saxony, from whom he had obtained the blood, presumably that of a Christian child, bore credential letters signed by "Mosè of Hol of Saxony, Iudeorum principalis magister". There appear to be no doubt that this "Mosè of Hol" was identical with Rabbi Moshè, head of the *yeshiva* at Halle, who, together with his family, enjoyed privileges granted by the archbishop of Magdeburg in 1442 and later by Emperor Friedrich III in 1446, including that of adorning himself with the title of *Jodenmeister*, i.e., the *principalis magister Judeorum*, as Mosè is described in Samuele da Nuremberg's deposition. We know that Mosè abandoned Halle (a particular apparently ignored by Samuele) as early as 1458 and had moved to Poznán in Poland, to pursue his rabbinical activity in that community.[55]

The text of the certificate of guarantee signed by Mosè of Halle, which accompanied the purse of dried blood sold by Orso (Dov) of Saxony, was quite similar to the text of an attestation commonly issued in relation to permissible food: "Be it known by all, that all that which is carried by Dov is *kasher*".[56] It is understandable that the script intentionally omitted any mention of the type of merchandise dealt in by Orso. Samuele, once he had bought the blood, wrote his name on the white leather of the purse, which featured a list of the German merchant's clients and a signature in Hebrew: *Rabbi Schemuel mi-Trient*.[57]

* * *

NOTES TO CHAPTER SIX

[1] "Accipiunt dictum sanguinem dictorum puerorum Christianorum et illu redigunt in pulverem, quem pulverem ipsi Iudei servant et postea, quando circumciserunt eorum filios, ponunt de sanguine pueri Christiani super preputiis circuncisourm [...] et si non possunt habere de sanguine pueri Christiani quando circumcidunt, ponunt de bolo Armeno et de sanguine draconis, et dicit quod dictus pulvis mirabiliter consolidat vulnera et restringit sanguinem" ["They take the blood of Christian boys and reduce it to powder, which powder these Jews use themselves, and later, when they circumcise their own children they use the blood of a Christian child to coagulate the flow of blood from the circumcision wound [...] and if they cannot obtain the blood of Christian boys for their circumcisions, they use Bolo of Armenia and Dragon's Blood, and say that the said power miraculously heals the wound and clots the flow of blood"]. Deposition of Angelo da Verona to the Trent judges on 8 April 1475. Cfr. A. Eposito and D. Quaglioni, *Processi contro gli ebrei di Trento, 1475-1478*; I: *I processi del 1475*, Padua, 1990, p. 288. On the Jewish custom of applying astringent powders such as dragon's blood on the circumcision wound, see J. Trachtenberg, *The Devil and the Jews*, Philadelphia (Pa.), 1961, pp. 150-151.

[2] "Magister Ioseph, qui habitat Ripe et qui circumcidit filios ipsius Angeli, tenet de sanguine predicto, quod postea utitur quando circumcidit" ["Master Joseph, a resident of Riva, who circumcised Angelo's sons, obtained blood, and then used it when he circumcised"] (cfr. Esposito and Quaglioni, *Processi*, vol. I, cit., p. 288). "Magister Iosephus phisicus", known as the "zudio gobo" [hunchbacked Jew], the circumcisor of the sons of the Angelo da Verona, appears to have been active at Riva del Garda, together with his son Salomone, at least until the end of 1496 (cfr. M.L. Crosina, *La communità ebraica di Riva del Garda, sec. XV-XVIII*, Riva del Garda, 1991, pp. 29, 33, 42-43).

[3] "Thobias [...] dicit quod (judei) accipunt sanguinem pueri Christiani et illum faciunt coagulare et deinde illum dessiccant et de eo faciunt pulverem" ["Tobias [...] said that (the Jews) take the blood of a Christian boy and cause it to coagulate and then they dry it and make a

powder of it"] (cfr. Esposito and Quaglioni, *Processi*, vol. I, cit., p. 318).

[4] "Pro ut Thobias inter alias confessus est, (pueros suos circumcisos) cum pulveribus dicti sanguinis coagulati medentur et statim altero vel tertio die santitatem recipiunt" ([Benedetto Bonelli], *Dissertazione apologetica sul martirio del beato Simone da Trento nell'anno MCCCCLVXXV dagli ebrei ucciso*, Trent, Gianbattista Parone, 1747, p. 113).

[5] Cfr. K. von Amira, *Das Endinger Judenspiel*, Halle, 1883, pp. 95-97; R. Po-Chia Hsia, *The Myth of Ritual Murder. Jews and Magic in Reformation Germany*, New Haven (Conn.)-London, 1988, pp. 20-21.

[6] Cfr. Po-Chia Hsia, *The Myth of Ritual Murder*, cit., p. 29.

[7] Anton Bonfin, in *Rerum Hungaricuarum Decades*, by K.A. Bel, dec. V.I. 4, 1771, p. 728.

[8] On this matter, see recently P. Billar, *View of Jews from Paris around 1300. Christian or Scientific?*, in D. Wood, *Christianiy and Judaism*, Oxford, p. 199; I.M. Resnick, *On Roots of the Myth of Jewish Male Menses in Jacques de Vitry's History of Jerusalem*, in "International Rennert Guest Lecture Series", III (1996), pp. 1-27. See moreover Trachtenberg, *The Devil and the Jews*, cit., pp. 50, 148.

[9] "Audivi a Judeis [...] quod omnes Judei, qui de eorum processerunt, singulis mensibus sanguine fluunt et dissenterium sepius patiantur et ea ut frequentius moriuntur. Sanatur autem per sanguinem hominis Christiani, qui nomine Christi baptizatus est" (*Historiae Memorabiles*, by E. Kleinschmidt, Cologne, 1974, p. 65).

[10] On the multiple uses of the blood, fresh or dried, human or animal, in the popular Christian pharmacopaeia of the Middle Ages until the early modern era, see the classic study by H.L. Strack, *The Jew and Human Sacrifice. Human Blood and Jewish Ritual*, London, 1909, pp. 43-88.

[11] Cfr. P. Camporesi, *Il sugo della vita. Simbolismo e magia del sangue*, Milan, 1988, p. 14. See also the recent study of this problem by B. Bildhauer, *Medieval Blood*, Plymouth, 2006.

[12] "Ex sanguine humano fieri potest oleum et sal, post haec lapis rubeus mirabilis efficaciae et virtutis; cohibet flux sanguinis, multasque infirmitates expellit" (*Theatrum chemicum*, Strasburg, heirs L. Zetzner, 1613, vol. I, p. 693).

[13] The quote is dealt with by Francesco Sirena, *L'arte dello spetiale*, Pavia, G. Ghidini, 1679, p. 86. See also Camporesi, *Il sugo della vita*, cit., pp. 20-21.

[14] Leon da Modena, *Historia de' riti hebraici*, Venice, Gio. Calleoni, 1638, pp. 95-96.

[15] Giulio Morosini, Derekh Emunah. *Via della fede mostrata agli ebrei*, Rome, Propaganda Fide, 1683, pp. 114-118.

[16] Raffaele Aquilino, *Trattato pio*, Pesaro, Geronimo Concordia, 1571, pp. 35v-36r. On the appearance and personality of Aquilino, whose previous Jewish name is unknown, but who was probably a rabbi, see F. Parente, *Il confronto ideologico tra l'ebraismo e la Chiesa in Italia*, in "Italia Judaica", I (1983), pp. 316-319.

[17] Paolo Medici, *Riti et costumi degli ebrei*, Madrid, Luc'Antonio de Bedmar, 1737, p. 11.

[18] Eliyahu Baal Shem, *Sefer Toledot Adam*, Wilhemsdorf, Zvi Hirsch von Fürth, 1734, c. 16r. The handbook was printed earlier, at Zolkiew in 1720, while there must have been many republications before that at Lemberg in 1875.

[19] Chaim Lipschütz, *Derekh ha-chaim*, Sulzbach, Aharon Lippman, 1703. Under the title *Sefer ha-chaim ha-nira Segullot Israel* and the attribution to Shabbatai Lipschütz, a similar work was printed in 1905 (the recipes in question are at cc. 19v and 20r) and at Jerusalem in 1991. The use of powdered blood on the circumcision wound is also recommended in the modern editions of the *Ozara ha-segullot* ("Treasure of Secret Remedies"), by A. Benjacov (Jerusalem, 1991, and in the *Refuah chaim we-shalom* ("Medicine, Life and Peace"), by S. Binyamini (Jerusalem, 1998). See also the manuscript code of *segullot*, reproduced by Y. Ytzhaky (*Amulet and Charm*, Tel Aviv, 1976 [in Hebrew], in which the prescription of powdered blood on the circumcision wound appears at p. 101.

[20] Scaharja Plongiany Simoner, *Sefer Zechirah*, Hamburg, Thomas Rose, 1709, M. Steinschneider (*Catalogus librorum hebraeorum in Biblioteca Bodleiana*, Berlin, 1852-1860, column 2249), translates the title: *Memoraie et specifica (medicamenta superstitiosa)*. The same quotation from Jeremiah 30:17 as a textual basis for the use of dried blood as a haemostatic is reported in the *Sefer-ha-chaim* by Lipschütz, who, after illustrating the treatment of the circumcision wound, recommends, in the event of nose bleed, "di fiutare il sangue in polvere come fosse tabacco" ["to insert it in the nose as if it were tobacco"].

[21] Strack (*The Jew and Human Sacrifice*, cit., pp. 139-144) records similar, sometimes identical, customs, present in the popular culture of the surrounding Christian society, but minimizes any consideration of the significance assumed by blood among the Jews, considering any such significance to be the product of tardy external influences of little importance.

[22] Anon., *Sha're' Zedq* ("The Doors of Justice"), by Nissim Modai, Salonicco, Nahman, 1792, c. 22v. The Gaonic response on the

perfumed waters of circumcision is reproduced and commented upon by Strack, *The Jew and Human Sacrifice*, cit., pp. 136-137.

[23] Morosini, *Derekh Emunah. Via della fede mostrata agli ebrei*, cit., pp. 114-115.

[24] Lipschütz, *Sefer ha-chaim ha-nikra Segullot Israel*, cit., Chaim Yoself David Azulay, *Machzik herakhah*, Leghorn, Castello and Sadun, 1785 (*Yoreh de'ah*, par. 79). Chaim Abraha Miranda, *Yad neeman*, Salonicco, Nahman, 1804.

[25] R. Ohana, *Sefer mar'eh ha-yeladim*, Jerusalem, 1990.

[26] On this matter, see G.A. Zaviziano, *Un raggio di luce. La persecuzione degli ebrei nella storia. Riflessioni*, Corfu, 1891, pp. 4-5; Trachtenberg, *The Devil and the Jews*, cit., pp. 150-155.

[27] Cfr. R. Straus, *Urkunden und Aktenstücke zur Geschichte der Juden in Regensberg, 1453-1738*, Munich, 1960, p. 78-79; Po-Chia Hsia, *The Myth of Ritual Murder*, cit., p. 75. The use of (animal) blood as a safeguard against the Evil Eye is also present among the traditions of the Jews of Kurdistan (cfr. M. Yona, *Ha-ovedim be-erez: Ashur: yehude' Kurdistan* ["Dispersed in the Land of Assyria: The Jews in Kurdistan"], Jerusalem, 1988, p. 59).

[28] Cfr. C. Guidetti, *Pro Judaeis. Riflessioni e documenti*, Turin, 1884, pp. 290-291; Zaviziano, *Un raggio di luce*, cit., p. 175.

[29] "Cum in X praeciptis Moisi a Deo ipsis Iudeis sit mandatum quod quempiam non interficiant nec sanguinem comedant; et propter hoc ipse Iudei secant gulas animalibus que intendunt velle comedere, ut magis exeat a corporibus animalium, et quod postea etiam salant carnes ut sanguis magis excicetur" (cfr. Esposito and Quaglioni, *Processi*, vol. I, cit., p. 351).

[30] Lipschütz, *Sefer ha-chaim ha-nikra Segullot Israel*, cit. The recipe of rabbit's blood to cure sterility in women is repeated by Ohana, *Sefer mar'eh ha-yeladim*, cit. A variant sometimes consists of the prescription that it should be the man, and not the woman, who should ingest the potion before having sexual relations. In this regard, see E. Bashan, *Yahdut Marocco 'avarah we-tarbutah* ("The Hebrewism of Morocco, Its Past and its Culture"), Tel Aviv, 2000, p. 216. On arresting excessive menstrual flow, a compound of fallow-deer's blood and powdered frog, diluted in almond oil, was sometimes recommended (Binyamini, *Refuah chaim we-shalom*, cit.).

[31] Elyahu Baal-Shem, *Sefer Toledot Adam*, cit., par. 6, 18, 43, 80. The prescription of the menstrual blood of a virgin as a cure for sterile women is repeated with several variants by Banjacov, *Ozar ha-segullot*, cit.

[32] Cfr. Amira, *Das Endinger Judenspiel*, cit., p. 97; Po-Chia Hsia,

The Myth of Ritual Murder, cit., p. 21.

[33] Cfr. Ytzhaky, *Amulet and Charm*, cit., p. 169.

[34] Cfr. Benjacov, *Ozar ha-segullot*, cit.

[35] Cfr. Strack, *The Jew and Human Sacrifice*, cit., pp. 201-205.

[36] In this regard, see M. Rubin, *Gentile Tales. The Narrative Assault on Late Medieval Jews*, New Haven (Conn.), pp. 190-195.

[37] "Dicit quod dictus sanguis valet mulieribus non valentibus portare partum ad tempus debitum, quia si tales mulieres bibunt de dicto sanguine, postea portant foetum ad tempus debitum [...] Et dicit quod dum ipsa Bella esset in camera in qua erat Anna, illuc venit Bruneta, quae in manibus habebat quoddam cochlear argenti et praedictum illum ciatum argenti, quem Samuel in die Paschae de sero habebat in coena, et de quo ciato argenti dicta Bruneta cum cochleari accepit modicum de vino et illud posuit super cochleari et miscuit illud modicum sanguinis cum vino et porrexit ad os Annae, quae Anna illud bibit" ([Bonelli], *Dissertazione apologetica*, cit., pp. 122).

[38] "Quod vidit Annam quadam alia vice comeder modicum de sanguine, quem sic comedit, ponendo illud in quodam ovo coctus" (ibidem).

[39] "Dixit quod quidam Magister Jacob Judaeus, modo sunt duo anni, dixit sibi Bonae et Dulcette, quod si quid acciperet de dicto sanguine et iverit ad aliquem fontem clarum et de illo projecerit in fonte, ex postea cum facie se fecerit supra fontem [...] et dixerit certa verba, sine dubio inducet grandines et pluvias magnas [...] et praedictus M. Jacob habebat quendam, super quo erant descripta omnia, ad quae sanguis pueri Christiani valet" (ibidem, p. 43).

[40] Deposition of Lazzaro da Serravalle dated 16 December 1475. "Quod Christianis, inimicis fidei Judaice, possunt Judeai facere omne malum et quod lex (Dei) [...] loquitur de sanguine bestiarum" ["That the Jews may do any evil unto Christians, who are the enemies of the Jewish faith, and that the law (of God) [...] speaks of the blood of beasts"] (ibidem, p. 53-54).

[41] On the Jewish attitude towards lending to Christians at interest, see H. Soloveitchik, *Pawnbroking. A Study in the Inter-Relationship between Halakhah, Economic Activity and Commercial Self-Image*, Jerusalem, 1985 (in Hebrew); *The Jewish Attitude in the High and Late Middle Ages*, in D. Quaglioni, G. Todeschini and G.M. Varannini, *Credito e usura fra teologia, diritto e amministrazione. Linguaggi a confronto (sec. XII-XVI)*, Rome, 2005, pp. 115-127; J. Katz, *Hirhurim 'al ha-yachas ben dat le-kalkalah* ("Considerations on the Relationship Between Religion and the Economy"), in M. Ben-Sasson (author); *Religion and Economy. Connection and Interaction*, Jerusalem, 1995,

pp. 33-46 (in Hebrew); A. Toaff, *Testi ebraici italiani all'usura dalla fine del XV agli esordi del XVII secolo*, in Quaglioni, Todeschini and Varannini, *Credito e usura*, cit., pp. 103-113.

[42] Deposition of Israel Wolfgang dated 3 November 1475. "Existimant Judaei non esset peccatum comedere aut bibere sanguinem pueri chistiani et dicunt quod lex Dei, data Moysi, non prohibitat eis aliquid facere aut dicere quod sit contra christianos aut Jesus Deum Christianorum, dicens quod ex dicta lege eis prohibitum est foenerari, et tamen tenent Judaei quod nullum sit peccatum foenerari christiano et christianum decipere quovis modo" ["The Jews do not consider it a sin to eat or drink the blood of Christian boys and that the law of God, the so-called Laws of Moses, do not prohibit doing or saying anything at all against Christians or against Jesus the God of the Christians, saying that the said law prohibits them from lending at interest, and yet the Jews do not consider it any kind of sin at all to lend money at interest to Christians and to deceive Christians in any manner whatever"] ([Bonelli], *Dissertazione apologetica*, cit., p. 53).

[43] Cfr. Camporesi, *Il sugo della vita*, cit., p. 14.

[44] Hebrew: *Mete' goim enam asurim ha'anaah; en asur ba-anaah ella mete Israel; met goy mutar ha'anaah afilu le-choleh she-en-bo sakkanah* ("One may also use the corpse of a non-Jew in curing a sick person who is not in danger of losing his life"). See David b. Zimra, *Sheelot w-teschuvot. Responsa*, vol. III, Fürth, 1781, no. 548 [= 979]; Abraham Levi, *Ghinnat veradim. Responsa* ("The Garden of the Rose"), Constantinople, Jonah b. Ja'akov, 1715, *Yoreh' de'ah*, vol. I, response no. 4; Jacob Reischer, *Shevut Ya'akov. Responsa* ("The Captivity of Jacob"), vol. III, Offenbach, Bonaventura de Lannoy, 1719, no. 94 (see also the following note). The responses on this topic are based on the opinion expressed in regards to the Tossaphists, the classical Franco-German commentators on the Talmud. In this regard, see also H.J. Zimmels, *Magicians, Theologians and Doctors*, London, 1952, pp. 125-128, 243-244.

[45] Reischer, *Shevut Ya'akov*, cit., vol. II, *Yoreh de'ah*, no. 70. For a detailed examination of this response, see D. Sperber, *Minhage' Israel*, ("The Customs of the Jewish People"), Jerusalem, 1991, pp. 59-65.

[46] In this manner, Haim Soloveitchik, intelligently and without reticence, as always, discusses the relationship between the customs of the Ashkenazi Jews and the norms of Jewish law, often in contradiction and mutually incompatible (cfr. *Pawnbroking*, cit., p. 111).

[47] See the illuminating comments in this regard by Daniel Sperber, who discusses and broadens the arguments presented by Soloveitchik (cfr. Sperber, *Minhage' Israel*, cit., pp. 63-65).

[48] H.O. Grodzinksi, *Sheelot w-teshuvot Achiezer. Responsa*, New York, 1946, vol. III, pp. 66-68 (par. 31).

[49] On the magical and necromantic practices of Medieval Ashkenazi Judaism, with particular reference to the creation of the Golem, the artificial anthropoid, see M Idel, *Golem. Jewish Magical and Mystical Traditions on the Artificial Anthropoid*, New York, 1990.

[50] On the ritual murder at Waldkirch (1504), see F. Pfaff, *Die Kindermorde zu Benzhausen und Waldkirch im Breisgau. Ein Gedicht aus dem Anfang des 16. Jahrhunderts*, in "Alemannia", XXVII (1899), pp. 247-292; Po-Chia Hsia, *The Myth of Ritual Murder*, cit., pp. 86-110.

[51] Cfr. Esposito and Quaglioni, *Processi*, vol. I, cit.

[52] "Predictia quibus (dictus Moises antiquus) emit sanguinem pueri Christiani habebant litteras testimonials factas a suis superioribus, per quas fiebat fides quod portantes illas litteras erant persone fide et quod illud quod portabant erat sanguis pueri Christiani" ["... (Moses the Old Man said) that those who sell the blood of Christian boys have testimonial letters prepared by their superiors, attesting that those who bear these letters are persons to be trusted and that that which they carried was the blood of Christian boys"]. Mosè da Würzburg added that, when he had been living at Monza fifty years before, he had used Christian blood from an authorized merchant named Süsskind of Cologne (cfr. ibidem, pp. 358-359).

[53] For this testimony by Isacco, Angelo da Verona's cook, see G. Divina, *Storia del beato Simone da Trento*, Trent, 1902, vol. I, p. 109; vol. II, pp. 21-23.

[54] On the life and death of Rabbi Shimon Katz, head of the *yeshivah* of Frankfurt, see R. Yoseph b. Moshè, *Leqet yosher*, by J. Freimann, Berlin, 1904, p. L1 (par. 132); *Germania Judaica*, III: *1350-1519*, Tübingen, 1987, pp. 365-366 (s.v. *R. Simon Katz v. Frankfurt am Main*). See also I.J. Yuval, *Scholars in Their Time. The Religious Leadership of German Jewry in the Late Middle Ages*, Jerusalem, 1984, pp. 135-148 (in Hebrew).

[55] On Rabbi Moshè of Halle and his rabbinical activity, see *Leqet yosher*, cit., vo. XVI (par. 101); *Germania Judaica*. III: *1350-1519*, cit., p. 501 (s.v. *R. Mosès von Halle*). See also Yuval, *Scholars in Their Time*, cit., pp. 197-207.

[56] On certificates of guarantee for permissible food, and in particular for those used at *Pesach*, in the Ashkenazi communities, see I. Halpern, *Constitutiones Congressus Generalis Judaeorum Maraviensium (1650-1748)*, Jerusalem, 1953, p. 91, no. 278 (in Hebrew and Yiddish): "(year 1650). The obligation to inspect foodstuffs of any

kind, both food and drink, originating from other communities, existed in every Hebrew community. Anyone taking foodstuffs outside a given community had to equip himself with a certificate of guarantee, written and signed (by the rabbinical authority), attesting that everything had been prepared according to the rules [*she-na'asah be-heksher w-betiqqun*] [...], such as, for example, foodstuffs used at Passover".

[57] "[...] litterae, quas Ursus habebat seu portatur, continebant inter alia ista verba in lingua hebraica: 'Notum sit omnibus illud quod portat Ursus est iustum'; et deinde in subscriptione legalitas dictarum litterarum, inter alia verba erant ista: 'Moises de Hol de Saxonia, Iudeorum principalis magister' [...] et dicit quod dictus vas erat coopertum de quodam coramine albo, super quo coramine erant scripta in hebraico hec verba: 'Moyses Iudeorum principalis magister', super quo coramine albo ipse Samuel etiam se subscripsit manu sua in litera hebraica, scribendo hec verba: 'Samuel de Tridento' " ["... the letters that Oros carried with him contained, among other things, these words in Hebrew: 'Be it known to all that everything carried by Oro is kosher'; and then, the inscription of the said letters, said as follows, among other things: 'Moses of Halle of Saxony, main head of the Jews', upon which Samuel then signed his name in Hebrew letters on the white leather, writing these words: 'Samuel da Tridento' "] (cfr. Esposito and Quaglioni, *Processi*, vol. I, cit., pp. 255-256).

CHAPTER SEVEN

CRUCIFIXION AND RITUAL CANNIBALISM: FROM NORWICH TO FULDA

On the eve of Passover, 1144, the mutilated body of William, a child of twelve years, was found in Thorpe's Wood, on the edge of Norwich, England. No witness came forward to cast light on the savage crime. The child's uncle, a cleric by the name of Godwin Sturt, publicly accused the Jews of the crime in a diocesan synod held a few weeks after the discovery of the body. The body of the victim of Thorpe Wood, where it had been initially buried, was taken to the cemetery of the monks shortly afterwards, near the cathedral, and became the source of miracles.

A few years later, between 1150 and 1155, Thomas of Monmouth, prior of the cathedral of Norwich, reconstituted, with plentiful details and testimonies, the various phases of the crime, [allegedly] perpetrated by local Jews, and prepared a detailed and extensive hagiographic report of the event.[1] These were the origins of what is considered by many to have been the first documented case of ritual murder in the Middle Ages, while, for others, it is the source of the myth of the "blood libel" accusation. The latter consider Thomas to have been the inventor and propagator of the stereotype of ritual crucifixion, soon to be rapidly disseminated, not only in England, but in France and the German territories as well, fed by in the information relating to the now famous tale of the martyrdom of William of Norwich by the Jews in the days of Passover.[2]

William was an apprentice tanner in Norwich and came from an adjacent village. Among the shop's clients were a few local Jews, who are thought to have chosen him as the victim of a ritual sacrifice to be performed during the days of the Christian Easter. On the Monday following Palm Sunday, 1144, during the reign of King Stephen, a man claiming to be the cook for the arch deacon of Norwich presented himself in the village of William, asking his mother Elviva for permission to take William with him to work as an apprentice. The woman's suspicions and hesitation were soon won over thanks to a considerable sum of money. The following day, little William was already traveling the streets of Norwich in the company of the self-proclaimed cook, directly to the dwelling of his aunt Leviva, Godwin Sturt's wife, who became informed of the apprenticeship undertaken by the child and his new patron. But the latter individual awakened numerous suspicions in the aunt, Leviva, who asked a young girl to follow them and determine their destination. The shadowing, as discreet as it was effective, took the child to the threshold of the dwelling of Eleazar, one of the heads of the community of Norwich, where the cook had little William enter the house with the necessary prudence and circumspection.

At this point, Thomas of Monmouth allowed another key witness to speak, one who had been strategically placed inside the Jew's house.

This was Eleazar's Christian servant, who, the following morning, had by chance, witnessed, with horror – through the crack of a door left inadvertently open – the cruel ceremony of the child's crucifixion and atrocious martyrdom, with the participation, carried out with religious zeal, of local Jews, "in contempt of the passion of our Lord". Thomas kept the date of the crucial event clearly in mind. It was the Wednesday following Palm Sunday, 22 March of the year 1144.

To throw off suspicion, the Jews decided to transport the body from the opposite side of the city to Thorpe's Wood, which extended to within a short distance from the last house. During the trip on horseback with the cumbersome sack, however, despite their efforts at caution, they crossed the path of a respected and wealthy merchant of the locality on his way to church, accompanied by a servant; the merchant had no difficulty realizing the significance of what was taking place before his eyes. He is said to have remembered, years later, on his death bed, and to have confessed to a priest, who then became one of the diligent and indefatigable Thomas's valued sources of information. Young William's body was finally hidden by the Jews among the bushes of Thorpe.

The scene now became the inevitable scene of miraculous happenings. Beams of celestial light illuminated the boy's resting place late at night, causing townspeople to discover the body, which was then buried where it was found . A few days afterwards, the cleric, Godwin Sturt, who, informed of the murder, requested, and was granted, permission to have the body exhumed. He then recognized his nephew William as the tragic victim. A short time afterwards, during a diocesan synod, Godwin got up to accuse the Jews of the crime. Thomas of Monmouth agreed with him and accused them of the horrible ritual of crucifixion of a Christian boy as the principal event of a Passover ceremony intended to mock the passion of Jesus Christ, a sort of crude and bloody Passover counter-ritual.

The outcome of the matter turned out to be anything but a foregone conclusion, particularly in comparison with the numerous similar cases occurring over the following years, in which the Jews, considered responsible for the horrible wickedness, met a cruel fate. In this case, the Jews of Norwich, invited to present themselves before the archbishop to respond to the accusations, requested and obtained the protection of the King and his agents. Protected by the walls of the sheriff's castle, in which they found refuge, they waited for the storm to pass, as in fact it did. In the meantime, little William's body was taken from the ditch in Thorpe's Wood to a magnificent tomb usually reserved for monks, in a sheltered spot behind the Cathedral, and began, as anticipated, to work miracles, as only a martyr worthy of being proclaimed a saint possibly could.[3]

The most disturbing of the testimonies gathered by Thomas of Monmouth for his file on the murder of little William was that of a converted Jew, Theobald of Cambridge, who had become a monk hearing the story of the miracles reported at the tomb of the victim of Norwich. The convert revealed that the Jews believed that, to bring redemption closer, and with it, their return to the Promised Land, they sacrificed a Christian child every year "in contempt of Christ". To carry out this providential plan, the representatives of the Jewish communities, headed by their local rabbis, were said to meet every year in council in Narbonne, in the south of France, to draw lots as to the name of the locality where the ritual crucifixion was to occur from time to time. In 1144, the choice fell by lot to the city of Norwich, and the entire Jewish community was said to have adhered to that choice.[4]

Theobald's confession has been considered by some to constitute the origin of the ritual murder accusation of Norwich, which was then collated, accompanied by suitable documentation, by Thomas of Monmouth.[5] The ex-Jewish monk was probably alluding to the carnival of *Purim*, also known as the "carnival of the lots", which, in the Jewish calendar precedes *Pesach*, Passover, by one month, since the macabre lottery was said to have taken place every year on *Purim*.[6]

The reason for drawing lots to select the Jewish community to be entrusted with the duty of carrying out the annual sacrifice of a Christian child appeared later, in the confessions of the defendants of a ritual murder committed at Valréas in 1247, and, with reference to another case at Pforzheim in Baden in 1261, gathered and disseminated by the friar Thomas of Cantimpré in his *Bonum universale de apibus* (Douay, 1627).[7] On that occasion, the Jews of the small village of the Vaucluse were accused of killing a two-year old girl, Meilla, "in a sort of sacrifice" for the purpose of collecting her blood, and then dumping the body in a ditch.[8] The testimonies, extorted by the inquisitors under torture, were said to have shown that "it is a custom of the Jews, above all, wherever they live in large numbers, to carry out this practice every year, particularly in the regions of Spain, because there are a lot of Jews in these places".[9] It should be noted that Narbonne, mentioned by the converted Jew, Theobald of Cambridge, as the meeting place of the representatives of the Jewish communities for the annual Passover lottery held to select the location of the next ritual homicide, was in France, but belonged to the Mark of Spain.

But was the case of William of Norwich truly the first ritual murder of a Christian reported during the Middle Ages? Was Thomas of Monmouth really the creator of the stereotype which became widespread, first in England and later in France and the German territories in the years after 1150, when Thomas is supposed to have composed his hagiographic account?[10] It is permissible to wonder. It appears in fact to have been demonstrated that the story of William and his sacrifice by the Jews had already become widespread in Germany in the years prior to the composition of Thomas of Monmouth's hagiographic account. The first documents relation to William's veneration as a saint are said to have originated, not in England, but in Bavaria, dating back to 1147.[11]

Latin chroniclers report that, in the same year, a Christian was reportedly killed by the Jews at Würzburg, where the martyr's body is said to have worked miracles.[12] Twenty one local Jews accused of committing the crime during the feast of *Purim* and Passover were said to have been put to death.

Rabbi Efraim of Bonn confirmed this report, stating that "On 22 August (1147) wicked men revolted against the Jewish community of Würzburg [...] making it the object of insinuations and calumnies, for the purpose of attacking them [the Jews]. Their accusation claims: 'We found the body of a Christian in the river, and it was you who killed him and then dumped him there. Now he is a saint and is working miracles'. Under this pretext, those wicked men, and people of the poorer classes, without any real motive, assailed (the Jews...) killing twenty one of them".[13]

It is rather probable that the Hebrew and Latin reports were alluding to a crime with ritual connotations, considering the time of year in which these crimes were said to have been committed, the collective guilt attributed to Jews, the consequent massacre of many of them, and finally, the miracles which were said to have flowed forth from the victim's body. It is therefore possible that the stereotype of homicide for ritual purposes was disseminated in Germany before it gained an inch of ground in England.[14]

Thomas of Monmouth's hagiographic report would appear to vindicate those who have maintained that the first ritual homicides in England, France and Germany for almost a century, starting with the Norwich murder in 1144, conformed to the stereotype of the crucifixion of Christians, without providing for the utilization of the victims' blood for ritual purposes. In other words, ritual crucifixion is said to have proceeded the so-called "ritual cannibalism" accusation in the origin, development and final fixation of the type of ritual child sacrifice [allegedly] perpetrated by Jews.[15] As early as the during the reign of Paul IV, the jurist Marquardo Susanni in his treatise *De Judaeis and aliis infidelibus* (Venice 1558), referred to William's murder and the second presumed ritual homicide at Norwich in 1235, alluding to ritual crucifixion, without any mention of the ritual use of the victim's blood.[16] But, if we examine the matter more closely, a careful reading of Thomas of Monmouth's text might point to other possible conclusions.

The Jew Eleazar of Norwich's Christian servant, the only eyewitness of the presumed ritual homicide of little William, claimed, in her deposition, that, while the Jews proceeded with the cruel crucifixion, they asked her to bring a pot full of boiling water "to staunch the flow of the victim's blood".[17] It seems obvious to us that, contrary to the maid servant's interpretation, the boiling water must, on the contrary, have been used for the opposite purpose, i.e., to increase the flow of blood. It therefore remains to be proven that blood was a secondary element in the so-called "sacrifice of the child at Norwich". The fact that the written traditions which have come down to us do not inform us of the manner in which they intended to utilize the blood of the crucified child in this case constitutes no proof in either direction.

Be that as it may, the accusation of ritual murder or the crucifixion of Christian boys spread from Norwich throughout England: from Gloucester in 1169, to Bury St. Edmunds in 1183, to Winchester in 1192, from Norwich – again – in 1235, to London in 1244, and, finally, to Lincoln in 1255, where the martyr was sainted.[18] As we shall see, there are reports of an anomalous case of plural ritual murder again at Bristol at the end of the 13th century.

The Gloucester case occurred almost a quarter of a century after the child murder of little William at Norwich. Yet, in this case as well, the sources are not sufficiently clear as to the date of the murder of little Harold. John Brompton's *Chronicle* speaks generally of an anonymous boy crucified by Jews near Gloucester in 1160, while the

Peterborough Chronicle, although confirming the crucifixion, places the crime during the days of Passover of the following year.[19] The author of the history of Saint Peter's monastery at Gloucester, seems more precise and better-informed, reporting the killing of a child, named Harold, referring to him as a "glorious martyr in Christ", and stating that the crime was committed in 1168 by Jews, who were said to have thrown the body into the Severn river.[20]

The body of an eight-year old child, Hugh, in the bottom of a well owned by Copino, a local Jew, at Lincoln in the summer of 1255. The judge, John of Lexington, hastened to establish precise analogies with the Norwich murder a century before. The victim had been abducted by Jews, tortured and crucified, exactly as in little William's case. In those days, the great affluence of foreign Jews into the city of Norwich, of modest size, seemed to confirm that something big was in the works, and that the link with Hugh's disappearance and killing was something more than a mere working hypothesis. The marriage of Rabbi Benedict (Berechyah)'s daughter, held there at the time, did not appear to deserve serious consideration by anyone wishing to demonstrate any other theory. But it was necessary to call upon the principal defendant, Copino, who, rather than respond to the accusations, was to confirm them.

The Jew, under torture, "sang" quickly, according to the pre-established script, confessing that the Jews of the Kingdom were accustomed to crucify cruelly a Christian child in contempt of the passion of Christ every year.

This year, it was the city of Lincoln's turn to be selected as the theatre of the sacred and macabre ceremony, and the child Hugh was simply the victim of bad luck in becoming the innocent martyr of Jewish depravity. Popular devotion thus acquired another saint.[21] Of the more than one hundred persons involved in the religious crime, about twenty were executed after summary trial. All the others were imprisoned in the Tower of London. All had their property confiscated, which in some cases amounted to huge fortunes, forfeit to the treasury of King Henry III. At the end of the 14th century, Chaucer, in his *Canterbury Tales*, was able to draw inspiration from the crime at Lincoln, describing the re-emergence, from a well, of another child, who, like Hugh the Saint, had been sacrificed by the infamous followers of the Jewish sect.[22]

The case of Adam, considered the victim of a ritual homicide occurring at Bristol at the end of the 13th century, provides us with a true and proper serial killer, the Jew Samuel, who, "in the days of King Henry, father of the other King Henry", is said to have killed three

Christian children in one year. Thereafter, with the collaboration of his wife and son, he is said to have gone on to kidnap another child, named Adam, who, tortured, mutilated (perhaps subjected to circumcision) and crucified, is said finally to have been skewered on a spit like a lamb and roasted over a flame. Samuel's wife and son are said to have repented, expressing the intention to bathe in the baptismal waters, but at this point the perfidious and criminal Jew is said to have killed them both as well.[23] As we see, sometimes the popular psychosis of ritual murder caused persons caught up in irrational fears to mistake one thing for another. And this regardless of the fact that perhaps these fears could have a some correspondence to actual crimes committed by individuals deranged by phobias and psychoses of a religious nature, transferred to the plane of action.

A few years after the crimes at Norwich and Gloucester, ritual murders made their appearance in grand style in France as well. These crimes, at least in the cases we know about, involved so-called "child crucifixions", which, once discovered and made public, led to the massacre of entire Jewish communities. It is thus said to have happened that, during the reign of Louis VII, the Jews of Joinville and Pentoise crucified a child named Richard in 1179, who then became the object of popular devotion and was buried in Paris.[24] When Philippe II, future King of France, was a child, around 1170, he is said to have listened in terror to contemporary tales told within the palace describing the Jews of Paris intent upon sacrificing a Christian child every year, in contempt of the Christian religion, butchering him in the slums of the city.[25]

The most famous, and most frequently studied, ritual homicide of which Jews in French territory were accused during this period is certainly that reported in 1171 in Blois, a central location on the main rout from Tours to Orleans, on the banks of the Loire. Here, the Jews of that community, suspected of killing a Christian child and then dumping the body in the waters of the Loire, were condemned to death, and thirty two of them met death at the stake after a summary trial.[26] In his memoirs, the rabbi Efraim of Bonn reconstituted that which, according to him, had been the tragic mix-up leading to the accusation of ritual murder brought against the Jews of Blois:

"Towards evening a Jew (who was hurrying along the street), bearing a bundle of hides to the tanner, without noticing that one of the hides had become separated from the others and could be seen protruding from the bundle. The groom's horse (which was being led to drink from the river), seeing the whitened skins in the darkness, began to paw the ground and then reared up, refusing to be led to the water.

The terrified Christian servant immediately returned to his lord's palace and reported: 'Know ye that I stumbled upon a Jew, as he was about to dump the body of a little Christian into the waters of the river' ".[27]

It seems obvious that waterways and tanners are recurrent elements in many supposed ritual child murder stories, and probably for good reason; this may be seen in many of the episodes we have already dealt with, from Norwich and Blois to Trent. The waters of rivers furrowing the regions of England and France and the German territories were considered silent accomplices, suggestive of cruel infanticides for religious purposes. In 1199, the upper waterways of the Rhine, near Cologne, were the scene of a presumed ritual murder, which was immediately punished with the usual massacre of all those considered responsible. Some Christians, traveling on a boat going upstream, discovered the lifeless body of a girl lying on the bank in the mists of Buppard. The perpetrators of the crime were soon identified. A short time later, as it happened, a group of Jews were observed on board a barge moving slowly in the same direction, while their other companions controlled its movements by means of ropes fixed to the bank. Their fate was sealed. Captured without hesitation, they were hurled into the turbid waters of the Rhine, where they drowned miserably.[28]

On a previous occasion, in 1187, the Jews of Magonza were accused of a ritual homicide and forced to swear that "they were not accustomed to sacrifice a Christian on the eve of *Pesach*", the Jewish Passover.[29] A few years later, in 1195, it was the turn of the Jews of Spira to be accused of killing a young Christian girl. Justice was soon done. The Jewish district was sacked by an infuriated mob, while the rabbi of the community, Isaac ben Asher, was lynched, together with eight other Jews, and their houses and the synagogue burnt down. As if according to script, once again, the tragedy was concluded on the river banks. The Torah rolls and other Hebraic books, removed from the place of worship, were thrown into the Rhine and disappeared beneath the waves.[30]

Two years afterward, as Jewish chronicles report, "God's rage struck His people when a Jewish madman killed a Christian girl in the city of Neuss, cutting her throat in front of everyone".[31] Popular vengeance was immediate, and did not limit itself to targeting the supposed madman. Another five Jews were in fact accused of complicity in the murder, which was obviously not dismissed as the mere result of the insanity of an individual.

Particular importance has been attributed to the ritual murder of which the Jews of Fulda were accused in Franconia at Christmas 1235.

Based on the report contained in the Annals of Erfurt:

"In this year, on 28 December, 34 Jews of both sexes were killed by the Crusaders because two of them, on the Holy Day of Christmas, had cruelly killed the five sons of a miller who lived outside the city walls. (The Jews) gathered the blood of the victims in waxed bags, and left the area after setting fire to the house. When the truth came to light, and after the Jews themselves had confessed to their guilt, they received the punishment they deserved".[32]

The Annals of Marbach, referring to the same events, explained that the Jews had committed the horrendous crime "to use the blood to cure themselves".[33]

Based on this unusual annotation, some people have identified the crime at Fulda as involving the birth of a new motive, intended to explain and characterize these religious child murders: so-called "ritual cannibalism". If, previous to this time, the Jews had been accused of crucifying Christians, at least during the Passover period, "in contempt of the passion of Christ", without the blood of the victims being attributed any particular significance, starting in Fulda in 1235, the blood presumably consumed by the Jews for ritual, magical or curative purposes, is said to have assumed a decisive and almost exclusive significance. The myth of the crucifixion of the Christian children is said to have arisen from the fertile imagination of Thomas of Monmouth, as a result of the murder of little William of Norwich in 1144. The myth of ritual cannibalism on the other hand, is said to have originated in the Fulda murder in 1235, tendentiously interpreted in this direction by clerical bodies headed by Conrad of Marburg, abbey of the imperial monastery of Fulda.[34] In support of this interpretation, broadly accepted today, people stress that hardly one year afterwards, Emperor Friedrich II created a commission of inquiry to verify whether or not the Jews had really nourished themselves on the blood of Christian children.[35]

To this theory a few objections may be raised, which appear of little importance. Precisely in the motivation adopted upon the creation of the *Annals of Marbach*, it is stated that its members were called upon to investigate "whether the Jews considered the consumption of blood to be necessary *during the Passover period*". We now know that the presumed ritual murder at Fulda was committed during the Christmas period and not at Easter, a sign that the German Emperor, although unaware of these recent facts, was thinking of the supposed ritual murders committed in the localities of Germany on Passover eve, when the ritual use of the blood was presumed, even if unverified.

Secondarily, the allegation that the Jews of Fulda collected their victim's blood "to cure themselves" (*ad suum remedium*) does not necessarily indicate oral ingestion, and, therefore, a form of ritual cannibalism. We have in fact seen that, according to the prosecutors, and sometimes even according to the defendants themselves, the Jews used blood, reduced to powder, to heal wounds, such as the circumcision wound, to staunch hemorrhages of various kinds, and to spread upon the body and face for purposes of exorcism. If these considerations are of any value, then the specific relevance of Fulda as the birthplace of supposed ritual cannibalism should certainly be revised, without prejudice to the fact that the ingestion of blood in the Passover celebrations was thereafter to become an increasingly recurrent and explicit motif in the accusations and trials.

It was Thomas de Cantimpré (1201-1272), who supplied his theological interpretation of the significance of attributing the value placed upon Christian blood by the Jews as the result of some prodigious and infallible medication. According to the friar of the monastery of Cantimpré, in the outskirts of Cambray, the Jews were the heirs of the curse falling upon their ancestors, guilty of crucifying the Redeemer. Jewish blood was irremediably polluted and an inextinguishable source of physical and moral suffering. The only infallible therapy for such horrors and painful infirmities lay in Christian blood, which was transfused into their bodies in order to cleanse them.[36] The confirmation of this unexceptionable truth, Thomas found, as might have been foreseen, in the zealous confessions of a learned Jew, recently purified by the sacred waters of baptism. This Jew is identified by some as the famous convert Nicholas Donin, responsible for the great bonfire of the Talmud in Paris in 1242, and perhaps linked to the anti-Jewish polemics following the ritual homicide at Fulda.[37] Donin is supposed to have informed Thomas that a Jewish wise man, esteemed by all for his prophetical gifts, was said to have bared his soul on his deathbed to confirm that the torments suffered by the Jews in body and soul could find certain remedy only through to the beneficial ingestion of Christian blood.[38] Whether in liquid form or powder, dried or in curdles, fresh or boiled – blood, this magical fluid with the ambiguous and mysterious fascination, made its arrogant presence known through stories of child sacrifice, in the folds of which it lay concealed, perhaps less successfully than often supposed, until then.

Ritual murder accusations became more widespread: from Pforzheim in Baden in 1261, to Bacharach in 1283 and Magonza in the same year, to Troyes in France in 1288. These crimes generally involved child murders, in which the method was not emphasized; at times, they still involved crucifixions, as in the Northampton cases of 1279 (*apud Northamptonam die Crucis adorate puer quidam a Judaeis crucifixus est*) and Prague in 1305, and perhaps that of Chinon, in Thuringia, in 1317. The sellers of Christian children to Jews to enable them to carry out their horrendous sacrifices were generally beggars, both men and women, who had few scruples when it came to earning a few coins; or unscrupulous nannies and wet nurses or unnatural parents. When the market supply was insufficient, the Jews were constrained to take direct action to abduct children for crucifixion, running not inconsiderable risks in such cases. Inquiries and trials generally concluded with the confession and the pitiless condemnation of the defendants, who were at all times considered *a priori* to be guilty. Justice was often administered in a summary manner, in which case massacres and burnings at the stake were inflicted upon the entire Jewish community, such as Munich in 1285, where two hundred Jews were burnt alive in the synagogue, accused by a stinking old woman of bribing her to abduct a boy for them. Another supposed ritual murder was recorded in that same Bavarian city in 1345.[39]

The use of blood by Jews for ritual purposes was explicitly mentioned in many cases, but not always in connection with Passover. The *Klosterchronik* of Zwettl refers, in the year 1293, to a ritual murder accusation brought against the Jewish communities of southern Austria, on the banks of the Danube, and mentions blood as the motive for the crime. "The Jews of Krems had obtained a Christian (boy) from those of Brünn; they therefore killed him in the cruelest manner to obtain his blood".[40] Thus, in the analogous case reported at Ueberlingen in Baden in 1332, the chronicler John of Winterthur revealed that the victim's parents had observed "signs of incisions in the internal organs and veins" of the body.[41]

In the Passover period of 1442, a blood accusation struck the small Jewish community of Lienz in the Val Pusteria, a city located on the confines between Kärnten and the Tyrol. The martyred body of a three-year-old girl named Orsa, a baker's daughter, was found in a canal.

Wounds and punctures observed on the body led people to believe that they had been inflicted to drain the victim's blood. It was therefore foreseeable that popular rumor would immediately conclude that the crime was one of ritual child murder, committed by the enemies of Christ. The Jews, arrested without delay and interrogated with the usual coercive methods, admitted the crime, which is said to have taken place among the wine kegs in the cellar of Samuele's house on Good Friday. The child had been purchased by the Jews from a beggar, a certain Margarita Praitsschedlin, who was arrested and taken to jail; she quickly confessed. The trial was summary. Samuele, the principal defendant accused of ritual murder, was suspended from the wheel and burnt; Giuseppe "the Old Man", the probable spiritual head of the small Jewish community, was hanged; finally, the beggar woman, guilty of the abduction of little Orsa, was burnt on the wheel, together with two former Jewesses, obviously considered accomplices in the crime. These tragic events, however, came to a happy and comforting conclusion; consisting of the baptism of five Jewish girls, four women and one male, to be exact.[42]

The only problem, although of secondary importance, regarding the so-called "Martyrdom of Orsola Poch" is the fact that the report lacks any contemporary documentation. The first document relating to crime at Lienz in Easter of 1442 consists of a posthumous report, drawn up in 1475 at the request of Giovanni Hinderbach, bishop of Trent.[43] We shall therefore have to wait until the beginning of the 18th century to encounter the first hagiographic reports relating to Orsola and her tragic death. Moreover, the attentive reader will not fail to notice the analogies – perhaps not accidental – relating to the involvement of Hinderbach, famous because of the Trent case. The name of the principal defendant in both cases is Samuele; Mosé "the Old Man" of Trent corresponds to Giuseppe "the Old Man" of Lienz; women appear to play a major role in both cases. Finally, Hebraic ritual cannibalism during the Passover period – in this case, committed on the person of an innocent girl – is poorly suited to the stereotype, which insists that the child martyr must be a boy, upon whom circumcision may be practiced during the cruel and homicidal ceremony.

A few years afterwards, in 1458, a murder accusation, probably for ritual purposes, was brought against the Jews of Chambéry in Savoy. On 3 April of that year, during the first night of *Pesach*, two Christian brothers, Leta, 12 years old, and Michel, aged five, were mysteriously killed, after having been seen traversing the Jewish quarter at nightfall. The examination of the bodies indicated that the two children had been savagely beaten and then strangled. Suspicion once again fell on the Jews, who were arrested en masse and tried without any further delay the following May. Nevertheless, precise proofs not having been presented against them during the hearings, the accused were acquitted and released.[44] In any case, it was clear that any child murder, especially if committed during the spring months, most particularly when the body was found near the Jewish quarter, would be automatically attributed to the Jews and linked to their secret Passover rites, drenched with blood.

Several Christian boys, sanctified in the popular devotion and who later became objects of veneration as supposed victims of the Jews over that same period, require separate discussion. We are referring to "Good Werner" of Oberwesel in the Rhineland, Rudolf of Bern, Conrad of Weissensee and Ludwig of Ravensburg.[45] Apart from the last, with regards to whom we know only that in 1429, at the age of 14, he is said to have fallen victim to the horrendous rites of the Jews on the banks of Lake Constance, in all the other cases the blood motif returns in an obsessive manner.

At Oberwesel on the Rhine, a boy named Werner, also fourteen, like Ludwig of Ravensburg, is said to have been tortured to death by the Jews for three days and then thrown into the waters of the river. His body is said to have floated miraculously upriver, against the current, and to have washed ashore at Bacharach, where it began to work miracles, curing the sick and suffering. The tradition, gathered by later hagiographers, reports that "Good Werner" had been hung by the feet, by Jews, and intentionally made to vomit the Host which he had previously swallowed in church; his veins are then said to have been cruelly opened, so that his blood might flow and be collected. In short, the whole tale was an extraordinary, perhaps rather redundant, concentration of accusations, intended to exalt poor Werner's halo of martyrdom, from crucifixion and ritual cannibalism to profanation of the Host.[46] And yet, over the 16th century, "good Werner" became transformed, from a victim of the Jews into the rubicund patron saint of the wine growers of the region extending from the Rhineland to the Jura and Auvergne.[47] The close kinship between blood and wine, constant over the centuries, permitted the holy martyr effectively to protect the Cabernets and Merlots of industrious and zealous French and German growers.

Another saint, Rudolf of Bern, killed in 1294, is said to have been tortured and decapitated in the basement of a palace owned by a rich Jew in the Swiss city of Jöli during the Passover period of that year.[48] The hagiographic reports of the early Eighteenth century state that this Christian victim was crucified and his blood drained off by Jews "intending to practice their damned superstitions".[49] More specifically, the violent death of Conrad, a schoolboy from Weissensee in Thuringia, not far from Erfurth, occurred in 1303 and was attributed to the Jews, according to chroniclers, in relation to the celebration of the Jewish Passover. In observation of the Passover norms prescribed by the cult, the murder of young Conrad, who is said to have become a popular saint in the regions of central Germany, is alleged to have had his veins opened to collect the precious blood.[50]

***

NOTES TO CHAPTER SEVEN

[1] See the text in *The Life and Miracles of St. William of Norwich by Thomas of Monmouth*, Now First Edited from the Unique Manuscript, by A. Jessopp and R.M. James, Cambridge, 1896.

[2] It would be possible to compile an extremely long and extensive bibliography on this topic. See, in particular, the extremely curious monograph by M.D. Anderson, *A Saint at Stake. The Strange Death of William of Norwich, 1144*, London, 1964, and the important works by Langmuir and McCullogh, to which we will return later: G.L. Langmuir, *Thomas of Monmouth, Detector of Ritual Murder*, in "Speculum", LIX (1984), p. 820-846; Id., *Toward a Definition of Antisemitism*, Berkeley – Los Angeles (Calif.) – Oxford, 1990, pp. 209-236; Id., *Historiographic Crucifixion*, in G. Dehan, *Les Juifs en regard de l'histoire. Mélanges en honneur de Bernard Blumenkranz*, Paris, 1985, pp. 109-127; J.M. McCullogh, *Jewish Ritual Murder, William of Norwich, Thomas of Monmouth and the Early Dissemination of the Myth*, in "Speculum", LXXII (1997), pp. 109-127. "We note that it was in England, in the German regions and in those Alpine regions, in which the devotion of the 'child martyrs' was most widespread, always presented as victims of the Jews", (A Vauchez, *La santità nel Medioevo*, Bologna, 1989, p. 104).

[3] "In England [...] various images remain of the child martyr William of Norwich (d. 1144), who was never canonized" (Vauchez, *La santità nel Medioevo*, cit., p. 454).

[4] Theobald's deposition, accompanied by other fragments from the written hagiography of Thomas of Monmouth, is recorded by J.R. Marcus, *The Jew in the Medieval World. A Source Book (315-1791)*, New York, 1974, pp. 121-126.

[5] Cfr. J. Jacobs, *St. William of Norwich*, in "The Jewish Quarterly Review", IX (1897), 748-755.

[6] In this regard, see G. Mentgen, *The Origins of the Blood Libel*, in "Zion", LIX (1994), pp. 341-349 (in Hebrew).

[7] Thomas de Cantimpré, *Bonum universale de apibus*, Douay, Baltazar Belleri, 1627, pp. 303-306. For Thomas's statements relating to the drawing of lots among Jewish communities for candidates to obtain the child who was destined to renew the supply of Christian blood, see H.L. Strack, *The Jew and Human Sacrifice. Human Blood and Jewish Ritual*, 1909, pp. 174-175.

[8] Cfr. A. Molinier, *Enquête sur un meurtre imputé aux Juifs de*

Valréas (1247), in "Le Cabinet Historique", n.s., II (1883), pp. 121-133; Strack, *The Jew and Human Sacrifice*, cit., pp. 179-182, 277-279; Langmuir, *Toward a Definition of Antisemitism*, cit., pp. 290-296.

[9] "Consuetudo est inter Judaeos et ubicunque maxima sit multitudo Judaeorum facere factum simile annuatorum et maxime in partibus Yspaniae, quia ibi est maxima multitudo Judaeorum".

[10] This is the argument set forth by Langmuir, who is often accepted and shared uncritically. "Ever since the ritual murder accusation was first made against the Jews in the Middle Ages, that is, from 1150 at Norwich, to 1235, for almost a century, the Jews of England and northern France were accused of crucifying Christian children, but not of ritual cannibalism (i.e., the consumption of their blood for ritual purposes). Absolutely no accusation of ritual cannibalism was ever made in Germany until the Fulda case in 1235, and when this accusation came to light it was a novelty. It is true that, between 1146 and 1235, the Jews of Germany were accused of killing children of different ages and as a consequence they were assaulted, but there is no evidence of the ritual cannibalism accusation before 1235 at Fulda" (cfr. *Toward a Definition of Antisemitism*, cit., pp. 266-267). On the recent arguments set forth by N. Roth, *Medieval Jewish Civilization*, New York-Lond, 2003, pp. 119-121, 566-570.

[11] Cfr. McCullogh, *Jewish Ritual Murder*, cit., p. 728.

[12] *Annales Herbipolenses*, in "Monumenta Germaniae Historica. Scriptores", XVI Hannover, 1859, p. 3.

[13] Cfr. A.M. Haberman, *Sefer ghezerot Ashkenaz we-Zarft* ("Book of Persecutions in Germany and France"), Jerusalem, 1971, p. 119; Id, *Sefer zechirah. Selichot we-qinot le-Rabbi Efraim b. Ya'akov* ("Book of Memory. Prayers and Elegies of the Rabbi Efraim di Bonn"), Jerusalem, 1970, pp. 22-23.

[14] This is the argument advanced by I.J. Yuval, *"Two Nations in Your Womb". Perceptions of Jews and Christians*, Tel Aviv, 2000, pp. 182-184 (in Hebrew), partially accepted by John McCullogh.

[15] "We read nothing about Jewish blood ritual [...] till right into the thirteenth century. It is mentioned for the first time in 1236 on the occasion of the Fulda case, but then already being generally believed in Germany" (cfr. Strack, *The Jew and Human Sacrifice*, cit., p. 277). As we have seen, Strack's arguments are accepted and taken up by Langmuir (*Toward a Definition of Antisemitism*, cit., pp. 266-267) and more recently by R.C. Stacey, *From Ritual Crucifixion to Host Desecration. Jews and the Body of Christ*, in "Jewish History", XII (1998), pp. 11-28.

[16] Marquardo Susanni, *Tractatus de Judaeis et aliis infidelibus*,

Venice, Comin da Trino, 1558, c. 25rv: "de illo Vuilelme puero in Anglia, qui fuit crucifixus a Judaeis in die Parasceves in Urbe Vormicho [...] quod Judaei degentes Nordovici quendam Christianum puerum furtim captum totum integrum annum enutriverunt, ut adventante Paschate cruci affigerent, qui tanti criminis convicti meritas dederunt poenas".

[17] Cfr. McCullogh, *Jewish Ritual Murder*, cit., pp. 702-703.

[18] Cfr. Strack, *The Jew and Human Sacrifice*, cit., p. 177; J. Trachtenberg, *The Devil and the Jews*, Philadelphia (Pa.), 1961, pp. 123-130, 143-144; Langmuir, *Historiographic Crucifixion*, cit., pp. 113-114; André Vauchez mentions the popular devotion for Herbert of Huntington, presumed victim of the Jews at about 1180 (cfr. Vauchez, *La santità nel Medioevo*, cit., p. 99). On ritual murders in England in general, see C. Holmes, *The Ritual Murder Accusation in Britain*, in "Ethnic and Ritual Studies", IV (1981), pp. 265-288.

[19] Johannes Brompton, *Chronicon*, in *Historiae Anglicanae Scriptores*, London, Jacob Flescher, 1652, vol. X, p. 1050; "anno 1160 [...] regisque Henrici Secundi quidam puer a Judaeis apud Gloverniam crucifixus est". *Chronicon Petroburgense*, by Th. Stapleton, London, 1894, p. 3: "anno 1161 [...] in hoc Pascha quidam puer crucifixus est apud Gloucestriam".

[20] *Historia Monasterii S. Petri Gloucestriae*, by W.H. Hart, London, 1863, in *Rerum Medii Aevi Scriptores*, vol. LIII, t. I, p. 20: "anno 1168 [...] Haraldum puerum [...] gloriosum Christo martirem sine crimine necatum [...] in amnem Sabrinem [Judaei] proiecerant".

[21] Cfr. G.L. Langmuir, *The Knight's Tale of Young Hugh of Lincoln*, in "Speculum", XLVII (1972), pp. 459-482; Vauchez, *La santità nel Medioevo*, cit., p. 99.

[22] Cfr. A.B. Friedmann, *The Prioresss's Tale and Chaucer's Anti-Semitism*, in "Chaucer Review", XIX (1974), pp. 46-54.

[23] Cfr. Stacey, *From Ritual Crucifixion to Host Desecration*, cit., pp. 11-28; C. Cluse, *"Fabula ineptissima". Die Ritualmordlegende um Adam von Bristol*, in "Ashkenas", 5 (1995), pp. 293-330.

[24] "Sanctus Richarus a Judaeis crocifixus fuit". Cfr. Vauchez, *La santità nel Medioevo*, cit., p. 99.

[25] The term used for the killing of the Christian boy by the Jews of Paris is *jugulabant*. Cfr. H.F. Delaborde, *Oeuvres de Rigord et Guillaume le Breton*, Paris, 1882, vol. V, p. 15.

[26] For an extensive bibliography on the ritual murder of Blois, see, among others, Sh. Spiegel, *"In monte Dominus videbitur". The Martyrs of Blois and the Early Accusation of Ritual Murder*, in *Mordecai K. Kaplan Jubilee Volume*, by M. Davis, New York, 1953, pp. 267-287 (in

Hebrew]; Marcus, *The Jew in the Medieval World*, cit., pp. 127-130; R. Chazan, *The Blois Incident of 1171. A Study in Jewish Intercommunal Organization*, in "Proceedings of the American Academy for Jewish Research", XXXVI (1968), in "Jewish History", XII (1998), pp. 29-46; and, lastly, Sh. Shwarzfuchs, *A History of the Jews in Medieval France*, Tel Aviv, 2001, pp. 117-123 (in Hebrew).

[27] Cfr. Haberman, *Sefer ghezerot Ashkenaz we-Zarfat*, cit., pp. 120-124.

[28] Cfr. ibidem, p. 126. On the massacre at Boppard, see Yuval, *"Two Nations in Your Womb"*, cit., p. 192; Roth, *Medieval Jewish Civilization*, cit., p. 568.

[29] Cfr. Haberman, *Sefer ghezerot Ashkenaz we-Zarfat*, cit., p. 161. See also Yuval, *"Two Nations in Your Womb"*, cit., p. 185.

[30] Cfr. Haberman, *Sefer Zechirah*, cit., pp. 42-43; Id. (same author), *Sefer ghezerot Ashkenaz we-Zarfat*, cit., pp. 231-232. On the facts of Spira, see also Yuval, *"Two Nations in Your Womb"*, cit., pp. 185, 192, and in particular, Roth, *Medieval Jewish Civilization*, cit., pp. 568-569.

[31] Cfr. Haberman, *Sefer Zechirah*, cit., p. 40.

[32] *Annales Erpherfurtenses*, in "Monumenta Germaniae Historica. Scriptores", XVI, Hannover, 1859, p. 31.

[33] *Annales Marbacenses*, ibidem, p. 178 ("ut ex eis sanguinem ad suum remedium elicerent").

[34] Hermann L. Strack was the first author to note that the belief in the ritual use of blood by the Jews, although widespread in Germany even beforehand, was mentioned explicitly for the first time in 1255, on the occasion of the Fulda case (cfr. Strack, *The Jew and Human Sacrifice*, cit., pp. 178, 277). Based on this consideration, Langmuir (*Toward a Definition of Antisemitism*, cit., pp. 263-281) maintains that the origin of the motive of that which is called "ritual cannibalism" may be found in connection with the facts of Fulda. Before that time, in all the cases reported, the crimes were said to have involved "ritual crucifixion", without any mention of the blood motif. This thesis seems today generally accepted (see, among others, Mentgen, *The Origins of the Blood Libel*, cit., pp. 341-349; Roth, *Jewish Medieval Civilization*, cit., pp. 119-120).

[35] "Utrum, sicut fama communis habet, Judaei christianum sanguinem in parasceve necessarium habeant". In this regard, see Strack, *The Jew and Human Sacrifice*, cit., pp. 178, 277, and, recently, Sh Simonsohn, *The Apostolic See and the Jews. History, Documents: 1464-1521*, Toronto, 1990, pp. 48-52.

[36] "Quod ex maledictione parentum currat adhuc in filios venam

facinoris per maculam sanguinis, importune fluidam proles impia inexpiabiliter crucietur, quosque se ream sanguinis Christi recognoscat poenitens et sanetur" (Tommaso da Cantimpré, *Bonum universale de apibus*, cit., pp. 304-305). See also Roth's arguments, *Jewish Medieval Culture*, cit., pp. 120-121.

[37] For the identification of Donin with the converted Jew mentioned in Thomas de Cantimpré, see Strack, *The Jew and Human Sacrifice*, cit., p. 175. For a convincing examination of the Hebrew texts placing the French apostate in relation with the anti-Jewish accusations made after the Fulda case, see, in particular, S. Grayzel, *The Church and the Jews in the XIIIth century*, Philadelphia (Pa.), 1933, pp. 339-340, and more recently, J. Schatzmiller, *Did Nicholas Donin Promulgate the Blood Libel?* in *Studies on the History of the People and the Land of Israel* presented in *Azriel Shochet*, 1987, vol. IV, pp. 175-182 (in Hebrew).

[38] "Certissime vos scitote nullo modo sanari vos posse ab illo, quo punimini verecundissimo cruciatu nisi solo sanguine Christiano" (Thomas da Cantimpré, *Bonum unverisale de apibus*, cit., p. 306).

[39] Cfr. Strack, *The Jew and Human Sacrifice*, cit., pp. 169-191; Roth, *Medieval Jewish Civilization*, cit., pp. 568-569.

[40] "Monumenta Germaniae Historica. Scriptores", IX, Hannover, 1848, p. 658.

[41] *Johannes Vitodurani Chronicon*, by G. von Wyss, Zurich, 1856, pp. 106-108.

[42] "Circiter anno quadregesimo secundo, vel tertio proxime elapso, hic in dicto oppido Leontio aliqui Hebraei, in duabus aedibus habitationem habuerint [...] cum illi Judaei dictae puellae (Ursulae) ut ex sequenti eorum inquisitione patet compotes facti, eandem dicto anno, die Parasceves martyrio affecerunt et occiderunt, et postea hic in aqua proiecerunt, ut tam enormem caedem et facinus occultarent [...] quod sanguis eius ex eodem corpusculo elicitus ac effusa fuerit [...] et ita Judaeos omnes sanguis eius ex eodem corpusculo elicitus ac effusus fuerit [...] et ita Judaeos omnes unanimiter fuisse confessos et effatos, quomodo dictam infantem die Parsceves anno praefato enecassent et martyrio affecissent (in cella vinaria)".

[43] See note above. On this document and the 18th century reports of ritual murder of Lienz, see [Benedetto Bonelli], *Dissertazione apologetica sul martirio del beato Simone da Trento nell'anno MCCCCLXXV dagli ebrei ucciso*, Trent, Gianbattista Parone, 1747, pp. 242-246; F. Rohrbacher, *Usula von Lienz: Ein von Juden gemartertes Christenkind*, Brixen, 1905.

[44] Cfr. R. Segre, *The Jews in Piedmont*, Jerusalem, 1986, vol. I, p.

[45] Cfr. Vauchez, *La santità nel Medioevo*, cit., pp. 99-100. In this regard, see, most recently, K.R.Stow's stimulating study, *Jewish Dogs. An Image and Its Interpreters*, Stanford (Calif.), 2006.

[46] Cfr. F.S. Hattler, *Katholischer Kindergarten oder Legende fur Kinder*, Freiburg, 1806. See also Strack's argument, *The Jew and Human Sacrifice*, cit., pp. 184-185; F. Pauly, *Zur Vita des Werner von Oberwesel. Legende und Wirklichtkeit*, in "Archiv für Mittelrheinische Kirchengeschichte", XVI (1964), pp. 94-109; Roth, *Medieval Jewish Civilization*, cit., p. 569.

[47] Cfr. H. de Grèzes, *Saint Vernier (Verny, Werner, Garnier) patron des vignerons en Auvergne, en Bourgogne et en Franche-Comptè*, Clermont-Ferrand, 1889; A. Vauchez, *Antisemitism e canonizzazione populare: San Werner o Vernier (1287), bambino martire e patrono dei vignaioli*, in S. Boesch Gajano and L. Sebastiani, *Culto dei santi, istituzioni e classi sociali in età preindustriale*, L'Aquila-Roma, 1984, pp. 489-508.

[48] Berner-Chronik, by G. Studer, Bern, 1871, p. 29. For the older sources relating to this ritual murder, cfr. Strack, *The Jew and Human Sacrifice*, cit., pp. 186-188.

[49] Cfr. Johann Rudolf von Waldkirch, *Gründliche Einleitung zu der Eydgenössischen Bunds- und Staats-Historie*, Basel, Thurneysen, 1721, vol. I, p. 135; J. Lauffer, *Beschreibung helvetischer Geschichte*, Zurich, Conrad Orell, 1706, vol. III. P. 108.

[50] Cfr. "Monumenta Germaniae Historica. Scriptores", XXV, Hannover, 1896, p. 717; XLII, Hannover, 1921, p. 29.

CHAPTER EIGHT

DISTANT PRECEDENTS AND THE SAGA OF *PURIM*

Ritual murder accusations have been made against the Jews for thousands of years. The murders were sometimes alleged to have been accompanied by ritual cannibalism, but not always. In every case, it is rather improbable that the testimonies which have come down to us from antiquity were known and disseminated in the Middle Ages and could constitute a significant point of reference for later accusations of crucifixion and ritual cannibalism.[1]

As early as the second century before Christ, the almost unknown Greek historian, Damocritus, who probably lived in Alexandria, recorded a violently biased anti-Jewish testimony, at that time referred to under his name in Suida's Greek dictionary. According to Damocritus, the Jews were accustomed to render worship to a golden head of an ass; every seven years, they abducted a foreigner to sacrifice him, tearing the body to pieces.[2]

This horrible rite is said to have taken place probably every seven years in the Temple of Jerusalem, sanctuary of the Jewish religion.

Damocritus's report is evidently intended to stress the barbarism of the Jews, the "haters of mankind", who practiced superstitious and cruel cults. It should nevertheless be noted that the Greek historian made no reference either to any need to collect the victim's blood or other forms of ritual cannibalism.

A report only partly similar to that reported by Damocritus is found in the polemical *Contra Apione*, by Flavius Josephus, quoting the tendentiously anti-Jewish rhetorician, Apione, who lived at Alexandria during the 1st century of the Christian era. According to Apione, Antiocchus Epiphane, entering the Temple of Jerusalem, is said to have been surprised to find a Greek, stretched on a bed and surrounded by exquisite foods and rich dishes. The prisoner's report was extraordinary and horrifying. The Greek said that he had been captured by the Jews and taken to the Temple and concealed from everyone, while they force-fed him on all sorts of foods. At first, it the unusual circumstances in which he found himself did not greatly displease him until the sanctuary attendants revealed the fate waiting in store for him:

he was fated to die, the predestined victim of homicidal Jewish sacrificial practices.

"(The Jews) carry out this (rite) every year, on a pre-established date. They catch a Greek merchant and feed him for a whole year. They later take him into a forest, kill him and sacrifice him according to their religion. They then savor the viscera, and in the moment of sacrificing the Greek, they swear their hatred of all Greeks. They then dump the remains of the carcass into a ditch".[3]

Flavius Josephus reports that the history recounted by Apione was not invented by him, but was, rather, derived from other Greek writers, an indication that its dissemination must have been much more widespread than we are led to imagine based on the two only surviving accounts, i.e., of Damocritus and Apion.[4]

Compared to the first, the second describes a number of variants which are undoubtedly important. The sacrificial ceremony is now annual, and held on a fixed date, even if the account does not specify the Jewish holiday on which it allegedly took place. Furthermore, ritual cannibalism is now stressed in an explicit and brutal manner, even if there is still no mention of any need for human blood, which, as we have seen, is said to have become the preponderant element starting with the Middle Ages. On the other hand, that both Greeks and Romans are alleged to have ended up as a meal for ravenous Jews is shown by the fact that Dio Cassius, writing of their rebellion at Cyrene (115 of the Christian era), hastened to mention, in disgust, that the Jews were accustomed to feasting upon the bodies of Greek and Roman enemies slain in battle. Not contenting themselves with the satisfaction of this alimentary predilection, they painted their bodies with the blood of their enemies and used their intestines as belts.[5]

A more delicate matter than the above seems to relate to a passage in the Talmud (*Ketubot* 102b) which might be interpreted as an indirect confirmation of the phenomenon of ritual murder during an ancient epoch, although we don't know how widespread or how widely approved it may have been. The passage concerns a so-called "outside" *baraita*, or *mishnah*, i.e., one not incorporated into the codified and canonical text of the *mishnah* (dating back approximately to the third century A.D.) – which seems to be one of the oldest – and may therefore be traced back to Palestine at the time of the second Temple.

"A man is killed, leaving a son of a tender age in the care of his mother. When the father's heirs approach and say, 'Let him grow up with us', and the mother says 'Let him grow up with me', he (the boy) should be left with the mother, and should not be entrusted to the care of anyone entitled to inherit from him. A case of this kind happened in the past and (the heirs) killed him on Passover Eve (Hebrew: *weshachatuhu 'erev ha-Pesach*)".[6]

We know that the Hebrew verb *shachet* has the meaning of "butcher", "kill", as well as to "immolate", as, for example, as a sacrifice (as for example, Exodus 12:21 "Thou shalt sacrifice the Passover lamb", *we-shachatu ha-pesach*). If in the case in question were merely a matter of a simple murder committed by heirs for profit, the statement that the murder was committed "on Passover Eve" would be quite superfluous. In fact, in support of the law providing that the child should be entrusted to the mother instead of persons entitled to inherit his property, it would have been sufficient merely to state that, in the past, a child had been killed by his heirs. When and how the murder occurred is in fact superfluous, except to remind the reader of a case, which was presumably well known, in which such a child murder, which deserved to be condemned, actually occurred, but only for material and egotistical motives.

At this point, it might be noted that the most ancient Christian authors appeared to make no use of this Talmudic passage in their anti-Jewish polemics, although the passage shows a relationship between the cruel killing of a child and the Jewish Passover, which might have been used by them in support of the ritual murder accusation. But perhaps their failure to do so was due to poor knowledge of Talmudic literature and rabbinical literature in general on the part of Christian polemicists, who were often ignorant of Talmudic and rabbinical language and interpretive categories.[7]

Be that as it may, it is advisable to stress that the reading "They killed (or immolated) him on Passover eve" (*we-shachatuhu 'erev ha-Pesach*), appears in all the manuscript and ancient versions of the *Ketubot* treatise in question, as well as in the first edition of the Talmud, printed at Venice in 1521 by Daniel Bomberg. Later, no doubt for the purpose of defending themselves against the ritual murder accusation brought by those who had, in the meantime, discovered the potential value of the embarrassing passage, the Jewish editors of the Talmud replaced the passage with a more anaemic, less embarrassing reading: "they killed him on New Year's Eve" (*'erev Rosh Ha-Shanah*), or "they killed him the first evening" (*'erev ha-rishon*).[8] The latter version might suggest that the child's heirs got rid of him in a violent way as early as the evening of the day upon which he was entrusted to them, with the obvious intention of getting their hands on the estate as soon as possible.

The editors of the famous Vilna edition of the Talmud (1835) justified their decision to adopt the reading "they killed him the first evening" in a *glossa* to *Ketubot* 102b, in which they rejected the preceding version – but without explicitly mentioning it – containing the reference to "Passover Eve", as the circumstance under which the unhappy child is said to have been cruelly killed. "Whoever preceded us in the Talmud", they stressed, "fell into error and preferred a reading completely torn out of context".[9]

That Christian Europe of the Middle Ages feared the Jews is an established fact. Perhaps the widespread fear that Jews were scheming to abduct children, subjecting them to cruel rituals, even antedates the appearance of stereotypical ritual murder which seems to have originated in the 12th century. As for myself, I believe that serious consideration should be given to the possibility that this fear was largely related to the slave trade, particularly in the 9th and 10th centuries, when the Jewish role in the slave trade appears to have been preponderant.[10]

During this period, Jewish merchants from the cities in the valley of the Rhône, Verdun, Lione, Arles and Narbonne, in addition to Aquisgrana, the capital of the empire in the times of Louis the Pious [Louis I]; and, in Germany, from the centers of the valley of the Rhine, from Worms, Magonza and Magdeburg; in Bavaria and Bohemia, from Regensburg and Prague – were active in the principal markets in which slaves (women, men, eunuchs) were offered for sale, by Jews, sometimes after abducting them from their houses. From Christian Europe the human merchandise was exported to the Islamic lands of Spain, in which there was a lively market. The castration of these slaves, particularly children, raised their prices, and was no doubt a lucrative and profitable practice.[11]

The first testimony relating to the abduction of children by Jewish merchants active in the trade flowing into Arab Spain, comes down to us in a letter from Agobard, archbishop of Lyon in the years 816-840. The French prelate describes the appearance at Lyons of a Christian slave, having escaped from Cordoba, who had been abducted from a Leonese Jewish merchant twenty four years before, when he was a child, to be sold to the Moslems of Spain. His companion in flight was another Christian slave having suffered a similar fate after being abducted six years before by Jewish merchants at Arles. The inhabitants of Lyons confirmed these claims, adding that yet another Christian boy had been abducted by Jews to be sold into slavery that same year. Agobard concludes his report with a comment of a general nature; that these were not considered isolated cases, because, in everyday practice, the Jews continued to procure Christian slaves for themselves and furthermore subjecting them to "infamies such that it would be vile in itself to describe them".[12]

Precisely what kind of abominable "infamies" Agobard is referring to is not clear; but it is possible that he was referring to castration more than to circumcision.[13] Liutprando, bishop of Cremona, in his *Antapodosis*, said to have been written in approximately 958-962, referred to the city of Verdun as the principal market in which Jews castrated young slaves intended for sale to the Moslems of Spain.[14] During this same period, two Arab sources, Ibn Haukal and Ibrahim al Qarawi, also stressed that the majority of their eunuchs originated from France and were sold to the Iberian peninsula by Jewish merchants. Other Arabic writers mentioned Lucerna, a city with a Jewish majority, halfway between Cordoba and Malaga in southern Spain, as another major market, in which the castration of Christian children after reducing them to slavery was practiced on a large scale by the very same people.[15]

Contemporary rabbinical responses provide further confirmation of the role played by Jews in the trade in children and young people, as well as in the profitable transformation of boys into eunuchs. These texts reveal that anyone who engaged in such trade was aware of the risks involved, because any person caught and arrested in possession of castrated slaves in Christian territories was decapitated by order of the local authorities.[16]

Even the famous Natronai, *Gaon* of the rabbinical college of Sura in the mid-9th century was aware of the problems linked to the dangerous trade in young eunuchs.

"Jewish (merchants) entered (into a port or a city), bringing with them slaves and castrated children [Hebrew: *serisim ketannim*]. When the local authorities confiscated them, the Jews corrupted them with money, reducing them to more harmless advisors, and the merchandise was returned, at least in part".[17]

But if one wishes to interpret the significance and scope of the Jewish presence in the slave trade and practice of castration, it is a fact that the fear that Christian children might be abducted and sold was rather widespread and deeply rooted in all Western European countries, particularly, France and Germany, from which these Jews originated and where the greater part of the slave merchants operated. Personalities in the clergy nourished that fear, conferring religious connotations upon it with an anti-Jewish slant, failing to account for the fact that slavery as a trade had not yet gone out of fashion morally and, as such, was broadly tolerated in the economic reality of the period. On the other hand, the abduction and castration of children, often inevitably confused with circumcision, which was no less feared and abhorred, could not fail to insinuate themselves in the collective unconscious mind of Christian Europe, especially the French and German territories, inciting anxiety and fear, probably solidified over time, believed, as a result, to have concretized itself, in a variety of ways and in more or less in the same places, as ritual murder.

In the Hebrew calendar, *Pesach*, Passover, comes one month after the feast of *Purim*, which commemorates the miraculous salvation of the Jewish people in Persia during the reign of King Ahasuerus I (519-465) from the threat of extermination linked to the plotting of the King's perfidious minister, Haman. The Book of Esther, which examines all these explosive matters and exalts the saving function of the Biblical heroine as well as that of Mordechai, Esther's uncle and mentor, concludes with the hanging of Haman and his ten sons, as well as with the beneficial massacre of the enemies of Israel. Leon da Modena in his *Riti*, describes *Purim* in precisely this manner, stressing a carnival-like atmosphere of celebrations and convivial opulence in which restraint and inhibition were dangerously weakened.

"On the 14th of Adar, which is March, is the festival of *Purim*, in memory of everything we read in the Book of Esther, which saved the people of Israel from being exterminated through the machinations of Haman, and he and his sons were hanged [...]. After the ordinary orations, with remembrance only of the escape which occurred at the hour of death, we read the entire History or Book of Esther, written in bulk, on parchment, like the *Panteuch*, and which we call *meghillah*, i.e., volume. And some hearing Haman's name mentioned, pound on the tables as a sign to curse him [...] They make much rejoicing festivities and banquets [...] an effort is made to serve the most sumptuous meal possible and eat and drink more than usual, after which friends go out to visit each other, with receptions, festivities and revelry".[18]

For a number of reasons, not least that of its not infrequent proximity to Holy Week, *Purim*, also called the "festival of the lots", came, in time, to acquire openly anti-Christian connotations and the related celebrations became openly suggestive in this sense, both in form and substance, sometimes audaciously and openly. Haman, equated with that other Biblical arch-enemy of the Jews, Amalek (Deut. 25: 17-19), whose memory was to be blotted out from the face of the earth, was transformed, over time, into Jesus, the False Messiah, whose impious followers were now threatening the Chosen People with extermination.[19]

Moreover, Haman was killed, hanged, as Jesus was said to have been, and there was no shortage of exegetic material reinforcing this paragon. In the Greek translation of the Septuagint as well as in Flavius Josephus (*Ant. Jud.* XI, 267, 280), Haman's gallows was interpreted as a cross, and the execution of King Ahasuerus's belligerent minister was described, in effect, as a true and proper crucifixion. The equation between Amalek, Haman and Christ was self-evidently obvious. Haman, who, in the Biblical text is referred to as *talui*, "the hanged one", was confused with Him who, in all anti-Christian Hebraic texts, was the *Talui* by antonomasia [the replacement of a proper name by an epithet], i.e., the crucified Christ.[20]

The sensational trial of the most prominent members of the Ashkenazi communities of northern Italy accused of vilifying the Christian religion was held in Milan in the spring of 1488. In reply to inquisitors demanding the name used by Jews with reference to Jesus of Nazareth, Salomone da Como, one of the accused, answered unhesitatingly: "Among ourselves we call him 'Ossoays' ('that man', from the Hebrew *oto' ha-ish*, according to the German pronunciation), or *Talui* ('the hanged one', 'the crucified one'), while, when speaking to Christians, we always refer to him as 'Christ' ".[21] It is not surprising that a text by 4th century writer Evagrius describes the Jew Simone, in an argument with a Christian, Theophilus, should have equated "the cursed and despised Passion of Christ" with Haman's "crucifixion".[22]

According to the great English anthropologist James George Frazer, Christ died while playing the role of Haman (the dying god) in a drama of *Purim* in which (Jesus) Barabbas, the double of Jesus of Nazareth, played the part of Mordechai (the god that resurges). In the model of the god that dies and is reborn – which is common in the Near East – Haman is said to have played the part of death and Mordechai that of life, while the celebration of *Purim* is said to constitute the Hebraic ritual of death and resurrection. Based on this consideration, one might hypothesize that, in the past, the Jews, at the culmination of the festival, might have been accustomed to putting a man to death in flesh and blood reality, and that Jesus was crucified in this context, playing the role of Ahasuerus's tragic minister, the arch-enemy of Israel.[23]

There is no shortage of testimonies of the celebration of rituals, within the framework of the carnival of *Purim*, intended to vilify and outrage the image of Haman, reconstituted in the semblance of Christ hanging from the cross. First, the emperor Honorius (384-423) and, in his footsteps, Theodosius (401-450), prohibited the Jews from the provinces of the Empire from setting fire to effigies of Haman crucified in contempt of the Christian religion. Probably to be associated with the preceding prohibitions is the report, mentioned by the late chronicler

Agapius [10th century] and dating back to 404-407 A.D., during the reign of Theodosius II [Flavius Theodosius, Roman Emperor of the East, 401-450 A.D.], that certain Jews of Alexandria, forced to submit to baptism, are said to have rebelled, giving rise to a sensational protest, stating that, in their eyes, such a ceremony possessed the fascination of a certain originality. They are said to have taken an image of the crucified Christ, heaping insults upon the Christians, mocking them with the words: "This is our Messiah?".[24] It is not impossible that the episode formed part of the framework of the Hebraic *Purim* celebrations.

Before 1027, at Byzantium [Constantinople, now Istanbul], baptized Jews were required to curse their ex-fellow-Jews "who celebrated the festival of Mordechai, crucifying Haman on a beam of wood, in the form of a cross, and then setting fire to it, accompanying the vile rite with a torrent of imprecations directed at those faithful to Christ". Again, in the very early 13th century, Arnol, prior of the monastery at Lübeck, censured the wickedness of the Jews in bitter terms "in crucifying the figure of the Redeemer every year, making him the object of shameless ridicule".[25]

Even the Hebrew texts do not seem to be sparing on information in this regard. The Talmudic dictionary *Arukh*, consisting of the rabbi Natan b. Yehiel of Rome in the second half of the 11th century, contains reports that the Jews of Babylon were accustomed to celebrate the festival of *Purim* in a particular way.

"It is the custom among the Jews of Babylon and the rest of the entire world for the boys to make effigies shaped like Haman and hang them on the roofs of their houses for four or five days (before the festival). In the days of *Purim*, they prepare a phallus and throw it among these images, while they stand around singing songs".[26]

The above mentioned rites were culinary, even symbolically cannibalistic in nature. The effigies of Haman-Christ were of sweet pastry, to be destroyed, avidly consumed by youngsters and children during the days of carnival.[27]

During the Middle Ages, the sweet delicacy enjoying absolute primacy in the sumptuous banquets of *Purim* was a typical biscuit, once again bearing the pathetic figure of Haman as a gastronomic butt of ridicule. The so-called "Haman's ears" (*onze' Aman*), presented in a variety of versions according to the various traditions of the Jewish community, gained a position of great importance in the feast of *Purim*. In Italy, they were strips of puff pastry shaped like ass's ears, fried in olive oil and powdered sugar, which quite resembled the Tuscan *cenci* and Roman *frappe* prepared during carnival time. Among Oriental and

North African Jews, the puff pastry was roasted and covered with honey and sesame seeds.[28]

The Italian Ashkenazim did not much care for the overly-Mediterranean taste of these biscuits, which they called *"galahim frit"* in contempt, "fried priests" (literally "people with the tonsure"), confirming the detestable relationship between Haman, Israel's bitter enemy, and the arrogance of Christianity, with its priests. Their version of the "ears" were called *Hamantaschen* or "Haman's pockets", and was more elaborate. These consisted of a large triangle-shaped cake of egg pasta filled with a sweet brownish mixture based on poppy seeds.[29] Nor should we be surprised to find that, even in the relatively recent past, there was no shortage of people in Germany who shared the belief, curious even if not very original, that the Ashkenazi stuffed their *Hamantaschen* with the coagulated blood of Christian boys martyred by them.[30] Modern anti-Semites gather and disseminate this cannibalistic fable today from their university chairs, particularly in the Arab countries, making it the subject of ridiculous pseudo-historical research.[31]

Turning back centuries, however, we must note, following Frazer, that the ritual of *Purim* did not always conclude with the bloodless hanging of a mere effigy of Haman. Sometimes, the "effigy" was a flesh-and-blood Christian, crucified for real, during the wild revelry of the Jewish carnival. One of the available sources in this regard is Socrates Scolasticus, history of the Church in the 5th century, which, from its *Historia Ecclestiastica* (VII, 16), refers to a case occurring in 415 at Inmestar, near Antioch, in Syria.[32] The local Hebrews, in their debaucheries and intemperate revelry to celebrate *Purim*, after getting suitably drunk, according to the prescriptions of the ritual, which provided that they must drink so much wine that they can no longer distinguish Haman from Mordechai:

"...took to deriding the Christians and Christ Himself in their boasting; they ridiculed the cross and anyone trusting in the crucifix, putting the following joke in practice.

"They took a Christian child, tied it to a cross and hanged him. Initially they made him the object of jokes and drollery; then, after a while, they lost control of themselves and mistreated him to such a degree that they killed him."

The report, which makes no mention of miracles occurring at the site of the relics of the martyred child, seems to possess all the indications of truthfulness. Moreover, as we have seen above, there are people who have viewed the immoderate celebrations of *Purim*, accompanied by anti-Christian insults and violence, as the core from which the belief in Jewish ritual homicide of Christian children is thought to have developed during the Middle Ages, as an integral part of a ritual centered around on the festival of *Pesach*, considered the ideal culmination of *Purim*.[33]

The case of Inmestar is not an isolated one. A Jewish source, the memoires of rabbi Efraim of Bonn, takes us to France, to Brie-Compte Robert, in 1191 or 1192.[34] A servant of the Duchess of Champagne was found guilty of the murder of a Jew and was being held in prison for that offense. The other Jews of the village decided to rescue the prisoner in exchange for money and executed him during the festival of *Purim*, hanging him.[35]

"A perfidious Christian killed a Jew in the city of Brie, which is in France. Then the other Jews, his relatives, went to the lord of the region (the Duchess of Champagne), and implored her (to hand over) the murderer, who was a servant of the King of France. They therefore bribed her with their money in order to be able to crucify the killer.[36] And they crucified him on the eve of *Purim*".[37]

The vengeance demanded in a loud voice by the Christians of Brie, headed by Philippe II August, King of France (1165-1223), was not long in coming. The entire adult Jewish population of the city, totaling about eighty persons, were tried and condemned to be burnt at the stake ("wealthy persons, rich and influential, some of them famous rabbis and people of culture, who refused to sully themselves [in the baptismal waters] and to betray the One God, were burnt alive proclaiming the unity of the Creator"). The children, who were Jews and circumcised, were taken en masse to the baptismal font to be made Christians. No festival of *Purim* ever concluded in a more tragic manner for the Jews, overturning and thwarting the saving and hope-giving meaning of the Biblical account of Esther and Mordechai.

The blasphemous parody of the Passion of Christ sometimes had the most tragic consequences. But this obvious fact did not always suffice to cool hot heads and restrain fanatical, agitated minds. The Christians were not too subtle about it, since they certainly didn't need excuses or pretexts to perpetrate indiscriminate massacres of Jews or to plunge Jewish children into the beneficial waters of baptism by force. The spiral of violence, having due regard to the discrepancies between the relative power and size of the two conflicting societies, could not be extinguished. The serpent bit its own tail, leaving its imprint of blood on the sand. Each society was, in a sense, its own victim, but neither noticed.

To give a few examples, on 7 February 1323, a few days before the festival of *Purim*, a Jew in the Duchy of Spoleto was condemned for striking and insulting the cross.[38] On 28 February 1504, precisely coinciding with the festival of *Purim*, a beggar from Bevagna accused the local Jews of the place, transformed into evil spirits, of having cruelly crucified him.[39] It was still in the days of *Purim*, in February 1444, that the Jews of Vigone, in Piedmont, were accused of having pretended to butcher an image of Christ Crucified as a joke;[40] again, it was in the month of February, this time in 1471, that a Jew from Gubbio brought a legal action to "scrape" the image of the Virgin Mary from the outside wall of his house.[41]

Purim was followed by *Pesach*, but the story, during that violent month, was no different, even without any strict need to play cruel and lethal tricks on Christian boys, or to stone Jews and their houses en masse during the "holy hailstorm of stones". On 21 March 1456, a Jew of Lodi entered the cathedral of San Lorenzo at nightfall with a drawn sword, directing himself without hesitation, where he walked straight up to the main altar and proceeded to make log wood and splinters out of the image of Christ Crucified, with the evident intention of chopping it to bits. His fate was sealed. The culprit was lynched on the spot, amidst the rejoicing of a jubilant crowd, and vengeance was wreaked. 21 March 1456 corresponded to the 15th of the Month of Nissan of the Jewish year 5216 and the first day of *Pesach*. The matter was thus described by the commander of Lodi to the Duke of Milan:

"In our dear city of Lodi, on the 21st day, 17 hours, of the present month [March], according to the common reports, a Jew entered the cathedral with sword in hand to cut the crucifix of Christ to pieces, for which offense the whole territory rose up against him and they ran to the Jew's house [...] and killed the above-mentioned Jew and dragged him on the ground".[42]

In the early modern age, the carnival-like festivities of *Purim* finally lost those qualities of aggressiveness and violence which had been characteristic since the early Middle Ages, but never renounced the clearly anti-Christian meaning it possessed according to tradition. Thus wrote Giulio Morosini, known as Shemuel Nahmias at Venice when he was still a Jew, a shrewd former disciple of Leon da Modena:

"During the reading [of the *megillah* of Esther], whenever Haman is named, the boys beat the benches of the synagogue with hammers or sticks with all their might as a sign of excommunication, crying out in a loud voice, *'May his name be blotted out and may the name of the impious rot.'* And they all cried *'Be cursed, Haman, Be blessed, Mordechai, Be blessed Esther, Be cursed Ahasuerus.'* And they continue like that until evening, just as on the morning of the first day, never ceasing to express their justified contempt for Haman and the enemies of Judaism at that time, covertly spreading poison against Christians, under the name of Idolaters [...] they therefore cry out in a loud voice, *'Be Cursed all the Idolaters'* ".[43]

But at an even earlier time, the illustrious jurist Marquardo Susanni, protected by Paolo IV Carafa, the fervent and impassioned founder of the Ghetto of Rome, mentioned the wild hostility of the Jews towards Christianity as well as the peculiar carnival-like characteristics of *Purim*. According to him, "during the feast of Mordechai", the Jews did not hesitate to greet each other by saying, in contemptuous tones:

"May the King of the Christians go down to ruin immediately, the way Haman went down to ruin".[44]

* * *

NOTES TO CHAPTER EIGHT

[1] Cfr. G.L. Langmuir, *Thomas of Monmouth. Detector of Ritual Murder*, in "Speculum", LIX (1984), p. 824.

[2] Cfr. Th. Reinach, *Textes d'auteurs grecs et romains relatifs au Judaisme*, Paris, 1895, p. 121, no. 60.

[3] Josephus, *Contra Apion*, II, 7-1: "et hoc illos facere singulis annis quodam tempore constituito. Et comprehendere quidem Graecum peregrinum, eumque annali tempore saginare et deductum ad quamdam silvam occidere quidem eum hominem, eiusque corpus sacrificare secundum suas solemnitates, et gustare ex eius visceribus, et iusiurandum facere in immolatione Graeci, ut inimicitas contra Graecos haberent, et tunc in quandam foveam reliqua hominis pereuntis abjicere", Cfr. Rheinach, *Textes d'auteurs grecs et romains*, cit., pp. 131-132, no. 63.

[4] For an examination of the story of Damocritus and Apione on the ritual homicides committed by the Jews in the Temple of Jerusalem, see, among others, J. Parkes, *The Conflict of the Church and the Synagogue*, 1934, p. 16; D. Flusser, *The Blood Libel against the Jews According to the Intellectual Perspectives of the Hellenistic Age*, in *Studies on Hellenistic Judaism in Memory of J. Levy*, Jerusalem, 1949, pp. 104-124 (in Hebrew); Id., *Moza 'alilot ha-dam* ("The Origins of the Blood Accusation") in "Manhanaim", CX (1967), pp. 18-21; J.N. Sevenster, *The Roots of Pagan Anti-semitism in the Ancient World*, Leyden, 1975, pp. 140-142.

[5] Cfr. Reinach, *Textes d'auteurs grecs et romains relatifs au Judaisme*, Paris, cit., pp. 196-197, no. 112.

⁶ Thus, the final passage of this *haraita* is translated by rabbi Dovid Kamenetsky, in the recent edition of the Babylonian Talmud, with a version in English (*Talmud Bavli, Schottenstein Edition, Tractae Ketubos, III*, New York, 2000, c. 102b and no. 32): "for it once occurred that a boy was entrusted to those fit to inherit him, and they butchered (or: slew) him on *Pesach* eve".

⁷ "In the Latin translation of extracts from the Talmud contained in Latin manuscript 16558 B.N., which is the principal source of knowledge of rabbinical literature in the Christian world in the 13th century, the *Ketubot* treatise is not explicitly mentioned [...]. It does not contain the passage which interests you (*Ketubot* 102b). I have never found it used in polemics; nevertheless, the link made between *Pesach* might very well have encouraged belief in 'ritual murder'; but the authors of the anti-Jewish accounts on this subject obviously know nothing about Jewish literature. [...]. Among the number of accusations made of ritual murder, I do not recall ever having found an argument based upon this Talmudic passage" [written communication dated 2 August 2001 from Professor Gilbert Dehan, to whom I wish to express my deepest thanks).

⁸ A. Steinzaltz notes, in this regard, that "in some later editions (of the Talmud), the *Rosh Ha-Shanah* (New Year's) version appears instead of *Pesach*, in the fear that this expression might constitute evidence to be used by those who accuse the Jews of ritual murder". (*Talmud Bavli, Ketubot*, Jerusalem, 1988, vol. II, p. 457). And nevertheless, the first writer to use the text of *Ketubot* in this sense seems to be the famous August Rohling, University professor and one of the more caustic Austrian anti-Semitic polemicists, author of *Der Talmudjude* (Munster, 1871). The passage of *Ketubot* 102b was revealed by him and publicized with ill-concealed satisfaction in a brochure entitled *Ein Talmud fur rituelle Schächten*, which saw the light in 1892. Hermann L. Strack replied to him, arguing passionately but only somewhat convincingly, in the fourth edition (London, 1892), of his classic essay on Jews and human ritual sacrifice (*The Jew and Human Sacrifice. Human Blood and Jewish Ritual*, pp. 155-168).

⁹ *Talmud Bavli*, Vilna, Menachem (Mendele) Man e Simcha Zimel, 1835. It should be noted that this edition preceded Rohling's "revelations" by more than half a century, in an act of surprising self-censorship. It is not impossible that the editors of the Vilna Talmud intended to respond to doubt and embarrassment within the Jewish world on the interpretation of this text in the original version, rather than reply to the external attacks which were still long yet to come.

¹⁰ In this regard, see Ch. Verlinden's now famous classic,

L'esclavage dans l'Europe medievale, Brugge, 1955, vol. I, pp. 702-716. For a rather over-simplified interpretation of the role of the Jews in the slave trade, see B. Blumenkranz, *Juifs et Chrétiens dans le monde occidental (430-1096)*, Paris 1960, pp. 18-19, 184-211, to which the same Verlinden replied (*A propos de la place des juifs dans l'économie de l'Europe occidentale au IXème siècles. Agobard de Lyon et l'historiographie arabe*, in *Storia e storiografia. Miscellanea de studi in onore di E. Dupré-Theseider*, Rome, 1974, pp. 21-37).

[11] Cfr. Verlinden, *A propos de la place des juifs*, cit., pp. 32-35.

[12] "Et cum precedens scedula dictata fuisset, supervenit quidam homo fugiens ab Hispanis de Cordoba, qui se dicebat furatum fuisse a quoda Judeo Lugduno ante annos IIti IIIor, parvum adhuc puerum, et venditum. Fugisse autem anno presenti cum alio, qui similiter furatus fuerat ab alio Judeo ante annos sex. Cumque huis, qui Lugdunesis fuerat, notos quereremus et invenirem dictum est a quibusdam et alios ab eodem Judeos furatos, alios vero eptos ac venditos; ab alio quoque Judeo anno presenti alium puerum furatum et venditum; qua hora inventum est plures Christianos a Christianis vendi et comparari a Judeis, perpatrarique ab eis multa infanda que turpia sunt ad scribendum" (*Epistolae Karolini aevi*, in "Monumenta Germaniae Historica", III, Hannover, 1846, p. 185). For an analysis of this text, see, in particular, B. Blumenkrantz, *Les auteurs chrétiens latins au Moyen Age sur les Juifs et le Judaisme*, Paris, 1963, pp. 152-168; Id., *Juifs et Chrétiens dans le monde occidentale*, cit., pp. 191-195; Verlinden, *A propos de la place des juifs*, cit., pp. 21-25.

[13] For a useful discussion of this topic, see Blumenkrantz, *Juifs et Chrétiens dans le monde occidental*, cit., pp. 194-195, no. 142; Id., *Les auteurs chrétiens*, cit., p. 163, no. 53.

[14] "Carzimasium autem greci vocant amputatis virilibus et virga puerum quod Virdunenses mercatores ob immensum lucrum facere et in Hispaniam ducere solent" ["Virgin boys whose genitals have been amputated are referred to by the Greeks as 'eunuchs'. These boys are castrated by merchants at Verdun at an immense profit and are usually taken to Spain"], cit., in Verlinden, *A propos de la place des juifs*, cit., p. 33).

[15] On the Arab sources attesting to the role of Jewish merchants in the eunuch trade, cfr. Verlinden, *L'esclavage dans l'Europe médiévale*, cit., p. 716; Id., *A propos de la place des juifs*, cit., pp. 22.

[16] On the rabbinical responses relating to the trade in castrated young slaves and on the role of Lucena [outside Cordoba] as a center for the castrations, see A. Assaf, *Slavery and the Slave-Trade among the Jews during the Middle Ages* (from the Jewish Sources), in "Zion",

IV (1939), pp. 91-125 (in Hebrew); E. Ashtor, *A History of the Jews in Moslem Spain*, Jerusalem, 1977, vol. I, pp. 186-189 (in Hebrew).

[17] The text of Natronai Gaon is reported in Assaf, *Slavery and the Slave-Trade*, cit., pp. 100-101.

[18] Leon de Modena, *Historia de' riti hebraici*, Venice, Gio. Calleoni, 1638, pp. 80-81.

[19] The first to have linked the rise of the Christian stereotype of ritual murder to the feast of *Purim* and to the hanging-crucifixion of Haman-Jesus was Cecil Roth in his now classic study (C. Roth, *Feast of Purim and the Origins of the Blood Accusations*, in "Speculum", VIII, 1933, pp. 520-526). Recently following in Roth's footsteps have been Elliot Horowitz and Gerd Mentgen, adding further documents attesting to phenomena of anti-Christian violence during the celebration of *Purim* (cfr. E. Horowitz, *And It Was Reversed. Jews and Their Enemies in the Festivities*, in "Zion", LIX, 1994, pp. 129-168, in Hebrew; Id., *The Rite to Be Reckless. On the Perpetration and Interpretation of Purim Violence*, in "Poetics Today", XV, 1994, pp. 9-54; G. Mentgen, *The Origins of the Blood Libel*, in "Zion", LIX, 1994, pp. 341-349; Id., *Über den Ursprung der Ritualmordfabel*, in "Aschkenas", IV, 1994, pp. 405-416). On the *status quaestionis*, see the precise summary of I.J. Yuval, *"Two Nations in Your Womb". Perceptions of Jews and Christians*, Tel Aviv, 2000, pp. 179-181 (in Hebrew), and the recent stimulating monograph of E. Horowitz, *Reckless Rites. Purim and the Legacy of Jewish Violence*, Princeton, (N.J., 2006.

[20] On this subject, see T.C.G. Thornton, *The Crucifixion of Haman and the Scandal of the Cross*, in "Journal of Theological Studies", XXXVII (1986), pp. 419-426; A. Damascelli, *Croce maledizione e redenzione. Un' eco di Purim in Galati 3, 13*, in "Henoch", XXIII (2001), pp. 227-241.

[21] "Quomodo (judaei) vocant Iesum de Nazaret quem adorant christiani? [...] Dicit quod (inter se) vocant Ossoays et Talui et quando locunt cum Christianis vocant Christo" ["How do the Jews speak of those who adore Jesus of Nazareth? [...] [Amongst themselves] they call him Ossays and Talui but when they are speaking to Christians, they call him Christ"] (cfr. An. Antoniazzi Villa, *Un processo contro gli ebrei nella Milano del 1488*, Milan, 1986, p. 111).

[22] The expression used in the text is "maledicta et ludibriosa passio" ["cursed and filthy passion"] (cfr. Damascilli, *Croce, maledizione e redenzione*, cit.).

[23] Cfr. J.G. Frazer, *The Golden Bough*, London, 1913, IX, pp. 359-368, 392-407 (translated as *Il ramo d'oro. Studio sulla magia e la*

religione, Turin, 1991).

[24] Cfr. Parkes, *The Conflict of the Church and the Synagogue*, cit., p. 234.

[25] Cfr. H. Schreckenberg, *Die christlichen "Adversos Judaeos". Texte und ihr literarisches und historisches Umfeld*, Frankfurt am Main – Bern, 1982, p. 543; Mentgen, *The Origins of the Blood Libel*, cit., pp. 341-343. This last essay stresses the link between *Purim*, known as the "feast of the lots", and the date upon which the annual lottery of the Jewish community to establish the location of which to carry out the annual ritual murder (Norwich, Valreas, etc.).

[26] Natan b. Yechiel, *Arukh*, Pesar, G. Soncino, 1517, cc. 162v-163r (s.v. *shwwr*). See also *Shoshanat ha' amaqim. 'Emeq ha-Purim. Ozar minhagin we-hanhagot le-chag Purim* ("Treasure of the Rites and Customs of the Feast of *Purim*"), Jerusalem, 2000, pp. 111-112.

[27] The custom is reported in the ritual scripts of rabbi Chaim Palagi, *Mo'ed le-chol chay* ("A Time Established for Every Living Thing?"), Smyrna, B.Z. Rodit, 1861, c. 243rv.

[28] In this regard, see my *Mangiare alla giudia. La cucina ebraica in Italia dal Renascimento all'età moderna*, Bologna, 2000, pp. 166-167.

[29] Cfr. ibidem, p. 166. On the *Hamantaschen* in particular, see N.S. Doniach, *Purim or the Feast of Esther. An Historical Study*, Philadelphia (Pa.), 1933, p. 103.

[30] The reference occurs in J. Trachtenberg, *The Devil and the Jews*, Philadelphia (Pa.), 1961, p. 154, no. 43.

[31] To give an example, the 13 March 2002 Saudi daily newspaper "Al-Ryad" carried an article on the Jewish feast of *Purim*, authored by a zealous professor at the university named after King Faysal. The historian Umaya Ahmed Al-Jalahama, his article, claimed that in the preparation of the Jewish sweets known as "Haman's ears", Jews must provide themselves with the coagulated blood, in the form of lumps or powder, of a Christian boy, or even a Moslem boy. As we have seen, this addition is as bold as it is unhistorical, which nevertheless seems fully understandable, considering the scope of the essay as established by the author, and the public for whom he was writing.

[32] For a description and evaluation of Socrates' text on the facts of Inmestar, see, among others, Strack, *The Jew and Human Sacrifice*, cit., p. 176; J. Juster, *Les Juifs dans l'Empire romain; leur condition juridique, économique et sociale*, Paris, 1914, vol. II, p. 204; Parkes, *The Conflict of the Church and the Synagogue*, cit., p. 234; Trachtenberg, *The Devil and the Jews*, cit., pp. 127-128; Blumenkranz, *Les auteurs chrétiens*, cit., p 58; M. Simon, *Verus Israel. Etude sur les*

relations entre chrétiens et juifs dans l'Empire romain (135-425), Paris, 1964, p. 160.

[33] The hypothetical derivation of the stereotype of the blood accusation at *Pesach* based on Jewish behavior at *Purim*, maintained by Roth (cfr. Roth, *Feast of Purim*, cit., p. 521; "It would not have been altogether unnatural had the coarser spirits among the Jews themselves introduced into the proceedings a spirit of mockery of the [Christian] religion", and of the many who follow Roth, among them, recently, Mriri Rubin, with reference to the accusation of the desecration of the Host (cfr. M. Rubin, *Gentile Tales. The Narrative Assault on Late Medieval Jews*, New Haven, Conn, 1999, p. 87: "That Jews, roused by festivity and fellowship, may have played about, even played a practical joke on their neighbors and their beliefs is all too believable"), is rejected with disdainful presumption by Langmuir. The affair of ritual murder, in both its variants of the crucifixion and the consumption of blood, is said to have been a brilliant, entirely ecclesiastical and medieval Christian invention. Those historians, in particular, those Jewish historians, attempting to link these accusations with real Jewish behavior, even if misinterpreted, are said to have fallen into error intentionally, for fear of facing Christian historiography openly, which is believed to be incapable of understanding the power of the irrational in the human mind, or, worse, because these historians have become befuddled by the fanciful presumption that the Jews play a role of some weight in history (cfr. Langmuir, *Toward a Definition of Antisemitism*, Berkely – Los Angeles – Oxford, 1990, pp. 209-296: "Whether they were insensitive to the powers of irrationality, reluctant to attack Christian historiography too openly, or concerned to attribute an active role in history to Jews, they were predisposed to believe that something Jews had done – however misinterpreted by Christians – must have been a major cause of the charge [...] exuberant Jewish conduct at *Purim* cannot be used to explain the accusation.").

[34] The village in question is Brie-Compte-Robert in the Isle-de-France, as shown in the works by William C. Jordan and Shim'on Schwarzfuchs, referred to in the note below, and not Bray-sur-Seine, as claimed by the majority of preceding scholars.

[35] The episode is discussed, not only in the works by Roth, Horowitz and Trachtenberg, already cited, but by W.C. Johnson, *The French Monarchy and the Jews. From Philip Augustus to the Last Capetians*, Philadelphia (Pa.), 1989, pp. 36, 270-271; Id., Jews, *Regalian Rights and the Constitution in Medieval France*, in "AJS Review", XXIII (1998), pp. 1-16; Sh. Schwarzfuchs, *A History of the Jews in Medieval France*, Tel Aviv, 2001, pp. 155-156 (in Hebrew).

[36] The text uses here the verb *talah* (*li-tlot, wa-yitlu*), which, as we have seen, may be indifferently translated as "to hang".

[37] The quotation is taken from the *Sefer Zechirah* by Efraim of Bonn. Cfr. A.M. Haberman, *Sefer ghezerot Ashkenaz we-Zarfat* ("Book of Perscutions in Germany and France"), Jerusalem, 1971, p. 128.

[38] Manuele da Visso was accused and condemned "super eo quod dicebatur dixisse et fecisse aliqua illicita de Cruce" (cfr. A. Toaff, *The Jews in Umbria*, I: *1245-1435*, Leyden, 1993, p. 76-77).

[39] "Quod omnia eius brachia et etiam genua sibi dicti spiritus asperuissent et devasstassent cum quibusdam stecchis" (cfr. Toaff, *The Jews in Umbria*. III: *1484-1736*, Leyden, 1994, pp. 1116-1118; Id., *Il vino e la carne*, Bologna, 1989, p. 171-172).

[40] The Jewish defendants were held guilty "de jugulatione Christi in formam crucifixi" (cfr. R. Segre, *Jews in Piedmont*, Jerusalem, 1986, vol. I, pp. 171-172).

[41] Cfr. M. Luzzati, *Ebrei, chiesa locale, principe e popolo. Due episodi di destruzione di immagini sacre alla fine del Quattrocento*, in "Quaderni Storici", XXII (1983), no. 54, pp. 847-877; Toaff, *Il vino e la carne*, cit., pp. 156-158.

[42] Simonsohn, *The Jews in the Duchy of Milan*, Jerusalem, 1982, vol. I, pp. 199-200.

[43] Cfr. Giulio Morosini, *Derekh Emunah, Via della fede mostrata agli ebrei*, Rome, Propaganda Fede, 1683, p. 836.

[44] "Et in festo Mardochai quod adhuc (Judaei) celebrant XV Kalendas martii, ubi conterunt ollas in Synagogis, dicentes: sicut contritus est Aman, sic conteratur velociter regnum Christianorum" ["And during the feast of Mordechai, which the Jews still celebrate on the 15th of March, they smash jars in the synagogue, saying: thus Haman was destroyed, thus may the kingdom of the Christians rapidly be destroyed"] (Marquardo Susanni, *Tractatus de Judaeis et aliis infidelibus*, Venice, Comin da Trino, 1558, cc. 25v-26r).

CHAPTER NINE

SACRIFICE AND CIRCUMCISION: THE SIGNIFICANCE OF *PESACH*

The celebration of the festivals of the Jewish calendar marking the life of the people of Israel from ancient times has assumed primarily the character of historical-ritual repetition and "renewal of memory" (*zikkaron*) of the divine interventions in the history of the nation. In this sense, *Pesach*, the Jewish Passover, is celebrated as a "memorial", *zikkaron*, in the sense of being a ritual representation of the past.[1] More precisely, at *Pesach*, the events linked to slavery in Egypt, the persecutions suffered on the banks of the Nile, the miraculous exodus from the land of oppression, the divine vengeance on the enemies of Israel, and the laborious pathway towards the Promised Land and Redemption, are reviewed and projected into the present day. This is a pathway which has not yet been completed and perfected, pregnant with unknown factors and hazards, the happy outcome of which may be brought nearer by the actions of Man and the miraculous interventions of God in the history of Israel. What is more, the Jewish community, wherever it is located, is able to request the active involvement of the Divinity, intended to hasten the coming of Redemption, moving God through the sight of the sufferings of His Chosen People and impelling Him to act, defend, protect and wreak vengeance.

Blood is a fundamental and indispensable element in all the memorial celebrations of *Pesach*: the blood of the Passover Lamb and the blood of circumcision. In the *Midrash*, this relationship is continually stressed and demonstrated. God, having seen the of Israel in Egypt, bathed with the blood of the Passover lamb, is said to have recalled his Pact with Abraham, signed and sealed with the blood of circumcision. "Thanks to the blood of the Passover lamb and that of circumcision, the children of Israel were saved from Egypt". In fact, the Jews are said to have circumcised themselves for the first time precisely in concomitance with their exodus from the lands of the Pharaoh. And in this regard, adds the *Midrash*, "the blood of the lamb is mixed with that of circumcision".[2]

The German rabbis, for their part, placed particular stress upon the importance of that magnificent and fateful event, stating that the Jews transfused the blood of their circumcision into the same glass into which the blood of the Passover Lamb to be utilized in painting the door-posts of their doorways had been poured, according to God's orders, so that, together, they might become the distinctive symbols of their salvation and redemption. This is why the prophet Ezekiel is said to have twice repeated the wish, "And when I passed by thee, and saw thee polluted in thine own blood, I said unto thee, when thou wast in thy blood, Live; yea, I said unto thee when thou wast in thy blood, Live." (Ezekiel 16:6), intending to refer both to the blood of the Passover lamb and that of circumcision. In the *Midrash*, the German rabbis found the references necessary to establish beyond any doubt the close relationship between blood (of the Passover lamb and that of circumcision) and the final redemption of the people of Israel. "God has said: I have given them two precepts so that, fulfilling them, they may be redeemed, and these are the blood of the Passover lamb and that of circumcision".[3]

In the *Sefer Nizzachon Yashan*, a harsh anonymous anti-Christian polemical publication compiled in Germany at the end of the 13th century, the themes of which are repeated in the liturgical invocations of Rabbi Shelomoh of Worms, the exodus of the people of Israel from Egypt is taken as a pretext to outline a dispute intended to contrast the saving power of the Passover blood and of circumcision to the powers of the cross.

"It is written: 'And ye shall take a bunch of hyssop, and dip it in the blood (of the Passover lamb) that is in the basin, and strike the lintel and the two side posts with the blood that is in the basin' (Ex. 12:22).

"The Christians distance themselves even further from this passage and claim to find a reference to the Cross in it, since it recalls three places (the lintel and the two door-posts). This therefore tells us: It is thanks to the Cross that (your fathers in the exodus from Egypt) gained their salvation.[4]

"One must reply to them by rejecting an interpretation of this kind. In fact, the truth is in these words of God: 'Through the merit of the blood, poured into different occasions, I shall remember you, when I see your houses tinted with blood. This is the blood of circumcision of Abraham, of the blood of the sacrifice of Isaac, when Abraham was about to immolate his son, and of the blood of the Passover lamb'. It is for this reason that the blood returns three times in the verse of the prophet Ezekeiel (16:6). 'And when I passed by thee, and saw thee polluted in thine own blood, I said unto that when thou wast in thine own blood, Live; yea, I said unto thee when thou wast in thy blood, Live' ".[5]

The reference to the sacrifice of Isaac would appear out of place, considering that, in the Biblical account, Abraham did not really immolate his son, as he was prepared to do, but was stopped by the miraculous Divine intervention which stayed his hand, holding the sacrificial knife.

But this conclusion should certainly be revised. The *Midrash* even advances the hypothesis that Abraham really shed Isaac's blood, sacrificing him on the precise spot upon which the Altar of the Temple of Jerusalem was later to be built. The pious patriarch is then believed to have proceeded to reduce the body to ashes, burning it on the pyre which he is said to have previously prepared for that purpose. Only later is God supposed to have rectified Abraham's action, returning Isaac to life.[6] Elsewhere, the analogy between Isaac, who bears the burden of the bundles of wood intended for his own holocaust on Mount Moriyah, and Christ, bent double under the weight of the Cross, is clearly shown.[7] Explaining the verse of Ex. 12:13 ("And I when I see the blood, I will pass over you, and the plague shall not be upon you to destroy you, when I smite the land of Egypt"), the *Midrash* asks us which blood God is to see on the doors of the Children of Israel, and unhesitatingly responds: "God will see the spilt blood of the sacrifice of Isaac". On the other hand, the Jewish month of Nissan, during which the festivity of *Pesach* falls, in the tradition of *Midrash*, is considered the month of Isaac's birth, as well as that of his immolation.[8]

Isaac was sacrificed for the love of God and his blood gushes onto the altar, coloring it red. This is the historical-ritual memory, transfigured and updated, which the Judaism of the German lands, reduced in numbers by the suicides and mass child murders committed during the Crusades "for the sanctification of the Lord's name" wished to preserve, situating it at Passover and in relation to the exodus from Egypt. In one of his elegies, Ephraim of Bonn described not only the ardor and the zeal of Abraham in immolating his son, butchering him on the altar, but also the abnegation of Isaac, happy to serve as the holocaust.[9] After the saintly boy was carried back to life by God himself, Abraham is said to have sought to sacrifice him a second time in an overflowing backwash of fervent faith. It was precisely these elements which, according to the Jews of the Franco-German communities, correlated the prayer for the dead (*zidduk hadin*) with the sacrifice of Isaac.

"The verse 'When He seeth the blood upon the lintel, and on the two side posts, the Lord will pass over the door, and will not suffer the destroyer to come in unto your houses to smite you' (Ex. 12:23) recalls the sacrifice of Isaac, while the verse 'I said unto thee when thou wast in thy blood, Live; yea, I said unto thee when thou wast in thy blood, Live!' (Ez. 16:6) possesses the same numerical value (*ghematryah*) as the name Isaac, Izchak. For this reason, the text of the prayer for the dead, *ziddu, ha-din*, came to include the following wish: 'Through the merit of Him who was sacrificed like a lamb (Isaac), Thou, oh God, lend an ear and act accordingly'. In fact, Isaac, was killed and appeared in the divine presence (*schechinah*). Only after he was already dead did the angel cure him, restoring him to life".[10]

In conclusion, the German Jews, who, during the first crusade in 1096, sacrificed their sons to avoid forced baptism, intending to imitate the sacrifice of Isaac by the hand of Abraham, his father. Deliberately ignoring the Biblical conclusion of the episode, which stressed God's aversion to human sacrifice, they preferred to refer to those texts of the *Midrash* in which Isaac actually met a cruel death on the altar. The German Jews thus conferred new life upon these new texts in search of moral support for the their actions, which appeared unjustifiable and might easily be condemned under the terms of ritual law (*halakhah*).[11]

The Biblical account of Jeptha was generally interpreted in this sense as well. The exegetic tradition of the *Midrash* has no hesitation of any kind in stating that the brave judge of Israel who solemnly promised to sacrifice the first creature he met upon victorious return from the battle against the Ammonites (Judges 11:31), actually kept his vow, sacrificing on the altar his only daughter, who ran out to celebrate the happy outcome of the epic battle with him (Judges 11:35).[12] Nor did the Medieval exegetics of the German territories show any kind of embarrassment in dealing with this problematical tale, since they were all intent on minimizing the seriousness of the action of this Jewish leader from Galahad.[13] It is, however, a fact that, while reference to the sacrifice of Isaac is frequently made, heavily charged with significance in the historical-ritual memory of Ashkenazi Judaism, that of Jeptha's daughter never rose to the rank of moral precedent of reference.

As we have said, the memorial celebration of *Pesach* was indissolubly linked with the sacrifice of the lamb and the blood of circumcision.

The latter arose as a symbol of the pact between God and the people of Israel, signed in the flesh of Abraham, while the blood of the Passover lamb was the emblem of salvation and redemption. As Yerushalmi notes, the Passover dinner or *Seder* has always constituted the exercise of memory par excellence of the Jewish community, wherever it existed.

"Here, during the meal around the family dining table, ritual, liturgical and culinary elements were orchestrated in such a way as to transmit the most vital sense of the past from one generation to another. The entire *Seder* is the symbolic staging of an historically founded scenario, divided into three main sections, corresponding to the structure of the *Haggadah* (the account of the stories of *Pesach* and about *Pesach*), which are to be read aloud: slavery, liberation, final Redemption. [...] words and gestures which are intended to awaken, not simply memory, but a harmonious merging of the past and present. Memory is no longer something to be contemplated from afar, but represents a true and proper representation and updating".[14]

The wine drunk during the *Seder* symbolizes the blood of the Passover lamb and the circumcision, and it is not therefore surprising that the Palestinian Talmud associates the four glasses of wine, which absolutely must be drunk during the *Seder*, with the four phases of Redemption. What is more, the text presents the *charoset*, the fruit preserve kneaded with the wine, intended to bring to mind the past, as a "blood memorial" of the clay and mortar used by the Jews when engaged in slave labor during their long captivity in the land of the Pharaohs.[15]

If the blood of the Passover lamb was distilled from a sacrifice, so, in a certain sense, is the blood of circumcision. The *Midrash* states that "a drop of the blood (of circumcision) is as pleasing to the Holy One – may His name be blessed – as that of sacrifices".[16] But it was the rabbis and the medieval exegetics, particularly, those of the Franco-German territories, who developed and broadened this concept. The Provençal Aharon di Lunel (13th century) did not hesitate to affirm that "He who offers his own son for circumcision is similar to the priest who presents the farinaceous offering and sacrifices a libation on the altar". His contemporary, Bechayah b. Asher of Zaragoza, a famous moralist, also stressed the close relationship between sacrifice and circumcision: "The precept of circumcision is equivalent to a sacrifice, because a man offers the fruit of his loins to the blessed God for the purpose of fulfilling His command (to circumcise the son); and, just as sacrificial blood is used for expiation, thus the blood of circumcision heals wounds [...] It is, in fact, thanks to this obligation, that God promised Israel salvation from Gehenna".[17]

Even more explicit is Yaakov Ha-Gozer ("the Cutter") who lived in the 13th century in Germany, in his essay on the rite of circumcision.

"Come and consider how pleasing is the precept of circumcision before the Holy One, may His name be blessed. In fact, every Jew who sacrifices by means of circumcision in the morning is considered as if he had presented the daily holocaust of the morning. Before God, the blood of circumcision is as valuable as the sacrifice of the lamb on the altar every day: one in the morning and the other in the evening, and his son is perfect and immaculate like the lamb of one year".[18]

Circumcision is therefore considered equal to the sacrifice and the blood poured out during this holy act of surgery thus came to assume the same value as the uncorrupted blood of the perfect and innocent lamb, butchered on the altar and offered to God. This sacrifice was at the same time individual and collective, because, as Bechayeh b. Asher observed, it was considered capable of providing automatic and infallible salvation from the torments of *gehenna* [hell], regardless of the conduct of the individual and the community. It was a kind of sacramental mystery of certain efficacy and proven power.[19]

In this sense, circumcision came, with time, to assume the character of an apotropaic [warding off evil] and exorcistic rite. The blood of the circumcised child and the providential cutting of the foreskin provided protection and salvation, as taught in the Biblical account – which is otherwise short on detail – of Moses, mortally assailed by God and miraculously saved by virtue of his own circumcision and that of his son.

This was said to have been performed immediately, although a bit crudely, by Moses' wife Zipporah. "And it came to pass by the in the inn, that the Lord met him and sought to kill him. Then Zipporah took a sharp stone, and cut off the foreskin of her son, and cast it at his feet, and said, 'Surely a bloody husband art thou to me. So He let him go'; then she said, 'A bloody husband thou art, because of thy circumcision' " (Ex. 4: 24-26).

Circumcision defended and liberated from danger, and the blood shed on that occasion possessed infallible exorcistic significance. The *Gheonim*, heads of the rabbinical academies of Babylon, "circumcised in the water", i.e., they taught that the bloody foreskin was to be thrown into a recipient containing water perfumed with spices and myrtil [a red flower]. The young males present at the ceremony hastened to wash the hands and face in the sweet-smelling fluid as a counter-spell intended to bring good luck and serve as a propitiatory sign of stupendous success in love and numerous and healthy descendants.[20]

In the Middle Ages, particularly, in the German-speaking territories, circumcision came to assume, with particular clarity, the value of an apotropaic and exorcistic rite, which, in the synagogue, was free to express itself without hindrance of any kind against the background of community life. As we have seen, during the ceremony, the blood of the circumcised foreskin was mixed with the wine and tasted by the *mohel* himself, by the child and his mother, and the libation was accompanied by the prophetic wish "Thanks to your blood, you live!" The famous German rabbi Jacob Mulin Segal (1360-1427), known as *Maharil*, who also lived at Treviso for some time, in his weighty handbook of customs in use in the Ashkenazi communities of the valley of the Rhine, reported that it was a widespread custom to pour whatever remained in the cup, together with the wine and the blood of the circumcised child, before the Ark with the rolls of the Law, located in the synagogue. This act was intended to exorcise the exterior dangers hanging over the Jewish world and the tragedies threatening its existence.

In the 17th century, this custom was still in force in the Jewish community of Worms. "Soon after the *mohel* has completed the operation [...] whatever remains of the content of the glass, together with the wine and blood of the circumcised child, is poured onto the steps before the Ark with the rolls of the Law in the synagogue".[21] Among Ashkenazi Jews therefore, on a popular level, the salvation represented by the blood of circumcision was essentially understood, by both the individual and the collective, in a magical sense. That blood was able to provide protection from the constant threat of the Angel of Death, while functioning as an antidote to the ills of this life and serving as a health-giving potion during the rites of passage, charged with unknown dangers.[22]

Another curious testimony in this regard may be found in the writings of the so-called "Cutter", the *mohel* Yaakov Ha-Gozer. The German rabbi described the custom of his Jewish contemporaries (obviously, in the 13th century) of hanging the cloth used by the *mohel* to clean his hands, from the lintel of the entranceway to the synagogue upon completion of the operation.

"Therefore, the cloth used by the *mohel* to clean his hands and mouth, which are full of blood, is placed on the door to the synagogue. The meaning of the custom of hanging the cloth in the entrance to the temple was explained to me by my uncle, rabbi Efraim of Bonn. In effect, our elders told us that the children of Israel left the land of Egypt thanks to the blood of the Passover sacrifice and the blood of circumcision.

"On that occasion, the sons of Israel colored the lintels of their doorways with blood so that the Lord would prevent the Angel of Death from striking their houses and for the purpose of manifesting the miracle. For this reason, the circumcision cloth, stained with blood, is hung in the door of the synagogue to indicate the sign linked to circumcision and to make manifest to all the precept, as is said, 'It shall be a sign between thee and me' ".[23]

The custom of hanging the cloth used by the *mohel* to clean his hands and mouth of blood of the child in the synagogue doorway also appears in the so-called *Machazor Vitry*, written around the 12th century. This ancient French liturgical text in fact states that, in the Ashkenazi Jewish communities, the cloth used by the *mohel* to clean off the blood "shall be hung at the entrance to the synagogue".[24]

Jewish mystical texts also stress the relationship between the blood of the Passover lamb and that of circumcision and the meanings of *Pesach*. The *Zohar*, "the blood of splendor", the classical text of the *Cabbalah* attributed to rabbi Shimon bar Yochai and set in Palestine of the 2nd century of the Christian era, but, in reality, composed in Spain at the end of the 13th century, stresses, in its peculiar language, the centrality of the motif of blood in the ceremonial commemoration of the exodus of the Jews from Egypt.

"The blood of the circumcision corresponds to the divine quality of absolute piety, because the Holy One, may His name be blessed, upon seeing the blood of the circumcision, feels compassion for the world; the blood of the Passover lamb, on the other hand, indicates the divine quality of judgment, because the sacrifice of the Passover is performed with the lamb, which corresponds to the Zodiacal sign of the ram, the god of Egypt [...] therefore, the blood of the circumcision and that of the Passover lamb, which are to be seen on the door, corresponded to the two *sefirot* (the divine attributes) of piety and power (or justice), which had awakened to dominance in the heavens at that moment. In fact, the blood of circumcision represents the divine quality of compassion, while the blood of the Passover lamb represents the qualities of justice and power. Therefore, piety was kindled to pity the children of Israel so that they wouldn't die [...] while justice was kindled to wreak vengeance on the first born of the Egyptians".[25]

For the Cabballah, the blood of circumcision and that of the Passover lamb therefore possessed opposite meanings. The first indicated the piety of God, ready to show compassion towards the Jews and save them from dangers and death. The second, on the other hand, represented the power and severity of Divine justice, which wreaked vengeance on the peoples of Egypt, killing their children. The motif of the blood of the circumcision, capable of protecting the children of Israel, effectively removing the threats to its existence, annulling the instinct of evil and hastening the hour of Redemption, returns, further along in the Zohar, in connection with the memorial of *Pesach*.

"When the Holy One, may His name be blessed, having come down from Egypt to smite the first born, saw the blood of the Passover sacrifice marking the doors (of Israel), and also sees the blood of the pact (of circumcision) and that both are found on the door [...] To drive away the influx of evil spirits he sprinkled it (in those places) using a hyssop branch. In the future, in the hour of Israel's redemption, sublime and complete, the Holy One, may His name be blessed, shall take unto himself the instinct of evil and shall butcher it, thus removing the spirit of impiety from the earth".[26]

For the *Zohar*, God, passing by the doors of the children of Israel, daubed with blood, is not only said to have saved the Jews from the Angel of Death, but He is said to have cured the wounds of their circumcision, collectively performed by the Jews for the first time.

"It is written: 'God smote Israel, he smote it and he cured it' (Is. 19:22), wishing to signify that he smote Egypt and cured the Israelites, i.e., not only that Israel's salvation only occurred simultaneously with the slaying of the first born (of the Egyptians), but that Israel's healing occurred at the same time. If one were to wonder what the children of Israel were to recover from, we shall respond that, after being circumcised, they needed to be healed, and were cured through the appearance of the Divine Presence (*ghilui schechinah*). While the Egyptians were being smitten, at that exact same moment, the children of Israel were being cured of the wound caused by circumcision. In fact, what does the verse: 'And God passed by the door' (Ez. 12:23) mean? [...] the answer is that He passed by the door of the body. But what is the door of the body? And we shall respond: the door of the body is the place of circumcision. We shall conclude by saying that when the Holy One, may His name be blessed, passed by the door (of the children of Israel), in Egypt, they were cured of the wound of circumcision".[27]

The symbolic meaning of the Passover lamb offered in sacrifice is stressed by the *Zohar*, which places it in relationship with a significant, corresponding sacrifice performed in the secret and sublime world of the reality of God. When the children of Israel shall have immolated the Passover lamb, only then shall God in his firmament sacrifice the corresponding Lamb of Evil, responsible for the tragedies of Israel on earth and for the repeated exiles afflicting the Jews throughout history.

"Sayeth the Holy One, may His name be blessed, to the children of Israel: carry out this action below (on earth) and go and take the lamb and prepare it for sacrifice on the 14th of this month [of Nissan]; then I on high (in my heaven) shall destroy his power [...] Observing the precept of the sacrifice of the Passover lamb below (on earth), the children of Israel have caused to be reduced to impotence the slag of evil (*kelippah*) of the lamb on high (in the divine firmament), which is responsible for the four exiles suffered by the children of Israel (in Babylon, in Media, in Greece and in Egypt). Thus it is written: 'I will utterly put out the remembrance of Amalek from generation to generation' (Ex. 17:14), has this significance: You, children of Israel, shall blot out the memory of Amalek below (on earth) through the sacrifice of the Passover lamb, as it is written: 'Thou shalt cancel out the memory of Amalek', and thanks to this your action I shall blot out its memory on high (in my firmament)".[28]

The sacrifice of the Passover lamb therefore came to assume a cosmic significance in the texts of Jewish mysticism. Its blood, poured on the altar and applied to the door-posts of the houses, was intended to impel God to sacrifice the Lamb of Evil in His world, responsible for the successive troubles and misfortunes marking the history of Israel.

The link between the blood of the circumcision and that of the Passover lamb came to assume additional meanings during the Middle Ages, particularly in the German-speaking territories, and no longer alluded merely to the blood by virtue of which sin is expiated. The latter blood came to be added to the blood shed by Jewish martyrs, who offered their own lives and those of their dear ones "to sanctify the name of God" (*'al kiddush ha-Shem*), rejecting the waters of baptism. Thus, the blood of circumcision, that of the Passover lamb, and that of those killed in defense of their own faith became mixed together and confounded, hastening the final redemption of Israel and persuading God to wreak His atrocious vengeance on the children of Edom, the Christians, responsible for the tragedies suffered by the Jewish people. The Jews in Germany who, during the first crusade, sacrificed their own children 'as Abraham sacrificed Isaac his son', were perfectly convinced that their own blood, together with that of the two other sacrifices – circumcision and the Passover lamb – all offered to God in abnegation, would not be lost, but would constitute the powerful fluid from which the well-deserved and predicted revenge and the much-desired Redemption would ferment.[29]

Thus, in a distorted logic borne of suffering and distorted by passion, one might even arrive at aberrant analogies which might nevertheless appear justifiable from the point of view of the persons concerned. In the ceremony of the *milah*, a few drops of blood from the circumcised child, poured into wine, possessed the power to transform the wine into blood; therefore, the wine was drunk by the child, his mother and the *mohel* himself, with propitiatory, well-auguring and counter-magical meanings.[30]

By the same logic, during the Passover ceremony of the *Seder*, a few drops of the child's blood, the symbol of Edom (Christianity) and of Egypt, dissolved in the wine, had the power to transform the wine into blood, intended to be drunk and sprinkled onto the table as a sign of vengeance and as a symbol of the curses directed at the enemies of Israel as well as a pressing call to Redemption.

Again, in connection with *Pesach*, vengeance on the children of Edom – Christianity – representing Edom renewed, at Rome, the city of impurity – was also eagerly sought in the Zohar, even if in deliberately convoluted language:

"It is written 'Who is He who comes from Edom, with the garments tinted red from *Bozrah*?' (Is. 63:6). The prophet predicts that the Holy One, may His name be blessed, shall wreak vengeance against Edom, and that the minister who represents the reign of Edom on high (in the celestial firmament) shall be the first to die. The prophet is in fact speaking with the language of ordinary people, observing that when they kill someone, blood squirts upon their garments. For this reason, he refers to them as if they asked: 'Who is he who comes from Edom, with his garments tinted with blood; that is, from the armed city (Hebrew: *bezurah*, a pun, recalling the name *Bozrah* of the verse of Isaiah, which is the great metropolis of Rome)?' This is, therefore, the meaning of that which is written: in the future, the Holy One, may His name be blessed, shall reveal his powers of judgment and of blood in all their obviousness to wreak his vengeance on Edom".[31]

The fact that this fragment of the *Zohar* – which contains not one explicit reference to the memorial of Passover – is found in the section dealing with the exodus of the Jews from Egypt, clearly indicates that blood – linked to the vengeance against Edom, the symbol of arrogant and triumphant Christianity – was a major element in the updated historical-ritual celebration of the *Pesach*.

As we have seen, the preserve of fresh and dry fruit (apples, pears, nuts and almonds), kneaded with the wine, intended to represent the building materials used by the people of Israel during their captivity in Israel, and which was to be eaten and drunk during the Passover dinner of the *Seder*, took the name of *charoset* and was considered a memorial of the blood.[32] In other words, the clay and mortar with which the Jews had built the city on the banks of the Nile were mixed with the blood flowing from their bodies, covered with sores and suffering. It is not, therefore, surprising that the Jews, in their history (yet again, we are speaking of Ashkenazi-origin Jews) have sometimes been accused of murdering Christian children to eat the body and drink the blood in the *charoset* during a repulsive cannibalistic repast.

In 1329, in the Duchy of Savoy, a Jew, Acelino da Tresselve, and a Christian, Jacques d'Aiguebelle, were accused of abducting Christian boys in numerous cities of the region, such as Geneva, Rumilly and Annecy. Several other Jews in the Duchy were involved in the inquiry, including a certain Jocetus (Yoseph) and Aquineto (Izchak). The inquiry finally forced them to confess, at least partially under torture, to sacrificing five children to knead their heads and viscera into the *charoset* (indicated in the confessions under the correct term of *aharace*), which they are then alleged to have been eaten, presumably during the *Seder* dinner. According to their statements, this collective ritual constituted a surrogate Easter sacrifice, and was, as such, able to bring closer the hour of Redemption.[33] In relation to these facts, it might be noted that some of the Jews expelled from England in 1290 in the times of Edward I emigrated to Savoy, reinforcing the Jewish community of the Duchy from a demographic, cultural and religious point of view. Jews from Norwich, Bristol and Lincoln were now to be found at Chambéry, Bourg-en-Bresse and Annecy, bringing with them traditions and stereotypes charged with implications.[34] The accusation of preparing the *charoset* of *Pesach* with the blood of Christian children was repeated with regards to the Jews of Arles in 1453.[35]

Another child murder, that of Savona, the particulars of which were revealed around 1456 to Alfonso de Espina, confessor to the King of Castille, by one of the participants in the cruel ritual, desiring to obtain pardon and baptism, appears to have revolved around the preparation of the *charoset* for the celebration of the *Pesach*.[36] The victim's blood, gathered in the cup ordinarily used to collect the blood of Jewish infants following circumcision, was said to have been poured into the kneaded dough of a pastry consisting of honey, pears, nuts, hazelnuts and other fresh and dried fruits, which all persons present at the ceremony were alleged to have gulped down hastily with an appetite born of religious zeal.[37]

The *charoset*, according to these reports – the reliability of which we would not be inclined to swear upon – was thus transformed into a kind of sacred human black pudding, capable of wonderfully enriching the list of the foods of the Passover dinner and, at the same time, of bringing to the table the exotic savor of Redemption, soon to come. It is therefore plausible that, whoever placed the *charoset* in the forefront of the ritual murder accusations was quite aware of the fact that tradition considered it a memorial of blood. In this sense, it constituted an element perfectly well suited to serve as a basis for arguments alleging that the Jews used the blood of children in their Passover rites.

Circumcision, Passover lamb, sacrifice of Isaac, martyrdom for love of God, memorial of the *charoset*. A true and proper river of blood flowed towards *Pesach*, both on the table of *Seder* and in the pages of the *Haggadah*, the liturgical-convivial celebration of the stories of the exodus from Egypt. But that was not all. In addition, the first and the most characteristic of the ten plagues smiting the lands of the Pharaoh, guilty of culpably holding the Jews captive against their will, was linked to blood, *dam*. Moses and Aronne smote the sacred waters of the beneficial Nile with their staff and, by the will of God, the waters were transformed into venomous serpents (Ex. 7:14-25). These waters, now toxic and no longer potable, gave birth to abandonment, desolation and death.

In popular culture, carried along by a thousand rivulets within the traditions and customs of Jews in the Western word, the troublesome phenomenon of the waters of the rivers and the lakes, basins of water, fountains, and mountain springs capable of transforming themselves without warning into lethal agents, were an unfortunately recurrent theme. At least four times a year, with every change in the season (*tekufah*), for four days, blood was said to be have become mixed with the potable water (i.e., this cannot refer to the waters of the sea, but rather, to rivers, wells and fountains), menacingly jeopardizing the health of men. The uncertainty and dismay which accompanied the moments and the phases of passage, such as the approach of the seasons, once again evoked the obsessive menace of blood. Blood at birth, blood at circumcision, blood in matrimony, blood at death, blood at each change of the seasons. Superficial carelessness or inadvertent negligence was fraught with danger. Once again, the classical references to Isaac's cruel sacrifice (i.e., the sacrifice actually carried out), the transformation of the Nile into blood and Jeptha's tragic vow, became both customary and mandatory, finding well-considered, welcome acceptance in the texts containing the most ancient traditions of Franco-Germanic medieval Judaism, from the *Machazor Vitry* to the late 17th century writings of Chaim Chaike Levi Hurwitz, rabbi of Grodno.[38]

In the *Sefer Abudarham*, a famous liturgical compendium based on the popular traditions of the Sephardic world, both Sephardic, Provençal and Ashkenazim, makes open reference to the dangers threatening man whenever one season replaces another. David Agudarham, rabbi at Seville, who compiled his heavy handbook in 1340, advised, although with some hesitation, against the drinking of water during the days of the change of seasons (*tekufah*), for fear of its contamination by blood.

"I have found it written that one must be careful during any of the four changes of seasons, so as to avoid harm and danger. In the season of Nissan (spring, the Passover period), the waters of Egypt were actually transformed into wine; in the season of *Tamuz* (summer), when God commanded Moses and Aaron to speak to the rock, so that waters might flow forth from it, and they disobeyed, striking the rock instead [Num. 20:8-12], they were punished, and blood flowed forth from the rock [...]; in the season of *Tishri* (autumn), because then Abraham sacrificed his son Isaac and from his knife fell drops of blood, which alone were sufficient to transform all waters; and in the season of *Tevet* (winter), because it was then that the daughter of Jeptha was sacrificed and all the waters became blood [...]. It is for this reason that the Jews, living in the lands of the Occident, completely abstain from drinking water during any change of the seasons".[39]

Even at the end of the 16th century, the Marranos of Bragança, in northern Portugal, on trial before the Inquisition of Coimbra, proved themselves perfectly well aware of the dangers lurking in the night air upon the approach of any change of season. It was then that, according to the ancient traditions of the Judaizers [Christians who believe in circumcision], rays and veins of blood (*rai e veie di sangue*) penetrated the waters of wells and fountains at the setting of the sun. A wonderful and extraordinary phenomenon was observed at this point, because the "waters turned into wine"; and anyone drinking of them would undoubtedly lose his life in the cruelest way. It then became necessary to have recourse to particularly effective and powerful antidotes, identified by tradition in the ceremony of "tempering", which consisted of throwing three glowing-hot coals into the polluted waters; or of "ironing" the same waters by dipping a red-hot horseshoe into them.

Neglecting these precautions was said to cause certain death to anyone drinking those toxic and pestiferous potions. Death was said to fall upon the victim at the first onset of winter, "when his vines lose their last leaf".[40]

Sabato Nacamulli (Naccamù), a Jew of Ancona who later converted to Christianity under the name of Franceso Maria Ferretti, provided a critical summary of the rites relating to the change of seasons (*tekufah*), when the waters were capable of dangerously transforming themselves into deadly blood.

"Four times in the year, they pray that God might, at any moment, [at any] point or minute [of the compass], turn all the waters into blood; they therefore abstained from drinking water at such times, because they firmly believed that if anyone drank the water at that moment, his abdomen would certainly swell, and he would die a few days afterwards; they, therefore, keep bread, a piece of iron, or something else in those waters at such times, and this, in their vanity, they called *tecufà*".[41]

Perhaps linked to these popular beliefs was the custom among relatives in mourning to pour out, onto the ground, all water contained in recipients kept in the house of a dead person. In German-ritual Jewish communities, they actually believed that the Angel of Death intended to immerse his deadly sword in those waters, transforming them into blood, and thus threatening the lives of the relatives and all persons known by the deceased.[42]

In the German-language territories, rivers, lakes, rivers and torrents possessed an ambiguous and disturbing fascination. Many of the presumed ritual murder victims had emerged from those very same waters, cast forth onto the river banks of Saxony by floods and currents.

The muddy waters of the Severn and the Loire, the Rhine and the Danube, the Main and Lake Constance, with their ebb and flow, revealed that which was intended to remain hidden, becoming the fulcrum of many tales awaiting discovery.

Moreover, even the Christian populations of the regions traversed by these waterways were convinced, from ancient times, as Frazer tells us, that the spirit of the rivers and lakes claimed their victims every year, particularly during precise periods, such as the days around Assumption Day.[43] People considered it dangerous to bathe in the waters of the Saale, the Sprea and the Neckar, and even Lake Constance, for fear of becoming involuntary sacrifices to the cruel gods of the river. Thus, on St. Johns' Day, at Cologne, Schaffhausen, Neuburg in Baden, as well as at Fulda and Regensburg in Swabia, as well as in the Swiss valley of Emmenthal, there was wide-spread fear that new victims of the lethal waters of the rivers and lakes would be added to those of previous years, to satisfy the demands of the imperious spirits hovering over the waves. Jews and Christians observed the ebb and flow, fearful and simultaneously bewitched, possessed by an overwhelming fascination. No ritual homicide ever occurred, nor could it occur, at the seaside.

* * *

NOTES TO CHAPTER NINE

[1] In this regard, see A. di Nola, *Antropologia religiosa*, Florence, 1971, pp. 91-144; R. Le Deaut, *La nuit pascale*, Rome, 1963, p. 281.

[2] *Midrash Shemot Rabbah* 17, 3-5, 19, 5; *Ruth Rabbah* 6; *Shir Ha-shirim Rabbah* 1, 35; 5; *Midrash Tanchumah* 55, 4; *Pesiktah de-Rav Kahah* 63, 27.

[3] In this regard, see *Haggadat ha-midrash ha-mevor. Haggadah shel Pesach* by Z. Steinberger, P. Barzel and A.Z. Brillant, Jerusalem,

1998, pp. 65-69; N. Rubin, *The Beginning of Life. Rites of Death, Circumcision and Redemption of the First-Born in the Talmud and Midrash*, Tel Aviv, 1995, pp. 102, ss (in Hebrew); I.G. Marcus, *Circumcision (Jewish)*, in J.R. Strayer, *Dictionary of the Middle Ages*. III: *Cabala-Crimea*, New York, 1983, pp. 401-412; Sh. J.D. Cohen, *Why Aren't Jewish Women Circumcised? Gender and Covenant in Judaism*, Berkely (Calif.), 2005, pp. 16-18.

[4] A useful argument, intended to link the meanings of redemption, implemented through the sign of the blood of the Passover lamb on the doors of the houses of the Jewish people of Egypt, with the saving meaning of the Cross, may be found in Justin Martyr (Trifone, 111).

[5] Cfr. *Sefer Nizzachon Yashan (Nizzahon Vetus). A Book of Jewish-Christian Polemic*, by M. Breuer, Ramat Gan, 1978, p. 50 (in Hebrew). For the same argumentation on the links between the blood of circumcision, that of the sacrifice of Isaac and that of the Passover lamb, see also Shelomoh di Worms, *Siddur* ("Book of Prayers"), Jerusalem, 1972, p. 288.

[6] Cfr. H.E. Adelman, *Sacrifices in the History of Israel*, http://www.achva.ac.il/maof.2000_9.doc (google), pp. 5-6. See also the chapter dedicated to this argument in the thesis presented by my assistant in the Department of Jewish History at Bar-Ilan University, I. Dreyfus, *Blood, Sacrifice and Circumcision among the Jews of the Middle Ages*, Ramat Gan, 2005, pp. 11-16.

[7] In this regard, see J. Parkes, *The Conflict of the Church and the Synagogue*, London, 1934, pp. 116-117. The paragon between Isaac and Jesus was known, among the Fathers of the Church, by Origen: "and his use of it suggests that he knew it was quoted in the synagogue".

[8] *Midrash Mechiltah, Pascha* 7, 11; *Shemot Rabbah* 12, 13, 15, 11.

[9] Cfr. Sh. Spiegel, *Me-haggadot ha-'akedah: piyut 'al shechitat Izchak we-te-chiyato' le-R. Efraim mi-Bonn* ("Of the Story of Sacrifice of Isaac: A poetical composition on the immolation of Isaac and his resurrection, written by the rabbi Efraim of Bonn"), in M. Marx, *Alexander Marx Jubilee Volume*, New York, 1950, pp. 493-497 (in Hebrew). It is significant that Yiddish theater traditionally represents the sacrifice of Isaac as a drama of death and resurrection (cfr. M. Klausner, *The Sources of Drama*, Ramat Gan, 1971, p. 186 (in Hebrew).

[10] *Tosofot ha-shalaem* 22, 14. The term "tossaphists" [rabbinical commentators], the rabbi to whom the establishment of this liturgical custom is attributed, refers to the learned of the Talmudic academies in the Franco-German lands between the 12th and 14th centuries.

[11] On this argument, see, in particular, S. Spiegel, *The Last Trial*, New York, 1967; I.G. Marcus, *From Politics to Martyrdom. Shifting Paradigms in the Hebrew Narratives of the 1096 Crusade Riots*, in "Prooftext", II (1982), pp. 40-52; I.J. Yuval, *"Two Nations in Your Womb". Perceptions of Jews and Christians*, Tel Aviv, 2000, pp. 173-175 (in Hebrew); H. Soloveitchik, *Religious Law and Change. The Medieval Ashkenazic Example*, in "AJS Review", XII (1987), pp. 205-221; Id., *Halakhah, Ermeneutics and Martyrdom in Medieval Ashkenaz*, in "The Jewish Quarterly Review", XCIV (2004), pp. 77-108, 278-299.

[12] *Midrash Beresit Rabbah* 60, 3; *Wairah Rabbah* 37, 4; *Kohelet Rabbah* 10, 15; *Midrash Tanchumah (Bechukkutai)* 7. See also Josephus, *Ant. Jud.* 5, 10.

[13] In this regard, see J. Berman's recent study, *Medieval Monasticism and the Evolution of Jewish Interpretation to the Story of Jepthah's Daughter* in "The Jewish Quarterly Review", XCV (2005), pp. 228-256; E. Baumgarten, *"Remember that Glorious Girl". Jepthah's Daughter in Medieval Jewish Culture*, in "The Jewish Quarterly Review", XCVII (2007).

[14] Cfr. Y.H. Yerushalmi, *Zakhor. Storia ebraica e memoria ebraica*, Parma, 1983, pp. 57-58.

[15] In this regard, see L.A. Hoffmann, *Covenant of Blood. Circumcision and Gender in Rabbinic Judaism*, Chicago (Ill.), pp. 95-135.

[16] *Midrash Tachumah* 57, 6.

[17] Aharon b. Yaakov Ha-Cohen, *Orchot Chayim* ("The Paths of Life"), Berlin, 1902, vol. I, p. 12; Bechayeh b. Asher, *Kad ha-kemach* ("The Amphora of Flour"), Venice, Marco Antonio Giustinian, 1546, s.v. *milah* (circumcision); Id., *Beur 'al ha-Torah* ("Comment on the Penteuch"), Naples, Azriel Ashkenazi Gunzenhauser, 1492, on Genesis 17:24.

[18] Yaakov Ha-Gozer, *Zichron berit ha-rishonim* ("On Circumcision"), by Yaakov Glassberg, Berlin-Cracow, 1892, p. 5.

[19] Cfr. M. Klein, *'Et la-ledet. Mihagim we-masorot be-'edot Israel* ("A Time to Give Birth. Traditional Customs and Uses of the Community of Israel"), Tel Aviv, 2001, pp. 157 ss.; A. Gross, *Taame' mizwat ha-milah. Zeramim we-hashpa' ot historiot biyme' ha'benaym* ("The Motives for the Precept of Circumcision. Historical Currents and Influences in the Middle Ages"), in "Da' at", XXI (1989), pp. 93-96; I.G. Marcus, *Tikse' yaldut. Chanichah we-limmud ba-chevrah ha-yehudit biyme' ha-benaym* ("The Ceremonies of Girlhood. Initiation and Learning in Jewish Society of the Middle Ages"), Jerusalem, 1998,

pp. 20-21, 34; Dreyfus, *Sacrifice and Circumcision*, cit., pp. 11-16; Cohen, *Why Aren't Jewish Women Circumcised?*, cit., pp. 31-32.

[20] Anon, *Sha'are' Zedeq*, cit., c. 22v; Aharon b. Yaakov Ha-Cohen, *Orchot chayim*, cit., pp. 13-14; Yaakov Ha-Gozer, *Zichron berit harishonim*, cit., pp. 14-21; Izchak b. Avraham, *Sefer ha-eshkol. Hilkot milah, yoledot, chole' we' gherim* ("Book of the Precepts of Circumcision, etc."), Halberstadt 1868, p. 131. In this regard, see also H.L. Strack, *The Jew and Human Sacrifice. Human Blood and Jewish Ritual*, London, 1909, pp. 136-137.

[21] Jacob Mulin Segal (*Maharil*), *Sefer ha' ha-minhagim. The Book of Customs*, by Sh. Spitzer, Jerusalem, 1989, pp. 482 ss (in Hebrew); Yuspa Shemesh, *Mihage' Warmaisa* ("The Customs of Worms"), Jerusalem, 1992, vol. II, p. 71. In this regard, see also J. Trachtenberg, *Jewish Magic and Superstition. A Study on Folk Religion*, Philadelphia (Pa.), 1939, pp. 154; 170; Cohen, *Why Aren't Jewish Women Circumcised?*, cit., pp. 32-40.

[22] In this regard see Hoffman, *Covenant of Blood*, cit., pp. 96-135.

[23] Yaakov Ha-Gozer, *Zichron berit-ha-rishonim*, cit., p. 61. See also in this regard S. Goldin, *The Ways of Jewish Martyrdom*, Lod, 2002 (in Hebrew).

[24] *Machazor Vitry*, by H. Horovitz, Jerusalem, 1963, p. 626.

[25] *Zohar* (*parashat Bo*), c. 35b.

[26] Ibidem, c. 41a.

[27] Ibidem., c. 36a.

[28] Ibidem, cc. 39b-40a.

[29] In this regard, see Yuval, *"Two Nations in Your Womb"*, cit., pp. 109-150; *Blood and Sacrifice*, cit., pp. 28-30.

[30] On this point, see in particular Hoffman, *Covenant of Blood*, cit., pp. 96-135.

[31] *Zohar* (*parashat Bo*), c. 36a.

[32] On the meaning and origins of the charoset, understood as "memorial of blood", see in particular Yuval, *"Two Nations in Your Womb"*, cit., pp. 258-264.

[33] On the rather extensive bibliography on ritual murders of 1329 in the Duchy of Savoy, linked to the preparation of the *charoset*, see, among others, Strack, *The Jew and Human Sacrifice*, cit., pp. 190; J. Trachtenberg, *The Devil and the Jews*, Philadelphia (Pa.), 1961, pp. 130 ss; M. Rubin, *Gentile Tales. The Narrative Assault on Late Medieval Jews*, New Haven (Conn.), 1999, p. 108; M. Esposito, *Un procès contre les Juifs de la Savoie en 1329*, in "Revue Historique", XXXIV (1938), pp. 785-801. According to the text of their confessions, the Jews of Savoy had carried out that rite consuming the human

charoset "loco sacrificii" [at the sacrifice location] at *Pesach*, considering that they were approaching Redemption in so doing ("credunt se esse salvatos").

[34] The arrival in Savoy of the English Jews expelled in 1290 is documented by R. Segre, *Testimonianze documentarie degli ebrei negli Stati Sabaudi (1297-1398)*, in "Michael", IV (1976), pp. 296-297. In the lists of Jews in the Dukedom, there appears the name of "Manisseo (Menasheh) anglico, Crestecio (Ghershon) anglico, Elioto (Elahu) anglico, etc." See O. Ramírez's recent study, *Les Juifs et le crédit en Savoie au XIVe siècle*, in R. Bordone, *Credit e società: le fonti, le techniche e gli uomini. Secc. XIV-XVI*, Asti, 2003, pp. 55-68.

[35] In this regard, see R. Ben Shalom, *Un' accusa di sangue ad Arles e la missione francescana ad Avignone nel 1453*, in "Zion", XVIII (1998), pp. 397-399 (in Hebrew).

[36] Alphonsus de Spina, *Fortalitium fidei*, Nuremberg, Anton Koberger, 10 October 1485, cc. 190-192.

[37] Ibidem, c. 192: "Copiosissime vivus sanguis Infantis effundebatur in predicto vase (in quo Judaei consueverunt recipere sanguinem Infantium circumcisorum [...] et deinde fructibus diversis, scilicet pomus, piris, nucibus, avelanis et ceteris, que habere potuerunt, in partes minuitissimas dividentes, sanguinem illius Infantis Christiani in predicto vase miscuerunt et de illa confectione horribili omnes illi Judaei comederunt" [Approximately: "The living blood of the child flowed copiously into the vessel (in which the Jews were accustomed to capture the blood of their circumcised children [...] and then they mixed various fruits, like apples, pears, nuts, hazelnuts, etc., whatever they might have had on hand, cut into extremely fine bits, into the vessel containing the blood of the Christian child and then all the Jews ate of that horrible confection"].

[38] On the tradition of the *tekefot* (literally, "seasons"), rooted among the Jews of the German-speaking lands, above all starting in the years following the First Crusade, see in particular Trachtenberg, *Jewish Magic and Superstition*, cit., pp. 275-258; E. Baumgarten, *Mothers and Children. Jewish Family Life in Medieval Europe*, Princeton (N.J.), 2004, p. 238, no. 130; Ead., *"Remember that Glorious Girl"*, cit. (which examines a broad range of Medieval Ashkenazi sources, in large part manuscript, on this topic).

[39] *Abudarhamha-shalem*, b A.J. Wertheiemer, Jerusalem, 1963, pp. 311-312. On the religious texts of Ashzenazi Judaism, which include the tradition of the *tekufot*, from the *Machazor Vitry* to the manuscript of the work *Kevod ha-chuppah* ("The Honour of the Nuptials") by Chaike Hurwitz, see ibidem, p. 413.

[40] On the testimonies of the Marranos of Bragança relating to the *tekufot*, recorded in the protocols of the Inquisition of Coimbra, see in detail the pioneering study by my excellent student C.D. Stuczynski, *A "Marrano Religion"? The Religious Behaviour of the New Christians of Bragança Convicted by the Coimbra Inquisition in the Sixteenth Century (1541-1605)*, Ramat Gan, Bar-Ilan University, 2005, pp. 32-35 (cum laude doctoral thesis).

[41] Francesco Maria d'Ancona Ferretti, *Le verità della fede christiana svelate alla Sinagoga*, Venice, Carlo Pecora, 1741, pp. 342-343.

[42] Cfr. Y. Bergman, *Ha-foklor ha-yehudi* ("Jewish Folklore"), Jerusalem, 1953, p. 38; Ch. B. Goldberg, *Mourning in Halachah. The Laws and Customs of the Year of Mourning*, New York, 2000, pp. 56-59 ("It is customary that people pour out all the water that is in the house, where the deceased is dying, because the Angel of Death whets his knife on water, and a drop of the blood of death falls in").

[43] Cfr. Frazer, *The Golden Bough*, cit., VII, pp. 26-30.

CHAPTER TEN

BLOOD, LEPROSY AND CHILD MURDER IN THE *HAGGADAH*

Over the course of the first two evenings of *Pesach*, during the ritual dinner of the *Seder*, all persons at the table read the *Haggadah*, a liturgical text containing the account of the exodus of the people of Israel from Egypt based on the Biblical narration and rabbinical materials, together with the benedictions concerning the foods symbolic of the Jewish Passover, among them the unleavened bread (*mazzot*), *charoset*, bitter herb (*maror*), and lamb's foot. The text of the *Haggadah* is often ornamented by miniatures, tables and woodcuts illustrating the salient stages of the history of the Jews in the land of the Pharaohs, as well as to the events linked to their miraculous salvation and the perilous journey undertaken towards the Promised Land. The illustrations were not selected by accident; in addition to reflecting the artistic tastes of the Jews of various epochs and localities, the illustrations were intended to stress and focus upon particular historical or legendary events and underlying messages made indirectly perceptible through these images, while updating their content.[1]

Very rarely do the illustrations distance themselves from the text of the *Haggadah* and refer to legends of the *Midrash* presenting a few similarities with the Passover. One of these passages, which is anomalous insofar as it concerns the matter under discussion, but was surprisingly widespread despite its difficult and delicate nature, is the passage describing the Pharaoh, stricken with leprosy and cured by the blood of Jewish boys, cruelly killed for that very purpose. The *Midrash Rabbah* in fact reports that the Pharaoh was punished with leprosy by God, and that his physicians advised him to cure himself by means of health-giving baths in the blood of Jewish children. One hundred and fifty children of the nation of Israel are said to have been killed every day, from morning till night, to supply the Egyptian despot with the precious medicament. Cries of pain and desperation of the children of Israel, as well as of their fathers and mothers, bereaved of their tender offspring, are said to have risen to high heaven, accompanied by prayers for redeeming vengeance.[2]

The anonymous *Sefer Ha-Yashar*, an ethical text composed in the

13th century, illustrated the tragic legend with a plethora of detail, extending the dimensions of the massacre and transforming it into authentic history.

"When God smote the Pharaoh with the illness, the latter turned to his magicians and wise men so that they might cure him. The latter, so that he might be cured, prescribed that the sores be covered with the blood of children. At this point, the Pharaoh, heeding their counsel, sent his functionaries to the land of Goshen so that they might abduct Jewish children. The order was carried out, and the infants were taken by force from their mother's laps to be presented to the Pharaoh every day, one by one, it was then that his physicians killed them and, with their blood, bathed the sores on his body, repeating the operation for days at a time, so that the number of butchered children reached the number of three hundred seventy five".[3]

The grisly legend of the massacre of the Jewish children sacrificed to restore health to the monarch of Egypt, while it remained almost ignored by Iberian, Italian and Oriental Judaism, met with predictable success and a warm reception among Jews of the Franco-German territories and the Ashkenazi communities of northern Italy. As early as the 11th century, the famous French exegetist Rashi (R. Shelemoh Izchaki) of Troyes reminded his readers that the Pharaoh "contracted leprosy and (to get well) killed the children of Israel to take baths in their blood".[4] This account was followed by later, other well-known rabbis and commentators, such as Yehudah Loeb of Prague and Mordekhai Jaffe of Cracow. The *topos* [traditional theme or motif] was definitively established and was to enjoy a long life in Hebrew and Yiddish.[5]

Finally, and this is hardly surprising, the legend of the Pharaoh bathing in Jewish blood became very closely linked to the ritual of *Pesach*.

The texts of Medieval Ashkenazi Judaism therefore hastened to place this innocent blood in precise relationship with the tradition of mixing the red wine into the dough of the *charoset*, the fruit preserve eaten during the *Seder* dinner as a "memorial of blood".[6] Izchak ben Moshe, 13th century Austrian ritualist, explicitly stated that "The precept to drink wine of a red color (during the *Seder* dinner) is in remembrance of the leprosy said to have struck the Pharaoh, to cure himself of which he immolated suckling infants (of the Jews) and moreover in remembrance of the blood of the Passover lamb and the blood of circumcision".[7]

After the blood of the circumcision, the Passover lamb, the sacrifice of Isaac, the sacrifice of martyrs for the faith, the pure and innocent blood of Jewish children sacrificed to the therapeutic requirements of the enemies of Israel, an open path, safe and promising, led to the ritual celebrations of the *Seder* of the Jewish Passover. But to enable the *topos* to become even more deeply rooted, in all its mysterious and disturbing aspects, in the popular mind, conveying what were in fact alternative messages, accompanied by polemics of burning contemporary interest, the legend needed to be cemented in place through the crude force of images, fantastic and unreal in outward appearance only. These were the origins of the woodcuts of the Jewish victims of perverse infanticide in the illustrations of the *Haggadah*.[8]

The first testimonies to this iconographic topic are handed down to us in five Hebrew manuscripts, all originating in Bavaria and the centers of the Rhineland (Nuremberg in particular) and may be chronologically situated in the second half of the 15th century, i.e., the period of the most widespread dissemination of ritual murder accusations in the German-speaking lands. The miniatures are of crude workmanship, restricted to reproducing, often only suggesting, the essential elements of the tale, which was presumed to be well known to the reader.[9]

A rather more detailed and revealing example of the iconography of the leprous Pharaoh appears in the most famous and oldest *Haggadot* with printed illustrations: that of Prague in 1526 (there is a second edition with important variants, dating back to the end of the century), of Mantua in 1560 (republished in 1568) and Venice in 1609.[10] In the *Haggadah* of Prague, the image is used to illustrate that section of the text which describes the sufferings and laments of the children of Israel forced to perform forced labor in Egypt. The woodcut depicts a scene of amazing crudity.[11] On the right the crowned Pharaoh, curled up in a large tub of wood with staves, is enjoying a bath of fresh blood, poured in by an obliging domestic servant by means of a suitable recipient. On the left and in the center of the panel, some armed thugs, monstrous and cruel, dressed as soldiers and German peasants, are shown massacring innocent children, decapitating them, quartering them, and skewering them like thrushes on pikes and swords. Other children await their tragic fate with resignation. The points of the lances emerge from the open gash of the circumcision wound, while dismembered little bodies litter the ground.

In the so-called "second *Haggadah*" of Prague, the scene is repeated with some redundant and lachrymose added touches. In the center of the picture, a desperate mother, with her breasts exposed, attempts hopelessly to flee, carrying her unhappy infants with her.[12]

The butchery of the preceding edition is further confirmed with an abundance of detail. I believe there can be little doubt that this image is modeled after the Massacre of the Innocents during King Herod's reign in Palestine (Matthew 2:16), as depicted in a woodcut of the *Ultraquist Passional*, published in Prague in 1495. The latter was a Bohemian adaptation of the *Passional Sanctorum* of Jacopo de Voragine (1230-1298), while the scene in question is very similar, in terms of both crudity of detail and persons depicted (with the natural exception of the Pharaoh engaged in these cruel ablutions), to that in the *Haggadah*, published in that same Bohemian city decades later.[13]

In the *Haggadah* of Mantua (1560 and 1568), the image of the Pharaoh's bath is not so crude and is better organized; in some ways, it is rather more interesting and instructive.[14] The woodcut is divided into three sections; the scene takes place in a sumptuous palace, illuminated by large windows and divided by portals and columns. In the right-hand panel, some soldiers and functionaries are taking babes in arms away from anguished mothers, while, in the left-hand panel, the Pharaoh is seen taking his bath of blood in a wooden tub, assisted by two servants. The central section of the scene, the most detailed, depicts the hall of the palace, resembling a place of worship. Here, the children are shown being brought in by soldiers, and delivered to a personage responsible for butchering the victims. These persons butcher them with a knife, placed on an altar standing at the end of the room, causing the blood to gush forth in streams, collected in a suitably prepared vessel.[15] The analogies with the classical iconography relating to ritual murder are surprisingly precise here, and certainly intentional.

The scene of the bath of blood appears with a few major differences in the *Haggadah* of Venice published in 1609.[16] On the left, armed soldiers take children by force from the Jewish mothers, while on the right, a crowned Pharaoh with his pock-marked body, emerges erect from his wooden bathtub. This time, the butchers cut the throats of the children in such a way that the blood flows directly onto the diseased body of the Egyptian monarch, without bothering to collect it in vases or recipients kept ready for the purpose. The important novelty in this scene consists of the fact that the pitiless assassins are shown dressed like Turks, their heads covered with typical turbans. The artist, presumably working at Venice, where the *Haggadah* was printed, obviously considered it preferable, out of justifiable prudence, to associate the authors of this savage crime with Islam and the Koran of Mahomet, with the soldiers of the Great Turk and the unpopular Ottoman Empire, rather than depict them as good Christians subjects of the Serenissima.

But the message of these images is substantially identical, and provides an answer to the question of why Ashkenazi Judaism should have chosen precisely this legend, out of so many in the *Midrash*, as its very own, linking it by force to the rites of the Passover. It is certainly true that the account presupposes the same ambiguous attraction to the mysterious and fascinating curative powers of blood, and children's blood in particular, as did surrounding Christian German society. This attraction and fascination often developed into a true and veritable obsession. Those writers attempting to stress the love-hate relationship (or, more cautiously, a hostility-intimacy relationship) linking Jews and Christians in this context are therefore correct. We refer to those writers who lived side by side in the Alpine valleys and along the river banks furrowing the regions in which German was the mother tongue and the Jews spoke Yiddish.[17]

But that is not all. These images were intended to provide a response, of irrefutable historical obviousness and vivid suggestiveness, to the ritual murder accusation linked with the celebration of the rituals of the *Pesach*. The accusation was therefore turned on its head, or generally subordinated to the crime of child murder for ritual or curative purposes, which was then demoted in the scale of seriousness, as an aberration of which the enemies of the Jews (including the Christians) were also guilty.

Circumcised children of Israel had also been sacrificed by superior order so that their blood might be drained from their bodies in their hour of martyrdom and thus be capable of ensuring Redemption.

One intention of analogous indication emerges in all its obviousness from the illustration accompanying the aggressive invocation against nations refusing to accept the God of Israel (*Shefoch*, "Pour out your wrath against the peoples who do not recognize you..."), a characteristic liturgical formula, with openly anti-Christian meanings, recited after the Passover meal, which we shall dwell upon further along. In this case, the scene contained in the *Haggadah* of Venice of 1609[18] depicts a group of necromancers, dressed as Moors, with their typical oriental turbans, surrounded by crowds of demoniacal, dancing Negroes, while magicians and enchanters attempt to raise the dead on the other hand. The caption, written in rhyme, is significant, and revelatory of the underlying message: "Consumed be the ignorant kingdoms/ which serve demons and believe in necromancy".[19]

Now, the accusation made against the Jews of practicing magic and necromancy, often confused with the practical Cabbalah and assimilated to it, was public knowledge, as was the close relationship, often uncritically presupposed, between necromancy, ritual murder and the magical uses of blood. Even Pope Pius V Ghisleri, when he decided to expel the Jews from the Pontifical State by the bull *Hebraeorum gens* in 1569, making an exception for those of Rome, Ancona and Avignon, accused them of practicing divinatory and magical rites with pernicious and diabolical consequences for Christians.[20] The illustration accompanying the invective against the nations who refused to accept the God of Israel, the Goyim, was intended to turn the accusation around: it was not the Jews who were the necromancers and magicians, the spell-weaving charlatans of prodigious potions, the seductive soothsayers and macabre exorcists, but also, and above all, the other nations and peoples who did not accept the God of the Israelites. In any case, Jews were not the only people who practiced vain and dangerous sciences of this kind; on the contrary, the Jews were in authoritatively good company, together with the Moslems and Christians.

Once again, the iconography of the *Haggadah* implied the emergence, from the narrative and liturgical texts, of every possible debating point useful in analyzing the message of the *Pesach*, prudently camouflaged within a historical framework. Its readers must have understood this.

Another tragedy inflicted upon the children of Israel emerges from the Biblical text of Exodus. The cruel order of the Pharaoh to drown all new-born Jewish males in the Nile so that their people might not multiply (Ex. 1:22) promptly found easily recognizable equivalents in the iconography of the *Haggadah*. In the edition of Prague of 1526, the scene is depicted on a bridge with turreted piers and typically German medieval architecture, like many bridges on the Rhine, the Rhône and the Danube. Here, a few peasants are depicted flinging defenseless infants into the waters below, while a mother, also on the bridge, is depicted as seized with desperation.[21] The broad panel depicting this episode from the *Haggadah* of 1560, shows infants being thrown from the bridge into the waters of the river while a few mothers rush down onto the exposed gravel riverbed in a hopeless attempt to reach the bank and save their children from the rapids, while others give way to despair, raising their arms to Heaven.[22]

The *Haggadah* of Venice of 1609 contained two interesting illustrations of this episode. The first scene depicts the inside of a Jewish home, in which the husband and wife sleep in separate beds to avoid sexual relations, precursor of tragedy: the birth of a son might, in fact, lead to his inevitable killing by the Egyptians. In confirmation of their justifiable concern, the merest glimpse of an exterior scene is depicted, showing a few figures on the river bank, while the waters sweep away the bodies of drowned infants.[23] In the second scene, which takes place in the presence of the Pharaoh, seated on the throne, a few servants on the river bank throw poor nursing infants into the river, torn from their mother's bosom, while the heads of the miserable drowned babes are seen protruding from the raging waters.[24]

The reminder of the problematical relationship between waterways and human sacrifice and the many victims of mysterious child-killings revealed by the ebb and flow of the rivers, propelling the bodies of the victims onto the banks, and the miracles performed by the holy martyrs of ritual murder, [alleged to be] capable of floating upriver, against the current, in a stupendous manner and returning miraculously to the surface, was certainly present, in this case, in both the minds of the person illustrating the images and the readers looking at them, repeatedly, each succeeding year, during the convivial and liturgical *Pesach* celebration. The underlying message was dazzlingly obvious, and often of immediate current interest. The Children of Israel, too, had been martyred, torn from their mothers and thrown into the mysterious and deadly waters of the Nile, the river *par excellence*, the river of paradigmatic significance. The role of the victims and butchers was anything but fixed and established in a clear and definitive manner.

The iconography of the *Haggadah* obviously could not fail to contain a scene depicting the sacrifice of Isaac, who was thus closely connected to the ritual of *Pesach*. In fact, in the *Haggadah* published in Venice of 1609, young Isaac is depicted as down on his knees before the pyre, with his arms folded, as if in silent and resigned prayer, waiting for Abraham, with his knife raised above his body, to carry out the inevitable sacrifice.[25] A similar attitude towards death may be found in a miniature taken from a Jewish code, originating in Germany, and dating back to the third decade of the 15th century.[26] Here, the scene, located in a forested countryside, shows a Jew (probably a rabbi) with a thick head of hair and flowing beard, in patient submission, waiting to be executed. Behind him, the executioner is preparing to strike off his head with his sword. The victim, like Isaac, in the scene of the *Haggadah*, in depicted as down on his knees with his hands joined in prayer, prepared to die "for the sanctification of the name of God".[27]

It is interesting to note that another illustration taken from the same code depicts the same scene, presumably located in the same place, of another young Jew, this time with a thick head of hair but beardless, placed on a wooden table to be tortured by fire. The executioner is at his side and is heating the pincers red-hot.[28] The victim's body is nude and blood gushes forth from the stumps of his legs, which are cut off at the feet, and his arms, which are now without the two hands. More blood flows from the place of circumcision, which the young man hopelessly attempts to hide with the stumps of the hands, indicating that he has been cruelly castrated. Of similar workmanship, certainly cruder than the depiction of the sacrifice of Isaac in the *Haggadah* of Venice, is a woodcut unexpectedly contained in the first edition of the responses of the medieval German ritualist, Asher b. Yechiel, published in 1517.[29] Here, Abraham, with a grim expression and a dark, stiff-brimmed hat pressed down on his head, like a brigand, and wearing a cloak with long fluttering hems, brandishes a huge butcher knife and looms over poor Isaac, prepared to slaughter his son for the love of God. The boy, nude on an enormous stack of wood, appears anything but resigned to his sad fate, raising his legs in a terrified one last hopeless effort at self-defense. The iconography in this case is obviously German, crude and pitiless.[30]

Nor is there any shortage of representations of poor Simon of Trent, of equal crudity, on the Christian side. One little-known woodcut, contemporary with the Trent crime and probably manufactured in Alpine Italy, the poor child, disheveled and stretched out on his side on a crude table, is being pitilessly butchered as if he were a hog – which he actually resembles, right down to his features. Around him, a group of Jews, with sinister, gory faces, with the distinctive sign on their clothing, within the folds of which the image of an abominable sow is visible, appear intent upon cruelly vivisecting him. The butchers are wearing eyeglasses to protect their vision during the cruel operation, protecting the eyes from the victim's spurting blood. The overall image is frankly repulsive, and not at all likely to arouse sentiments of piety and compassion.[31]

It should be noted that, in the concept of the Christianity of the German territories during the Middle Ages, the circumcision of Christ, his crucifixion and the ritual murder, were considered symmetrical agonies.[32]

It should not surprise us that sacred art would assimilate this vision, translated into images. Thus, in one painting depicting the circumcision of Jesus, originating in Salzburg or the central Rhineland and dated 1440, the amputation of the Messiah's foreskin is depicted as an odious and almost lethal surgical operation. Around the Christ child, engaged in a helpless effort to escape the mortal incision, press several bearded and cowled Jews. The *mohel*, his head covered with the ritual mantle (*tallit*), is depicted as a cruel and menacing. Similarly, in an altar painting in the Liebfrauenkirche in Nuremberg, dating back to the mid-16th century and depicting the same subject, the godmothers, with caricature-like Jewish faces, crowd around the poor child with the terrorized face. The Jews wear the ritual mantle, bearing Sybillene writings in the holy language, while the *mohel*, dressed in black, resolute and pitiless, is about to lower the knife on the defenseless body.[33]

An iconography of the circumcision of Jesus of this type may be observed to be similar, in both design and execution, to the representation of the martyrdom of Little Simon of Trent in a painting of the Alto Adige school, dating back to the first half of the 16th century. Here as well, a large group of bearded, big-nosed Jews, with a grim appearance and caricature-like features, crowd around the naked, glorious body of the little martyr, the new Christ, intent on performing their cruel Passover rite on his miserable body.[34] The themes of blood, circumcision, the crucifixion and ritual murder were closely linked in the collective imagination, eagerly reflected in the artistic expressions of the Germanic world of the late Middle Ages, among both Jews and Christians.[35]

* * *

NOTES TO CHAPTER TEN

[1] On the illustrations of the *Haggadah* in the manuscripts and printed editions, there is an exceptionally extensive bibliography. See, among others, C. Roth, *The Illustrated Haggadah*, in "Studies in Bibliography and Booklore", VII (1965), pp. 37-56; B. Narkiss, *Medieval Illuminated Haggadot*, in "Ariel", XIV (1966), pp. 35-40; M. Metzger, *La Haggadah enluminée*, Leyden, 1973; Y.H. Yerushalmi, *Haggadah and History*, Philadelphia (Pa.), 1975.

[2] *Shemot Rabbah*, 1, 34. In this regard, see L. Ginzberg, *The Legends of the Jews*, Philadelphia (Pa.), 1946, vol. II, pp. 296-304.

[3] Anon., *Sefer Ha-Yashar*, Furth, 1768, c. 94a.

[4] Rashi (R. Shelomoh Izchaki di Troyes), *Perush la-Torah* ("Comment on the Pentateuch"), with reference to Esther 2:23.

[5] It should be noted that none of the classical Biblical exegetists of Sephardic Judaism, from Abaham Ibn Izra to Moshe ben Nachman, from Levi ben Gherson to Izchak Arama, to Izachak Abravanel, paid any attention to this legend.

[6] See, in particular, the arguments of I.J. Yuval, *"Two Nations in Your Womb". Perceptions of Jews and Christians*, Tel Aviv, 2000, p. 258-264 (in Hebrew).

[7] Izchak b. Moshe, *Or Zarua*, Zhitomir, 1862, c. 117b. See also M.M. Kasher, *Haggadah Shelemah*, New York, 1961, p. 95.

[8] See, in particular, the excellent and well-documented argument of

D.J. Malkiel, *Infanticide in Passover Iconography*, in "Journal of the Warburg and Courteauld Institutes", LVI (1993), pp. 85-89.

[9] Cfr. ibidem, p. 88-89.

[10] *Haggadah shel Pesach*, Prague, Ghershom Cohen, 1526; *Haggadah shel Pesach*, Mantua, Giacomo Rufinelli, 1560, *Seder Haggadah shel Pesach*, Mantua, Ya'akov Shalit Ashkenazi, 1568; *Seder Haggadah shel Pesach*, Venice, Giovanni De Gara, 1609. On the second *Haggadah* of Prague, see C. Abramsky, *Two Prague Haggadahs*, Verona, 1978.

[11] See fig. 1

[12] See fig. 2. One rare copy of the second *Haggadah* of Prague is conserved at the Valmadonna Trust Library in London.

[13] *Ultraquist Passional*, Prague, Jan Camp, 1495, c. 24a. Cfr. Ch. Wangrow, *Haggadah and Woodcut*, New York, 1967, pp. 109-110. See fig. 3.

[14] See fig. 4

[15] See fig. 6.

[16] This is the thesis advanced by Malkiel, *Infanticide in Passover Iconography*, cit., pp. 96-99.

[17] See fig. 7.

[18] The caption of the scene is in Italian in Hebrew characters.

[19] The caption of the scene is in Italian in Hebrew characters.

[20] "Omnium perniciosissimum est, sortilegiis, incantationibus magisque superstitionibus et maleficiis dedititi (sc. Judaei) quamplurimos incautos atque inforos Satanae praestigiis inducunt" [approximately: "The worst thing of all is that the Jews are dedicated to spells, incantations and great superstitions, leading many incautious persons to be deceived by the wiles of Satan"]. The bull *Hebraeorum gens* was promulgated on 26 February 1526 (*Bullarium Romanum*, Turin, 1852-1872, vol. VII, pp. 740-742). See in this regard K.R. Stow, *Catholic Thought and Papal Jewry Policy (1555-1593)*, New York, pp. 34-36.

[21] See fig. 8

[22] See fig. 9

[23] See fig. 10

[24] See fig. 11. In this regard, see Yerushalmi, *Haggadah and History*, cit., plates 25, 51-52, B. Narkiss, *The Passover Haggadah of Venice 1609*, Jerusalem, 1974, p. 12.

[25] See fig. 12.

[26] Hamburg, Staats- und Universitätsbibliothek, Cod. Hebr. 37. The manuscript is dated 1427-1428.

[27] See fig. 13.

[28] See fig. 14.
[29] Ahser b. Yechiel (Rosh), *Sheelot w-teshuvot. Responsa*, Constantinople, 1517.
[30] See figures 15 and 16. This woodcut of the sacrifice of Isaac was reprinted in the second half of the Sixteenth Century in the editions of Isac Prossnitz at Cracow (cfr. A. Yaari, *Hebrew Printers' Marks*, Jerusalem, 1943, pp. 29, 141.
[31] See fig. 17. The image is reproduced by A.M. Hind, *Early Italian Engraving*. II: *Florentine Engravings and Anonymous Prints of Other Schools*. Figs. 1-171, New York – London, 1938, fig. 74, and subsequently reproduced in *Occhiali da vedere. Arte, scienze e costume attraverso gli occhiali*, Carl Zeiss Foundation, Istituto e Museo di Storia della Scienza, Cataloghi di mostre, Florence, 1985, vol. II, p. 30, no. G1, in H. Schreckenberg, *The Jews in Christian Art*, Göttingen, 1996, p. 280, fig. 6j.
[32] In this regard, see L. Steinberg, *The Sexuality of Christ in Renaissance Art and in Modern Oblivion*, New York, 1983, pp. 57-65.
[33] See figure nos. 19 and 20. The two images are reproduced in Schreckenberg, *The Jews in Christian Art*, cit., pp. 144-145, figures 1 and 3.
[34] See fig. 22. The table is conserved at the Museo provinciale d'Arte di Trento. Cfr. L. Dal Pra, *L'immagine di Simonino nell'arte dal XV al XVIII secolo*, in L. Rogger and M. Bellabarba, *Il principle vescovo Johannes Hinderbach (1465-1486), fra tardo Medievo e Umanesimo*, Atti del Convegno promosso dall Biblioteca Communale di Trento, 2-6 October 1989, Bologna, 1992, pp. 445-481, table 19.
[35] On the relationship between the circumcision of Christ, blood and ritual homicide in late Medieval Christian iconography in the German-speaking territories, see B.Blumenkranz, *Juden und Judentum in der mittelalterlichen Kunst*, Stuttgart, 1965, p. 85; W.P. Eckert, *Motivi superstiziosi nel processo agli ebrei di Trent*, in Rogger and Bellabarba, *Il principe vescovo Johannes Hinderbach*, cit., pp. 390-391.

CHAPTER ELEVEN

THE DINNER AND INVECTIVE: THE *SEDER* AND THE CURSES

In the depositions, and, if you wish, the confessions under torture, of the Trent defendants under indictment for Simonino's so-called ritual murder, ample space, at the request of the inquisitors, was given to the preparation of the *Seder* of *Pesach* in the respective houses, to the reading of the *Haggadah* and the particular rites of the festival. The inquisitors inquired about the order of the prayers, their content, the salient phases of the celebration, the foods eaten, and the various roles played by the participants in the collective ritual. The persons under interrogation responded, apparently without reticence, here dwelling at length to illustrate in detail the unfolding of the *Seder*, here more succinctly, restricting themselves to the most significant moments.

At this point, the question must be raised whether these descriptions and reports, extorted under torture, were authentic and real; whether they were the fruit of suggestive pressures brought to bear by the inquisitors, intended to confirm their prejudices, the stereotypes and the superstitions which they carried in their minds and in those of the Christian society of which they were the expression, and to evaluate the assumptions of the accusation which were at the origin of the trials. In other words, an attempt should be made to determine whether these crude and embarrassing confessions were largely the result of suggestion, and were, so to speak, recited and written under dictation. To do so, we must, first of all, strip the matter of its most delicate component, consisting of the admitted use of the blood of a Christian child, dissolved in wine and mixed in the dough of the unleavened bread, while restricting ourselves to a mere verification of the details of the depositions in all other respects, of which these admissions constitute the broad corpus.

Tobias da Magdeburg, the Jewish physician and expert ophthalmologist, according to those who knew him, both Jews and Christians, among the numerous patients he had in the Fossato district, was a bad-tempered and unpleasant individual. From the Jewish point of view, he was considered ignorant; he had a very poor knowledge of the holy language and his adherence to Jewish laws was anything but scrupulous. Samuele da Nuremberg, the recognized head of the small Jewish community of Trent, certainly did not consider him a saint, but he, Samuele, was prepared to supply him, Tobias, more or less voluntarily, with indispensable religious services. At *Pesach*, then, to enable Tobias to celebrate the *Seder* at home according to the rules, Samuele supplied him with the crisp unleavened bread and, above all, the *shimmurim*, the so-called "solemn unleavened bread", prepared with particular care and pierced by the finger of the head of the house, his wife and servants, before being put in the oven.[1]

The *shimmurim*, three for each of the first two evenings of the Jewish *Pesach* during which the *Haggadah* was read and the *Seder* was held, were prominently displayed in a pan as the symbolic main course of the feast, to be eaten by the guests during the most important phase of the liturgical ceremony.[2] Tobias knew that when the unleavened bread had been kneaded, it had to be placed in the oven immediately, to avoid over-heating it or allowing it to get soggy, thus causing it to ferment and become unsuitable for the ritual. It was then that Samuele was able to make the following long-anticipated solemn announcement: "This unleavened bread has been prepared according to the rules".[3]

This same Samuele referred to the traditional first appearance of the Passover dinner. It was then that the head of the family sat at the head of the table and poured out the wine into the beaker, upon which he had recited the benediction and sanctification of the festival (*kiddush*), while the other guests poured themselves wine, each into their cups. The pan with the three solemn unleavened loaves (*shimmurim*) were placed in the center of the table, awaiting the collective recitation of the *Hagadah*.[4] Tobias descended into greater detail, stating that:

"In the first days of the Passover, during the evening, before dinner, and also on subsequent days, in the evening, before dinner, the head of the family, seated at the head of the table, mixed the wine in the cup and so did the other guests; then they placed a basin or pan in the middle of the table, into which the three unleavened loaves were placed, one after the other; in the same pan, they placed an egg, meat and other foods which were to be eaten during the dinner".[5]

At this point, as Mohar (Meir), the son of Mosè "the Old Man" of Würzburg, recalled in his deposition, all the participants in the ritual banquet raised the pan with the three *shimmurim* and the other foods, together, and recited, together, the introductory formula of the *Haggadah*, composed in Aramaic, which opened with the words *Ha lachmà aniya*, "This is the bread of affliction which our fathers ate in the land of Egypt".[6]

He then added one of the culminating and most significant moments of the entire *Seder*, when the tension was broken, fantasy broke free from its bonds and the words were distinctly pronounced, one by one, to be savored and tasted in their full significance: the ten plagues of Egypt, or as the Ashkenazi Jews called them, the ten curses. *Dam*, the blood, opened the list, to be followed by the frogs (*zefardea*), lice (*kinim*), and ferocious animals (*'arov*); then came the plagues of the animals (*dever*), the ulcers (*shechin*), hail (*barad*), locusts (*areh*), darkness (*choshekh*). In a terrible and deadly crescendo, the plagues concluded with the death of the first born Egyptians (*makkat bechorot*). According to the custom long established among the Ashkenazi Jews, the head of the family then solemnly dipped the index finger of the right hand into the cup of wine, which was before him, and as he announced each individual plague, he moved his finger inside the glass, towards the outside, rhythmically splashing the wine onto the table.

Samuele da Nuremberg had no difficulty in reciting the names of the ten plagues, in Hebrew, from memory and in order, explaining that "these words meant the ten curses which God sent to the Egyptians, because they didn't want to liberate His people".[7] The Christian Italian notaries had obvious difficulty in transcribing that machine-gun burst of Hebraic terms, pronounced with a heavy German accent, into Latin characters, but they did their best, almost always obtaining moderately satisfactory results. The record gives Samuele's list as follows: *dam*, *izzarda* (the frogs, *zefardea*, was apparently too harsh for their ears), *chynim*, *heroff* (for *'arov*, with a variant of little importance), *dever*, *ssyn* (for *schechin*, ulcer), *porech* (*barad*, hail, pronounced in the German way, *bored*, were inadequately understood), *harbe*, *hossen* (for *choshekh*, darkness) and finally, *maschus pchoros* (*makkat bechorot*), which rendered the term of the plague according to the Ashkenazim diction, *makkas bechoros*). But it was all more or less comprehensible, both in words and meanings.

In one of the depositions taken from Anna of Magdeburg, Samuele's daughter-in-law, she recalled her mother-in-law sprinkling the wine onto the table, plunging her finger into the glass and reciting the ten curses, but she did not remember the precise order. A *Haggadah* was then produced and Anna took it and read the text quickly, starting with *dam*, blood, translating the various terms correctly.[8]

Tobias, for his part, was able to repeat the precise order of liturgical functions in which the head of the household accompanied the reading of the ten curses while splashing the wine onto the table with his finger. He had no difficulty in reciting the ten plagues of Egypt, which he obviously knew by heart, in Hebrew, in the correct sequence. But he got mixed up when he tried to translate or interpret the various terms, revealing a rather poor knowledge of Hebrew. He thus confused *'arov*, the plague of the multitude of the wild beasts, with *ra'av*, famine, and *arbeh*, the locusts, with the word *harbe'*, which sounds similar, and means "a lot" in Hebrew. In his own way, he interpreted the plague of the pestilence of animals, *dever*, as the destruction of persons, and *harad* (*porech* for *bored*, again), as "storm at sea", instead of in the sense of "hail". And again, for him, the death of the first-born children was to be considered an epidemic of general plague.[9]

In sum, Tobias was certainly not very cultivated in Hebraic studies, which he had perhaps somewhat neglected in order to concern himself with medicine. At any rate, he had the ritual formulae well in mind, reciting them automatically as he did each year. The interpretations were his own, even the more abstruse, as well as the grammatical errors in Hebrew, a language which he knew rather badly, in contrast to Samuele da Nuremberg, Mosè "the Old Man", of Würzburg and Angelo da Verona.[10] Like the inquisitors, the notaries who were in this case responsible for transcribing [what were certainly] his words, were interested in learning more about the *Seder* and its rituals; they cannot have been responsible for his interpretive blunders and linguistic mistakes.

At this point, in the traditional reading of the *Haggadah*, according to the custom of the Ashkenazi Jews, the curses against the Egyptians were transformed into an invective against all the nations and enemies hated by Israel, with explicit reference to the Christians. "From each of these plagues may God save us, but may they fall on our enemies". Thus recited the formula reported by rabbi Jacob Mulin Segal, known as *Maharil*, active at Treviso around the last twenty years of the 14th century, in his *Sefer ha-minhagim* ("Book of Customs"), which unhesitatingly identified the adversaries of the Jewish people with the Christians, who deserved to be cursed. It seems that this custom was in force among German Jews even before the First Crusade.[11] The sprinkling of the wine, which was a surrogate for the blood of the persecutors of Israel, onto the table, simultaneously with the recitation of the plagues of Egypt, recalled the cruel punishment said to have come from the "vengeful sword" of God.[12]

A famous contemporary of *Maharil*, Rabbi Shabom of Wiener Neustadt, has also confirmed the anti-Christian significance of the sprinkling of the wine during the reading of the plagues of Egypt.

"When they name the ten plagues of Egypt, each time, they dip the finger into the cup of wine standing in front (of the head of the family) and they pour a little bit of it out, onto the table [...] saying: 'From this curse may God save us'. The reason is that the four cups of wine (which must be drunk during the recitation of the *Haggadah*) represent a wish for the salvation of the Jews and a curse against the nations of the world. Therefore (the head of the family) pours the wine out of the glass with his finger, signifying that we Jews shall be saved from such curses, which shall, by contrast, fall upon our enemies".[13]

It should be noted that the ritual of the wine and the curses was practiced only in Jewish communities of German origin, while it was quite unknown among Jews of Iberian origins (Sephardim), or Italian and Oriental Jews.

The old man, Mosè da Würzburg recalled times past, when he was the head of the family at Spira and then Magonza. During the Passover evening, he had sat at the head of the table with the guests and directed the *Seder* and the reading of the *Haggadah*, sprinkling the wine onto the table while he clearly pronounced the names of the ten plagues of Egypt. He then informed his inquisitors that, according to the Ashkenazi tradition, "the head of the family added these words: 'Thus we implore God that these ten curses may fall on the gentiles, enemies of the faith of the Jews', a clear reference to the Christians".[14] According to Israel Wolfgang, who was, as usual, well informed, the famous and influential Salomone da Piove di Sacco, as well as the banker Abramo da Feltre and the physician Rizzardo da Regensburg at Brescia, all complied with the ritual of reciting the ten curses and symbolically pouring out the wine against the nations hostile to Israel.

Mosè da Bamberg, the wandering Jewish guest in the Angelo da Verona's house, testified to this custom, at which he had been present during the *Seder* in Leone di Mohar's house at Tortoa. Mosè the master of Hebrew, who lived at the expense of Tobias, the physician, remembered well, from the time in which his house was located in the district of the Jews of Nuremberg.[15]

Tobias himself, as the head of the family, had directly guided those parts of the *Seder* and recalled the details, which were furthermore repeated every year at Passover without variation. He therefore announced to the judges at Trent that "when the head of the family had finished reading those words (the ten plagues), he then added this phrase: 'Thus we implore God, that you shall similarly send these ten plagues against the Gentiles, who are the enemies of the religion of the Jews', intending to refer, in particular, to the Christians".[16]

For his part, Samuele da Nuremberg, sprinkling the wine onto the table from the inside of his chalice, also took as his starting place the tragedies of the Pharaohs to curse the Christian faith unambiguously:

"We invoke God that he may turn all these anathemas against the enemies of Israel".[17]

The *Seder* thus became a scandalous display of anti-Christian sentiment, exalted by symbolic acts and significances and burning imprecations, which was now using the stupendous events of the exodus of the Jews from Egypt simply as a pretext. In Jewish Venice during the 17th century, the ritual characteristics related to the reading of this part of the *Haggadah* were still alive and present, as shown by the testimony of Giulio Morosini, which is to be considered quite reliable.

"When the head of the family refers to these ten blows, he is brought a bowl or basin, and at the name of each one, dipping the finger into his glass, he sprinkles the wine, and continues, gradually emptying the glass of wine as a sign of the curses against the Christians".[18]

Subsequently, the head of the family, after drinking another glass of wine, invites the guests to eat part of the three solemn unleavened loaves, the *shimmurim*, first all by itself and then together with the *charoset* and the bitter herbs, reciting the mandatory benedictions. At this point, the dinner true and proper began. Samuele reported that the "head of the family took the unleavened bread and divided it one by one, giving one piece to each (of the guests), then drank the wine in his cup, and the others did likewise; after which they all started to eat, and thus they did the next day".[19]

Similarly, Tobias da Magdeburg recounted that "the head of the family took the first unleavened loaf in the pan and gave part of it to each person present, and did the same with the second and third unleavened loaf (the *shimmurim*), giving a part of it to each person present. He then took a glass full of wine [...] and gulped it down, and immediately afterwards, the other guests also took their glasses and drank the wine, each from his own glass. Then the dinner started".[20]

When the meal was finished and the related benediction had been recited, before drinking the fourth glass of wine, the wine with which the advent of final redemption augured itself, the participants in the ritual united in reciting, all together, a new series of violent invective against the peoples having rejected the God of Israel, in a clear allusion to the Christians. The formula opened with the words *Shefoch chamatecha el ha-goim asher lo yeda'ucha* and, in the Ashkenazi ritual, contained particularly virulent overtones: "Vomit your anger onto the nations which refuse to recognize you, and their kingdoms, which do not invoke your name, which have devoured Jacob and destroyed his seat. Turn your anger upon them, reach them with your scorn; persecute them with fury, cause them to perish from beneath the divine heaven".

This was one of the most potent, explicit and incisive curses against the gentiles contained in the Passover liturgy of the *Seder*. This invective appears to have been unknown in ancient times, and it is first found in the *Machazor Vitry*, composed in France between the 11th and 12th centuries. In all probability, the text, of one hundred verses extrapolated from various Psalms, was introduced into the *Haggadah* of the Franco-German Jewish communities during the Medieval period.[21]

The meaning was obvious. Messianic redemption could only be built upon the ruins of the hated Gentile world. In reciting the curses, the door of the room in which the *Seder* was kept half-ajar, so that the prophet Elias would be enabled to intervene and announce the promised rescue. The anti-Christian invective was intended to prepare and facilitate Elias' entry. As we shall also see below, the magical cult of the outrage and anti-Christian evil omen was one of the principal elements characterizing the religious fundamentalism typical of the Franco-German environment of the Middle Ages, and its so-called "passive Messianism", which was aggressive and ritualized.[22]

Maestro Tobias, according to his statements to the judges at Trent, after dinner, devoutly recited the formula of the curses of *Shefoch* and did the same on both evenings during which the *Seder* was performed and the Passover *Haggadah* read.[23] Israel Wolfgang, as well, who had participated in Samuele da Nuremberg's ritual dinner, recalled the moment in which they had solemnly pronounced *Shefoch* ("Oh God, send your anger against the peoples which do not wish to glorify you"), cursing the Christians.[24]

The custom of reciting the curses of the *Shefoch* attributing anti-Christian connotations to them was still in force among the Jews of Venice in the 17th century, as Giulio Morosini attests with reference to the Ashkenazi formula:

"Each one raises his glass of wine [...] they curse the Christians and the other nations, all included under the name of *Ghoim*, Gentiles, all intoning these words, after they have eaten their fill and are very drunk: 'Cast thy anger upon the *Ghoim*, Gentiles, which have not recognized you and on the kingdoms which have not invoked your name. Cast your anger upon them and may the fury of your anger consume them. Persecute them with your fury and destroy them' ".[25]

The reading of this second series of curses was perhaps accompanied by demonstrative actions, such as that of flinging the wine from the basin into which it had been poured during the recital of the ten plagues of Egypt out of the windows and into the street: Egypt was thus transformed into Edom, and the persecutors of Israel were now solidly identified with the representatives of the surrounding Christian world.

The convert Paolo Medici reported on the existence of these rather picturesque customs, which also featured stentorian invectives against the Gentiles.

"The head of the house intones aloud verse 6 of Psalm 78: 'Effunde iram tuam in gentes, quae te non noverunt'. (*Shefoch chamatecha el hagoim asher lo yeda'ucha*), and one person in the house runs to the window, takes the basin containing the wine of the curses, which was poured into the basin during the recitation the ten plagues inflicted on Egypt by God, and throws the wine into the street, the meaning of which, by way of this verse of the Psalm, was to inflict thousands of curses on all those who were not members of Judaism, and against the Christians in particular".[26]

In substance, the so-called "confessions" of the defendants during the Trent trials relating to the rituals of the *Seder* and the Passover *Haggadah* are seen to be precise and truthful. Apart from the details of the use of blood in the wine and the unleavened bread, of which we shall speak somewhat further along, the sporadic insertion of which into the text is insufficient to invalidate the general picture, the facts described are always correct. The Jews of Trent, in describing the *Seder* in which they had participated, were not lying; nor were they under the influence of the judges, who were presumably ignorant of a large part of the ritual being described to them. If the accused dwelt at length upon the virulent anti-Christian meaning which the ritual had assumed in the tradition of that Franco-German Judaism to which they belonged, they were not indulging in unverifiable exaggeration. In their collective mentality, the Passover *Seder* had long since transformed itself into a celebration in which the wish for the forthcoming redemption of the people of Israel moved from aspiration to revenge, and then to cursing their Christian persecutors, the current heirs to the wicked Pharaoh of Egypt.

* * *

NOTES TO CHAPTER ELEVEN

[1] On the preparation of the unleavened break and the *shimmurim*, the unleavened bread, under supervision and most important, see A. Toaff, *Mangiare alla giudia. La cucina ebraica in Italia dal*

Rinascimento all'età moderna, Bologna, 2000, pp. 147-149.

[2] The pan with the symbolic *Pesach* foods generally contained, in addition to the three *shimmurim*, i.e. the "solemn unleavened loaves", hard-boiled eggs, the lamb's hoof, the *charoset*, i.e., the fresh and dried fruit preserve, bitter herbs, lettuce and celery (cfr. R. Bonfil, *Haggadah di Pesach*, Milan, 1962, pp. XXXII-XXXVI). To these foods, some people added "various other things, including other types of bitter herbs and two types of meat, roast and boiled, and fish and egg, and almonds and walnuts" (cfr. Giulio Morosini, *Derekh Emunah. Via della fede mostrata agi ebrei*, Rome. Propaganda Fide, 1683, pp. 551-552).

[3] "Quia ipse Thobias non habet clibanum in domo sua ad coquendo fugatias nec panem, eo tempore quo faciunt dictas fugatias seu azimas predictas, subito quamprimum sunt facte oportet quod ponantur in clibano, ut bene sint azime et quod Samuel habet clibanum in domo sua [...] dicto tempore Samud dedit sibi de fugatiis azimis, qui Samuel quando sic dabat fugatias dicebat: Iste fugatiae sunt aptate sicut debent" (cfr. A. Esposito and D. Quaglioni, *Processi contro gli ebrei di Trento, 1475-1478. I: I processi del 1475*, Padua, 1990, p. 328). For his part, Samuele da Nuremberg "interrogatus quin pinsavit pastam temporibus preteritis in domo ipsius Samuelis, cum qua fecerunt azimas predictas, respondit quod famuli ipsius Samuelis fecerunt azimas et pinsaverunt pastam cum qua fecerunt azimas; dicens tamen, quod nihil refert an masculi vel femine faciant dictas azimas" (cfr. ibidem, p. 252).

[4] "Ante cenam paterfamilias se ponit in capite mense et accipit unum ciatum in quo est de vino et quem ciatum ponit ante se [...] et alii de familia circum astantes habent singulum ciatum plenum vino; et in medio mense ponit unum bacile, in quo bacili sunt tres fugatie azimate [...] quas tres azimas ponunt in dicto bacili et in eodem bacili etiam ponunt aliquid modicum de eo quod sunt commesturi in cena" (cfr. ibidem, p. 252). Israel Wolfgang referred to the *shimmurim* as *migzos* (recte: *mazzot*, *mazzos* according to the Asnhenazi pronunciation), solemn unleavened bread (cfr. G. Divina, *Storia del beato Simone da Trento*, Trent, 1902, vol. II, p. 18).

[5] "In die Pasce eorum de sero, ante cenam, et etiam in die sequenti de sero, antecenam, paterfamilias judeus se ponit ad mensam et omnes eius familie se ponunt circa mensam. Qui paterfamilias habet ciphum plenum vino, quem ciphum ponit ante se, et omnes alii circumstantes habent singulum ciatum plenum vino; et deinde in medio mense ponunt unum bacile seu vas, in quo ponunt tres azimas sive fugatias [...] ponendo dictas fugatias unam super aliam; in quo bacili etiam ponunt de ovis, de carnibus et de omnibus aliis de quibus volunt comedere in illa cena" (cfr. Esposito and Quaglioni, *Processi*, cit., vol. I, pp. 325-

326).

⁶ "Dicit quod benedicunt postea dictas fugatias [...] dicendo hec verba: Holcheme hanyhe (recte: Ha la-chmà aniyà) et certa alia verba que ipse ignorat, que verba significant: 'panis iste', et nescit quid aliud significent" (cfr. ibidem, p. 379).

⁷ "Et paterfamilias ponit digitum in ciatum suum et illum balneat in vino [...] et deinde aspergit cum digito omnia que sunt in mensa, dicendo hec verba in Hebraico, videlicet dam, izzardea, chynim, heroff, dever, ssyn, porech, harbe, hossen, maschus pochoros, que verba significant decem maledictiones quas Deus dedit populo Egiptiaco, eo quod nolebat dimittere populum suum" ["And the head of the family places his finger in his glass and bathes his finger therein [...] and then sprinkles all those present at table with it, saying these words in Hebrew, that is, dam, izzardea, chynim, heroff, dever, ssyn, porech, harbe, hossen, maschus pochoros, which words mean the ten curses that God inflicted on the Egyptians who did not want to let His people go"] (cfr. ibidem, p. 252).

⁸ Cfr. [Benedetto Bonelli], *Dissertazione apologetica sul martirio del beato Simone da Trento nell'anno MCCCCLXXV dagli ebrei ucciso*, Trento, Gianbattista Parone, 1747, pp. 151-152.

⁹ "Et postea (paterfamilias) ponit digitum indicem manus dextrae in ciphum et intingit seu balneat digitum predictum in vino [...] et deinde cum eodemmet digito balneato in vino, ut supra, paterfamilias aspergit ea que sunt super mensa, dicendo hec verba in Hebraico, videlicet: dam, izzardea, chynim, heroff, dever, ssyn, porech, harbe, hossech, maschus pochoros, que verba significant in Latino istud, videlicet: dam, sanguis – izzardea, rane – chynym, pulices – heroff, fames – dever, destructiones personarum – ssyn, lepra – porech, fortuna in mari seu procella – harbe, multum – hossech, tenebre – maschus pochoros, pestilentia magna. Que omnia verba suprascripta dicuntur per dictum patremfamilias in commemoratione illarum decem maledictionum, quas Deus dedit Pharaoni et toto populo Egypti, quia nolebant dimittere populum suum" ["And after (the head of the family) put the index finger of the right hand in his glass and having bathed his finger in the wine [...] and, using the finger bathed in wine, as stated above, the head of the family sprinkles those at table, saying these words in Hebrew, namely, izzardea, chynim, heroff, dever, ssyn, porech, harbe, hossech, maschus pochoros, which words mean in Latin the following, to wit, dam, blood – izzardea, frogs – chynym, fleas – heroff, famine – dever, the destruction of persons – ssyn, leprosy – porech, loss of wealth in storms at sea – harbe, multitude – hossech, darkness – maschus pochoros – great pestilence. All of these words are

spoken by the head of the family in memory of the ten curses which God inflicted on the Egyptians and on the whole population of Egypt, because they did not want to let His people go"] (cfr. Esposito and Quaglioni, *Processi*, cit., vol. I, p. 326).

[10] Tobias did not hesitate to confess to the Trent judges to the limitations of his own Hebraic culture: "ipse Thobias est illetteratus homo et quod docti in lege suo hoc scire debent" ["that Tobias was uneducated and that the doctors in law should know that"] (ibidem, p. 318).

[11] Cfr. Jacob Mulin Segal (Maharil), *Sefer ha-minhagim* ("Book of Customs"), by Sh. Spitzer, Jerusalem, 1989, pp. 106-107. On the anti-Christian meaning of these invectives, contained in the *Haggadah* according to the custom of the German Jews, cfr. I.J. Yuval, *"Two Nations in Your Womb". Perceptions of Jews and Christians*, Tel Aviv, 2000, pp. 116-117 (in Hebrew).

[12] In this regard, see Sh. Safrai and Z. Safrai, *Haggadah of the Sages. The Passover Haggadah*, Jerusalem, 1998, pp. 145-146 (in Hebrew).

[13] Cfr. Shalom of Neustadt, *Decisions and Customs*, by Sh. Spitzer, Jerusalem, 1977, p. 134 (in Hebrew).

[14] "Postea dictus paterfamilias dixit suprascripta verba, idem paterfamilias iungit hec alia verba: 'Ita imprecamur Deum quod similiter immittat predictas .X. maledictiones contra gentes, que sunt inimice fidei Iudeorum', intelligendo maxime contra christianos, et deinde dictus paterfamilias bibit vinum" ["After the head of the family said these words, he added these other words: 'Thus we pray God to inflict ten similar curses on the Gentiles, who are enemies of the Jewish faith', meaning the Christians, more than anything else, and then the head of the family drank the wine"] (cfr. Esposito and Quaglioni, *Processi*, cit., vol. I, p. 363). "Et (Thobias) dicit quod quando dictus paterfamilias dixit suprascripta verba, postea etiam addit hec alia: 'Ita imprecamur Deum quod similiter immittat suprascriptas decem maledictiones contra gentes quod adversantur fidei Iudaice', intelligendo maxime contra Christianos" ["And (Tobias) said that when the head of the family said these words, after that he added these other words: 'Thus we pray God that He may inflict ten similar curses on all the people who are enemies of the Jewish faith' "] (cfr. Esposito and Quaglioni, *Processi*, cit., vol. I, p. 326).

[15] Cfr. Divina, *Storia del beato Simone da Trento*, cit., vol. II, pp. 16-32.

[16] "Et (Thobias) dicit quod quando dictus paterfamilias dixit suprascripta verba, postea etiam addit hec alia: 'Ita imprecamur Deum

quod similiter immittat suprascriptas decem maledictiones contra gentes quod adversantur fidei Iudaice', intelligendo maxime contra Christianos" ["And Tobias said that when the head of the family said the above mentioned words, after that he added the following, among other things: 'Thus we call upon God similarly to inflict the above mentioned curses against the Gentiles (or people) who are enemies of the Jewish faith', meaning, most of all, against the Christians"] (cfr. Esposito and Quaglioni, *Processi*, cit., vol. I, p. 326).

[17] "Et que verba postea quem dicta sunt per patremfamilias, idem paterfamilias dicit hec alia verba: 'Ita nos deprecamur Deum quod immittat omnes predictas maledictiones contra eos qui sunt contra fidem Iudaicam', intelligendo et imprecando quod dicte maledictiones immittantur contra Cristianos" ["And that after the head of the family said these words, he said these other words: 'Thus we pray God that He may inflict all these curses on those who are enemies of the Jewish faith', meaning and praying that these curses would befall the Christians"] (cfr. ibidem, p. 352). In the light of the Hebrew sources, such as *Maharil* and Shalom of Wiener Neustadt, who testify to the ancient custom of the Ashkanazi Jews of cursing the Christians during the recitation of the ten plagues of Egypt, W.P. Eckert is therefore in error on this point (*Motivi superstiziosi nel processo agli ebrei di Trento*, in I. Rogger and M. Bellabarba, *Il principe vescovo Johannes Hinderbach, 1465-1486, fra tardo Medioevo e Umanesimo*, Atti del Convegno held by the Biblioteca Comunale of Trent, 2-6 October 1989, Bologna, 1992, pp. 393-394) considers this to be a truth presumed by the Trent judges and suggested to the defendants by coercive means.

[18] Cfr. Morosini, *Derekh Emunah. Via della fede mostata agli ebrei*, cit., p. 559.

[19] "Et hiis dictis, paterfamilias accipit dictas fugatias et unamquamque dividit de unaquaque fugatia partem suam unicuique, et deinde ipse paterfamilias bibit vinum quod est in ciato suo, et similiter alii astantes bibunt vinum suum et postmodum omnes cenant, et similiter faciunt die sequenti de sero" (cfr. Esposito and Quaglioni, *Processi*, cit., vol. I, pp. 252-253).

[20] "Et post suprascripta paterfamilias accipit primam fugatiam que est in bacili, ut supra, et unicuique ex astantibus dat partem suam, et similiter facit de secunda et de tertia fugatia, dando partem suam unicuique. Et deinde accipit ciphum plenum vino [...] et illud vinum bibit; et deinde omnes alii circumstantes accipiunt ciatos suos plenos vino, ut supra, et unusquisque bibit de ciato suo, postque cenant omnes" (cfr. ibidem, pp. 326-327).

[21] On the initial introduction of the curses of *Shefoch* into the text of the *Haggadah* of the medieval Ashkenazi environment, see, among others, M.M. Kasher, *Haggadah Shelemah*, New York, 1961, pp. 177-180; E.D. Goldshmidt, *Haggadah shel Pesach*, Jerusalem, 1969, pp. 62-64; R. Bonfil, *Haggadah di Pesach*, Milan, 1962, pp. 122-123 ("It may nevertheless be presumed that the custom became widespread during the Middle Ages, during the period of the first great persecutions, during the Crusades [...] during the period in which the first accusations of ritual murder were made against the Jews. The custom of opening the door [...] probably also dates back to that period, in which such an act was caused by the fear that behind the door there might be placed the body of some murdered child and that the murder might be blamed on the Jews").

[22] In this regard, see, in particular, G.D. Cohen, *Messianic Postures of Ashkenazim and Sephardim*, in M. Kreutzberg, *Studies of the Leo Baeck Institute*, New York, 1967, pp. 117-158; Yuval, *"Two Nations in Your Womb"*, cit., pp. 140-145; Safrai and Safrai, *Haggadah of the Sages*, cit., pp. 174-178.

[23] "Et finita cena, paterfamilias dicit hec verba: *Sfoch chaba moscho hol ha-goym*. Similiter dicit quod fit in die sequenti de sero, post Pascha" ["And after dinner, the head of the family pronounces these words, *Sfoch chaba moscho hol ha-goym*. He does the same the evening of the following day, after Passover"] (cfr. Esposito and Quaglioni, *Processi*, cit., vol. I, p. 327). It should be noted that the Hebrew words are recorded by the Italian notary according to Tobias' Ashkenazi pronunciation, and therefore *chamatechà*, "da tua ira", is rendered as *chamoschò* (chaba moscho).

[24] Cfr. [Bonelli], *Dissertazione apologetica*, cit., p. 149; Divina, *Storia del beato Simone da Trento*, cit., vol. II, p. 18. Even in the case of Israel Wolfgang, the formula of *Shefoch*, reported according to the Ashkenazi pronunciation, is distorted by the notary's record (*Sfoco hemosco hai hagoym honszlar lho ghedalsecho*), but seems entirely intelligible.

[25] Cfr. Morosini, *Derekh Emunah. Via della fede mostrata agli ebrei*, cit., p. 559.

[26] Cfr. Paolo Medici, *Riti e costumi degli ebrei*, Madrid, Luc'Antonio de Bedmar, 1737, p. 171.

CHAPTER TWELVE

THE MEMORIAL OF THE PASSION

The use of the blood of Christian children in the celebration of the Jewish Passover was apparently the object of minute regulation, at least according to the depositions of all the defendants in the Trent trials. These depositions describe exactly what was prohibited, what was permitted, and what was tolerated, all in meticulous detail. Every eventuality was foreseen and dealt with; the use of blood was governed by broad and exhaustive case law, almost as if it formed an integral part of the most firmly established regulations relating to the ritual. The blood, powdered or dessicated, was mixed into the dough of the unleavened or "solemn" bread, the *shimmurim* – not ordinary bread. The *shimmurim* – in fact, three loaves for each of the two evenings during which the ritual dinner of the *Seder* was served – were considered one of the principal symbolic foods of the feast, and their accurate preparation and baking took place during the days preceding the advent of *Pesach*.

During the *Seder*, the blood had to be dissolved into the wine immediately prior to recitation of the ten curses against the land of Egypt. The wine was later poured into a basin or a cracked earthenware pot and thrown away. The performance of the ritual required only a minimum quantity of blood in powdered form, equal in quantity to a lentil.

The obligation to procure blood and to use it during the Passover ritual was the exclusive responsibility of the head of the family, i.e., a responsible male with a dependent wife and children. Bachelors, widowers, guests and employees, all those without dependent family, were exempt. In view of the difficulty of procuring such a rare and costly ingredient, it was anticipated that the wealthiest Jews would provide blood for the poorest Jews, an eccentric form of charity benefiting heads of families disinherited by fate.

Samuele da Nuremberg reported that:

"The evening before *Pesach*, when they stir the dough with which the unleavened bread (the *shimmurim*) is later prepared, the head of the family takes the blood of a Christian child and mixes it into the dough while it is being kneaded, using the entire quantity available, keeping in mind that the measure of a lentil is sufficient. The head of the family sometimes performs this operation in the presence of those kneading the unleavened bread, and sometimes without their knowledge, based on whether or not they can be trusted".[1]

Maestro Tobias restricted himself to recalling that "every year, the blood, in powdered form, is kneaded into the dough of the unleavened bread prepared the evening before the feast, and is then eaten on the solemn day, i.e., the day of Passover".[2] This testimony was confirmed by Mohar (Meir), the son of Mosè "the old Man" of Würzburg,[3] as well as by the convert Giovanni da Feltre, who had seen his father Schochat (Sacheto) perform the ritual while still living at Landshut in Bavaria.[4]

Isacco da Gridel, Angelo da Verona's cook, admitted to kneading the *shimmurim* containing blood for eight years, preparing it for the celebration of the *Seder*. Joav of Franconia, Tobias' domestic servant, recalled the custom from as much as seventeen years back, when she was in service with a rich Jew from Würzburg. Mosè da Bamburg, the traveler staying with Angelo of Verona, in his long deposition, stated that he had personally performed this operation when he was head of the family in Germany. Later, when he moved to Italy, he had seen it performed at Borgo San Giovanni, in the Piacenza region, in the home of money lender Sacle or Sacla (Izchak), who inserted the blood into the unleavened bread while his wife Potina kneaded the dough. Vitale, Samuele da Nuremberg's agent, attested to the custom as a result of having seen it performed for three consecutive years by his uncle, Salomone, at Monza.

The subject matter of these depositions was also confirmed by the women involved. Bella, the wife of Mayer da Würzburg, reported that she had seen her father preparing the *shimmurim* from the time she was a child at Nuremberg, in preparation for the first two evenings during which the *Seder* used grains of dried blood in the dough. Sara, Tobias's wife, recalled that her first husband, Elia, whom she married at Marburg, had used blood for this purpose, and that she had also seen the practice in many Jewish homes in Mestre.[5] Bona, Angelo da Verona's sister, stated that she had seen the brother placing the [dried] blood, [dissolved and] diluted in water, into the dough of the unleavened and so-called solemn bread, the *shimmurim*, which was kept under surveillance, and had to be eaten during the first two evenings of the festival, during the *Seder*. "Angelo himself, took a bit of the Christian child's [dried] blood and dissolved it in water, then poured the water containing the blood into the dough with which they then made the unleavened loaves, three of which Angelo and the other members of his family and Bona herself ate during the Passover evening feast, while the other three members ate it the evening of the next day".[6]

Angelo da Verona's report was rather more detailed. After briefly recalling that the Ashkenazi Jews "take a small quantity of the blood and they put it in the dough with which they later make the unleavened bread which they eat during the solemn days of the Passover".

He went on to provide a detailed description of the rite of preparing the *shimmurim* "with blood".[7] First of all, he explained to the judges, the ritual action was carried out "as a sign of outrage against Jesus Christ, whom the Christians claim is their God". He then continued, supplying whatever clarification he considered dutiful and necessary: "Eating unleavened bread with Christian blood in it means that, just as the body and powers of Jesus Christ, the God of the Christians, went down to perdition with His death, thus, the Christian blood contained in the unleavened bread shall be ingested and completely consumed".

How much truth there was to this key anti-Christian interpretation of the presumed Jewish haematophagia [blood-eating] through the medium of unleavened bread, and just how much was invented to please the inquisitors concerned, is unknown. It is however a fact that Angelo supplied a very colorful and credible representation of the ritual, utilizing the correct formulae from the classical Jewish liturgy.

"They place the blood in their unleavened loaves in this manner: after placing the blood in the dough, they knead it and stir it around to prepare the unleavened bread (the *shimmurim*). Then they poke holes in it, pronouncing these words: *Chen icheressù chol hoyveha*, which, translated, means 'Thus may our enemies be consumed'. At this point, the unleavened loaves are ready to be eaten".[8]

This Hebrew invective is not an invention. It may in fact be found among the blessings and curses pronounced during the so-called "*Haggadah* of the Jewish New Year" (*Rosh Ha-Shanah*) just before the feast dinner. On this occasion, the reading of the various formulae was accompanied by the consumption of vegetables and fruit, in addition to fish and a lamb's head, recalling, by means of a pun on their Hebrew names, the type of blessing or curse which the reader intended to pronounce. Leeks are called *cartì*, and the invective associated with its name was known as *she-iccaretu* (*iccaresu* in the Ashkenazi pronunciation) *col hoyevenu*, that is, "may all our enemies be exterminated ("consumed" according to Angelo)".[9] The original inspiration was, as usual, Biblical and prophetical (Mich. 5:9) "And all thine enemies shall be cut off" (*we-chos hoyevecha iccaretu*). At this point, it becomes much more difficult to dismiss the insertion of these

255

Hebrew-language execrations into the ritual of the Christian blood added to the solemn unleavened bread as merely the extemporaneous and extravagant invention of Angelo da Verona, "softened up" with torture.

From Samuele da Nuremberg and Angelo da Verona, from Maestro Tobias and Anna da Montagnana, all the accused at Trent were agreed in affirming that the head of the family, who was required to perform the task of directing the reading of the *Haggadah*, did not shake the blood into the wine before starting the *Seder* or during the initial phases of the celebration, but only when they were about to recite the ten curses of Egypt. Recalling the years of his stay in the Jewish quarter of Nuremberg with various employers such as Lazzaro, Giosia and Moshè Loff, Mosè da Ansbach, the teacher of Tobias's children, stated that the head of the family placed the blood in the wine at the precise moment of the commemoration of the so-called "ten curses", i.e., the plagues of Egypt.[10]

The learned Mosè da Würzburg, "the Old Man", explained that:

"The head of the family takes a bit of the blood of the Christian child and drops it in his glass full of wine [...] then, putting his finger in the wine in which the blood of the Christian child has been shaken, he sprinkles the table and food with it, pronouncing the Hebraic formula in commemoration of the ten curses, which God sent to the refractory Egyptian people who refused to liberate the Jewish people. At the end of the reading, the same head of the family, referring to the Christians, utters the following words (in Hebrew): 'thus we beseech God that he may similarly direct these ten curses against the gentiles, who are enemies of the Jewish faith' ".[11]

Giovanni da Feltre, the converted Jew, recalled the years of his youth, spent in lower Germany, when his father performed the ritual of the *Seder* of Passover, "Both evenings, my father took blood and shook it into his chalice of wine before beginning the Passover dinner, then sprinkled it on the table cursing the Christian religion".[12]

After the reading of the last part of the *Haggadah*, the head of the family performed the act of adding the blood to the wine to transform the wine into a potion symbolically intended to represent the cruel death of Israel's enemies, immediately before the ten curses. This part of the text of the *Haggadah* opens with the words: "(The Lord) made us leave Egypt with a strong hand, with the arm extended, with immense terror, with signs) and with prodigies: this is the blood (*zeh ha-dam*)".[13] The reason why the haematic fluid of the Christian boy was dissolved in the "wine of the ten curses" at this point was revealed by Angelo da Verona:

"The Jews performed this act in remembrance of one of the ten curses which God inflicted upon the Egyptians when they held the Jewish people in bondage: one of the plagues was God's transformation into blood of all the waters in the land of Egypt".[14]

As usual, Israel Wolfgang provided some sense of order for these various rituals. The young painter recalled participating in a *Seder* held in the house of a certain Jew named Chopel, at Günzenhausen, near Nuremberg, in 1460. Chopel used coagulated, pulverized blood, shaken into the wine prior to the recitation of the ten plagues. This was accompanied by the following declaration in Hebrew: "This is the blood of a Christian child", (*zeh-ha dam shel goi katan*). According to what may be gathered from Israel Wolfgang's account, after the reading of this fragment of the *Haggadah*, which began with the words *zeh ha-dam*, "This is the blood", the head of the house brought the ampoule containing the powdered blood to the table, added a bit of the contents to the wine in his chalice, and recited the analogous formula beginning with the same words, *zeh ha-dam*, but in reference to the blood of the Christian child, not in reference to the first plague of Egypt.

He then went on to the reading of the ten curses, the sprinkling of the wine onto the table, and the recitation of the invectives against the goyim – the Christians. Obviously, the formula, "This is the blood (*zeh ha-dam*) of a Christian child" was transmitted [from generation to generation] orally; the text of the *Haggadah* was alleged not to contain this text.

Israel Wolfgang's revelations continued. In 1474, he [said he] had participated in the celebration of the Jewish Passover at Feltre, at Abramo's house (Abramo being a money lender in that city). On that occasion, Wolfgang had seen the head of the family add the blood to the dough of the solemn unleavened bread (*migzo* = *mazzot*), that is, the *shimmurim*. During the evening ritual of the *Seder*, Abramo da Feltre, in preparation for the reading of the ten curses, came to table with a glass phial containing a small quantity of dried blood, the size of a nut, and shook a pinch of it into the wine, pronouncing the usual formula of the *zeh ha-dam*: "This is the blood of a Christian child". He then began the recitation of the plagues, pouring the wine onto the table and cursing the gentiles hostile to Israel.[15]

Lazzaro, employed at Angelo da Verona, also told the judges that he had seen the rite performed by his uncle Israel, the influential Ashkenazi banker at Piacenza, who occupied the function of treasurer in the Jewish community of the Duchy of Milan.[16] According to him, Israel, during the recitation of the plagues, diluted the blood into the wine, pronouncing the Hebrew words which meant: "This is the blood of a Christian child" (*zeh ha-dam shel goi katan*).[17] In this regard, Mosè of Bamburg confirmed the descriptions of the other defendants, referring to Leone of Mohar, a money lender active at Tortona, with whom he had stayed as a guest in the past, during the *Seder* of Passover.[18] As often happened, Leone, in the act of adding the dried blood to the wine before the recitation of the ten curses, turned to his guests with the required Hebrew phrase: *zeh ha-dam*, "This is the blood of a Christian child".

It should be obvious that only someone with a very good knowledge of the *Seder* ritual, an insider, could describe the [precise] order of gestures and operations as well as the Hebrew formulae used during the various phases of the celebration, and be capable of supplying such [a wealth of] detailed and precise descriptions and explanations. The judges at Trent could barely follow these descriptions, forming a vague idea of the ritual, which was so foreign to their experience and knowledge that they could only reconstitute it in [the form of] nebulous and imperfect images. The Italian notaries, then, had their work cut out for them in [attempting] to cut their way through this jungle of incomprehensible Hebrew terms, pronounced with a heavy German accent. But on the other hand, what interested them, beyond the particulars of difficult comprehensibility, was establishing where these Jews used Christian blood in their Passover rites, adding it to the unleavened bread and the wine of the libation. Imagining that the judges dictated these descriptions of the *Seder* ritual, with the related liturgical formulae in Hebrew, does not seem very plausible.

Goi katan, "little Christian", the expression used in referring to the ritual murder victim, who was usually nameless, is said to have been used during the act of adding his blood to the symbolic foods to be exhibited and consumed in the *Seder* dinner. This expression, although not at all neutral in view of the negative and pejorative connotations attributed to Christians in general, was certainly less contemptuous than the term normally used by German Jews with reference to a Christian child. [For example], the word *shekez* possesses the sense of "something abominable", while the feminine, *shiksa* or *shikse*, is a neologism used, in particular, in reference to Christian girls engaged in romantic relations with young men of the race of Israel.[19] The diminutive [Italianized] term of endearment, "*scigazzello*", was in use among the Ashkenazi Jews of Venice until relatively recent times. At any rate, the words *shekz*, *sheghez*, or *sceghesc*, employed in a contemptuous manner to refer to the children of those faithful in Christ, viewed as some of the [most] abominable expressions of [all] creation, was in widespread use in all cities with communities of German Jews, even in Northern Italy.[20]

It should be noted that the term is absent from the records of the Trent trials; but the terms *goi* (literally, "people" "nation"), with reference to Christians generally, and *goi katan* ("little Christian"), in the sense of a child belonging to the faith in Christ were used instead.

In his fierce invective against the Jews, the Venetian convert Giulio Morosini did not fail to censure the virulently anti-Christian education imparted by Jews to their children, according to Morosini, as well as the offensive terminology utilized by Jews in Hebrew to insult Christian children and their churches.

"You are accustomed to instilling in those little children, along with their mother's milk, the observance and the concept of the Law and the holy language, with Hebrew names for many things [...] This is so that they may easily and soon understand the Law and Bible. But at the same time, you inculcate hatred against the *Goyim*, that is, the Gentiles, by which name you refer to the Christians, never missing a chance to curse them, and make your children curse them. Thus, the name most frequently used against [Christian] children is *Sciekatizim*, that is, Abominations, which is also the word you use in reference to the 'Idols', as you are accustomed to call them. In the same manner, you abominate our Churches with your synonym, *Tonghavà*, which also means Abomination. And you very often warn them to flee the *Tonghavà*, not to speak to the *Sceketz* and other, similar terms of abuse".[21]

In the eyes of the Ashkenazi Jews of Trent, it was obvious that the ritual obligation to use the blood of Christian children in the Passover celebrations was exclusively incumbent upon heads of families, and not on other members of the community. The rule, enounced to the judges by Israel, the son of Samuele da Nuremberg, was that "Jewish fathers of families in the feast of *Purim*, before dinner, take a small quantity of the blood of a Christian child, put it in their cup full of wine and sprinkle the table with it".[22] Angelo of Verona placed it in the category, not of ritual regulations, but of customs (Hebrew, *minhagh*, Latin *mos*) and, always with patience and in a summary manner, explained that "the established custom is that the head of the family, and no one else, must place the powdered blood in the unleavened bread in the time of the Passover".[23]

Mosè da Würzburg, for his part, reported that, up to the time when he had been the head of a family in various places in Germany, it had been considered obligatory to provide blood for the Passover rites. Subsequently, since he no longer occupied the role of head of family, he had been exempted from performing this duty.²⁴ Mosè da Bamberg also stated that, as long as he had been the head of the family in Germany, he had procured the blood for the Passover *Seder*. He then went into service with various Jewish families at Ulm and other centers in Franconia, and was considered exempted from this custom.²⁵

In this regard, it should be noted that the pre-eminent role of the head of family (*paterfamilias*, a rendering of the Hebrew *ha-al ha-bait*, "patron of the house"), in the celebration of the Passover rites, particularly, in the medieval Ashkenazi environment, is attested to by many manuscript and printed texts with comments on the *Haggadah* of *Pesach*. Among other things, these texts stress that the obligation of the ritual washing of the hands (*netilat yadaim*) at the beginning of the *Seder* was only incumbent upon the head of the family, almost exclusively entrusted with the reading of the *Haggadah*, while all the guests were exempt. Beniamin di Meir of Nuremberg, at the beginning of the 16th century, testified to the existence of this custom, stating that he had observed it to be widespread in all the Jewish communities of Germany. "I have noticed that, most of the time", wrote the German rabbi, "the ritual washing of the hands (in the Passover *Seder*) is performed only by the head of the family, while the guests do not wash their hands at all".²⁶

On the other hand, procuring the raw material required for performance of the blood ritual was not an easy job, involving costs which the heads of poorer families could not afford. It was therefore anticipated that the heads of poorer families were exempt from a task which proved too costly for them, as was unhesitatingly admitted by the ancient expert Mosè of Würzburg when he explained to the inquisitors of Trent that "the Jews naturally require the blood of a Christian child, but if they were poor and could not afford any blood, they were relieved of the expense".²⁷

Rich Jews, often in a mixed spirit of prodigality and magnanimity, took over the beneficial task of assisting the poorer Jews by supplying the precious fluid required, although obviously in minute amounts. Isacco da Gridel, Angelo of Verona's cook, recalled that, when he was in service with the head of a family at Cleberg, a rich relative of his wife supplied them with a small preparation of dried blood at no charge, stating that "it was customary to do this for the poor". The blood had been acquired from the well-known rabbi Shimon of Frankfurt.²⁸ Mosè of Bamberg, the professional traveler, also recounted that he had had a dependent family until 1467, and, since his indigence was well known to all, he was supplied with powdered blood "of a size equal to a nut" by Salomone, a rich merchant from lower Germany, and sometimes by Cervo, a wealthy Jew from Parchim in Mecklenburg, who gave him no more than half a spoonful.[29]

The rite of the wine, or blood, and curses had a dual significance. On the one hand, it was intended to recall the miraculous salvation of Israel brought about through the sign of the blood of the lamb placed on the door-posts of Jewish houses to protect them from the Angel of Death when they were about to be liberated from slavery in Egypt. It was also intended to bring closer final redemption, prepared by means of God's vengeance on the gentiles who had failed to recognize Him and had persecuted the Jewish people. The memorial of the Passion of Christ, relived and celebrated in the form of an anti-ritual, miraculously exemplified the fate destined for Israel's enemies. The blood of the Christian child, a new *Agnus Dei*, and the eating of his blood, were premonitory signs of the proximate ruin of Israel's indomitable and implacable persecutors, the followers of a false and mendacious faith.

The old man, Mosè da Würzburg, stressed both the significance of the blood rite and the curses, from the positive memorial of the blood of the lamb on the door-posts of the houses and the negative memorial of the passion of Christ, scorned and abhorred.

"According to the laws of Moses, it is commanded of the Jews that, in the days of the Passover, every head of family should take the blood of a perfect male lamb and place it (as a sign) on the door-posts of the dwellings. Nevertheless, since the custom of taking the blood of the perfect male lamb was being lost, and, in its place, (the Jews) now used the blood of a Christian boy [...] and they do this and consider it necessary as a negative memorial (of the Passion) of Jesus, God of the Christians, who was a male, rather than a female, and who was hanged and died on the cross in torment, in a shameful and vile manner".[30]

Israele, Samuele of Nuremberg's son, referred to the rite's ancient value in a response to his judges relating to the significance which came to be attributed, over time, to the mixing of the blood into the unleavened bread. "We consume it in the unleavened bread" he said, "as a memorial of the blood with which the Lord commanded Moses to paint the door-posts of the doors of Jewish houses when they were the slaves of the Pharaoh".[31]

On the other hand, Vitale of Weissenburg, Samuele's agent, preferred to confer a second meaning upon the rite, that is, that of an upside-down memorial to the Passion of Christ, considered as an emblem and paradigm of the fall of Israel's enemies and of divine vengeance, forewarning of final redemption. "We use the blood", he declared, "as a sad memorial of Jesus [...] in outrage and contempt of Jesus, God of the Christians, and every year we do the memorial of that passion [...] in fact, the Jews perform the memorial of the Passion of Christ every year, by mixing the blood of the Christian boy into their unleavened bread".[32]

The origins of the ritual of the use of blood in the Passover dinner are not very clear; nor do we know the names of the rabbinical authorities who presumably taught it. The only defendants in the Trent trials able to shed any light on the subject were Samuele da Nuremberg and Mosè da Würzburg, both of whom possessed a high degree of Hebrew culture, the fruit of many years of arduous study in the most famous Talmudic academies (*yeshivot*) in Germany. Neither Samuele nor Mosè were able to provide precise answers in this regard, entrenching themselves behind the hypothesis that the ritual was based on ancient traditions which were only transmitted orally, for obvious reasons of prudence, and that no written traces of it remain in the texts of ritual law. Just when these traditions were formed, and why, was, for them, an unresolved mystery, enveloped in the mists of the past.

Samuele vaguely attributed these traditions to the rabbis of the Talmud (*Iudei sapientiores in partibus Babiloniae*), who were said to have introduced the ritual in a very remote epoch, "before Christianity attained its present power". Those scholars, united at a learned congress, were said to have concluded that the blood of a Christian child was highly beneficial to the salvation of souls, if it was extracted during the course of a memorial ritual of the passion of Jesus, as a sign of contempt and scorn for the Christian religion. Over the course of this counter-ritual, the innocent boy, who had to be less than seven years old and had to be a boy, like Jesus, was crucified among torments and expressions of execration, as had happened to Christ.[33] Another praiseworthy addition was circumcision, to make the symbolic similarity more obvious and significant. We do not know how firmly convinced Samuele was of what he said; but it seems certain that the judges were highly gratified with this kind of macabre confession. This does not detract from the fact that the allegations of this Jew, at least in historical and ideological terms, if not in relation to the practical application of the [alleged] ritual in the case of little Simon, were quite plausible.

Mosè, "the Old Man" of Würzburg, was even vaguer than Samuele, noting that the blood ritual was not recorded in any of the ritualistic scripts of Judaism, but was transmitted orally, and in secret, by rabbis and scholars in Jewish law. Mosè nevertheless confirmed that the Christian boy who was to be crucified during the rite in commemoration of the Christ's shameful Passion had to be less than seven years old and of the male sex.[34]

In accordance with Samuele da Nuremberg's statements ("we believe that the blood of the sacrificed Christian boy is of great benefit in the salvation of our souls"), it was the custom, attributed to the participants in the blood ritual, to perform collective acts, even if only symbolic, to stress their intervention in the ceremony, such as that of touching the victim's body. "All those present placed their hands, now one and now the other, as if to suffocate the child, because the Jews believe that they render themselves meritorious before God by demonstrating their participation in the sacrifice of a Christian child". Isacco da Gridel, Angelo da Verona's cook, in effect, affirmed this in his confession, by describing his own participation in a ritual child murder committed at Worms in 1460, according to him.[35]

In a certain sense, this behavior recalled the collective funereal rituals proper to the Judaism of the German territories during medieval times, testified to, among other things, in the writings of Rabbi Shalom of Wiener Neustadt. These writings include a description of the *hakkafoth*, the circular procession around the coffin of the deceased by the persons present at the funeral to drive evil spirits away from the soul of the deceased, which reveals undoubted links with the Cabbalah; the collective custom of placing the hand on the casket or the tomb to implore divine mercy in favor of the deceased; and finally, the custom of placing a tuft of grass, a clod of earth, or a stone or pebble on the mound to testify to their own presence at the burial.[36]

While Samuele da Nuremberg remained more or less deliberately vague with regards to the origins of the custom of using the blood of the Christian child in the rituals of the Jewish Passover, he was very precise in discussing the persons who had transmitted and taught him these regulations orally. David Sprinz had actually been his rabbi and teacher, with whom Samuele had studied lovingly and with great success thirty years before, in the *yeshivah* of Bamberg, and later in the *yeshivah* of Nuremberg. Samuele knew that Sprinz had since moved to Poland, but didn't know whether or not he was still alive.[37]

David Tebel Sprinz was actually a rather well-known rabbi. Born in 1400, he had governed the Talmudic academy of Bamberg until 1448, and moved to Nuremberg around the middle of the century, taking control of the local *yeshiva*. He was still alive in 1474, carrying on his activity at Poznán in Poland.[38] Samuele's information in this respect was therefore correct, although we have no way of knowing how much truth there might be in his assertions relating to the subject of the teachings which Sprinz is alleged to have imparted orally in relation to the blood rituals. It is, however, a fact that three German rabbis, all of top-level importance, were implicated in the Trent trials in various ways relating to the transmission of traditions connected to ritual child murder, the use of blood in the Jewish Passover and the contemptuous commemoration of the Passion of Christ. Together with David Tebel Sprinz of Bamberg, we find the names of *Jodenmeister* Moshè of Halle, who also moved to Poznán just like his predecessor, and Shimon Katz, president of the rabbinical tribunal of Frankfurt am Main. It seems hardly accidental to me that none of the Ashkenazi rabbis – from the most famous to the least well-known – active in the German-origin Jewish communities of northern Italy are mentioned in the trial records; the only rabbis mentioned are ones whose activity was always carried on in Germany.

The observation that neither Italian Jews nor Italian Jewish communities were ever accused of committing ritual child murders compelled the Trent judges to investigate this phenomenon in order to determine whether or not the Italian Jews were simply unaware of the custom or rejected it as contrary to the principles of Judaism, in contrast to the Jews of Germanic origin.

If he had been able to speak freely, Samuele, from the lofty height of his Hebraic doctrine of Ashkenazi origin, might have replied with ill-concealed scorn that Italian Jews were not authoritative because they were ignorant in terms of rabbinical culture, not very observant, and very careless about the observation of ritual standards.[39] Instead, he restricted himself to admitting that Italian Jews did not possess this custom in their texts, nevertheless adding, immediately afterwards, that "it appeared in the texts of Jews from overseas", an intentionally inexact term, perhaps an allusion to the Judaism of Babylonia and, indirectly, to Ashkenazi ultramontane Judaism.[40]

On the other hand, even if we consider the confessions of Samuele and the other defendants to have been sincere and valid, and even accepting the realities of the dissemination of a ritual of this kind among the Jews of Medieval Germany, it appears beyond doubt that – as also emerges from the records of the Trent trials – in the world of Ashkenazi Judaism, there were people who rejected this ritual, considering it in conflict with Jewish law. The persons responsible for the scandalous plural child murders at Endingen, in Alsace, in 1462, confessed that they had feared that any one of them might have revealed the details of the crime to the elders of the local Jewish community, knowing that the elders would have unhesitatingly reported them to the police authorities.[41]

Returning to the facts of the Trent case, [at least] according the confession of Samuele da Nuremberg, in the days preceding the Jewish Passover, the defendants are alleged to have instructed Maestro Tobias to meet two German Jewish travelers passing through Trent in those days to inquire whether they were prepared to agree to abduct a Christian boy and conceal him in Samuele's house. But the two Ashkenazi Jews, David and Lazzaro "of Germany", decisively rejected the proposal, notwithstanding the fact that it was accompanied by an offer of the considerable sum of one hundred ducats. They had no intention of getting mixed up in matters of this kind.

The words of the two travelers clearly reveal their capacity as emissaries from the Jewish communities of Germany, who were, as usual, invited to Italy every year, in the spring, to arrange for the purchase of cedars for the autumnal feast of the "Capanne" or "Frascate" ["little sheds" and "covered market stalls"; the Jewish Feast of the Autumn Harvest] (*Sukkot*). In general, the objective of these specialist wholesale suppliers of ritual oranges for German Judaism was the Italian Riviera, particularly, San Remo. Lazzaro and David, on the other hand, were headed for Riva on the Lago di Garda, where they knew that what they needed could be found in the green orchards surrounding that delightful body of water.[42]

Even the commemorative pamphlet on little Simon, who was now a saint, published in Rome one hundred years after his death, with the obvious intention of recalling the facts relating to his martyrdom through education and admonishment, found space to praise the noble act of these two Jews in denouncing a ritual which they found detestable, considering it a true and proper betrayal of Jewish teachings. The consideration that precisely a clearly hagiographic source, such as the *Summary of the Life and Martyrdom of Saint Simon, Child of the City of Trent*, a text which is moreover openly anti-Jewish, should preserve and translate their words in a sense of positive appreciation, constitutes grounds for reflection. If nothing else, it sounds like a confirmation of the existence of a general belief that Ashkenazi Judaism was anything but monolithic in this sense.

"They (Lazzaro and David) prudently responded that they did not wish to commit similar follies and that they (with Moshè) wished them ill, because God did not command such things; on the contrary, He says, 'Thou shalt not kill', and that child murder was a new ceremony and against the law, which did not wish God's followers to shed innocent blood, such as that of a child, just because the child was a Christian. And if they thought about these things properly, they would discover that they were entirely invented, because there was no basis for them in the texts. Apart from that, they said that it was not right for a Jew to eat blood, as these men wished to do, by kneading the unleavened bread with a certain amount of blood".[43]

This same Giovanni da Feltre, the converted son of Shochat da Landshut, a person far from inclined to find anything justifiable in Jews and Judaism, had no difficulty in admitting that, in Germany, the ritual of using the blood of Christian children in the ceremonies of the Jewish Passover was only practiced by fundamentalist orthodox Ashkenazi sects. The same *Summary of the Life and Martyrdom of Saint Simon* briefly reports the ex-Jew's explicit notes in this regard. "The convert Giovanni said that not all the Jews do this; but that sometimes, they do it out of contempt for Christ and in revenge for the tribulations which they suffer because of that same Christ, our Lord".[44] It goes without saying that the problem did not even exist among Italian Jews, the Sephardim, or oriental Jews, who made up the overwhelming majority of the medieval Jewish world. But this majority was not always the most self-assertive, experiencing a serious inferiority complex compared to an Ashkenazi Judaism which considered itself the inimitable prototype of true religious orthodoxy (which was, moreover, created in its own image and resemblance).[45] Medieval Ashkenazi Judaism made up a hermetically sealed orthodoxy, which fed upon itself, confined by a myriad of minute ritualistic regulations, which they considered binding on all, the mere memorization of which constituted an arduous and almost impossible task.

According to Samuele da Nuremberg, the blood ritual was a secret rite, the rules of which were only transmitted with due prudence and circumspection.[46] The convert Giovanni da Feltre confirmed this.[47] Entering into increasingly greater detail, Mosè da Würzburg recalled a presumed rabbinical recommendation to keep the rite a secret from women and girls not having yet reached their religious majority, i.e., any age less than thirteen, "because they are fatuous and incapable of keeping a secret".[48] The inferiority of women and minors on a religious level, in addition to idiots and lunatics, was contemplated by Jewish ritual law (*halakhah*), which discriminated between these categories while largely or completely exonerating them from compliance with the positive precepts of Jewish law.

It is advisable at this point to mention the most significant text of anti-Christian polemics, the *Toledot Yeshu* (literally, "The Stories of Jesus"), or "The Jewish Counter-Gospel". This was a virulently defamatory biography of Jesus dating back to between the 4th and 8th century, disseminated first in Aramaic and later in Hebrew, in slightly different, or grossly divergent versions of the same text, written with the obvious intention of distorting the Christian religious identity by demolishing and ridiculing its memory. Systematic contempt for the figure of Christ and the Virgin Mary, described as a woman of easy virtue, formed the basis of a satirical and mocking tale, presented as a sort of side-show rivaling the Gospels themselves.[49]

It is not surprising that this classic of anti-Christian polemical writing found an attentive and highly satisfied readership among Jews all over the world, from the Islamic countries to Spain and Italy. It is even less surprising that the Jews of Germany adopted this text both enthusiastically and devoutly, as attested by the fact that almost all manuscripts of the *Toledot Yeshu* appear to have been written by Ashkenazi copyists, and that all of the translations of this text into Judeo-Hebraic dialect are in Yiddish. In one Yiddish manuscript of the *Toledot Yeshu*, the scribe admonishes the reader to be cautious and practice the necessary circumspection.

Hidden dangers might lurk unexpectedly as a result of excessive trust, as well as of unjustifiable complacency. Women, children and the feeble-minded were to be kept at a safe distance, as well as overly curious and intriguing Christians. "This treatise should be transmitted orally, and should not be read in public; nor should it be read to women or children, all the less so to feeble-minded persons. Its reading in the presence of Christians who understand German should certainly be avoided".[50]

In another manuscript, also of German origin, containing the *Toledot Yeshu* together with other anti-Christian scripts, which I recently held in my hands personally, the warnings are even more explicit. The oral transmission of secret texts was energetically enjoined upon all readers to avoid serious hazards and to ward off the serious problems which might possibly originate in surrounding Christian society.

" 'Ask thy elders, and they will tell thee' (Deut. 32:7). This booklet contains a tradition transmitted orally, by one person to another; it may be put in writing but not printed, for reasons due to our bitter exile. Beware of reading this text before children and persons of scanty understanding, or all the more so before the uncircumcised who understand German. For this reason, he who is wise shall know how to understand and maintain silence, because these are unpropitious times. If he is able to keep silent, he shall receive mercy (from God); God's just reward shall be upon him, and his work shall be before him. Publicizing this text is an extremely serious matter, and it cannot be revealed to all, because we can never know what tomorrow has in store for us and we can trust no one. I have written the text in intentionally allegorical and obscure language, because we have been selected as the Chosen People and we are permitted (by God) to use mysterious imagery".[51]

Mosè da Würzburg certainly know which precedents to mention in describing the recommendation to avoid discussion of the counter-ritual of the Passion of Christ and the use of the blood of Christian children in the Passover celebrations among women, children and the feeble-minded, "who are unable to keep a secret". Among the Jews of Germany, these precautions were quite understandable. Their violent anti-Christian feelings and expressions, both ideological and ritualistic, in which these feelings found an outlet and a reflection, necessarily had to be surrounded by a protective aura of secrecy and *omertà* [fatalistic manliness] because any indiscretion in this regard, either deliberately or through naiveté, could be the precursor of struggle and tragedy.

* * *

NOTES TO CHAPTER TWELVE

[1] "In vigilia Pasce sui, dum pinsatur pasta de qua postea faciant azimas, paterfamilias accipit de sanguine dicti pueri Cristiani et de illo sanguine ponit paterfamilias in pasta dum pinsatur, et sic ponitur et plus et minus prout paterfamilias habeat multum de sanguine predicto; et quod si poneret tantum quantum est unum granum lentis, sufficit; et quod sic paterfamilias ponit dictum sanguinem in pasta, aliquando videntibus illis qui pinsant panem (sc. pastam) et aliquando non; et quod si illi qui pinsant panem (sc. pastam) sunt persone fide, paterfamilias ponit sanguinem videntibus illis qui pinsant, et si non sunt fide ponit secrete" [Approximately: "On the eve of their Passover, when they are kneading the dough for the unleavened bread, the head of the family takes the blood of a Christian child and places some of it in the dough which they are kneading, in greater or lesser quantities according to whether the head of the family had a lot of it or not; and that if he adds as much a single lentil, it is enough; and that thus the head of the family places the said blood in the dough, sometimes those kneading the dough see him do it and sometimes he does it in secrecy"] (cfr. A. Esposito and D. Quaglioni, *Processi contro gli ebrei di Trento, 1475-1478*. I: *I processi del 1475*, Padua, 1990, pp. 251-252).

[2] "Et dicit quod (Iudei) accipiunt sanguinem pueri Cristiani et illum faciunt coagulare et deinde illum exiccant et de eo faciunt pulverem, quem pulverem postea ponunt singulis annis in pasta azimarum, quas faciunt in vigilia Paschae sui, quas azimas postea comedunt in die solemni, videlicet in die Paschae eorum" ["And he said that (the Jews) take the blood of Christian boys and allow it to coagulate and they dry it and make a powder of it, and place it in the dough of the unleavened

bread every year, on the eve of their Passover, and eat it on the solemn day, namely, during their Passover"] (cfr. ibidem, p. 318).

[3] "(Iudei) ponunt (sanguinem) in azimis suis seu fugatiis, quas comedunt in festo Pasce sui" ["(The Jews) place (blood) in their unleavened bread, which they eat during their Passover feast"] (cfr. ibidem, pp. 378-379).

[4] "Pater ipsius [...] de dicto sanguine ponebat in pasta, de qua pasta faciebat fugatias, et hoc ante festum Pasce eorum; quas fugatias ipsi Iudei postea comedebant in dicta die Pasce" ["The father [...] placed some of the blood in the dough, from which they make the unleavened bread, and does so before the Passover feast; which these Jews ate on Passover day"] (cfr. ibidem, p. 125).

[5] Cfr. G. Divina, *Storia del beato Simone da Trento*, Trent, 1902, vol. II, pp. 1-32.

[6] Wien, Österr. Nationalbibl., Ms. 5360, cc. 186r-189v. Information and translation by D. Quaglioni.

[7] "(Iudei) de dicto sanguine accipiunt aliquam particulam et ponunt in pasta, de qua pasta postea faciunt fugatias azimas, et de quibus fugatiis açimis postea comedunt inter se in die solemni, videlicet in die Pasce" ["(The Jews) take a few particles of the blood and place it in the dough, from which they make their unleavened bread, and later they eat it amongst themselves on the solemn day, namely, on Passover"] (cfr. Esposito and Quaglioni, *Processi*, cit., vol. I, p. 287).

[8] "(Iudei) ponunt illum sanguinem in eorum azimis et illum postea comedunt [...] in contemptum Iesu Cristi, quem Cristiani dicunt esse Deum suum; et quod ideo ponunt in eorum azimas sanguinem, quia posteaquam positus est sanguis in pasta, illam pastam pinsant et graminant, et deinde faciunt fugatias, quas fugatias postea punetant dicendo ista verba: *Chen icheressù chol hoyveha*. Que verba sonant in lingua Latina: 'Così sya consumadi li nostri inimizi'. Et postea dictas fugatias commedunt, que commestio fagatiarum cum sanguine significat quod ita corpus et virtus Iesu Cristi Dei Cristianorum ita penitus morte consumptum est et consumpta, sicut iste sanguis qui est in fugatiis ex commestione penitus consumitur" [Approximately: "(The Jews) place the blood in their unleavened bread and afterwards they eat it [...] in contempt of Jesus Christ, whom the Christians say is their God, and that the reason they put the blood in their unleavened bread, is because after the blood is placed in the dough, they knead the dough and shape it, and make their unleavened bread out of it, and they eat it, saying these words: *Chen icheressù chol hoyveha*, which means in Latin: 'Thus may all our enemies be consumed'. And then they eat the unleavened bread, and in eating it with the blood in it, it means that the

body and virtue of Jesus Christ, the God of the Christians, was thus punished by death and consumed, thus, the blood in the unleavened bread is thus consumed at a common meal"] (cfr. ibidem, p. 293). For the Hebrew words which appear in the text, see [Benedetto Bonelli], *Dissertazione apologetica sul martirio del beato Simone da Trento nell'anno MCCCCLXXV dagli ebrei ucciso*, Trent, Gianbattista Parone, 1747, p. 145.

[9] *Machazor le-Rosh Ha-Shanah* ("Liturgical Form for the Jewish New Year"), *Yehì razon shel Rosh Ha-Shanah* ("New Year's Wishes"), s.v. *cartì* ("leeks"). On the so-called "*Haggadah* of the Jewish New Year" and its content, see A. Toaff, *Mangiare alla giudia. La cucina ebraica in Italia dal Rinascimento all'età moderna*, Bologna, 2000, pp. 134-135.

[10] The depositions from Mosè da Ansbach, "a young person nineteen years old", on this matter are reported in detail in Divina, *Storia del beato Simone da Trento*, cit., vol. II, pp. 20-21.

[11] "In die Pasce ipsorum Iudeorum, ante cenam, unusquisque Iudeus paterfamilias accipit modicum de sanguine pueri Cristiani et illum ponit in uno ciato pieno vino, quem ciatum postea ponit super mensa, circa quem mensam omnes de dicta familia circumstant; et paterfamilias ponit digitum in ciato suo, in quo est commixtus sanguis pueri Cristiani, et deinde curo eodem digito balneato in vino aspergit totam mensam et ea omnia que super mensa sunt, dicendo certa verba Hebraica, per que in effectu commemorantur decem maledictiones quas Deus dedit Pharaoni et Egiptiis, quia nolebant dimittere populum Iudaicum; dicens quod posteaquam dictus paterfamilias dixit suprascripta verba, idem paterfamilias iungit hec alia verba: 'Ita imprecamur Deum quod similiter immittat predictas .X. maledictiones contra gentes, que sunt inimice fidei Iudeorum', intelligendo maxime contra Cristianos" ["On the Jewish Passover, before dinner, each Jewish head of a family takes a small quantity of the blood of a Christian child and places it in a glassful of wine, and they put the glassful of wine on the table, around which all members of the family are sitting; and the head of the family places his finger in his glass, containing the wine mixed with the blood of a Christian child, and then, after bathing his finger in it, he sprinkles the entire table around which the people are sitting, saying certain words in Hebrew, by means of which they commemorate the ten curses which God inflicted on the Egyptians, who didn't wish to release the Jewish people, after which each Jewish head of a family says the above words, after which he adds these words: 'Thus we pray God that he may inflict ten similar curses against the peoples who are enemies of the Jewish people', meaning,

most of all, the Christians"] (cfr. Esposito and Quaglioni, *Processi*, cit., vol. I, p. 356).

[12] "Pater ipsius [...] in die Pasce Iudeorum, ante cenam et etiam in die sequenti post Pascha ante cenam, accipiebat de dicto sanguine et de illo ponebat in ciato suo, in quo erat vinum, et deinde aspergebat mensam maledicendo fidem Cristianorum" ["Their father [...] on Passover, before dinner as well as before dinner the following day, takes some of the blood and puts it in his glass, containing wine, and sprinkles the table, cursing the Christian faith"] (cfr. ibidem, p. 125).

[13] The brief text of the *Haggadah* is the following: "Con prodigi, questo è il sangue (*zeh ha-dam*), come è detto: 'Farò prodigi in cielo e in terra' " ["With miracles, this is the blood (*zeh ha-dam*), as it is said: 'I will do miracles in the Heaven and Earth' "] (cfr. R. Bonfil, *Haggadah di Pesach*, Milan, 1962, pp. 62-63).

[14] "Hoc fecerunt in memoriam unius ex .x. maledictiones quas dedit Deus Egyptiatiis quando retinebant populum Hebraicum in servitute et quod inter ceteras maledictiones Deus convertit omnem aquam terre Egypti in sanguinem" ["This they do in memory of the ten curses inflicted by God on the Egyptians when they held the Hebrews captive and that, among these multiple curses, God changed all the water of Egypt into blood"] (cfr. Esposito and Quaglioni, *Processi*, cit., vol. I, p. 287).

[15] Israel Wolfgang's long and detailed report by is reproduced in Divina, *Storia del beato Simone da Trento*, cit., vol. II, pp. 16-19.

[16] Israele di Lazzaro managed the principal lending bank at Piacenza from 1449 until at least 1472 and was the treasurer of the Jewish community of the Duchy of Milan in the years 1453-1454. In 1479, he was still alive and represented the heirs of Benedetto da Como in the negotiations for renewal of the money lending permit in the city of Como (cfr. Sh. Simonsohn, *The Jews in the Duchy of Milan*, Jerusalem, 1982, vol. I, pp. 126, 131-133 etc.).

[17] On Lazzaro's deposition, cfr. Divina, *Storia del beato Simone da Trento*, cit., vol. II, pp. 23-25.

[18] Cfr. ibidem, pp. 25-32, presenting an exhaustive exposition of the details of Mosè Bamberg's long deposition.

[19] In this regard, see E. Carlebach, *The Anti-Christian Element in Early Modern Yiddish Culture*, in "Braun Lectures in the History of the Jews in Prussia", Ramat Gan, Bar-Ilan University, X (2003), 2003, p. 17.

[20] For the introduction of the term *shegez*, *shekez* ("cosa abominevole") [something abominable] to indicate the Christian children in Judeo-Italian dialect, see, among others, G. Cammeo, *Studi*

dialettali, in "il Vessillo Israelitico", LVII (1909), p. 214; A. Milano, *Glossario dei vocaboli e delle espressioni di origine ebraica in uso nel dialetto giudaico-romanesco*, Florence, 1927, p. 254; V. Colorni, *La parlata degli ebrei mantovani, in Id., Judaica Minora. Saggi sulla storia dell'ebraismo italiano dall'antichità all'età moderna*, Milan, 1983, p. 614 (the author attempts to provide a less problematical and embarrassing connotation of the term, proposing that it be translated as "street urchin" or "little rascal, scamp").

[21] Cfr. Giulio Morosini, *Derekh Emunah. Via della fede mostrata agli ebrei*, Roma, Propaganda Fide, 1683, p. 157.

[22] "Iudei patresfamilie in festo Pasce ante cenam, accipiunt modicum de sanguine pueri Cristiani et de illo ponunt in suo ciato pieno vino, et cum eo aspergunt mensam" ["The head of the Jewish family, before the Passover dinner, takes a small quantity of the blood of a Christian child and places it in his glassful of wine, and sprinkles the table with it"] (cfr. Esposito and Quaglioni, *Processi*, cit., vol. I, p. 192).

[23] "Ita est de more, ut patresfamilias ponunt pulverem sanguinis Cristiani in dictis açimis in dicto tempore" ["It is their custom to place the blood of a Christian child in their unleavened bread at that time"] (cfr. ibidem, p. 295).

[24] "Ipse non curavit habere sanguinem, quia non erat paterfamilias, quia soli patresfamilias sunt illi qui debent habere (sanguinem) et qui utuntur" ["He was not worried about obtaining any blood, because he was not the head of a family, because only the heads of families had to obtain it (blood) and possess it"] (cfr. ibidem, p. 358).

[25] Cfr. Divina, *Storia del beato Simone da Trento*, cit., vol. II, pp. 25-30.

[26] On this argument and on the preeminent role of the head of the family in the celebration of the rites of *Pesach* in the Ashkenazi environment, see, in particular, Sh. Safrai and Z. Safrai, *Haggadah of the Sages. The Passover Haggadah*, Jerusalem, 1998, p. 106 (in Hebrew).

[27] "Sanguis pueri Cristiani est summe necessarius ipsis Iudeis, videlicet patribusfamilias ipsorum Iudeorum. Et si esset aliquis pauper Iudeus, qui non possit haberi de sanguine, excusaretur" ["The blood of a Christian boy is absolutely necessary for these Jews, namely, the heads of Jewish families; anyone who cannot obtain blood, is excused"] (cfr. Esposito and Quaglioni, *Processi*, cit., vol. I, p. 356).

[28] Cfr. Divina, *Storia del beato Simone da Trento*, cit., vol. II, pp. 22-23. *La biografia di Shimon Katz, rabbino a Francoforte sul Meno dal 1462 al 1478*, is found in I.J. Yuval, *Scholars in Their Time. The*

Religious Leadership of German Jewry in the Late Middle Ages, Jerusalem, 1984, pp. 135-148 (in Hebrew).

[29] Cfr. Divina, *Storia del beato Simone da Trento*, cit., vol. II, pp. 26-27.

[30] "Secundum legem Moisi, precipiebatur ipsis Iudeis quod in die Pasce unusquisque paterfamilias acciperet de sanguine agni masculi sine macula, et de illo sanguine poneret super liminaribus hostiorum domorum suarum; et quod inter ipsos Iudeos est sublata illa consuetudo de accipiendo sanguinem dicti agni masculi sine macula, ut supra dixit, et in eius locum modo utuntur sanguine pueri Cristiani [...] et hoc faciunt et ita dicunt esse necessarium in pessimam commemorationem Iesu, Dei Cristianorum, qui fuit suspensus et qui fuit masculus et non femina, et qui vituperose et turpiter in cruce et in tormentis mortuus est" ["According to the laws of Moses, the Jews were commanded that each head of the family should take the blood of male sheep without fault and paint the lintels of their doorways with it, and that these Jews, having neglected this custom, of taking the blood of a male sheep without fault, as set forth above, instead, they use the blood of Christian boys [...] and they do this and say that this is necessary in bad memory of Jesus, the God of the Christians, who was hanged and who was a male and not a female, and who was shamefully and vilely hanged on the cross and died in torment"] (cfr. Esposito and Quaglioni, *Processi*, cit., vol. I, p. 357).

[31] "Illa esio sanguinis Cristiani et quare ita illum comedunt in fugatiis [...] est commemoratio sanguinis quem Dominus dixit ad Moisem ut deberet spargere super liminaria hostiorum domorum Iudeorum, quando ipsi Iudei erant in servitute Pharaonis" (cfr. ibidem, p. 186).

[32] "(Iudei) haberent sanguinem [...] in (malam) memoriam Iesu [...] in contemptum et vilipendium Iesu, Dei Cristianorum, dicens quod omni anno faciut memoriam dicte passionis [...]; ipsi Iudei faciunt memoriam dicte passionis Iesu omni anno, quia ponunt de sanguine pueri Cristiani omni anno in eorum azimis sive fugatiis" [Approximately: "(The Jews) obtain blood [...] in bad memory of Jesus [...] in contempt and outrage of Jesus, the God of the Christians, saying that every year, they perform a memorial of the said Passion [...]; these Jews perform a memorial of Jesus, because they place the blood of a Christian boy in their unleavened bread every year"] (cfr. ibidem, p. 220).

[33] "Quod iam multis et multis annis (et aliter nescit dicere quot anni sint, nisi quod credere suo fuit antequam fides Cristiana esset in tanta potentia), quod Iudei sapientiores in partibus Babiloniae seu locis

vicinis, ut dicitur, fecerunt consilium inter se, et ibi deliberatum fuit, quod saluti animarum ipsorum Iudeorum; et quod talis sanguis non poterat prodesse nisi extraheretur de puero Cristiano; et qui puer Cristianus, dum sic extraheretur sanguis, interficeretur ea forma qua fuit interfectus Iesus, quem Cristiani colunt pro Deo; et qui puer Cristianus debeat esse etatis annorum septem vel infra et quod non sit maioris etatis .VII. annis, sed potius sit minoris etatis; dicens quod si esset femina Cristiana non esset bona ad sacrificium suum, videlicet ad extrahendum sanguinem, et talis sanguis mulieris, licet minoris etatis .VII. annis, non esset bonus. Et ratio quia curo Iesus, quem nos Cristiani colimus pro Deo, fuerit crucifixus et in eius contemptum et vilipendium hoc faciant, conveniens putant ipsi Iudei quod ille a quo extrahant sanguinem debet esse masculus et non femina" [Approximately: "He said that many, many years ago (he didn't know how many, but he believed that it was before the Christian faith became so powerful), the Jewish wise men in parts of Babylon or nearby, it is said, held a council and decided that the blood of Christian boys killed in this manner was good for the souls of the Jews, and that this blood could only be extracted from a Christian boy; and that the Christian boy, when his blood was extracted, had to be killed in the same manner as Jesus, whom the Christians claim is their God, and that the Christian boy must be seven years of age or less, and that he could not be older than seven, but that he could be younger, saying that if it was a girl it was no good for their sacrifice, i.e., to extract the blood, and that the blood of such a girl, even if she was less than seven years of age, was no good. And the reason for this is that Jesus, whom the Christians claim is their God, was crucified, and they do this in contempt and outrage against them, since these Jews think that the person from whom one extracts the blood must be a male and not a female").

[34] "Quod apud ipsos Iudeos non reperitur scriptum, sed inter ipsos ita dicitur apud doctos et peritos in lege, et istud habetur ex successione memorie, et tenetur pro secreto inter ipsos Iudeos [...] et quod necesse est quod talis sanguis sit sanguis pueri Cristiani masculi et non femine, et qui non sit maioris etatis 7 annorum" ["That no text will be found among those Jews, but that it was said among those same Jews and experts in the law, and that they handed it down from generation to generation in memory, and it was kept secret among those Jews [...] and that it was necessary for this blood to be the blood of a Christian boy and not a girl, and that he could not be more than 7 years old"] (cfr. ibidem, p. 357).

[35] "Quod omnes praedicti astantes posuerunt manum ad suffucandum illum, ponendo modo unus, modo alius manum, et quod

omnes praedicti Judaei adjuverunt ad interficiensum, quia existimant omnes Hebraei quod ille multum promereatur apud Deum, qui adjuverat ad interficiendum aliquem puerum christianum" ["That all those present placed their hands on him to suffocate him, some of them placing one hand, some of them both hands, and that all the above mentioned Jews helped kill him, because they thought that all those Hebrews would be promoted before God who helped kill that Christian boy in any way"]. Deposition of Isacco da Gridel of 28 November 1475. Cfr. [Bonelli], *Dissertazione apologetica*, cit., p. 144. On this argument, see also Divina, *Storia del beato Simone da Trento*, cit., vol. II, pp. 34-36. It should be noted that, according to the trial records, the defendants accused of the ritual murder at Valréas in 1247 claimed that they had performed the rite of crucifixion out of revenge against Jesus, responsible for the tragic exile of the Jewish people ("debebant eam crucifigere per illum prophetam, qui vocatur Jesus, per quem sunt in captivitate et in deffectu ipsius hec fecerunt") ["they must crucify him for the prophet whom they call Jesus, for whom they are in captivity and they did it because of that"] and that the participants had placed their hands on the child ("quod omnes tetigerunt puellam causa venie") ["and they all touched the child to obtain indulgence"]. Cfr. M. Stern, *Urkundliche Beiträge über die Stellung der Päpste zu den Juden*, Kiel, 1895, vol. II, p. 51.

[36] On these funeral rites, proper to German Judaism, see *Hilkhot w-minhage' R. Shalom mi-Neustadt* ("Rules and Customs of rabbi Shalom of Wiener Neustadt"), by Sh. Spitzer, Jerusalem, 1997, p. 188; A. Unna, *Miminhage' yahadut Ashkenaz* ("Among the Customs of the Jews of Germany"), in A. Wassertil, *Yalkut minhagim*, Jerusalem, 1976, vol. II, p. 34.

[37] "Et dicit ipse Samuel se scire predicta et ea didicisse non quod legerit in scripturis suis, sed quia dici audivit et didicit a quodam preceptore Iudeo qui vocabatur magister David Sprinç, qui regebat scolas in Bamberg et in Nurremberg, sed quo preceptore ipse Samuel didicit iam .XXX. annis preteritis. Et dicit interrogatus, quod dictus magister David ivit postea in Poloniam et nescit an vivit vel sit mortuus" (cfr. Esposito and Quaglioni, *Processi*, cit., vol. I, p. 253).

[38] On the life and rabbinical activity of David Tebel Sprinz at Bamberg, Nuremberg and Poznán, see *Germania Judaica*, Tübingen, 1987, vol. III: *1350-1519*, t. I, p. 76; vol. III, t. II, pp. 1014-1015; Yoseph b. Moshè, *Leqet yosher*, by J. Freimann, Berlin, 1904, p. XXV, par. 30; Yuval, *Scholars in Their Time*, cit., pp. 369-377.

[39] Samuele in fact is said to have claimed that ignorant Ashkenazi were not aware of this custom either. Maestro Tobia da Magdeburg, as

we have seen, although he was a physician, was not very well versed in Hebraic culture, seeking to persuade the inquisitors that he had become aware of the blood ritual only having come into contact, at Trent, with the same Samuele, with Mosè "the Old Man" da Würzburg and with Angelo da Verona. "Tobias [...] se numquam usum fuisse dicto sanguine nec unquam dici audivisse de dicto sanguine, nisi hiis diebus quibus Samuel, Moises et Angelus sibi dixerunt" (cfr. Esposito and Quaglioni, *Processi*, cit., vol. I, p. 318).

[40] "Et dicit quod ipsi Iudei Italici non habent istud in scripturis suis, sed bene dicitur quod de hoc est scriptura inter Iudeos qui sunt ultra mare" (cfr. ibidem, p. 251).

[41] On this argument, see K. von Amira, *Das Endinger Judenspiel*, Halle, 1883; R. Po-Chia Hsia, *The Myth of Ritual Murder. Jews and Magic in Reformation Germany*, New Haven (Conn.) – London, 1988, pp. 18-22.

[42] "(Lazarus and David de Alemania) responderunt se nolle intromittere in illa re, quia dicebant se esse impeditos ad faciendum alia, quia volebant ire in Riperiam territorii Brixiensis ad emendum de citronis, causa portandi illos in Alemaniam" ["(Lazarus and David of Germany) said they didn't want to get mixed up in this business, because they said they were prevented from doing otherwise, because they wanted to go to Riva in the Brescian region and buy citrus fruit, to take it to Germany"] (cfr. Esposito and Quaglioni, *Processi*, cit., vol. I; p. 242). Many Central European Jewish communities provided themselves with the palm (*tulavim*) and cedar (*etroghim*) leaves necessary for the celebration of the festivities of the Capanne (Sukkot), purchasing them at San Remo and on the Italian Riviera. The 1435 statutes of San Remo provided for the sale of cedar and palm leaves to Jews, who were granted the option of choosing cedars in compliance with the ritual requirements, when the leaves were still attached to the trees (cfr. R. Urbani and G. Zazzu, *Ebrei a Genova*, Genoa, 1984, p. 22). Other destinations favored by these emissaries of the Ashkenazi Jewish communities responsible for purchasing the ritual cedar leaves, were the Lago di Garda region, celebrated in the responses of rabbi Mordekhai Jaffe in the mid-16 century, followed by Puglia and the Florentine countryside (cfr. A. Toaff, *Il vino e la carne. Una comunità ebraica nel Medioevo*, Bologna, 1989, pp. 124, 127, and, above all, Sh. Schwarzfuchs, *De Gênes à Trieste. Le commerce millénaire des cédrats*, in G. Todeschini and P.C. Ioly Zorattini, *Il mondo ebraico. Gli ebrei tra Italia nord-orientale e Impero asburgico dal Medioevo all'Età contemporanea*, Pordenone, 1991, pp. 259-286).

[43] *Ristretto della vita e martirio di S. Simone fanciullo della città di*

Trento, Rome, Filippo Neri alle Muratte, 1594, pp. 9-10.

[44] Ibidem, pp. 26-27.

[45] In an important essay, Isadore Twersky (*The Contribution of Italian Sages to Rabbinic Literature*, in "Italia Judaica", I, 1983, p. 390) stresses "the sturdy, sometimes aggressive, Ashkenazi sentiment of allegiance which characterizes central and Eastern Europe at this time, where Ashkenazi origins are flaunted and the scrupulous rigidity of Ashkenazi precedent is held aloft".

[46] "(Iudei) habent istud pro secreto, et unus narrat alteri ex successione, et aliter non reperitur scriptura inter ipsos Iudeos" [Approximately: "(The Jews) keep this a secret, and tell it from generation to generation, and that otherwise it was not written down among these Jews"] (cfr. Esposito and Quaglioni, *Processi*, cit., vol. I, p. 251).

[47] "Et dicit quod alii Iudei similiter ita faciunt, prout ipse vidit fieri et audivit, dicens quod predicta fiunt secretissime inter ipsos" ["And he said that the other Jews did the same, just as he saw and heard it being done, saying that it was a big secret among them"] (cfr. ibidem, p. 125).

[48] "Secundum consilium doctorum Iudeorum dicitur quod mulieres nec masculi minores .XIII. annis non debent interesse quando dicti pueri interficiuntur, nec etiam illud debent scire, quia mulieres et minores tredecim annis sunt faciles et leves et nesciunt tenere secreta" (cfr. ibidem, pp. 357-358).

[49] In the vast bibliography relating to the *Toledot Yeshu*, see, in particular, S. Krauss, *Das Leben Jesu nach jüdischen Quellen*, Berlin, 1902; Hugh Schonfield, *Toledot Yeshu According to the Hebrews*, London, 1937; R.Di Segni, *Il Vangelo del Ghetto. Le "storie di Gesù": leggende e documenti della tradizione medievale ebraica*, Rome, 1985; D. Biale, *Counter-History and Jewish Polemics against Christianity. The "Sefer Toldot Jeshu" and the "Sefer Zerubavel"*, in "Jewish Social Studies", VI (1999), pp. 130 ss.; Carlebach, *The Anti-Christian Element in Early Modern Yiddish Culture*, cit., pp. 8-17.

[50] Cfr. Krauss, *Das Leben Jesu nach judischen Quellen*, cit., pp. 10-11.

[51] The manuscript, a late copy of the *Toledot Yeshu* and other anti-Christian polemic writings, is in Hebrew and appears under the name of *Ma'asè ha-Nozrì* ("The Truth About the Nazarene"). It appears to have been copied in Germany around 1740 on a somewhat older copy of the text. It was put up for sale at Jerusalem by the Judaica Jerusalem auction house on 5 January 2005. For a summary description of the text in English, see the auction catalogue (p. 58, n. 122).

CHAPTER THIRTEEN

TO DIE AND KILL FOR THE LOVE OF GOD

In the late 14th century or early 15th century, a woman from Esztergom, in northern Hungary, wrote to the authoritative rabbi Shalom of Wiener Neustadt with an urgent and pathetic inquiry. Some years previously, in her native country, on a Sabbath day, the local Christians had assaulted the Jews, threatening to baptize their children by force. Seized by despair, the poor woman, to prevent her children from forced conversion, seized a knife and piously killed them. She then fled, taking refuge in Poland. But she was now seized by remorse and was turning to the learned rabbi to find out how to expiate her guilt and earn God's pardon. Shalom of Wiener Neustadt had no hesitations of this kind and promptly reassured the woman that, in this kind of tragic situation, the Jewish mother had acted for the better and in an appropriate manner, and did not therefore deserve to be punished in any way.[1]

Years before, in April 1265, when the Christians assaulted the Jewish district of Coblenz, in the Lower Rhineland, a Jew, fearing his family might be baptized by force, decided to kill his wife and four children, cutting their throats with a knife.[2] He then turned to Rabbi Meir of Rothenburg, one of the greatest authorities of Ashkenazi Judaism, asking if he should do penitence for that cruel action.

"Suicide for the sanctification of God is certainly permitted", replied the rabbi, "while, as regards the killing of other persons for the same reason, one must search for and find evidence in the texts. Any action of this type has been considered acceptable and even permissible for some time. We have personally learned and verified as true the fact that many illustrious Jews have killed their own children and wives (under similar conditions)".[3]

The fact that the mother from Esztergom and the father from Coblenz questioned the rabbi at all, asking what type of repentance was required, under Jewish law, for persons guilty of killing their own children to protect them from baptism, thus sacrificing them for the love of God, is a clear indication of a fear on their part that such actions might be quite incompatible with the dictates of the *halakhah*, the ritual laws of Judaism. This fear, or if one prefers, this sense of uncertainty, must have been rather widespread among the Jewish populations of the German territories, as well as among their rabbis, as in the case of Meir of Rothenburg, since, rather than justify such behavior on the basis of Jewish law, they preferred to recall illustrious precedents, which had, in effect, rendered these actions permissible by adoption. The call to suicide and mass child murder, as well as to examples of collective martyrdom, such as that of Coblenz in 1096, was indirect, but nevertheless obvious.

In fact, the phenomenon of martyrdom among German Jews at the time of the First Crusade had no significant precedents in Judaism capable of explaining and justifying the phenomenon. Jewish chronicles written subsequent to those events, intended to describe the behavior of the Jews of the communities of the Valley of the Rhine in these situations, offered no excuse at all, nor did they appear to feel the need for justification of any kind. Under such tragic and exceptional circumstances, the choice to act contrary to the innate instinct to survive, and to love and care for one's children, was irrational, spontaneous and unpremeditated. The rational dictates of Jewish law could have no influence in such a situation.[4]

German Jews were terrorized by the possibility of forceful conversion to Christianity. They were even more frightened of the possibility, which became a tragic reality in many cases, of seeing their own children violently dragged to the baptismal font. With obsessive insistence, the German Jewish communities, from the beginning of the Crusades, addressed repeated and often useless appeals to their rulers so that their children might be protected from forced baptism.[5] Supplications to this effect are said to have been repeated over the following centuries, wherever there were Jewish nuclei of German origin, even in the regions of Northern Italy, becoming one of the distinctive features of Ashkenazi conduct.[6]

To the teachers who killed their pupils, the mothers who cut the throats of their children, the fathers who killed their wives and children, conversion to Christianity represented a repellent and abhorrent eventuality. From their earliest childhood, the Jews of the Franco-German territories had been taught to view the Christian faith as a despicable religion, barbarous and idolatrous, dedicated to the worship of images and holy cadavers. Baptism and the forced conversion of the Chosen People to the religion of their cruel and ignorant persecutors was surely the quickest passport to a base and corrupt life, deserving the severest divine punishment in both this world and the next. Death, death without hesitation of any kind, was to be considered a beneficial and desirable alternative.[7]

In view of the intolerable menace hanging over the souls of the tender infants, born to be brought up in the love of the True God and according to His sacred dictates, yet fated to be immersed against their will in the contagious waters of baptism, the lethal blade was the sole adequate response. The blood shed by these innocent children, put to death for the love of God, was said to have served to bring forward the time of redemption. Their sacrifice, like that of the uncontaminated lambs offered as a holocaust on the altar of the Temple, was thought to help arouse Divine vengeance against their idolatrous persecutors. This vengeance was to be consummated from on High, in the Heavens, but needed to be prepared on Earth. God's vengeance, and that of the fathers and mothers, compelled to shed the precious blood of their children by the extreme arrogance of the Christians.[8]

Sometimes the synagogue was destined to be chosen as the favorite location for the sacrifice of these children and the sanctification of God's name. The place of prayer conferred solemnity and rituality upon the drama being performed. The Holy Ark with the rolls of the Law (*Aron ha-kodesh*), the pulpit, also called the *almemor* (or *himah* or *tehah* in Hebrew),[9] the benches upon which the faithful were accustomed to sit, were all bathed in the blood of the uncontaminated victims, while laments combined with invocations, litanies and imprecations, opening the way to Heaven. The sacred nature of the Temple failed to slow the arm of those who rose up to immolate, nor did the act reek of sacrilege. Quite the contrary, these surroundings constituted the most appropriate theatre for this act of sublime martyrdom. The story of Isacco, son of David, sacristan (*parnas*) of the synagogue at Magonza, who committed suicide during the first Crusade killing his children and mother and setting fire to the place of prayer, seems illuminating in this regard.[10]

In those days, the great majority of the Jewish population of Magonza, after uselessly seeking refuge in the bishop's palace, met death in an indiscriminate massacre. Few of their lives were spared. Among them, Isacco, the sacristan of the synagogue, had personally been compelled to accept conversion to Christianity. But after a few days, the poor convert, assailed by remorse and repentance, dreamed up a delirious ritual of expiation based on a series of human sacrifices intended to move the Eternal to vengeance in a bath of blood.

First of all, Isacco, seized by fervent hallucinations, put his mother to death, burning her alive in her house. He then dragged his children, "not yet of an age capable of discerning good from evil" into the synagogue. Here, on the pulpit, the *almemor*, before the Ark containing the rolls of the Law, with his own hands, he slaughtered them all, one by one, offering a sacrifice to God. "And as the blood of the unhappy children spurted from their mortal wounds, painting the door-posts of the Ark of the Law, the sacristan devoutly recited: 'May this blood serve as an expiation for all my sins' ". Immediately afterwards, he set fire to the synagogue, running from one side of the hall to another, his hands raised to Heaven in an act of prayer, his chanting voice clearly audible outside the holy sanctuary. And among the flames, before the holy Ark, the miserable Isacco finally found the death he so desired".[11]

A psychopath? A lunatic suffering from homicidal religious fits of insanity? A poor soul driven mad by desperation and seized by a self-destructive mania? A madman and masochistic fanatic? The anonymous author who reports this tragic tale has absolutely no doubt at all of this kind: Isacco was a "wholesome and upright person, pious, merciful, and God-fearing". His behavior deserved to be pointed out as an example to later generations, and all types of censure in this case were to be considered absolutely unjustified and inopportune. Isacco had decided to sacrifice his own children on the *almemor*, before the Ark of the Law, the holiest place in the synagogue, according to a ritual, recalling, on the one hand, the holocaust offered on the altar of the Temple of Jerusalem, and, on the other hand, the Biblical sacrifice of Isaac, which, according to the *Midrash*, had actually been carried out. The grisly example of the pious sacristan of Magonza appeared to inspire enthusiastic and zealous imitators. The synagogue itself was thus transformed, in time, into a sort of sacred slaughterhouse, in which, among moans and prayers, the blood of the women and children, sacrificed for the love of God, gushed forth in torrents: Holy Ark, pulpit, women's gallery, benches and steps were all stained red, as was the altar of the Temple.

At Vienna in 1421, during that city's violent riots against the Jews, accused of favoring and supporting the Hussites, the rabbi Natan Eger visited all the local Jewish boys in their own homes, and instructed their mothers to slaughter them without remorse if the Christians attempted to baptize them *en masse*. One Yiddish chronicle reports that, on that occasion, the Jewish community gathered a great number of children together in the synagogue to prevent their forced conversion, as vehemently demanded by an apostate.

"The Jews of the community at this point began to cry in a loud voice: 'Alas, (the Christians), may God forbid, intend to contaminate our children, holy and immaculate'. They therefore deliberated to deprive them of their lives in order to sanctify the name of God the Blessed.

"They drew lots and selected the pious rabbi Jonah Ha-Cohen, who was responsible for putting the decision into action. This happened during the Festival of the Capanne (*Sukkot*).

"While the entire community murmured the formula of the call to repentance in a low voice, turning from one to another, the rabbi placed himself in front of the Ark containing the rolls of the Law, and cut the throats of all the children, one after the other. This occurred in the great hall, intended for men's prayers. The women were also slaughtered, one by one, in the antechamber of the synagogue, intended for them, and this to sanctify the name of God. The last woman waiting to be sacrificed turned to Jonah, the rabbi, asking him to butcher her (without entering the women's hall, but) causing his arm to pass through the grid, which separated the two halls. Then Johan the rabbi, having no more strength to kill himself, removed the rafters in the synagogue, made a stack of them, and poured oil on them, asking God to pardon him for that which he had done to save their souls. Finally, he curled up on the *almemor*, setting fire to them from on top, and met death in the midst of the flames".[12]

The blood of the sacrifice, far from contaminating the place, was to serve as an irresistible call to God, exhorting Him to implacable vengeance against His enemies and those of the Chosen People, as the necessary preamble to the much-desired Messianic redemption. The blood of the innocent children, shed in the synagogue "in sanctification of the name of God", or "as a sign of contempt and abomination of the heretical crucifix", therefore served the same function, or, more exactly, served as two symbolic and successive phases of the very same process towards final redemption.

The depositions of the defendants in the Trent trial were all in agreement as to the fact that the murder of little Simon was said to have been committed on Friday, inside the synagogue, located in the dwelling of Samuele da Nuremberg, and, more exactly, in the antechamber of the hall in which the men gathered in prayer. This area, which was separated from the synagogue, properly speaking, by a door, was intended for women's prayers, since there was no women's gallery. The door, however, remained half-ajar; during the Sabbath liturgy, the women peeped in while the rolls of the Law were raised and exhibited by the person officiating at the *almemor*, before the reading of the weekly fragment of the Penteuch. On that occasion, the women placed their fingers to their lips and blew kisses in the direction of the rolls, open and placed on show. There, as the physician Tobias da Magdeburg informed the judges, "according to their customs the women gather in the antechamber of the synagogue and come forward at the door, when the (rolls with) the precepts of Moses were raised, which happens every Sabbath based on their rites".[13]

Simon's crucifixion was alleged to have been committed on a bench located in the so-called "women's synagogue". The boy's body, now lifeless, was then alleged to have been removed to the central hall of the synagogue and placed on the *almemor* for the ceremonies of the Sabbath. Tobias confirmed that, during the Sabbath liturgy, "he had seen the boy's body stretched out on the *almemor*, which is a table in the middle of the synagogue, on which they place books".[14] Angelo da Verona stated that "*almemor* is a Hebrew term equivalent to the Latin term 'seat of prayer'; in fact, the *almemor* is the table upon which they place the five books of Moses and is located in the midst of the School. The child's body lay supine on the *alememor* (during the offices of the Sabbath)".[15]

The body was wrapped in a *mappah* (wimple) of variegated silk and embroidery, a fine cloth the size of a hand towel used to cover the rolls of the Law after the reading.[16]

Israel Wolfgang testified before the Inquisitors of Trent in relation to the ritual child murder of Regensburg of 1467, at which he had personally participated, according to his own statement. In this case as well, the monumental ritual was alleged to have been committed in the antechamber of the synagogue; later, the body of the victim was said to have been transferred into the prayer room and placed in the *almemor*, so that the faithful might in some way participate in the significant ceremony.[17]

Probably in an attempt to detract from the overly obvious anti-Christian connotations of the ritual of the child's crucifixion, Angelo da Verona transformed it into an emblematic commemoration of the epic tale of the exodus from Egypt, explicitly linking it to the celebration of the *Pesach*. The wound inflicted on the victim's jaw was said to have been required to recall Moses' useless appeals to the Pharaoh to free the people of Israel from the land in which they were being held prisoner. The wound on the tibia was said to have been a symbolic reference to the Egyptian army's pursuit of the Jews in flight towards the Red Sea, and the terror and desperation with which the Jews were allegedly inflicted in those days. The amputation of the foreskin was said to have possessed an even more obvious commemorative function, recalling the mass circumcision of the Jewish people for the first time when they were about to leave Egypt, at God's command.[18] The punctures in the victim's body were said to have been inflicted to be taken as a symbol of the physical punctures inflicted by God upon the Egyptians, cruelly punished and suffering from a variety plagues.[19]

Nevertheless, Angelo da Verona's elaborate explanations, obviously intended to link the rite to the Biblical events celebrated in the Jewish Passover, hardly appear convincing. The defendants' depositions actually provide obvious indications of the obvious intention to transform the child's crucifixion into a symbolic commemoration of the Passion of Christ, referred to contemptuously as *Tolle Iesse mina* (= *Talui, Ieshu ha-min*), i.e., "the hanged one, Jesus the heretic".[20]

In effect, the so-called "Jewish formulae", which were said to have been pronounced on that occasion, cannot be dismissed as the mere expression of a mysterious, imaginary language, intended to confer Satanic connotations upon the cruel tale of ritual murder to satisfy the wishes of the inquisitors.[21] With some effort, due to the crude transliteration by Italian notaries of long and complicated phrases spoken in Ashkenazi Hebrew with a thick German accent, the formulae can be reconstructed rather satisfactorily, revealing their markedly anti-Christian tenor.

For example, the phrase in Hebrew recorded by Samuele of Nuremberg (*lu herpo, lu colan, lu tolle Yesse cho gihein col son heno*) and translated by Samuele as: "In contempt and shame of the hanged Jesus, and thus may it happen to all our enemies", is only apparently incomprehensible, due to inevitable errors of transcription by the notary. The phrase should in fact be reconstructed as *le-cherpah, li-klimah la-talui Yeshu, cach* (or *coh*) *ihye' le-col soneenu*, in the German pronunciation (and therefore *herpoh* instead of *herpah*), precisely the same significance as attributed to it by Samuele, who had a good knowledge of Hebrew.[22]

Mosè da Würzburg, "the Old Man", reported that during the rite, some of those present recited a Hebrew formula which meant: "Thou shalt be martyred as Jesus, the hanged God of the Christians, was martyred: and thus may it happen to all our enemies". At this point, all persons present responded in unison: "*Amen*". The actual phrase, in mangled Hebrew, is as follows: "*Hato nisi assarto fenidecarto cho Iesse attoloy le fuoscho folislimo cho Iesso*".[23] In view of the fact that the Hebrew was rendered according to the Ashkenazi pronunciation, the invective should be reconstructed as follows, leaving little room for doubt:

Attà nizlvatà we-nikartà ke-Ieshu ha-talui le-boshet we-li-klimà (35th Psalm, 26), *ke-Ieshu*, which, literally translated, would sound like:

"You have been crucified and pierced like 'Jesus the Hanged', in ignominy and shame, like Jesus".[24]

For the participants in the ritual, the Christian child seems to have lost his identity (if he ever had any in their eyes) and had actually been transformed into Jesus the "crucified and hanged". So many Jewish boys baptized by force in Christ's name in the German territories, beginning with the Crusades; so many others slaughtered by their fathers and mothers to avoid that holy abuse of power, bathing the *almemor* and the steps of the Ark with the rolls of the Law in the synagogue with their innocent blood – now, in turn, those who considered themselves the descendents of the victims of forced baptism imagined that a cruel but holy representation of the memorial of the Passion was capable of redeeming the descendants from their unforgettable trauma, with the God of redemption, severe and pious, capable of vengeance and pardon, involved and satisfied, as a privileged witness.

* * *

NOTES TO CHAPTER THIRTEEN

[1] Shalom of Neustadt, *Decisions and Customs*, by Sh. Spitzer, Jerusalem, 1977, p. 137 (in Hebrew).

[2] Cfr. S. Salfeld, *Das Martyrologium des Nürnberger Memorbuches*, Berlin, 1898, p. 15.

[3] Meir of Rothenburg, *Responsa, Decisions and Customs*, by Y.Z. Kahana, Jerusalem, 1960, p. 54 (in Hebrew).

[4] In this regard, see the acute observations contained in H. Soloveitchik, *Halakhah, Hermeneutics and Martyrdom in Medieval Ashkenaz*, in "The Jewish Quarterly Review", XCIV (2004), pp. 77-105 ("the correctness of their conduct was axiomatic to them [...] and it was no less axiomatic to their successors [...]. Convinced of the palpable reality of the afterlife, feeling its almost graspable closeness [...] husbands killed wives and parents dispatched their children with a swift stroke of the knife, certain that they were bestowing upon them the gift of eternal bliss").

[5] Cfr. B.Z. Kedar, *The Forcible Baptism of 1096. History and Historiography*, in K. Borchardt and E. Bünz, *Forschungen zur Reichs-, Papst- und Landesgeschichte. Peter Herde zum 65. Geburtstag*, Stuttgart, 1998, pp. 187-200.

[6] In this regard, see A. Toaff, *Migrazioni di ebrei tedeschi attraverso i territori triestini e friulani fra XIV e XV secolo*, in G. Todeschini and P.C. Ioly Zorattini, *Il mondo ebraico. Gli ebrei tra Italia nord-orientale e Impero asburgico dal Medioevo all'Età*

contemporanea, Pordenone, 1991, pp. 10-11; A. Toaff, *Gli insediamenti ashkenaziti nell'Italia settentrionale*, in *Storia d'Italia. Annali*. XI: *Gli ebrei in Italia*, t. I: *Dall'Alto Medioevo all'età dei ghetti*, by C. Vivanti, Turin, 1996, pp. 160-161.

[7] Cfr. Soloveitchik, *Halakhah, Hermeneutics and Martyrdom in Medieval Ashkenaz*, cit., pp. 105-106 ("Every aspect of the Christian religion was subject to ridicule and disgust. Much of the intuitive rejection of conversion in Ashkenazi communities come from the revulsion of Christianity instilled from childhood [...] their suffering filled them with bitterness [...]. Having one's children brought up as Christians meant not only having them raised as savages, worshipping idols and venerating corpses, but also becoming the blood-stained persecutors of the Chosen People; and after a barbaric and sin-filled life, they would be condemned to an eternity of death; a swift stroke of the sword was perhaps seen as the greatest kindness that a parent could bestow upon a child").

[8] In this regard, see, among others, I.J. Yuval, *Vengeance and Damnation, Blood and Defamation. From Jewish Martyrdom to Blood Libel Accusations*, in "Zion", LVIII (1993), pp. 33-90 (in Hebrew); Id., *"The Lord Will Take Vengeance, Vengeance for His Temple". Historia Sine Ira et Studio*, in "Zion", LIX (1994), pp. 351-414 (in Hebrew). For a contrary opinion, see E. Fleischer, *Christian-Jewish Relations in the Middle Ages Distorted*, in "Zion", LIX (1994), pp. 267-316 (in Hebrew). See also M. Minty, *Kiddush Ha-Shem in German Christian Eyes in the Middle Ages*, in "Zion", LIX (1994), pp. 266-269 (in Hebrew).

[9] From the 13th century onwards, the tribune of the synagogue, (*bimah, tevah*), seat of the person officiating, was also referred to as the *almemor*, a term derived from the Arabic, *al-minbar*, "pulpit", exemplifying the forms and functions of the pulpit. The tribune contained the table (*dukhan*) bearing the roles of the Law during the weekly liturgical readings. It is curious to note the manner in which the term *almemor*, of Arabic origin, was also adopted by the Ashkenazi synagogues (cfr. Th. Metzger and M. Metzger, *Jewish Life in the Middle Ages. Illuminated Hebrew Manuscripts of the XIIIth to the XVIth Centuries*, Freiburg, 1982, pp. 71-74).

[10] The chronicle containing the tale of the tragedy of Isaac, the *parnas* [sacristan] of the synagogue at Magonza, is reproduced by A.M. Haberman, *Sefer ghezerot Ashkenaz we-Zarf at* ("Book of the Persecutions in Germany and France"), Jerusalem, 1971, pp. 36-38.

[11] For a detailed examination of the affair with historical and ideological references, see J. Cohen, *The Persecutions of 1096. From*

Martyrdom to Martyrology. The Sociocultural Context of the Hebrew Crusade Chronicles, in "Zion", LIX (1994), pp. 185-195 (in Hebrew); for an opinion closer to my own, see I.J. Yuval, *"Two Nations in Your Womb". Perceptions of Jews and Christians*, Tel Aviv, 2000, pp. 159-161 (in Hebrew).

[12] Cfr. S. Bernfeld, *Sefer ha-dema'ot* ("The Book of Tears"), Berlin, 1924, p. 169. In this regard, see Yuval, *"Two Nations in Your Womb"*, cit., pp. 199-200 and, more recently, A. Gross, *Struggling with Tradition. Reservation about Active Martyrdom in the Middle Ages*, Leyden, 2004, pp. 1-44.

[13] "Interrogatus ubi erant mulieres ipsorum Iudeorum, respondit quod non erant in sinagoga, quia non est de more eorum quod mulieres intrant sinagogam. Interrogatus ubi stant mulieres quando celebrantur offitia sua, respondit quod mulieres tunc stant in camera que est ante sinagogam. Interrogatus an mulieres stantes in dicta camera possint videre in sinagogam et maxime ea que sunt super almemore, respondit quod non, nisi veniant super ostium per quod intratur in sinagogam. Et dicit, interrogatus, quod secundum eorum consuetudinem mulieres, que se reperiunt in camera que est ante sinagogam, se reducunt super ostium quando elevantur precepta Moisi in sinagoga. Et dicit, interrogatus, quod dicta die Sabbati de sero precepta deberunt elevati, quia omni die Sabbato de sero elevantur, secundum eorum ordines" (cfr. A. Esposito e D. Quaglioni, *Processi contro gli ebrei di Trento, 1475-1478. I: I processi del 1475*, Padua, 1990, pp. 324-325).

[14] "Vidit cadaver dicti pueri extensum super almemore, qui est discus positus in medio sinagoge, super quo ponunt libros" ["He saw the body of the boy lying on the almemor, placed in the middle of the synagogue, which is where they place their books"] (cfr. ibidem, p. 324).

[15] "Et die Sabbati [...] ipse Angelus ivit ad domum Samuelis et intravit dictas scolas et vidit quoddam cadaver pueri mortui positum super almemor, quod est verbum Hebraicum, quod est dicere in lingua latina 'locus sermonis'; qui almemor est discus quidam super quo ponuntur quinque libri Moisi. Qui discus sive almemor era positus in medio Scole, super quo disco erat cadaver dicti pueri, quod cadaver iacebat resupinum" ["And on the Sabbath [...] this Angelo went to Samuele's house and entered their school and saw the body of the dead boy placed on the almemor, which is the Hebrew word for what is called in Latin 'the place where we give our sermons', which almemor is the chest upon which they place books"] (cfr. ibidem, p. 286).

[16] Vitale, Samuele da Nuremberg's agent, stated "quod illud (i.e., Little Simon's body) sic vidit in dicto die Sabbati, de mane, in sinagoga

super almemore, et quod illud erat coopertum quodam palleo de sirico diversi coloris; et similiter illud vidit dicta die, de sero, tempore quo dicebantur offitia in eorum sinagoga" ["that they saw it (the body) that Sabbath, in the morning, in the synagogue, on the almemor, and that it was covered with a cloth of various colors, and they also saw it that day, in the evening, when they have their religious services"] (cfr. ibidem, p. 220). Samuele da Nuremberg confirmed that "dictum corpus pueri erat coopertum una tovalea, qua tovalea solent uti super suo altari [...] et post coperto dicto corpore et illo stante in almemore, venerunt omnes alii Iudei in sinagogam et ibi dixerunt offitia sua" (cfr. ibidem, p. 248).

[17] "Corpus illud fuit portatum [...] in quadam cameram contiguam Synagogae et illud corpus posuit in quadam capsam. Et dicit quod mane sequenti venerunt plures alii Judaei ad videndum dictum corpus et in qua die sequenti de sero idem corpus fuit sublatum de capsa et portatum in Synagogam praedictam [...] corpore stante extenso super Almemore" ["The body was taken [...] into the chamber adjacent to the synagogue and placed on the chest. And he said that in the morning several other Jews came and saw the body and that on the following day the body was taken from the chest and taken into the synagogue [..] and placed on the almemor"] (cfr. [Benedetto Bonelli], *Dissertazione apologetica sul martirio del beato Simone da Trento nell'anno MCCCCLXXV dagli ebrei ucciso*, Trent, Gianbattista Parone, 1747, p. 141).

[18] The circumcision of the Jews on the occasion of the exodus from Egypt, when they are said to have complied with this precept for the first time, is mentioned in the *Midrash: Shemot Rabbah* 17, 3-5; 19, 5; *Ruth Rabbah* 6; *Shir ha-shirim Rabbah* 1, 35; 5; *Tanchumah* 55, 4; *Pesiktah de-Rav IV: Kazhanah* 63, 27.

[19] "Interrogatus quod dicat quid importat aut significat illud vulnus quod factum fuit puero in maxilla dextra, respondit quod hoc significat quod Moyses per os suum pluries dixit Pharaoni quod debere dimittere populum suum Israheliticum; et quod vulnus quod habebat puer in tibia dextra, fit ad significationem quod Pharao et populus Egiptiacus, qui persequebantur ipsos Iudeos, quod in eorum itineribus fuerunt infelices; et quod vulnus quod habebat puer in virga significat circumcisionem eorum et quod punctiones que fiunt per corpus pueri significant quod populus Egiptiacus in omni parte corporis sui fuit percussus" ["When asked the meaning of the injury to the boy's right jaw, he answered that this meant that the laws of Moses told the Pharaoh orally several times to let the Israelites go; and that the injury to the boy's right shinbone meant that the Pharaoh and the people of Egypt, who were persecuting

the Jews, who were unhappy in their wanderings, and that the injury to his penis referred to their circumcision and that the puncture wounds to the boy's body meant that the people of Egypt were inflicted with suffering in all parts of their body"] (cfr. Esposito and Quaglioni, *Processi*, cit., vol. I, p. 291).

[20] Bonaventura (Seligman) di Mohar, Mosè da Würzburg's young nephew, maintained that he had heard those present at the rite pronounce the words *Tolle, Iesse mina*, "que verba ipse Bonaventura nescit quid important" (cfr. ibidem, p. 157). Israel Wolfgang (and his statement in this regard was confirmed by Joav da Ansbach, Tobias the physician's servant) had, on that same occasion, heard the same words *Tolle, lesse mina* from the mouth of Mosè "the Old Man" da Würzburg. At this, Bishop Hinderbach noted in the margin: "verba enim praedicta significant tantum 'suspensus' Jesus hereticus" (["the aforesaid words mean as much as 'the hanged one', Jesus the heretic"], cfr. [Bonelli], *Dissertazione apologetica*, cit., pp. 149-151). For his part, Bonaventura (Seligman), Samuele da Nuremberg's cook, recalled that he had heard the words *memmholzdem talui*, perhaps a distorted rendering of the Hebrew *mamzer talui*, "the hanged bastard" (cfr. Esposito and Quaglioni, *Processi*, cit., vol. l, p. 138).

[21] Anna Esposito maintains in this regard that the phrases "reproducing the curses of the Jews against the Christians, sometimes rendered in transliterated Hebrew, more often in a sort of pseudo-Hebrew, and then translated into Latin, and often into Italian as well" were intended to "augment, through the introduction of words in an obscure foreign language, the sensation of mystery and fear which were already, by the very nature of things, afflicting the Hebraic world". The insertion of such phrases in fact "seems to have been effected precisely to confirm, first of all, in all readers of the trial records, the impression of an obscure Satanic rite smelling of witchcraft" (cfr. Esposito and Quaglioni, *Processi*, cit., vol. I, pp. 70-71). For a similar opinion, see D. Quaglioni, *Propaganda antiebraica e polemiche di Curia*, in M. Miglio, F. Niutta, C. Ranieri and D. Quaglioni, *Un pontificato ed una città. Sisto IV (1471-1484)*, Atti del Convegno, Roma, 2-7 December 1984, Città del Vaticano, 1988, p. 256. W.P. Eckert (*Motivi superstiziosi nel processo agli ebrei di Trento*, in I. Rogger and M. Bellabarba, *Il principe vescovo Johannes Hinderbach, 1465-1486, fra tardo Medioevo e Umanesimo*, Atti del Convegno held by the Biblioteca Comunale di Trento, 2-6 October 1989, Bologna, 1992, p. 393) states that "the Jews had to be made to look ridiculous because ridicule produces a lethal effect" and that, to attain this objective, the Trent judges demanded "an exact explanation of incomprehensible

Jewish terms".

[22] "Dicebant hec verba in Hebraico, videlicet: *Lu herpo, lu colan, lu tolle Yesse cho gihein col son heno*; que verba significant: 'In vituperium et verecundiam [translation error for "vilipendium"] illius suspensi Iesu, et ita fiat omnibus inimicis nostris', intelligendo de Cristianis" ["He said these words in Hebrew, that is, *Lu herpo, lu colan, lu tolle Yesse cho gihein col son heno*, which means, 'In insults and contempt for the hanged Jesus, and may this be done to all our enemies', meaning the Christians"] (cfr. [Bonelli], *Dissertazione apologetica*, p. 149; Esposito and Quaglioni, *Processi*, cit., vol. I, p. 247). In the breadth of anti-Christian Jewish literature, it should be noted that Yannai, for example, poet and composer of liturgical songs, who lived in Palestine in approximately the 5th century, was the author of an invective against the believers in Christ to be read during the prayers of Yom Kippur, the solemn fast of expiation. His concluding words were: "may they (the Christians) be covered with ignominy, contempt and shame (*bushah, cherpah w-klimah*)". Cfr. A. Shanan, *Otò ha-ish. Jesus through Jewish Eyes*, Tel Aviv, 1999, pp. 47-50 (in Hebrew). On the image of Jesus in anti-Christian literature, in which He is referred to as *talui* ("the hanged one"), *mamzer* ("the bastard"), *min* ("the heretic"), see, among others, M. Goldstein, *Jesus in the Jewish Tradition*, New York, 1950; T. Walker, *Jewish Views of Jesus*, London, 1974; W. Jacob, *Christianity through Jewish Eyes*, Cincinnati (O.), 1974; T. Weiss-Rosmarin, *Jewish Expressions on Jesus*, New York, 1997.

[23] "Et aliqui ex suprascriptis dicebant hec verba Hebraica, videlicet: Hatto nisi assarto fenidecarto cho lesse attoloy le fuoscho folislimo cho lesso, que verba significant: 'Tu martiriçaris sicut fuit martirizatus et consumptus Iesus Deus Cristianorum suspensus, et ita fieri possit omnibus nostris inimicis' " ["And all the above mentioned persons said these Hebrew words: Hatto nisi assarto fenidecarto cho lesse attoloy le fuoscho folislimo cho lesso, which means: 'You will be tortured to death and eaten as was Jesus Christ of the Christians the hanged one, and thus may it be with all our enemies' "] (cfr. [Bonelli], *Dissertazione apologetica*, cit., p. 149; Esposito and Quaglioni, *Processi*, cit., vol. I, p. 354).

[24] In Hebrew pronounced the German way, the phrase sounds like this: *Atto nizfavto fenidecarto co-Iesho hattoloy* ecc. "Jesus crucified and pierced", as an expression of offensive meaning, is found in numerous anti-Christian Hebraic compositions, widespread in medieval Ashkenazi Judaism (cfr. Shanan, *Gtò ha-ish. Jesus through Jewish Eyes*, cit., p. 61).

CHAPTER FOURTEEN

"DOING THE FIG": OBSCENE RITUALS AND GESTURES

Lazzaro, Angelo da Verona's servant, recalled that, as an introduction to the contemptuous commemoration of Christ's Passion, enacted upon the body of the infant Simon, the zealous Samuele da Nuremberg had intended to prepare and incite those present with a mocking sermon ridiculing the Christian faith. In the improvised sermon, Jesus was described as being born of adultery, while Mary, a woman of notoriously easy morals, was said to have been impregnated during her menstrual period, against all the rules of propriety and custom.[1]

While the whole theme of Jesus' adulterous generation was not at all new, this was not because of any claim that the Virgin was impregnated during her menstrual period. In fact, this only appeared in a few versions of the *Toledot Yeshu* – the so-called "Hebraic counter-Gospels", written in the German-speaking territories between the 15th and 16th centuries. Samuele's reference to the anti-Christian text containing the accusation that Christ was "a bastard conceived by an impure woman" (*mamzer ben ha-niddah*) was therefore chronologically somewhat premature and doubtlessly characteristic of the intolerant climate of a certain section of late medieval Ashkenazi Judaism.[2] It is inconceivable to imagine that the naïve Lazzaro da Serravalle should have given free rein to his fantasy by inventing the anti-Christian thematic details contained in Samuele's sermon. It is even less plausible to imagine that the Trent judges and inquisitors might have been expert connoisseurs of the various texts of the *Toledot Yeshu*.

A few years later, in 1488, the Jews of the Duchy of Milan, on trial for contempt of the Christian religion, were asked by the judges whether or not they actually referred to Jesus as a bastard and the son of a menstruating woman. In particular, they demanded whether any expressions of this kind, which originated in the texts of the Toledot Yeshu, appeared in a liturgical composition beginning with the words *ani, ani ha-medabber* ("It is I, I who speak..."), and in the form of the secondary feasts of the German rite.[3] Many of the defendants responded in the affirmative and admitted that, in that prayer, Jesus was indeed referred to as having been "born of a woman having her menstrual period", and "born of a polluted woman, that is, one who was menstruating". In fact, the oldest versions of the Ashkenazi handbook of prayers for ceremonial solemnities contains a commemorative elegy for the martyrs, massacre victims and suicides in sanctification of God's name, entitled *ani, ani ha-medabber*, "It is I, I who speak...", attributed to Rabbi Efraim di Isacco da Regensburg, and intended for recital during the Fast of Expiation (Kippur). The elegy contains an explicit reference to Jesus as "conceived of a menstruating woman", in conformity with a motif which was widespread in the German versions of the *Toledot Yeshu*.[4]

Not surprisingly, this line of invective rapidly gained ground in the world of Ashkenazi Judaism, both in Germany and in the more or less recently settled regions of sub-Alpine Italy.

Elena was the widow of Raffaele Fritschke, analogous to the German family name Fridman, rendered into Italian as Freschi or Frigiis.[5]

Her husband, a famous physician and rabbi from Austria or Bohemia, had become one of the most influential and esteemed personages of the Jewish community of the German rite of Padua by the end of the 15th century and the early 16th century. His death is thought to have occurred in the city of Venice around 1540. A few years later, Raffaele and Elena's son, Lazzaro Freschi, later a friend and esteemed colleague of Andreas Vesalius, graduated with brilliant medical credentials from the Studio di Padova, and was invited to occupy the chair of surgery and anatomy in that university, accepting the job and occupying that position from 1537 until 1544. No later than 1547, Maestro Lazzaro Freschi moved to the old ghetto of Venice, together with his mother, and was admitted as a member of the local Ashkenazi community.

A dramatic turning point came a few years later, before the end of 1549, when Lazzaro, physician son of Rabi Raffaele Fritschke, converted to Christianity for reasons unknown. To avoid doing things by halves, the Paduan physician also persuaded his mother Elena to visit the baptismal font and embrace the religion of Christ. From that moment on, Lazzaro, now known as Giovanni Battista Freschi Olivi, became a severe critic of his former religion and an open accuser of the Jewish world from which he originated. Thanks to his zealous and indefatigable polemical efforts, the Talmud was placed on the Index and finally burnt by the public hangman in the Piazza San Marco on 21 October 1553 by decision of the Council of Ten.[6]

But while Giovanni Battista Freschi Olivi gave all outward signs of having enthusiastically embraced the Christian religion, his aged mother Elena, who must have been at least seventy years old, proved herself rather less convinced of the wisdom of the step taken. The virulently anti-Christian religious upbringing which she had received during her year in the Ashkenazi environment had left an indelible imprint and continued to influence her spontaneous mental attitudes, even after her conversion.

In 1555, Elena was brought before the Holy Office of Venice under the accusation of having publicly given vent to blasphemous expressions regarding Christianity. Only the authoritative intervention of her son, who was compelled to plead his mother's mental infirmity for purposes of defense, sufficed to get her out of trouble.[7] One Sunday in March of that year, Elena, while attending Mass in the Church of San Marcuola, just as the priest was reciting the Credo, had been unable to refrain from mockery, expressing her outrageous contempt with malevolent terms of speech. Jesus, she alleged, was not conceived by the Virgin Mary by the virtue of the Holy Spirit at all, but was the bastard son of a whore.

"Last Sunday (17 March 1555) [...] finding herself at the said Mass (in the Church of San Marcilian) [...] the mother of meser Zuan Baptista, a Hebrew physician having become a Christian, just as the priest was saying the Credo: *Et incarnatus est de Spiritu Sancto ex Maria Virgine et homo factus est*, said the following, or similar, words: 'You're lying through your teeth. Jesus was the bastard born of a whore' ".[8]

The anti-Christian sentiments expressed through the texts of the *Toledot Yeshu* and assimilated by the old Paduan Jewish woman thus found an uncontrollable outlet, in church, in an automatic and perhaps involuntary reflex. Poor Elena's basic personality was still Jewish and Ashkenazi, and would probably remain so forever afterward.

A few years later, two other Ashkenazi Jews were tried by the Inquisition of Venice for insulting the Christian faith, and once again, the accusation turned on the allegation of Jesus' spurious birth as the son of a menstruating woman. Aron and Asser (Asher, Anselmo) were two aimless and unaccomplished youths having arrived in the ghetto of Venice around 1563, the one from Prague and the other from Poland. They later decided to convert to Christianity and enter the Casa dei Catecumeni [Church institution for the conversion of Jews and infidels] to try to make ends meet by means of a self-interested and calculated baptism. But they obviously proved to be rather poorly convinced of the basics of the Christian religion, since they were indicted by the Holy Office for uttering unspeakable insults against Jesus and the Virgin Mary.[9] The two Ashkenazi youths appeared to have been nurtured upon massive doses of the anti-Christian motifs characteristic of the *Toledot Yeshu*.

"Esso (Asser) began to say that the Lord God was a bastard son of a whore, saying in the Hebrew language that the Lord God was engendered while the Madonna was having her menstrual period, and, what is even more insulting, saying *mamzer barbanid*,[10] which means what I said above [...] He uttered opprobrious words offensive to the Divine Majesty and the glorious Virgin Mary, asserting that Christ was a bastard born by carnal sin when the Madonna Virgin Mary was having her menstrual period".[11]

Almost a century had passed since the Trent trials and the polemical motifs of Samuele da Nuremberg's sermon over the corpse of little Simon-Jesus, taken from the *Toledot Yeshu* – which had now become a classical text – were still alive and well in the Ashkenazi environment of the valleys of the Loire and the Rhône, the Rhine and Danube, the Elba and the Vistula, and all communities having migrated down from the other side of the Alps to the plains of the Po and the gulf of Venice.

Another outrageous assertion about the Christian religion very widespread among Jews of German origin was based on the Talmudic dictum that Jesus was to suffer punishment in the coming world, condemned to immersion in "boiling excrement".[12] The Jewish bankers of the Duchy of Milan accused of contempt for the Christian faith in 1488 were asked whether their texts claimed that Jesus was condemned to the pains of Hell and placed in a pot full of excrement. Salomone Galli da Brescello, a Jew from Vigevano, had no difficulty in admitting that he had indeed read that malodorous prophecy in a little notebook which passed through his hands in Rome during the Pontificate of Sixtus IV.[13] Salomone, a Jew from Como, and Isacco da Parma, a resident of Castelnuovo Scrivia, confirmed that they, too, were aware of the Hebraic texts asserting that Jesus, in the future world, was destined to be immersed in a bath of steaming feces ("Jesus the Nazarene [...] is being punished in excrement, in boiling shit").[14]

It should be noted in this regard that the Hebraic sources refer to a significant and revealing episode linked to the sanguinary massacre of the Jewish community at Magonza in 1096. On that occasion, David, son of Netanel, the person responsible for the synagogue services (*gabbay*), is said to have turned to the Crusaders about to kill him cruelly, wishing them the same fate as Jesus, "punished by immersion in boiling excrement".[15] When it came to anti-Christian polemic, Ashkenazi Jews didn't beat around the bush, and the tragic events of which they were the victims served as a justification for an uncompromising hatred, verbally insulting and violent in action, at least whenever possible.

On the other hand, the Christians, too, loved the idea of the pious Jew, the scrupulous observers of the Law, immersed up to the neck in baths of excrement, as a well-deserved punishment for their arrogant blindness. Friar Luisi Maria Benetelli of Venice, lecturer in Hebrew at Padua and later at Venice, reported, with ill-concealed satisfaction, a malodorous anecdote of ancient origin describing a Jew, devote observer of the Sabbath, compelled to pass the week-end among the miasmas of a filthy cesspool due to his obtuse religiosity.

"Mr. Salomone, having fallen into the bog of a ditch, so as not to violate the feast day of the Sabbath, rejected the charity of a Christian who offered to pull him out. *Sabbath sancta colo, de stercore surgere nolo* [I must adhere to the Sabbath, and do not wish to be pulled out of the shit]. The following day, the same good man passed by again, and the Jew beseeched him for assistance in getting out of the ditch, but the Christian excused himself saying, 'Yesterday was your feast day, today is mine', and left him there to enjoy that aromatic stench all Sunday. *Sabbatha nostra quidem Salomon celebrabis ibidem*".[16]

For many, the synagogue, particularly, during the most significant moments of the liturgy, was the most suitable place to confer solemnity and sacral effectiveness upon anathemas, invective and contempt, often accompanied by the dramatic exhibition of aggressive and mocking gestures. One of the most important days of the Jewish calendar among the Jews of the German territories during the Middle Ages was the feast of *Pesach*, when they opened the doors of the holy Ark to extract the rolls of the Law. It was then, in the context of prayers for the festivity, that they cursed the Christians in stentorian voices, "uttering imprecations to which one cannot listen".[17] But the insults and the contempt were also pronounced by the litigious faithful, who had, or who considered themselves to have, reciprocally outstanding accounts to settle. In the early 16th century, the rabbi Jechiel Trabot lamented the widespread wickedness of taking advantage of the ceremonies of the synagogue to engage in furious verbal disputes, which sometimes concluded with recourse to fisticuffs. These violent disputes, accompanied by insults and curses, usually occurred "with the *Seder* open", that is, when the rolls of the Law were exhibited and placed, open, upon the *almemor* for reading.[18]

The [Ashkenazi] Jews possessed a vast range and picturesque catalogue of anathemas against Jesus and the Christians, generally reinforced by appropriate gestures of mockery and contempt, often taking the form of obscene and scurrilous jests. Offensive and obscene gestures, ritualized and sanctified by the holy temple in which they were performed, constituted an effective instrument of communication, directed at their own community, to request and obtain the anticipated and complacent approval, or at least silent complicity. The insults and scurrilous gestures most frequently resorted to [by Jews] during the Middle Ages, right down to the end of the early modern age, include the rhythmic stamping of the feet to create an ear-splitting din intended to drown out any mention of the memory or even the very voice of the adversary; the act of sticking out the tongue and/or making faces, the act of spitting in the face, the act of uncovering the buttocks and the gesture of "doing the fig". The latter, considered a particularly insulting gesture of contempt, was performed by displaying the hands with the thumb tightly inserted between the index and middle fingers, a symbolic allusion to the female genital organ during the act of copulation.[19]

When, in the weekly readings of the *Pentateuch*, they reached the fragment relating to the Amalek (Deut. 25: 17-19), considered Israel's implacable enemy and persecutor par excellence throughout history, the participants in the liturgy of the synagogue stamped their feet violently, accompanied by a deafening noise to drown out any mention of their name. This often occurred during the recitation of the *meghillah*, the roll of Esther, during the feast of *Purim*, at every mention of Haman, Assuerus's cruel minister, inventor of the plan to exterminate the Jewish people in the land of Persia. The hubbub was also renewed at any mention of *Zeresh*, Haman's faithful consort, and his numerous children, in the liturgical text. In this connection, Leon da Modena recalled that "some people, at the mention of Haman's name, beat on the benches of the synagogue as a sign that they were cursing him", a custom the existence of which was confirmed by the convert Giulio Morosini, who stated that, at Venice, the Jews pounded violently on the flat surfaces of their wooden benches in the synagogue as a sign of execration of the hated enemy, "pound on the benches of the synagogue with all their strength as a sign of excommunication, saying in a loud voice, 'May his name be blotted out', and 'May the name of the impious putrefy' ".[20]

One of the most widespread prayers of the Jewish ritualistic formulary was doubtlessly the one beginning with the words *'Alenu leshabbeach* ("We must praise the Lord"), which was to be recited several times a day and during feasts and solemnities. This text, sometimes called a sort of "Credo of Judaism", not surprisingly contained expressions particularly critical of Jesus and Christianity. Ecclesiastical censure therefore dealt severely with this prayer, erasing all polemical mention of the faith in Christ from the manuscripts and prohibiting any printing of the full text. Yet, nonetheless, during the persecutions of the Middle Ages, it was precisely this prayer which was most frequently shouted at their persecutors by Jews when the time case to sacrifice their lives to God.

In the tradition of the German Jews, at the phrase "So that they (the Christians) may prostrate themselves and turn their prayers to vanity and nullity, to a God which is not the Savior", it was the custom to perform gestures of reproof and contempt, such as stamping the feet, shaking the head or jumping up and down on the ground.[21] Giulio Morosini reported that, even in his time, when the Jews of Venice recited the liturgical hymn *'Alenu le-shabbeacuh*, which he described as "contumelious against Christ and Christians [...] some attest that, when saying these words, they are accustomed to show abomination by spitting".[22] Insulting and scurrilous gestures and obscene acts, even, and most particularly, if performed within the holy confines of the synagogue, lost their negative connotations and served to underline and stress their passionate hatred and implacable contempt.

On the Sabbath right after little Simon's murder, when the child's body was placed on the *almemor*, the Jews of Trent, gathered in the synagogue, abandoned themselves to excessive gestures absolutely without inhibition or restraint. According to the deposition of Angelo da Verona's servant, Lazzaro, Samuele da Nuremberg, after concluding his fiery anti-Christian sermon against Jesus and His Mother, rushed up to the *almemor*, and, after "doing the fig", slapped the boy in the face and spat on him. Not to be outdone, Angelo de Verona imitated these outrageous gestures, spitting and slapping the corpse, while Mosè "the Old Man" da Würzburg "did the fig", mockingly showing his teeth, while Maestro Tobias allowed himself to be carried away in the performance of other acts of violence, with no shortage of slapping and spitting.

This scandalous spectacle was crowned by the other participants, led by Isacco, Angelo's cook, and Mosè da Bamberg, the traveler, Lazzaro and Israel Wolfgang, the painter, and Israel, Samuele's son, who, in addition to "doing the fig" like the others, stuck out his tongue and made faces. For their part, Joav da Ansbach, Maestro Tobias's scullery boy, had no hesitation in performing obscene gestures, and, coarsely raising his caftan, displayed his buttocks [and genitals] shamelessly, a blasphemous act sometimes reserved solely for the passing of holy processions.[23] Joav himself, in his confession, added that he had bitten the child's ear in an attempt to imitate or outdo Samuele da Nuremberg.[24] Anna da Montagana, the latter's daughter-in-law, confirmed that she had indeed been present at this unedifying scene.[25]

Bella, wife of Mayer, son of Mosè of Würzburg, recalled that she had been present at the exhibition of similar insulting gestures, always at Trent, three or four years earlier, on the occasion of another child murder, also committed in Samuele's house. In this case as well, the outrageous ritual had been performed in the synagogue during the hour of prayer.[26] For his part, Israel Wolfgang described the details of the 1467 ritual murder at Regensburg in which he claimed to have participated personally, stating that "the same insulting acts as those at Trent, in Samuele's house", were performed in Sayer's *stiebel* [parlor] in the presence of the child's body [as in 1467].[27]

Giovanni Hinderbach summarized the Trent defendants' depositions relating to the scene of the outrageous acts performed in the synagogue in a letter sent to Innsbruck in the fall of 1475, addressed to the orator of the Republic of Venice before Sigismundo, Archduke of Austria, written in a kind of Italian which was unusual for him and somewhat crude:

"The said Jews, or some of them, the said body having been placed on the *almemor*, said the following, or similar words, in the Hebrew language: 'This be in contempt and shame of our enemies', referring to us Christians. Quite a few others 'did the fig' in the eyes of the corpse, while others raised their hands to heaven and stamped their feet on the ground, while others spat in the face of the said body, saying these other words: 'Go to the God of Jesus, your God, and Mary, may she help you; pray to her to free you, and may she rescue you from our hands' ".[28]

The bishop of Trent was either suffering from a memory lapse or was committing a more or less intentional error here, because the Jews could not have defied Jesus and the Madonna to come to the assistance of the poor child on that occasion. In fact, in their eyes, the boy lying on the *almemor* and the Crucified Christ were one and the same person. Simon did not exist – if he had ever existed – and, in his place, they saw the *Talui*, Jesus the hanged, and the *Teluiah*, the hanged or crucified woman, as Mary was called in an extemporaneous Hebraic neologism. To them, he was the Christ, and whoever had engendered Him – the detestable embodiments of Christianity, responsible for their miserable Diaspora, their bloody persecutions and forced conversions. Almost trance-like, they cursed and swore, performed contemptuous and obscene gestures, each one recalling tragic family memories and the many sufferings of those who, in their eyes, had embraced the cross as an offensive weapon.

The indignities heaped upon this innocent, sacrificed child in some ways resembled the Cabalistic rite of the *kapparot* ("The [Fast of] Expiation"), an established custom among German Jews on the eve of the solemn fast of Kippur. On that occasion, young white free-range roosters were whirled around the head of the sinner to assume the sinner's transgressions. The roosters were later sacrificed, taking punishment upon themselves on behalf of the guilty-minded transgressors.[29] This ritual was intended to bring about the symbolic transfer of a person's sins onto an animal, which was then sacrificed, serving a similar function to that of the expiatory goat [scapegoat]. Where the cock assumed the guilt of the entire community, the rooster of the cabbalistic, magical *kapparot* served as a receptacle for the sins of the individual, erased through the killing of the innocent bird. The custom of the *kapparot*, widespread among the Ashkenazi Jews of Venice, was vividly described, as usual, by Samuele Nahmias, alias Giulio Morosini.

"All the males and females in the house go out and look for white chickens: the men look for a white rooster, while the women look for a white hen, and then they whirl these chickens around their heads several times, saying these words [...] 'This be in exchange for myself, may this take my place, this be my expiation, may this bird go to its death while I go on living'. After the ceremony, they butcher the birds and eat them, and then they give some of the meat to some poor person, in charity, in the belief that if God had condemned any of them to death, He would now have to settle for the rooster or hen in exchange [...]. They all practice this ritual, particularly in the Levant and in Germany".[30]

Once again, at the beginning of the 18th century, the Minorite friar Luigi Maria Benetelli severely censured those Jews of Venice, presumably belonging to the German community, who unperturbedly maintained the custom of the *kapparot* on the eve of the Fast of Expiation. According to him, these Jews intended to transfer the ballast of their own sins onto the white roosters, condemned to be sacrificed, while irreverently imitating the Passion of Christ.

"Many of you, on that day, dress in white and search for a white rooster without a single reddish feather (since red is the color of sin), and, clutching it by the neck and whirling it around your heads three times, pray that the rooster may expiate their sins; they torment the rooster by pulling its neck, they butcher it, throw it violently on the ground, and finally, they roast it; denoting, by means of the first torment, that they themselves deserve to be strangled; by means of the second torment, that they themselves deserve to be killed with a noose;

in the third, that they themselves deserve to be stoned; and in the fourth, that they themselves deserve to be burnt for their sins. Not all (and for this reason, I said 'many') practice this ceremony even today. To me, it is enough that many of them, although unintentionally, admit, in fact, that the Messiah, which is white for its divinity and red for Humanity, should expiate sin".[31]

Similarly, as with the *kapparot*, in the case of the Christian child, his crucifixion transforms the child into Jesus and into Christianity, symbolically allowing the community to savor that vengeance against the enemies of Israel which is a necessary, although insufficient, preamble to their final redemption. The crescendo of insults and contemptuous gestures in front of the *almemor* of the synagogue was not, paradoxically, directed against the innocent boy, but rather, against Jesus, "the hanged one", whom the boy personified. Whether by 'doing the fig', spitting on the ground, grinding their teeth or stamping their feet, all the participants in the spectacular representation, alive and charged with tension, repeated the Hebrew wish, *ken ikkaretu kol oyevecha*, which means, "thus may our enemies be consumed".[32]

The women also had their role to play in the ritual of vilification, and their role was not one of secondary importance. Their enthusiastic participation in the display of verbal and gestural contempt during the functions of the synagogue was well known to everyone and caused no surprise. Rabbi Azriel Diena, in a ritual response sent to the heads of the Jewish community of Modena in the month of November 1534, censured the bad habits of the women, who, in the synagogue, as well as on the Sabbath and during the festivities, "when the solemn moment arrives in which the rolls of the Torah were extracted from the Ark, they rise up, as if they were infuriated, launching a barrage of insults and curses against all those whom they hated".[33] Beniamin Slonik, rabbi of Grodno in the Grand Duchy of Lithuania, in his manual of honest female behavior in the Ashkenazi communities, which was translated into Italian several times, attempted, in an effort to teach them to restrain themselves and cool their burning ardor, to explain the predisposition of Jewish women to imprecate and fling endless anathemas. According to the scholarly Lithuanian, the women suddenly restrained themselves "when they curse with *kalalot* (anathemas), which the women are very accustomed to doing, because they cannot revenge themselves physically due to their lack of strength, and start to curse and swear at all other persons who have displeased them in some way".[34]

Even the Jewish chronicles of the Crusades, which exalted the heroism and readiness for martyrdom of German Jewish women, stressed the manner in which they disdainfully rejected "conversion to the faith of the crucified bastard (*talui mamzer*)" and, showing praiseworthy courage and surprising temerity, did not hesitate to shout insults and curses at their Christian aggressors.[35]

Bella, the wife of Mayer and daughter-in-law of Mosè of Würzburg, in her deposition dated 6 March 1476, recalled the women's active participation in the contemptuous ritual allegedly performed in the synagogue of Trent during the child murder committed the year before.

The same Bella, together with Brunetta, Samuele of Nuremberg's wife, and Anna, his daughter-in-law, Brünnlein, Angelo da Verona's mother, Anna, Maestro Tobias's first wife, now deceased, all appeared at the threshold of the synagogue during the ceremonies to see the child's body, which lay stretched out on the *almemor*. They then enthusiastically joined the ritual of imprecations, spontaneously begun by the men, waving their arms and shaking their heads as a sign of censure and spitting on the ground.[36]

These acts were accompanied by the ever-present scurrilous gesture of "doing the fig", which was exalted and almost sanctified by the fact that it was being performed in a place of worship, whether a synagogue or a church. It is not, therefore, surprising that the display of those contemptuous gestures was one of the charges brought by the Holy Office of Venice against the elderly Elena Freschi (Fritschke), survivor of a poorly digested conversion to Christianity. According to the testimony of the Venetian patriarch Donna Paola Marcello, in fact, that Sunday, during Mass in the church of San Marcuola, just as the priest had started reciting the Credo, the arrogant Paduan convert "got very angry and made ugly faces and said bad words, and, among other things, I heard her say: 'You're lying through your teeth'. And I saw her 'do the fig' towards the altar where the priest was saying Mass".[37] The clash of religions therefore occurred on several different levels simultaneously, passing from ideological diatribe, with scholarly and religious features, to sneering and curses, accompanied by codified gestures of proven and obvious effectiveness, with obscene and insolent meanings.

* * *

NOTES TO CHAPTER FOURTEEN

[1] "Samuel fecit quandam predicationem et dixit non esse verum quod Iesus Christus fuisset ex vergine natus, sed quod eius mater,

videlicet beata virgo Maria, fuerat meretrix et adultera et Christus ex adultera natus et quod fuerat exginta tempore quo menstrua patiebatur" ["Samuele declared that it was not true that Jesus Christ was born of a virgin, but that His mother, i.e., the Virgin Mary, was a whore and an adulteress and that Christ was born of an adulteress and that He was conceived while she was having her menstrual period"] (Archivio di Stato di Trento, Archivio Principesco Arcivescovile, sez.lat., capsa 69, n. 163).

[2] In this regard, see R. Di Segni, *Due nuove fonti sulle "Toledot Jeshu"*, in "La Rassegna Mensile di Israel", LV (1989), pp. 131-132. The author stresses that "the importance of the information inferred from the Trent trial lies in the fact that, for the moment, it is the oldest source which explicitly considers Jesus to be the son of a menstruating woman" and records, as "worthy of note, the German origin of the narrator, which could cause one to assume that the information is of the same origin as well". It seems implicit that Riccardo Di Segni does not consider the tale of Samuele of Nuremberg's anti-Christian sermon as the fruit of suggestive pressures of the Trent judges upon the accused, but he places it in relationship with the reasons for the anti-Christian polemic present in contemporary Ashkenazi Judaism with peculiar sociocultural characteristics. On the story of Jesus the "bastard, son of a menstruating woman" in the *Toledot Yeshu* and on its importance, see Id., *Il Vangelo del Ghetto. Le "storie di Gesù": leggende e documenti della tradizione medievale ebraica*, Rome, 1985, pp. 120-123.

[3] The defendants were required to respond in relation to the "verba scripta in dicto libro Mazor (*recte: Machazor*, the liturgical form for the feasts) sibi ostensa in capitulo quod incipit: *Anni, anni amezaber* (recte: *anì, anìha-medabber*), videlicet in lingua latina: Io sonno quello che parla" (cfr. A. Antoniazzi Villa, *Un processo contro gli ebrei nella Milano del 1488*, Milan, 1986, pp. 132-135).

[4] *Machazor le-yamim noraim le-fì minhage' bene' Ashkenaz* ("Handbook of solemnities according to the custom of the German Jews"). II: *Yom Kippur*, by E.D. Goldshmidt, Jerusalem, 1970, pp. 555-557.

[5] On the Ashkenazi name Frishke, Fritschke, Frits, Fritse, Fridman, rendered into Italian as "Freschi" or "de Frigiis". See A. Beider, *A Dictionary of Ashkenazic Given Names*, Bergenfield (N.J.), 2001, p. 315.

[6] On the personage of Maestro Lazzaro di Raffaele Freschi, his conversion to Christianity and his anti-Jewish activity at Venice, see S. Franco, *Ricerche su Lazzaro ebreo de Frigeis, medico insigne ed amico di Andre Vesal*, in "La Rassegna Mensile di Israel", XV (1949), pp.

495-515; F. Piovan, *Nuovi documenti sul medico ebreo Lazzaro "de Frigeis"*, *collaboratore di Andrea Vesalio*, in "Quaderni per la storia dell'Università di Padova", XXI (1988), pp. 67-74; D. Carpi, *Alcune nuove considerazioni su Lazzaro di Raphael de Frigiis*, in "Quaderni per la storia dell'Università di Padova", XXX (1997), pp. 218-225.

[7] The trial of the Holy Office at Elena Freschi Olivi is reported and transcribed by P.C. Ioly Zorattini, *Processi del S. Uffizio contro ebrei e giudaizzanti*. I: *1548-1560*, Florence, 1980, pp. 51-52, 151-224. On this case, see also B. Pullan, *The Jews of Europe and the Inquisition of Venice (1550-1670)*, Oxford, 1983, pp. 282-289.

[8] Cfr. Ioly Zorattini, *Processi del S. Uffizio contro ebrei e giudaizzanti*, cit., vol. I, p. 152.

[9] The trial of Aron and Asser before the Inquisition of Venice is transcribed by P.C. Ioly Zorattini, *Processi del S. Uffizio contro ebrei e giudaizzanti*. II: *1561-1570*, Florence, 1982, pp. 17-19, 31-48. In this regard, see also Pullan, *The Jews of Europe and the Inquisition of Venice*, cit., pp. 296-297.

[10] The Hebrew expression *mamzer barbanid* is an obvious corruption of *mamzer bar ha-niddah*, "bastard son of a menstruating woman", and not, as maintained by Ioly Zorattini, "*mamzer barchanit*" (?), "turncoat bastard, deserter" (cfr. Ioly Zorattini, *Processi del S. Uffizio contro ebrei e giudaizzanti*, cit., vol. II, p. 33).

[11] Cfr. ibidem, pp. 33, 46.

[12] Babylonian Talmud, Ghittin, c. 57a.

[13] "Interrogatus si dicunt Iesum Christum damnatum est in inferno et ibi positum est in vase uno pleno stercore et si habent predicta scripta in libris eorum vel aliis scripturis, respondit et dicit quod semel in civitate Romana et tempore papis Sisti audivit predicta verba et vidit predicta in uno quinterncto ct verba ea legit" ["In reply to the question of whether it is said that Jesus Christ is in hell and was placed in a vase full of excrement there and whether such words appeared in their books or other scriptures, he answered and said that he had read the aforementioned words in Rome, in a booklet during the reign of Pope Sixtus"] (cfr. Antoniazzi Villa, *Un processo contro gli ebrei nella Milano del 1488*, cit., p. 102).

[14] Salomone da Como stated "quod comprehendere ipsius quod (Iesu) sit iudicatus in stercore calido" ["that he understood that (Jesus) was being punished in hot excrement"] (cfr. ibidem, pp. 112-114).

[15] Cfr. A.M. Haberman, *Sefer ghezerot Ashkenaz we-Zarf at* ("Book of the Persecutions in Germany and France"), Jerusalem, 1971, p. 36.

[16] Luigi Maria Benetelli, *Le saette di Gionata scagliate a favor*

degli Ebrei, Venice, Antonio Bortoli, 1703, p. 410.

[17] In this regard, see S. Krauss, *Imprecation against the Minim in the Synagogue*, in "The Jewish Quarterly Review", IX (1897), pp. 515-517.

[18] In this regard, see Y. Boksenboim in Azriel Diena, *Sheelot w-teshuvot. Responsa*, by Y. Boksenboim, Tel Aviv, 1977, vol. I, p. 12 note 5, and, more recently, R. Weinstein, *Marriage Rituals Italian Style. A Historical Anthropological Perspective on Early Italian Jews*, Leyden, 2004, pp. 225-226.

[19] In this regard, see P. Burke, *Insulti e bestemmie*, in Id., *Scene di vita quotidiana nell'Italia moderna*, Bari, 1988, pp. 118-138; Id., *L'art de l'insulte en Italie au XVIe et XVIIe siècle*, in J. Delumeau, *Injures et blasphèmes*, Paris, 1989, pp. 249-261.

[20] Leon da Modena, *Historia de' riti hebraici*, Venice, Gio. Calleoni, 1638, pp. 80-81; Giulio Morosini, *Derekh Emunah. Via della fede mostrata agli ebrei*, Roma, Propaganda Fide, 1683, p. 836. On gestural language in Jewish liturgy, see, recently, U. Ehrlich, *The Non-Verbal Language of Jewish Prayer*, Jerusalem, 1999 (in Hebrew).

[21] On the expressions and anti-Christian meanings of the hymn *'Alenu le-shabbeach*, see, most recently, I.J. Yuval's exhaustive treatment in *"Two Nations in Your Womb". Perceptions of Jews and Christians*, Tel Aviv, 2000, pp. 206-216 (in Hebrew).

[22] Morosini, *Derekh Emunah. Via della fede mostrata agli ebrei*, cit., pp. 277-278.

[23] "Samuel stans apud *Almemor* coepit facere ficas in faciem pueri et illud colaphis caedere et in faciem expuere. Moyses antiquus similiter faciebat ficas, quas dum sic faceret, ostendebat dentes, irridendo et Angelus expuendo in faciem pueri, illud colaphis caedebat. Tobias cum manu sinistra coepit capillos pueri et cum caput eiusdem pueri quateret super *Almemor*, tenendo capillos per manum cum alia manu pluries colaphizavit faciem pueri, in illamque expuit. Et Israel, filius Samuelis, tenendo os apertum, emittebat linguam et fecit ficas et Ioff, elevatis pannis, ostendit posteriora et pudibunda [displayed his buttocks and genitals], et Isaac, coquus Angeli, similiter fecit ficas et colaphis cecidit puerum. Et Moyses forensis fecit ficas, et Israel pietor similiter fecit ficas et similiter omnes alii Judaei ibi adstantes fecerunt aliquos actus illusorios [...] et Lazarus fecit ficas et semel cum manu aperto percussit faciem pueri et per capillos cepit puerum et eius caput quassavit". [Approximately: "Samuele, standing near the altar, started to 'do the fig' in the boy's face and then he started to strike him and spit in his face. Moses the Old Man also 'did the fig', and, while he was doing it, he showed his teeth, grimacing, and Angelo spat in the boy's

face, then started striking him. Tobias, with his left hand, held the boy by the hair, holding his hair in his left hand, and with the other hand he started to strike the boy in the face, on the altar, over and over again, and to spit in his face. And Israel, Samuele's son, opened his mouth, stuck out his tongue, 'did the fig' and Joff, raising his hem, displayed his buttocks and genitals [at least, if we assume that "pudibunda" = "filled with shame", feminine nominative or ablative singular, is an obvious translation error for "pudenda" = "genitals", neuter accusative plural; otherwise the sentence makes no sense, either grammatically or in context], and Isacco, Angelo's cook, also 'did the fig' and struck the boy. And Moses did the fig in front of everybody and Israel piously did the same, and so did all the other Jews who were there performed acts of mockery [...] and Lazarus 'did the fig' and struck the boy in the face and held the boy by the hair and shook his head violently"] Deposition of Lazzaro da Serravalle dated 20 November 1475 (cfr. [Benedetto Bonelli], *Dissertazione apologetica sul martirio del beato Simone da Trento nell'anno MCCCCLXXV dagli ebrei ucciso*, Trent, Gianbattista Parone, 1747, p. 119). Peter Burke (*Insulti e bestemmie*, cit., p. 127) maintains that the public exhibition of the private parts was a classical gesture of contempt during the passage of Christ in a procession.

[24] "Quo puero sic stante, Samuel cum dentibus momordit aurem dicti corporis et idem Joff cepit aurem praedicti corporis illam stringendo cum dentibus" [Approximately: "The boy being on the altar, Samuele bit the corpse on the ear with his teeth and Joff did the same, fastening his teeth tightly"] (cfr. [Bonelli], *Dissertazione apologetica*, cit., p. 119).

[25] "Die sequenti post festum Paschae (Anna) vidit corpus illius extensum super *Almemore* et vidit in Synagoga omnes infrascriptos [...] qui colaphis caeciderunt dictum puerum" ["The day after Easter (Anna) saw the body lying on the altar and saw all the above mentioned persons in the synagogue [...] who began to beat the above mentioned boy"] (cfr. [Bonelli], *Dissertazione apologetica*, cit., p. 121).

[26] "Modo possunt esse anni tres vel quatuor et nescit dicere praecise quot anni, fuit interfectus alius puer in domo Samuelis, qui quadam die in vigilia tunc Paschae ipsorum Judaeorum de sero fuit portatus per Tobiam in domum Samuelis [...] Et dicit quod postea die sequenti [...] ipsa Bella vidit corpus dicti pueri in Synagoga prius prandium, hora quo celebrantur officia; quo corpore sic stante omnes suprascripti Judaei et etiam alii Judaei advenae, qui tunc se repererunt in Civitate Tridenti, illuserunt contra corpus dicti pueri [...] illudendo et dicendo illamet verba: Tolle, suspensus, Tluyo, suspensa" (cfr. ibidem, pp. 121-122).

²⁷ "Qui omnes, corpore stante super *Almemore*, illuserunt in dictum corpus, faciendo quasi easdem illusiones, pro ut factum fuit Tridenti in domo Samuelis" ["Everybody ridiculed the body lying on the altar, making jokes..." (cfr. ibidem, p. 141).

²⁸ The text of Hinderbach's letter is reproduced in F. Ghetta, *Fra Bernardino Tomitano da Feltre e gli ebrei di Trento nel 1475*, in "Civis", suppl. 2 (1986), pp. 129-177.

²⁹ The formula recited in the act of whirling the white chickens around the head is as follows: "This is instead of me, it is in my place, this is for my expiation (*kapparah*); this cock shall go to its death while I will proceed towards a happy life with all Israel. Amen". On the rite of the kapparot in the customs of the Ashkenazi Jews, see *Siddur mi-berakhah* ("Correct order of benedictions according to the customs of the German Jews"), Venice, Pietro & Lorenzo Bragadin, 1618, cc. 35-36.

³⁰ Morosini, *Derekh Emunah. Via della fede mostrata agli ebrei*, cit., p. 665.

³¹ Cfr. Benetelli, *Le saette di Gionata scagliate a favor degli Ebrei*, cit., p. 222.

³² Angelo da Verona reported that "omnes dicebant infrascripta verba in lingua Hebraica: *chen icheressù chol hoyveha*, que verba in lingua Latina sonant: così sya consumadi li nostri inimizi" (cfr. A. Esposito e D. Quaglioni, *Processi contro gli ebrei di Trento, 1475-1478*. I: *I processi del 1475*, Padua, 1990, p. 290).

³³ Azriel Diena, *Sheelot w-teshuvot. Responsa*, cit., vol. I, pp. 10-14.

³⁴ *Mizwat nashim melammedah. Precetti da esser imparati dalle donne hebree, composto per Rabbi Biniamin d'Harodono in lingua tedesca, tradotto ora di nuovo dalla detta lingua nella Volgare per Rabbi Giacob Halpron Hebreo a beneficio delle devote matrone & Donne Hebree tementi d'Iddio*, Venice, Giacomo Sarzina, 1615, p. 98.

³⁵ Cfr. Haberman, *Sefer ghezerot Ashkenaz we-Zarf at*, cit., pp. 34, 38-39. For a rather vague discussion of this matter, see S. Goldin, *The Ways of Jewish Martyrdom*, Lod, 2002, pp. 119-121 (in Hebrew).

³⁶ "Et dicit se vidisse dictus corpus ut supra, dum ipsa Bella esset super hostio Synagogae, cum qua etiam aderant Bruneta, uxor Samuelis, Anna, ejus nurus, Bruneta, mater Angeli, et Anna, uxor tunc Tobiae, qua mortua est jam duobus annis vel circa. Quae omnes infrascripte mulieres et ipsa Bella illuserunt contra dictum corpus sic jacens super *Almemore*, ut supra, faciendo ficas et expuendo in terram, admovendo manus et quatiendo capita sua et dicendo praedicta verba" ["...and all the above mentioned women ridiculed the body lying on the

altar, 'doing the fig' and spitting on the ground, waving their arms and violently shaking the boy's head and repeating the above mentioned words"], (cfr. [Bonelli], *Dissertazione apologetica*, cit., pp. 121-122).

[37] Cfr. Ioly Zorattini, *Processi del S. Uffizio contro ebrei e giudaizzanti*, cit., vol. I, pp. 154-155.

CHAPTER FIFTEEN

ISRAEL'S FINAL DEFIANCE

Israel da Brandenburg, the young Saxon painter and miniaturist who arrived at Trent on the occasion of the fateful Passover of 1475 on one of his frequent trips to the cities of the Triveneto region in search of clients, Jews and Christians, was the first to opt for a rapid conversion to Christianity. He had already successfully braved the baptismal waters by the time the interrogations of the principal persons implicated in the child murder of Simon began in late 1475. Wolfgang was given a new name selected for him by Hinderbach, in honor of a saint for whom the prince bishop of Trent showed particular affection.[1] As Wolfgang was to confess at a later time, he had decided to abjure the faith of his fathers simply in the hope of saving his skin.[2] And the circumstances proved him right. Or at least, they proved him right, at first.

    Two months later, by the end of June, upon conclusion of the first phase of the trials, the principle defendants, nine in total, including Samuele da Nuremberg, Angelo da Verona and the physician Tobias da Magdeburg, were condemned to death and executed. The old man Mosè da Würzburg had died in prison before being sentenced to execution. The trials were then all temporarily suspended by order of the Archduke of Austria, Sigismund. A few of the minor defendants, all of them from among the servants to the two principal money lenders and the physician Tobias, were in prison waiting to learn their fate. By contrast, the women of the small community were confined under house arrests in Samuele's house, kept under surveillance by the bishop's gendarmes.

    Giovanni Hinderbach had taken a liking to the young convert, Israel Wolfgang, and had demonstrated his trust in him by admitting him freely to the castle and allowing him to sit at table among his servants and courtiers. But his trust was not entirely disinterested. In the summer of 1475, Wolfgang, the convert painter, was in fact the only Christian in Trent who could read and understand Hebrew. This knowledge was indispensable to the young bishop, who, having confiscated the goods of the condemned, found himself in need of someone capable of deciphering the bank ledgers of the Jews, drawn up, as was normally the case, in Hebrew. The value of the pledges and their ownership by the citizens of Trent or foreigners could only be determined by means of a correct interpretation of the entries appearing in those books. In early June, Hinderbach decided officially to entrust Israel Wolfgang with the paid task of supervising the restitution and redemption of the collateral amassed in the vaults of the Jewish banks.[3] The Saxon painter's new workplace was now the money lending shop formerly owned by the deceased Samuele da Nuremberg. Here, the young Wolfgang spent a great part of his time, working diligently and capably.

But at the same time, Israel Wolfgang had simultaneously decided to use his conversion as a disguise, permitting him more easily to help the Jewish women confined under house arrest, facilitating their escape and expatriation.[4] He secretly informed his influential and powerful protector of these intentions: Salomone da Piove di Sacco, who had allowed Wolfgang to stay in his home as a guest, allowing him to meet his family and learn their secrets. The nearby city of Rovereto, located in the high valley of Lagarina, which belonged to the Republic of Venice and was therefore outside bishop Hinderbach's jurisdiction, had been selected as the general headquarters of the representatives of the Ashkenazi community of the Veneto region for the task of making every effort to obtain the release of those defendants still in prison in Trent, and to invalidate the trials. Salomone Cusi, sent to Rovereto by Salomone da Piove, informed anyone who needed to know of Israel Wolfgang's full preparedness to bring about the prisoners' release, particularly the women, quickly, and without attracting attention.[5] Jacob of Brescia, Jacob di Bonaventura da Riva, and Cressone da Nuremberg, some of the more prominent exponents of the "lobby" gathered at Rovereto, were perfectly well aware of the dangerous mission which the bold young Saxon, camouflaged as a Christian, had voluntarily assumed.

Jacob da Brescia was the brother of Rizzardo, accused of being one of the principal recipients of the blood originating from the Regensburg child murder. The money lender did business at Gavardo, in the Bresciano region, and, in testimony of his authority, in 1467, Milanese officials referred to him as "the Jew who is the head of the other Jews".[6] For more than a decade, from 1475 to 1488, Jacob di Bonaventura da Riva was generally considered the most influential banker at Riva del Garda.[7] Cressone (Gherson) was another highly prominent Ashkenazi Jew. A native of Nuremberg, he had reached Rovereto around 1460, but he had only received authorization from the Doge Nicolò Tron to bring his daughter and the family's movable capital from his native city in 1471.[8] Starting in 1465, a patrician from Rovereto, Delfino Frizzi, had permitted him to live in his palace and to become associated with the Adige river navigation business.[9] In his spare time, Cressone da Nuremberg also worked successfully in the money trade, an activity which often took him to the principal centers of the zone, including Riva del Garda.[10]

In the summer of 1475, the air at Trent was charged with tension. The minds of both Jews and Christians were filled with uncertainty about the fate of the defendants still in prison, as well as concern for the executed defendants' wives and children. Israel Wolfgang and his diligent collaborators were concerned with the total confiscation of all the defendants' property, the redemption of the collateral deposited in their shops, the reimbursement of all sums borrowed – promptly convoyed in Hinderbach's strongboxes. In the meantime, as we have seen, the Dominican Battista de' Giudici, bishop of Ventimiglia, the Pope's delegate commissioner, moved from Rome to Trent to shed light on Simon's murder and to search for errors by the prince bishop, suspected of the trials towards the resulting conclusion. Before Pope Sixtus IV, Salomone da Piove insistently supported the sending of this commissioner to save those defendants still in prison and to muffle the undesirable scandal threatening to overwhelm the other German Jewish communities of northern Italy, jeopardizing delicate interests and laboriously captured positions while irremediably upsetting the political hinterland which had made these interests possible.

In August 1475, on the road to Trent, the commissioner of the Judges was crossing the Veneto with a small retinue of functionaries and collaborators. It seems that they were accompanied by three Jews, who joined them traveling from the region of Padua.[11] Two of these are easily identifiable as Salomone da Piove and Salomone Fürstungar. Perhaps the third was Rizzardo da Regensburg's brother, Jacob da Brescia, returning from Rovereto. Fürstungar, the unscrupulous wheeler-dealer and expert intriguer with a thousand resources and influential and multifarious contacts, was probably identical with one of the most prominent figures in German Jewry, transplanted to the Veneto region. This person was Salomone da Camposampiere, who, together with Salomone da Piove, a friend and colleague, maintained despotic control over the money trade at Padua and the district.[12]

Battista de' Giudici entered Trent in the early part of the month of September, taking up quarters at the Albergo Alla Rosa, in the Via delle Osterie Grandi, from which the Wharf of Buonconsiglio was quite visible. He courteously declined bishop Hinderbach's invitation to be his guest at the castle, probably intending to control his meetings and movements in this way, on the grounds that the inn, although German-owned, was well-known for its appetizing Italian cuisine, a quality particularly appreciated by the Dominican inquisitor, who considered himself a man of good taste, not one disposed to compromise in culinary matters.[13] De' Giudici was escorted by a small retinue, including his assistant Raffaele, a one-eyed notary, blind in one eye, who knew German and could act as an interpreter, and a mysterious priest, old and hunchbacked, who always wore a torn black frock-coat. The Albergo alla Rosa also hosted Salomone Fürstungar, the influential wheeler-dealer who accompanied the apostolic commissioner with prudence and circumspection, meeting him frequently and speaking Italian, without need for an intermediary of any kind.[14]

Israel Wolfgang was now required to respect the delicate and dangerous commitments which he had voluntarily assumed. The young Saxon had been duly warned of de' Giudidi's arrival by Salomone da Piove, and knew that Fürstungar would contact him [Wolfgang] immediately.

They met at night, in the stalls of the Albergo alla Rosa, far from prying eyes. Fürstungar informed Wolfgang that Gasparo, assistant to Sigismondo's steward, had procured a safe conduct for him [Wolfgang] to travel to Innsbruck and confer with the Archduke of Austria in order to obtain a definitive suspension of the trials and the release of the imprisoned women. He also asked Wolfgang to make himself available to the apostolic commissioner through the one-eyed notary, who knew German, and to deliver secret messages to the women, confined in Samuele da Nuremberg's house, messages to be transmitted to Wolfgang from the general headquarters of the Ashkenazi Jews, set up in Rovereto. The women were reassured, and informed of the good prospects of Wolfgang's mission before Sigismundo and the commissioner's full readiness to do everything possible to obtain their release. Fürstungar entrusted Israel Wolfgang with money for his expenses and trouble.[15]

The next day, it was the one-eyed notary's turn to take the initiative of meeting Israel Wolfgang. The location of the appointment was the "stube" near the fountain behind the Chiesa di San Pietro, a public bath in a discreet area of Trent where the streets were usually empty. The notary informed the young painter that he would soon be called upon to talk with the commissioner and, knowing that Wolfgang could freely enter the rooms of the castle of Buonconsiglio, he asked Wolfgang to spy on Hinderbach's movements and to inform him, the notary, Raffaele, of any rumors going around at the castle relating to the Jews still held in jail as well as on the eventuality of a resumption of the trials.

For his part, Israel Wolfgang warned the one-eyed notary that he intended to continue to avoid the Jews so as not to awaken suspicion, informing him, in the meantime, of what he had succeeded in gleaning from the information floating around. A rumor was current at Trent that the apostolic commissioner was in cahoots with the Jews and proposed to exonerate all those condemned for Simon's murder, and bring about the release of anyone still in prison, including the women. In this regard, Israel Wolfgang knew that Hinderbach was not at all prepared to permit Battista de' Giudici to meet the women for the purpose of interrogating them, and therefore expressed his intention to remove them from house arrest in Samuele's dwelling and throw them in prison, in separate cells.[16]

With his usual circumspection, Salomone Fürstungar, before leaving for Trent on his way back from Innsbruck, had contacted another person, considered a certain friend of the Jewish families. This was Roper, known as Schneider Jud, a German known as the "tailor to the Jews", who had for years frequented their houses and was linked to them through strong ties of solidarity. For these reasons, he was arrested during the first phase of the trials and subjected to torture. But he confessed nothing, obviously because he knew nothing. He had finally been released and remained a friend to the Jews, although with justifiable caution.

We must not, therefore, be surprised that Schneider decided to go to Rovereto to meet the representatives of the Ashkenazi Jews, offering them his assistance. During the meeting, he was informed by Salomone Cusi, Salomone da Piove's delegate, and Cressone da Rovereto of Fürstungar's planned mission before the Archduke Sigismondo. Now Fürstungar now assigned Schneider, directly, with the same tasks as Israel Wolfgang, i.e., first of all, that of keeping contact with the women, and bringing them letters and information.[17]

Israel Wolfgang and Roper Schneider had become the Jewish women's messenger boys, their only precious source of information, the only chink onto external reality. But they had to be careful to avoid discovery. The bishop's soldiers, in fact, occupied Samuele's house, in which the women were confined, guarding the external door. The Saxon painter could easily enter the house, since it contained some of the late banker's collateral, but if he was caught talking to the women he would arouse the gendarmes' justifiable suspicions. The solution was to communicate orally, in the courtyard located at the rear of the house, where the women faced a small balcony overlooking the stall. Any letters sent to them, as well as any letters written in response, by contrast, were exchanged through a chink dug in the surrounding wall.[18]

Sara, Maestro Tobias's widow, and with her, Bella and Anna, were informed by Israel Wolfgang of the commissioner's favorable attitude towards them, as well as his plans to liberate them and the hopes linked to Fürstungar's ambassadorship at Innsbruck. In the letters sent from Rovereto and written in Hebrew, Fürstungar himself, with Jacob of Arco and Cressone, asked the women for detailed information about the conditions of their imprisonment and any coercive methods employed by Hinderbach to make them confess. For his part, Israel Wolfgang was now fully committed, working diligently and enthusiastically in the desperate attempt to free Sara and the other prisoners. The intrepid Saxon painter was thus compelled, despite himself, to neglect the graces of his mistress, Ursula Oberdorfer, a prosperous local beauty with whom he was accustomed to entertain himself concealed at Angelo's tavern, in the San Pietro district. To seal his love, Israel had recently given the young lady, who was, of course, a Christian, a precious silver ring with a valuable stone, obviously taken from Samuele's pledges, which he was supposed to safeguard.[19]

The same apostolic commissioner convened Israel Wolfgang to his room in the inn, in the wee small hours of the morning, under maximum secrecy. All of de' Giudici's collaborators were there: Raffaele, the secretary responsible for drawing up the minutes; the one-eyed notary, who knew German and who acted as a translator, and the hunchbacked priest in a black cassock. Invited under oath to set forth his version of the facts, the young Jew, now nominally a Christian, told of the horrible tortures to which the accused, all innocent, had been subjected during trial, for the purpose of extorting their confessions. Hinderbach and his jailers were accused of orchestrating a colossal injustice accompanied by ignoble machinations, all for profit. The Jews of Trent were said to be the mere victims of a pitiless theorem [theorem = an indicative conditional: if A, then B], intended to demonstrate their guilt at all costs.[20]

Israel Wolfgang was later to admit that he lied to the commissioner, in his effort to be of some assistance to the poor women who were still in prison.[21] Interrupting the painter's "domesticated" report, the one-eyed notary asked him whether he could do something to help the women escape from their involuntary abode.

The response was in the negative. Gendarmes were everywhere and were determined to be effective guards, subjecting Sara and her companions in misfortune to strict supervision.

As early as late September, Salomone Fürstungar returned to

Trent, disillusioned by his meeting with Sigismundo at Innsbruck. The archduke had in fact refused to intervene to free the prisoners and was persuaded that the trials should resume for the purpose of arriving at a final determination of the defendants' guilt or innocence. The path was now free for Hinderbach, who had probably exerted pressure on Sigismundo to obtain a decision of this kind. For his part, Fürstungar, angered by the unexpected failure of his mission, was now resolutely determined to avenge himself upon the implacable bishop of Trent by dispatching him to his Creator, perhaps in the company of his collaborators. And he knew he had a bold assassin at hand, prepared to do the job.

Israel Wolfgang was urgently summoned to the usual meeting place, at night. In the stalls of the "alla Rosa" inn, Fürstungar informed Wolfgang of the negative outcome of the appointment with Sigismundo and asked him to carry out an immediate plan to terminate Hinderbach's existence by poisoning.[22] The poison was to be put in his food while circumventing the many precautions with which the prudent bishop had thought fit to protect his life. The young painter, eager to carry out the new mission entrusted to him, carefully examined Hinderbach's habits at table. All dishes and wine placed on the table were tasted by various persons on three occasions, i.e., by the cook, in the kitchen, by the steward, in putting the dish on the sideboard, and by the waiter, in placing it on table. The poison therefore had to be placed in the food after the last servant had tasted it. Israel Wolfgang said he was capable of choosing the right time, but needed to find the raw material, an effective and lethal poison. Upon his return to the castle at Buonconsiglio, he quickly set to work..[23]

Among the stationary materials in the office, Israel Wolfgang knew there was a box containing materials belonging to a friend and colleague who had recently died, Friar Pietro, a German who had earned his living as a painter, miniaturist, and occasionally as an alchemist. The ingredients used by the monk in preparing his colors were bound to include some solid arsenic. Israel Wolfgang was not mistaken: a respectable chunk of red arsenic, or cinnabar-colored arsenic sulfide, soon found its way into his pockets.

The next night, the Saxon painter hasted to meet Fürstungar again; with justifiable satisfaction, Wolfgang showed him the poison he had obtained. But the astute and expert German go-getter only needed a glance to realize that that Wolfgang's lump of bi-sulfide of arsenic was almost harmless, and would never have troubled the bishop of Trent with anything more serious than a passing belly-ache. At any rate, he offered to supply his young assassin as quickly as possible with good arsenic, capable of poisoning the bishop effectively.[24] But for a variety of reasons, the project, although never formally abandoned, was to take another course, and Israel Wolfgang is not thought to have seen Salomone Fürstungar again.

Battista de' Giudici wasn't discouraged either. Unable to meet the women and other defendants due to Hinderbach's refusal, he concluded that he could do little by remaining at Trent. The hostile and intimidating climate – as he saw it – in which he was compelled to work, actually prevented him from making the desired progress in his inquiry.[25] The failure of Salomone Fürstungar's mission to Sigismundo, of which de' Giudici had been duly informed, was only an obvious prelude to the imminent resumption of the trials, leaving him with very little time in which to work, carrying the dossiers to Rome with only moderate hope that the appeals process might be approved and that the defendants might be released before they suffered the anticipated punishment.

In very late September 1475, less than one month after de' Giudici's arrival in the city, the pontifical commissioner decided to leave Trent and move to Rivereto, outside Hinderbach's jurisdiction. The choice of city seemed a rather delicate one, since Rovereto was known as the established general headquarters of the Ashkenazi Jewish community of northern Italy, actively mobilized some time before, in their efforts to exonerate the accused from any responsibility in Simonino's murder. It was also foreseeable that the bishop would spare no pains in representing the apostolic functionary as being under the thumb of the Jews. And Hinderbach lost no time in stressing the unsuitability of de' Giudici's decision. In a letter to the humanist friend Raffaele Zovenzoni, the bishop of Trent [Hinderbach] noted that the reasons for the commissioner's [de' Giudici's] move to Rovereto were just phony excuses and that the presence of the Jews gathered in the city at that time was highly suspicious.[26]

Before leaving Trent, commissioner de' Giudici sent his one-eyed notary to Israel Wolfgang to inform him, Wolfgang, of his, de' Giudici's intentions and later availability. De' Giudici, who intended to leave for Rome as quickly as possible to confer with the Pope and try to get him to stop the trials, is said to have warned the Saxon convert just in time for Wolfgang to reach Rovereto. In fact, the commissioner wished to take Wolfgang with him to see Sixtus IV, considering Wolfgang's testimony of fundamental importance. At Rome, Israel Wolfgang is also thought to have been assisted financially, as usual, by Fürstungar. In the meantime, Wolfgang was to maintain his contacts with the commissioner and keep him informed of everything going on at Buonconsiglio, sending regular epistolary reports to his protector, Salomone da Piove, who was well able to make best use of them. But the most important recommendation was that Salomone should do everything in his power to enable the women to escape from their enforced confinement in Samuele's home.[27]

With the departure from Trent of Fürstungar, who continued, cautiously and with circumspection, to watch de' Giudici and his retinue in their every move, Israel Wolfgang became the only Jew, although formally converted, left in the city, able to render any assistance to the women and other detainees. He was perfectly aware of the delicate nature of this role. Although he was able to leave Trent without impediment, reaching liberty on other, safer shores, the young painter from Brandenburg was not prepared to abandon the dangerous mission which he had voluntarily assumed. He was certainly not lacking in either courage or recklessness. He is believed to have remained at Trent, engaged in his desperate attempt to save the women defendants, at the risk of his life, to the bitter end.

Immediately upon his arrived at Rovereto, the apostolic commissioner ordered the bishop of Trent to free the prisoners without delay, particularly, the women and children, and he prohibited subjecting them to torture. At the same time, the Jews presented Battista de' Giudice with an appeal disputing the validity of the trials, signed by Jacob da Riva and Jacob da Brescia.[28] They were ready to accept it, instructing Hinderbach to respond to thirteen counts in an indictment accusing him, among other things, of bringing the trials solely to misappropriate the property of the condemned, estimated at twenty thousand florins.

The efforts expended to cause problems for the inquisitorial machinery set up at Trent enjoyed an initial success on 12 October 1475, when Sixtus IV himself, at the request of the Jews gathered at Rovereto, instructed Hinderbach to release the incarcerated women and children, said to be confined in precariously unhealthy conditions, and whom Sixtus believed to be innocent.[29] De' Giudici, for his part, invited Giovanni da Fondo, the notary at the Trent trials, to appear before him to testify as a witness. The notary's refusal was clear and immediate. Giovanni in fact maintained that he feared for his life: the Jews at Rovereto would not hesitate to have him murdered.[30]

In the meantime, Fürstungar, alias Salomone da Composampiero, reaching Val Lagarina together with the apostolic commissioner, abandoned Rovereto immediately to travel to Verona in an attempt to procure the services of Gianmarco Raimondi, one of the best lawyers in the city. Having obtained an appointment, Fürstungar explained to the

Veronese jurist, Raimondi, that, in the cause of the Jews of Trent, he could count on the support of illustrious Roman prelates, and that even the apostolic commissioner himself had only arrived in the area thanks to the considerable financial commitments assumed by the German-origin Jewish community to ensure the commissioner's very appointment before the Pope. Raimondi was offered a fee at the rate of three florins a day to overcome his foreseeable hesitation, but to no avail: Raimondi had no intention at all of taking the case.[31]

At Trent, Israel Wolfgang had an unexpected meeting. Waiting for him one morning under the portico of Samuele's bank, was a German Jew whom Wolfgang had met some time back, in his uncle's house at Erlangen, near Nuremberg. The German Jew told him that he, too, had converted to Christianity, taking the Christian name of Giovanni Pietro by baptismal deed, registered at Mantua, but that he had remained faithful in one way or another to the faith of his fathers. To allay suspicion, he told people that he had been moved to visit Trent by the miracles of little Simon, but had, in reality, been sent by the general headquarters of the German Jews at Rovereto to make contact with Israel Wolfgang. In particular, he had been instructed on his mission in Trent by no less a personage than the usual Salomone da Piove, and with him, Aronne da Castelnoveto.[32] The latter was to be tried and condemned in 1488 for contempt of the Christian religion, together with the other heads of the Ashkenazi community of the Duchy of Milan.[33]

The Mantuan convert known as "Giovanni Pietro" asked Israel Wolfgang to place him in contact with the women detainees and to obtain useful information from them; he moreover wished to obtain first-hand news about the goings-on at Buonconsiglio. Promptly satisfied, he [Giovanni Pietro] was successful in meeting secretly with Brunetta, Samuele of Nuremberg's obstinate widow, and asked her whether she and the other prisoners had been subjected to torture, despite the intimations of the commissioner and the Pope.[34] But there was not much time left – not even to organize one last desperate attempt to arrange for the women's escape and conveyance to safety. The meeting between Israel Wolfgang and Giovanni Pietro da Mantova, the German Jew from Erlangen, was held on 18 October. Two days later, the Trent trials were officially re-opened, on Hinderbach's initiative, with the explicit consent of the court at Innsbruck.

One week after that, Israel Wolfgang was already in trouble, betrayed by Lazzaro da Serravalle and Isacco da Gridel di Vedera, Angelo da Verona's servants, as well as by Mosè da Franconia, teacher of Tobias's children, and Joav da Ansbach, the ignorant scullery boy in Tobias's kitchen, who, tortured and confessing, out of envy or spite, had accused the young Saxon painter of responsibility for little Simon's murder.[35]

Israel Wolfgang was arrested on 26 October while dining at the castle, calmly and with a good appetite, with the bishop's officials and courtiers. Immediately transferred to the prisons of the Buonconsiglio, he was subjected to an exuberant dose of torture to induce him to say whatever he knew or imagined.

The other defendants were condemned and publicly executed between 1 December 1475 and 15 January of the following year. At the foot of the scaffold, Mosè of Franconia and the coarse Joav both converted to the faith in Christ, in the hope of alleviating their own suffering.[36]

Wolfgang was, deliberately, the last to be executed, condemned by Giovanni Hinderbach's tribunal on 19 January 1476.

Offended and feeling betrayed, Hinderbach made no exception of any kind for Wolfgang, and punished him much more harshly than even the principal defendants on trial; his body, cruelly broken on the wheel, was devoured by animals. The young Saxon painter and miniaturist, "who said that he was less than twenty five years old, although he looked at least twenty nine", faced martyrdom without batting an eye, dying a death which, both in his eyes and from the point of view of that German Judaism to which he belonged, he had been taught to court to sanctify the name of God (*'al qiddush ha-Shem*).

His death was accompanied by unflaggingly indecorous anti-Christian grimaces and a scornful profession of polemical faith. The voluntary sacrifice of Israel Wolfgang, the boy from Brandenburg, counter-balanced, or, more exactly, flanked, the involuntary sacrifice of little Simon, in a holy tragedy in which the basic elements of the plot, cruel and bloody, had been composed centuries before, in Hebrew and Yiddish, in German and in Latin, in the valleys washed by the muddy waters of the Rhine and the Main, the Rhône and the Danube, the Adige and the Ticino, where it was said that the god of the rivers claimed their innocent victims every year.

"Yes, I am perfectly persuaded and convinced that killing Christian children and consuming their blood and swallowing it was a good thing [...] If I could obtain the blood of a Christian boy for our Passover feast, of course I would drink it and eat it, if I could do so without attracting too much attention. Know ye that, although I have been baptized, I, Israel, son of Meir, may he rest in peace, a Jew of Brandenburg, intend, and have established in my soul, that I wish to die a true Jew. I had myself baptized when I saw that I had gotten caught, and in doubt that I might be condemned to death, believing that I could avoid it, as actually happened. Know ye, therefore, that I, Israel da Brandenburg, Jew, do not consider anything believed and observed by the Christian religion to be true at all. I believe with an unshakeable faith that the religion of Israel is correct and holy".[37]

But not everything had gone wrong, at least from Israel da Brandenburg's point of view. Not a single week had passed since his arrest before the young Saxon Jew, in his cell, was informed that Hinderbach had finally given in, perhaps in part to counterbalance foreseeable criticism of his decision to reopen the trials, and had consented to release the incarcerated women's children. These were Mosè and Salomone, the children of Verona and of Dolcetta; Seligman, Meir of Würzburg's young boy; Samuele da Nuremberg's daughter-in-law Anna's young boy, still in diapers; and the numerous offspring of the late Tobias, whose four children were named Joske, Mosè, Chaim and David. An envoy from the apostolic commissioner appeared at the castle of Buonconsiglio on 2 November and took delivery of the children, who were later taken to Rovereto and entrusted to the Jews.[38]

Little is known of their fate. Many of them were probably taken back to Germany and adopted by relatives or persons known by them, and seem to have disappeared from the pages of history. Only Mosè and Salomone, Angelo da Verona's children, remained safely in Italy, entrusted to the Ashkenazi community which had worked so actively to obtain their release.[39] Following the confessions of Brunetta, Samuele da Nuremberg's widow, and the other women, followed by their conversion to Christianity, which occurred in January 1477, attempts to return the children to their mothers proved fruitless.[40]

Bella, Anna and Sara, who had, at the time, voluntarily entrusted their children to the Jews of Rovereto – now that they were converted and baptized under the names of Elisabetta, Susanna, and Chiara – wanted them back urgently, ceding to the pressures of those who wished them to have the children baptized. Pope Sixtus IV himself, by a bull of 20 June 1478, addressed to Hinderbach, exhorted him to take all steps to ensure that they might be returned to the recently converted women, together with their dowries; the children were to be baptized. But his attempts in this direction were too late; it was like closing the barn door when the horse has already been stolen.

"We still wish, and we enjoin you to it with the same authority, that you shall use all diligence to ensure that the children of the condemned Jews be returned to their baptized mothers, together with their dowry, wherever that might be found, compelling any opponent or rebel by means of ecclesiastical censure and other means granted by law".[41]

But the last scene of the drama was yet to be enacted. The drama finally concluded with the solemn appearance at the baptismal font of Salomone, the physician Tobias's feeble-minded servant. The poor imbecile, deemed incapable of understanding or consenting, had survived the trial for little Simon's murder because he gave no indication of knowing or remembering anything about it. Now, to mark the occasion of the feeble-minded Salomone's baptism, under the name of Giovanni, in a crowded ceremony in the Chiesa di San Pietro at Trent, it was the common desire of all that he might also recover the light of the intellect.[42] The body of the sainted little martyr Simon was invoked aloud to perform this one last appropriate miracle.

* * *

NOTES TO CHAPTER FIFTEEN

[1] Cfr. D. Rando, *Dai margini la memoria. Johannes Hinderbach (1418-1486)*, Bologna, 2003, p. 398.

[2] The podestà of Trent stated with some uncertainty "quod Wolfgangus asseruit se minorem 25 annis et licet ex aspectu videatur major annorum 28 vel circa" ["that Wolfgang said he was less then 25 years old, but you could see from his face that he was at least 28"]. At an earlier date, on 21 April 1475, a record was made in the trial documents "quod Israel Hebreus, qui ad praesens in carceribus detinetur, occasione q. Simonis interfecti, desiderat effici Christianus et Baptisma suscipere; idcirco praelibatus Reverendissimus Dominus mandavit dictum Israelem de carceribus relaxari pro nunc, ita quod de Castro non exeat, ad hoc ut in fide instrui possit et deinde si visum fuerit Baptizari" [Approximately: "that Israel the Jew, who is presently being held in jail in relation to the killing of Simon, wishes to become a Christian and undergo baptism; for this reason, the Prince Bishop commands him to be released for now, as long as he doesn't leave the castle, so that he might be instructed in the faith, and we therefore consent to his baptism"]. Israel Wolfgang later admitted that he had been baptized to escape condemnation to death, "quare ipse Wolfgangus fecit se baptizare, quia vidit se captum et dubitavit ne condemnaretur ad mortem, credens se illam evadere, ut evasit" (cfr. [Benedetto Bonelli] ["because this Wolfgang caused himself to be baptized because he saw that he had gotten caught and feared he might be sentenced to death, believing he could escape death, which in fact he

did"], *Dissertazione apologetica sul martirio del beato Simone da Trento nell'anno MCCCCLXXV dagli ebrei ucciso*, Trent, Gianbattista Parone, 1747, pp. 138, 140, 147). In this regard, see also G. Divina, *Storia del beato Simone da Trento*, Trent, 1902, vol. II, pp. 78 ss.; R. Po-Chia Hsia, *Trent 1475. A Ritual Murder Trial*, New Haven (Conn.), 1992, pp. 95-96.

[3] On 8 June 1475 it was announced that Hinderbach "praelibatus Reverendissimus Dominus, attento quod non sit aliquis, qui libros Hebraicos dictorum Judaeorum legere sciat, cum supradictis libris nomina omnium qui habent pignora apud Judaeos scripta sint in Hebraicis litteris, nec alius sit qui dictos libros legere valeat, de quo verosimilius confidi possit, quam de suprascripto Israele, nun facto Christiano et nominato Wolfgango, eidem Wolfgango licentiam dedit quod possit exire de Castro etc."] [Approximately: "since His Most Reverend Lordship saw that there was nobody else who could read what was written in the books of the Jews, said books containing notations as to all the pledges held by the Jews, written in Hebrew, and that nobody else who can be trusted is any good at reading them, except for the above mentioned Israel, who has now become a Christian and is called Wolfgang, he gave the said Wolfgang permission to leave the castle, etc."] (cfr. [Bonelli], *Dissertazione apologetica*, cit., p. 140).

[4] Israel Wolfgang confessed to the Trent judges that, taking advantage of his new condition as a Christian, "volebat adjuvare judaeos, si potuisset" ["that he wanted to help the Jews, if possible"] (cfr. ibidem, p. 147).

[5] Cfr. Divina, *Storia del beato Simone da Trento*, cit., vol. II, pp. 87-90.

[6] On Jacob da Brescia, see, in particular, F. Glissenti, *Gli ebrei nel Bresciano al tempo della Dominazione Veneta. Nuove ricerche e studi*, Brescia, 1891, pp. 714; A. Gamba, *Gli ebrei a Brescia nei secoli XV-XVI*, Brescia, 1938, p. 31; F. Chiappa, *Una colonia ebraica in Palazzolo a metà del 1400*, Brescia, 1964, p. 37; Sh. Simonsohn, *The Jews in the Duchy of Milan*, Jerusalem, 1982, vol. I, pp. 433, n. 1013 and 677, n. 1632.

[7] "Iacob Ebreus et socii habitator Ripae", ["Jacob the Jew, and associates, residents of Riva"], or "Iacob Ebreus et socii dantes ad usuram in Rippa" ["Jacob the Jew and his money-lending associates in Riva"], are very often recalled in the advisory orders of Riva del Garda and in the notarial documentation for the years 1475-1488 (cfr. M. Grazioli, *L'arte della lana e dei panni nella Riva veneziana del sec. XV in due documenti dell'Archivio Rivano e Riva veneziano. Le uscite ordinarie*, in "Il Sommolago", III, 1986, n. 1, pp. 109-120; IV, 1987, n.

3, pp. 5-54; M.L. Crosina, *La comunità ebraica di Riva del Garda, sec. XV-XVIII*, Riva del Garda, 1991, pp. 29-35). It is not entirely impossible that Jacob da Arco, of whom we know nothing, may be identical with this Jacob da Riva.

[8] The privilege of the Doge Nicolò Tron, relating to the transfer in 1471 of the daughter of Cressone da Nuremberg to Rovereto, is recalled by R. Po-Chia Hsia, *The Myth of Ritual Murder. Jews and Magic in Reformation Germany*, New Haven (Conn.) – London, 1988, p. 44.

[9] Cfr. G. Boldi, *Gli estimi della città di Rovereto (1449, 1460, 1475, 1490, 1502)*, Rovereto, 1988, pp. XXV, 92, 180, 343. Cressone, who at Rovereto lived in the Frizzi palace "under the Rock", possessed real property in the district.

[10] On Cressone's banking activity, which included patrician families among his clients, such as the Counts of Lodron, see C. Andreolli, *Una ricognizione delle comunità ebraiche nel Trentino tra XVI e XVII secolo*, in "Materiali di lavoro", 1988, n. 1-4, pp. 157-158. On his involvement in the Riva del Garda affairs, see Crosina, *La comunità ebraica di Riva del Garda*, cit., p. 29.

[11] Cfr. Divina, *Storia del beato Simone da Trento*, cit., vol. II, pp. 69-70.

[12] The reasons leading me to accept the proposed identification of Salomone Fürstungar with Salomone da Camposampiero, already advanced by Daniele Nissim (*La risposta di Isacco Vita Cantarini all'accusa di omicidio rituale di Trento*, Padua 1670-1685, in "Studi Trentini di Scienze Storiche", LXXIX, 2000, p. 830), are many, of considerable weight: 1) it seems implausible that a personality of major importance in the panorama of Ashkenazi leadership in the Veneto, like Salomone da Camposampiero, should be quite absent from the documentation relating to the efforts of the Jewish community to save the Trent defendants, in contrast to what happened with his friend and colleague Salomone da Piove; 2) Salomone Fürstungar, whose name does not appear in the documentation on the Jews of Padua having come to light so far, is described in the trial records as a recognized leader of the Paduan Jews, among whom he had been living for some time, so much so as to have a perfect knowledge of Italian, in addition to German (which fits Salomone da Camposampiero perfectly); 3) Fürstungar was able to dress "like a Christian", a privilege enjoyed only by Jewish physicians and bankers, including Salomone da Camposampiero. On Salomone da Camposampiero and his family, cfr. D. Jacoby, *New Evidence on Jewish Bankers in Venice and the Venetian Terraferma (c. 1450-1550)*, in A. Toaff and Sh.

Schwarzfuchs, *The Mediterranean and the Jews. Banking, Finance and International Trade (XIII-XVIII Centuries)*, Ramat Gan, 1989, pp. 160-177; D. Carpi, *L'individuo e la collettività. Saggi di storia degli ebrei a Padova e nel Veneto nell'età del Rinascimento*, Florence, 2002, pp. 61-110.

[13] The inn *alla Rosa*, "a good inn", among the most popular of Trent, located in the district of the German inns beyond the northern gate of San Martino, was managed by the Bavarian family of Michael di Konrad and his son Michael (cfr. E. Fox, *Storia delle osterie trentine*, Trent, 1975, pp. 84-87; S. Luzzi, *Stranieri in città. Presenza tedesca e società urbana a Trento, secoli XV-XVIII*, Bologna, 2003, pp. 229-236).

[14] Cfr. Divina, *Storia del beato Simone da Trento*, cit., vol. II, pp. 73, 86.

[15] Ibidem, pp. 78-79; Po-Chia Hsia, *Trent 1475*, cit., pp. 98-100.

[16] Cfr. Divina, *Storia del beato Simone da Trento*, cit., vol. II, pp. 79-80.

[17] Cfr. ibidem, pp. 87-90. On the interrogation and tortures to which Roper Schneider was subjected, see A. Esposito and D. Quaglioni, *Processi contro gli ebrei di Trento, 1475-1478. I: I processi del 1475*, Padua, 1990, pp. 38-40.

[18] Cfr. Divina, *Storia del beato Simone da Trento*, cit., vol. II, pp. 84-85.

[19] Cfr. [Bonelli], *Dissertazione apologetica*, cit., p. 148; Divina, *Storia del beato Simone da Trento*, cit., vol. II, p. 95.

[20] Cfr. Divina, *Storia del beato Simone da Trento*, cit., vol. II, pp. 81-83.

[21] "Wolfgangus interrogatus a dicto Monoculo (the one-eyed notary), illo Notario interprete D. Commissarii, respondit quod delato sibi juramento [...] nec ipsi, nec alii Judaei interfecerunt dictum puerum [...] et ideo dixit et testificatus est quia ipse Wolfgangus volebat adjuvare Judaeos si potuisset"] (cfr. [Bonelli], *Dissertazione apologetica*, cit., p. 147).

[22] "(Salomon) rogabat ipsum Wolfgangum quod debebat cogitare modum aliquem, per quem posset ulcisci. Et cum ipse Wolfgangus respondisset quod erat contentus quod ulcisceretur, si modo posset, praedictus Salomon dixit sibi Wolfgango quod deberet bene advertere et diligenter considerare castrum, videlicet bene advertere quem modum servabat Reverendissimus Dominus in bibendo; et si aliquo modo idem Reverendissimus Dominus posset venenari et quod bene debeat considerare ista et in reditu ejusdem Salomonis postea referre sibi Salomoni. Cui Salomoni ipse Wolfgangus ita promisit facere"

[Approximately: "(Salomone) told Wolfgang that he should think of some way to get revenge. And when Wolfgang told him he would be happy to get revenge, Salomone told him that he should take great care and study the castle carefully, and see who served His Most Reverend Lordship his drink, and see if there was any way that that he might be poisoned, and that he should think about this, and report back to Salomone later. Which Wolfgang promised to do"] (cfr. ibidem, p. 145). In this regard, see Divina, *Storia del beato Simone da Trento*, cit., vol. II, pp. 127-145; Po-Chia Hsia, *Trent 1475*, cit., pp. 101-102.

[23] "Salomon dixit sibi Wolfgango an posset venenare Reverendissimum D. Episcopum Tridentinum, cui Salomoni ipse Wolfgangus respondit quod praefatus Reverendissimus Dominus faciebat sibi fieri magnas custodias, faciendo sibi facere credentias, et quod ipse Wolfgangus tamen tentaret et videret si posset illum venenare. [...] Wolfgangus cogitaverat de venenando ipsum Reverendissimum Dominum et alios hoc modo, quia volebat conterere dictum venenum et postea se approximare credentiae, super qua deferentur fercula, quae postea deferuntur in mensam Reverendissimi Domini et tentare, si illud venenum poterat proijcere vel in vinum vel in fercula, et hoc interim dum dicta fercula starent super credentieria, pincerna aut aliis ibi existentibus non advertentibus" (cfr. [Bonelli], *Dissertazione apologetica*, cit., p. 146).

[24] "Wolfgangus vidit dictum frustum veneni super disco in Cancellaria et accepit tantum de dicto veneno, quantum esset una avellana, et illud portavit ad dictum Salomonem, qui Salomon respondit quod illud non erat de bono veneno ad interficiendum et quod idem Salomon bene portaret de bono veneno pro interficiendo" (cfr. ibidem, p. 146).

[25] The apostolic commissioner also lamented the true and proper climate of Trent, humid and rainy, which is said to have reduced him to a state of infirmity for three weeks (see Battista de' Giudici, *Apologia Iudaeorum. Invectiva contra Platinam*, by D. Quaglioni, Roma, 1987, pp. 49-59).

[26] In the missive, Hinderbach stressed that "Iudei et quidam doctores qui apud Rovredum, oppidum nobis vicinum, sunt, ubi etiam legatus ille seu commissarius se pretextu adverse valitudinis que illum et suos hic invasit pridem se reduxit" (Esposito and Quaglioni, *Processi*, cit., vol. I, p. 17).

[27] In this regard, see Divina, *Storia del beato Simone da Trento*, cit., vol. II, pp. 93-94.

[28] Cfr. ibidem, pp. 101-104; Esposito e Quaglioni, *Processi*, cit., vol. I, pp. 19-21.

²⁹ "Verum, exponitur nobis pro parte Iudeorum, quod illic adhuc nonnulli pueri et femine, de quorum innocentia nullum dubium esse dicitur, detineantur infirmi, non absque vite, propter infirmitatem huiusmodi, periculo, carcerati. Hortamur in Domino fraternitatem tuam, ut, si carcerati predicti circa eiusdem pegni negocium culpa carent, eosdem relaxare, et operam suam etiam apud ducem ipsum, si necessarium fuerit, in hoc efficaciter impartiri velit, ut pro iustitie debito relaxentur" (cfr. Sh. Simonsohn, *The Apostolic See and the Jews*. III: *Documents, 1464-1521*, Toronto, 1990, p. 1232). See also W.P. Eckert, *Aus den Akten des Trienter Judenprozesses*, in P. Wilpert, *Judentum im Mittelalter*, Berlin, 1966, p. 300.

³⁰ Cfr. Divina, *Storia del beato Simone da Trento*, cit., vol. II, pp. 112-113, n. 6.

³¹ The lawyer, Raimondi, hastened to write to Hinderbach a few days later, on 12 October 1475, informing him of Salomone Fürstungar's report during the meeting. "Nonnulli Judeorum hic commorantium, oblato non parvo pondere auri, patrocinium meum habere quaesierunt et dietim sedulo aureos tres pollicebantur, subjungentes quod apud Summum Pontificem favores plurimos Praelatorum consequebantur et Delegatum Apostolicum impetrasse magna exposita pecunia. Haec et alia verba, quae mihi somnia videbantur, percepi a Salomone, hic commorante". The letter was published by Bonelli (*Dissertazione apologetica*, cit., p. 145) and is reproduced by Divina (*Storia del beato Simone da Trento*, cit., vol. II, p. 105).

³² In this regard, see Divina, *Storia del beato Simone da Trento*, cit., vol. II, pp. 114-117; Po-Chia Hsia, *Trent 1475*, cit., pp. 99-100.

³³ On the 1488 trial of Samuele, a resident of Castelnoveto, and the other German Jews living in the Duchy of Milan, see Simonsohn, *The Jews in the Duchy of Milan*, cit., vol. II, p. 897; A. Antoniazzi Villa, *Un processo contro gli ebrei nella Milano del 1488*, Milan, 1986, pp. 107-108.

³⁴ Cfr. Divina, *Storia del beato Simone da Trento*, cit., vol. II, pp. 116-117.

³⁵ Cfr. ibidem, p. 135.

³⁶ Cfr. ibidem, pp. 57-60.

³⁷ "Quod ipse Wolfgangus tenet et firmiter credit quod sit bene factum interficere pueros christianos et comedere et bibere sanguinem [...] et quod si ipse Wolfgangus posset habere de sanguine pueri christiani in festo Paschae ipsorum Judaeorum, etiam de illo biberet et comederet, dummodo posset illum secrete comedere et bibere; et quod, licet sit baptizatus, tamen intendit et in animo suo statuit velle mori ut

realis Judaeus, et ipse Wolfgangus fecit se baptizare, quia vidit se captum et dubitavit ne condamnaretur ad mortem, credens se illam evadere, ut evasit [...] et ipse Wolfgangus nihil credit de his quae fides Christiana tenet et observat et quod tenet pro firmo quod fides Judaeorum sit justa et sancta" [Approximately: "That Wolfgang held and firmly believed that it was a good thing to kill Christian boys and eat and drink their blood [...] and that if he could obtain the blood of Christian boys during the Jewish Passover feast, he would eat and drink of it, as long as he could eat and drink of it in secrecy; and that it was lawful to be baptized, but that he intended and wished in his soul to die a real Jew, and that he had himself baptized because he saw he had gotten caught and was afraid he'd be condemned to death, and thinking he could get off, which he did [...] and that he didn't believe there was any truth in the Christian faith and that he firmly held that the faith of the Jews was holy and just."] (cfr. [Bonelli], *Dissertazione apologetica*, cit., pp. 147-148).

[38] In this regard, see Divina, *Storia del beato Simone da Trento*, cit., vol. II, p. 110. Battista de' Giudici is said to have been later accused of having delivered the children to the Jews of Rovereto instead of having them baptized ("in quantum tradidit sanguinem innocentem perfidis Iudeis, videlicet infantes illos, qui modo essent Christiani, quorum animae plus valerent quam totus mundus"). Vedi [Bonelli], *Dissertazione apologetica*, cit., p. 132.

[39] The ritual decisions of the well-known rabbi Israel Isserlein of Wiener Neustadt refer to a compromise relating to the sharing of the inheritance of Angelo da Verona (who here appears under the name of Engel mi-Trient) among the orphan children, in a dispute before a rabbinical tribunal, the judges of which were from Treviso, Verona and Padua (Israel Isserlein, *Pesaqim w-ketavim*, Fürth, 1738, c. 17b, par. 102-103). Since Isserlein died in around 1460, it is not possible that the response, obviously linked to a situation later than 1475, can be attributable to him; the response was probably erroneously included among his writings. In this regard, see I.J. Yuval, *Scholars in Their Time. The Religious Leadership of German Jewry in the Late Middle Ages*, Jerusalem, 1984, p. 261. In August of 1498, the brothers, Mosè and Salomone, Angelo's sons, appointed as their procurator Manuele da Rovigo to recover the loans forming part of their father's inheritance (cfr. Simonsohn, *The Jews in the Duchy of Milan*, cit., vol. IV, pp. 2847-2848). It should be noted that Mosè, son of the late Angelo da Verona, was still alive and presumably rather old by the mid-Sixteenth century. He lived at Cremona (cfr. Simonsohn, *The Jews in the Duchy of Milan*, cit., vol. II, pp. 1335, 1357).

[40] On the conversion of the women detained at Trent, see, in particular, [Bonelli], *Dissertazione apologetica*, cit., pp. 158-160; Divina, *Storia del beato Simone da Trento*, cit., vol. II, pp. 204-206.

[41] "Preterea volumus, et eadem tibi auctoritate iniungimus, quod omnem adhibeas diligentiam, ut infantes Iudeorum damnatorum filii, eorum baptizatis matribus, una cum dotibus matrum eorundem, apud quoscumque reperiantur deposite, omnino restituantur; contradictores quoslibet et rebelles per censuram ecclesiasticam, et alia iuris remedia compescendo" (cfr. Simonsohn, *The Apostolic See and the Jews*, cit., pp. 1246-1247). In this regard, see also Eckert, *Trienter Judenprozesses*, cit., p. 300. My text includes Divina's translation of the passage from the Papal bull, Divina (*Storia del beato Simone da Trento*, cit., vol. II, p. 212).

[42] (Comparuit) Joannes Neophytus, alias Salmon in Judaismo denominatus, genua sua humiliter et devote flectens, et manus suas versus eandem capsam, in qua corpus praefati Beati Simonis et Martyris conservatur, tendens [...] in signum contritionis ac votorum suorum Omnipotenti Deo ac Beato Simoni" ["Johann the convert, alias Salomon, his Jewish name, humbly and devoutly (appeared) on bended knee, with his hands extended towards the vault in which the body of the Holy Saint Simon is kept, as a sign of contrition and prayer to the Omnipotent God and Saint Simon"] (cfr. [Bonelli], *Dissertazione apologetica*, cit., pp. 159-160). See also Divina, *Storia del beato Simone da Trento*, cit., vol. II, p. 60.

BIBLIOGRAPHY

MANUSCRIPT SOURCES

Archivio di Stato di Venezia (ASV): *Consiglio dei Dieci.*
Maggior Consiglio, Deliberazioni, Libro Ursa (1415-1454).
Senato Mar.
Collegio, Notariato.
Avogaria di Comun, Raspe: *Avogaria di Comun*, regg. 3660-3700.
Inquisitorato agli Ebrei.
Biblioteca Marciana, Venice: *Mss. italiani.*
Archivio di Stato di Padova (Asp): Consiglio del Comune, Atti Estimo 1418.
Notarile: Giacomo Bono.
Francesco Giusti senior Nicolò Brutto.
Giannantonio da Mirano Francesco Fabrizio.
Luca Talmazzo.
Ambrogio da Rudena Agostino delle Conchelle.
Archivio di Stato di Trento (AST): *Archivio Principesco Vescovile*, sez. lat.

PRINTED SOURCES

Abudarham, Costantinopole, Astruc de Toulon, 1513.
Abudarham ha-shalem, by A.J. Wertheimer, Jerusalem, 1963.
Amira, K. von, *Das Endinger Judenspiel*, Halle, 1883.
Annales Erpherfurtenses, in "Monumenta Germaniae Historica. Scriptores", XVI, Hannover, 1859.
Annales Herbipolenses, in "Monumenta Germaniae Historica. Scriptores", XVI, Hannover, 1859.
Annales Marbacenses, in "Monumenta Germaniae Historica. Scriptores", XVI, Hannover, 1862.
Antoniazzi Villa, A., *Un processo contro gli ebrei nella Milano del 1488*, Milan, 1986.
Aquilino, Raffael, *Trattato pio*, Pesaro, Geronimo Concordia, 1571.
Asher b. Yechiel (Rosh), *Sheelot w-teshuvot. Responsa*,

Costantinopoli, 1517.

Azulay, Chaim Yosef David, *Machzik berakhah*, Leghorn, Castello & Sadun, 1785.

Baal Shem, Eliyahu, *Sefer Toledot Adam* ("Book of the Generations of Man"), Wilhelmsdorf, Zvi Hirsch von Fürth, 1734.

Barbarano, Francesco, *Historia ecclesiastica della città, terriitorio, e diocese di Vicenza*, 6 vol., Vicenza, Cristoforo Rosio, 1652-.[sic]

Bechayeh b. Asher, *Beur 'al ha-Torah* ("Commentary on the Pentatheuch"), Napoli, Azriel Ashkenazi Günzenhauser, 1492.

– *Kad ha-kemach* ("L'anfora della farina"), Venice, Marco Antonio Giustinian, 1546.

Benetelli, Luigi Maria, *Le saette di Gionata scagliate a favor degli Ebrei*, Venice, Antonio Bortoli, 1703.

Beniamino d'Harodono, *Mizwat nashim melammedah. Precetti da esser imparati dalle donne hebree*, Venice, Giacomo Sarzina, 1615.

Benjacov, Avraham, *Ozar ha-segullot* ("Treasure of Secret Cures"), Jerusalem, 1991.

Bernfeld, S., *Sefer ha-dema'ot* ("The Book of Tears"), Berlin, 1924.

Binyamini, Shelomoh, *Refuah chaim we-shalom* ("Medicine, Life and Peace"), Jerusalem, 1998.

Blumenkranz, B., *Les auteurs chrétiens latins au Moyen Age sur les Juifs et le Judaïsme*, Paris, 1963.

Boeninger, L., *La Regula bilingue della scuola dei calzolai tedeschi a Venezza del 1383*, Venice, 2002.

[Bonelli, Benedetto], *Dissertazione apologetica sul martirio del beato Simone da Trento nell'anno MCCCCLXXV dagli ebrei ucciso*, Trent, Gianbattista Parone, 1747.

Boldi, G., *Gli estimi della città di Rovereto (1449, 1460, 1475, 1490, 1502)*, Rovereto, 1988.

Breve informatione del modo di trattare le cause del S. Officio per li molto Reverendi Vicarii della Santa Inquisitione, Modena, Giuliano Cassiani, 1608.

Brompton, Johannes, *Chronicon*, in *Historiae Anglicanae Scriptores*, vol. X, London, Jacob Flesher, 1652.

Bullarium Romanum, 18 vols., Torino, 1852-1872.

Burcardo di Andwil, *Bellum Venetum, Bellum ducis Sigismundi contra Venetos (1487)*, in *Carmina varia*, by M. Welber, Rovereto, 1987.

Buttaroni, S. and Musial, S., *Ritual Murder. Legend in European History*, Crakow – Nuremberg – Frankfurt, 2003.

Capsali, Eliyahu, *Seder Eliyahu Zuta*, by A Shmuelevitz, Sh.

Simonsohn and M. Benayahu, 3 vols., Jerusalem, 1977-1983.

Cardoso, Isac, *Las excelencias da los Hebreos*, Amsterdam, D. De Castro Tartas, 1679.

Colon, Yoseph, *Sheelot w-teshuvot. Responsa*, Venice, Daniel Bomberg, 1519.

– *Responsa and Decisions*, by E. Pines, Jerusalem 1970 (in Hebrew).

Cornaro, Flaminio, *Creta sacra sive de episcopis utriusque ritus graeci et latini in insula Cretae*, 2 vols., Venice, 1755.

Chronica gestorum in partibus Lombardiae et reliquis Italiae, by G. Bonazzi, in *Rerum Italicarum Scriptores*, vol. XXII, t. III, Città di Castello, 1904.

Chronicon Petroburgense, by Th. Stapleton, London, 1894.

David b. Zimra, *Sheelot w-teshuvot. Responsa*, Fürth, 1781.

De Szombathely, M., *Libro delle Riformagioni o Libro dei Consigli (1411-1429)*, Trieste, 1970.

Delaborde, H.P., *Œuvres de Rigord et Guillaume le Breton*, Paris, 1882.

Di Segni, R., *Il Vangelo del Ghetto. Le "storie di Gesù": leggende e documenti della tradizione medievale ebraica*, Rome, 1985.

Diena Azriel, *Sheelot w-teshuvot. Responsa*, by Y. Boksenboim, 2 vols., Tel Aviv, 1977.

Divina, G., *Storia del beato Simone da Trento*, 2 vols., Trent, 1902.

Esposito, A and Quaglioni, D., *Processi contro gli ebrei di Trento (1475-1478)*. I: *I processi del 1475*, Padua, 1990.

Ferretti, Francesco Maria (Sabbato Naccamù), *Le verità della fede cristiana svelate alla Sinagoga*, Venice, Carlo Pecora, 1741.

Germania Judaica. III: *1350-1519*, t. I, Tübingen, 1987.

Giorgio Sommariva da Verona, Martyrium Sebastiani Novelli trucidati a perfidis Judaeis, Treviso, Bernardino Celario de Luere, 12 May 1480.

Ginzberg, L., *The Legends of the Jews*, 2 vols., Philadelphia (Pa.), 1946.

Giudici, Battista de', *Apologia Iudaeorum. Invectiva contra Platinam*, by D. Quaglioni, Rome, 1987.

Goldshmidt, E.D., *Haggadah shel Pesach*, Jerusalem, 1969.

Grayzel S., *The Church and the Jews in the XIIth Century*, Philadelphia (Pa.), 1933.

Grodzinski, H.O., *Sheelot w-teshuvot Achiezer. Responsa*, New York, 1946.

Guarinoni, Ippolito, *Triumph Cron Marter und Grabschrift des*

Heilig-Unschuldigen, Innsbruck, Michael Wagner, 1642.

Guidetti, C., *Pro Judaeis. Riflessioni e documenti*, Turin, 1884.

Haberman, AM., *Sefer Zechirah. Selichot we-qinot le-Rabbi Efraim b. Ya'akov* ("Book of Memory. Prayers and Elegies of Rabbi Efraim of Bonn"), Jerusalem, 1970.

– *Sefer ghezerot Ashkenaz we-Zarfat* ("Book of the Persecutions in Germany and France"), Jerusalem, 1971.

Haggadah di Pesach, by R Bonfil, Milan, 1962.

Ha-Cohen, Aharon b. Yaakov, *Orchot Chayim* ("The Paths of Life"), Berlin, 1902.

Ha-Cohen, Yoseph, *Sefer 'Emeq Ha-Bakha* (The Vale of Tears), with the Chronicle of the Anonymous Collector, by K. Almbladh, Uppsala, 1981.

Haggadat ha-midrash ha-mevoar. Haggadah shel Pesach, by Z. Steinberger, P. Barzel and A.Z. Brilant, Jerusalem, 1998.

Haggadah shel Pesach, Prague, Ghershom Cohen, 1526 (in Hebrew).

Haggadah shel Pesach, Mantua, Giacomo Rufinelli, 1560.

Haggadah shel Pesach, Mantua, Ya'akov Shalit Ashkenazi, 1568.

Haggadah shel Pesach, Venice, Giovanni De Gara, 1609.

Ha-Gozer, Yaakov, *Zichron berit ha-rishonim* ("On Circumcision"), by Y. Glassberg, Berlin-Kracow, 1892.

Halpern, I., *Constitutiones Congressus Generalis Judaeorum Moraviensium (1650-1748)*, Jerusalem, 1953 (in Hebrew and Yiddish).

Historiae Memorabiles, by E. Kleinschmidt, Köln, 1974.

Historia Monasterii S. Petri Gloucestriae, by W.H. Hart, in *Rerum Brit. Medii Aevi. Scriptores*, London, 1863.

Hugh Schonfield, J., *Toledot Yeshu According to the Hebrews*, London, 1937.

Hutner, J., *Quattro responsi rituali relativi ad un rabbino che aveva emesso un interdetto religioso che colpiva colui che lo aveva defraudato*, in *Memorial Volume in Honor of Rabbi J.B. Zolti*, Jerusalem, 1987 (in Hebrew).

Ioly Zorattini, P.C., *Processi del S. Uffizio contro ebrei e giudaizzanti*. I: *1548-1560*; II: *1561-1570*, Florence, 1980-1982.

Isserlein, Israel, *Pesaqim w-ketavim* ("Decisions and Writings"), Fürth, 1738.

Izchak b. Avraham, *Sefer ha-eshkol. Hilkhot milah, yoledot, chole' we-gherim* ("Book of the Precepts of Circumcision, etc."), Halberstadt, 1868.

Izchak b. Moshè, *Or Zarua*, Zhitomir, 1862.

Johannis Vitodurani Chronicon, by G. von Wyss, Ziirich, 1856.

Kasher, M.M., *Haggadah Shelemah*, New York, 1961.

Klein, M., *'Et la-Iedet. Minhagim we-masorot be-'edot Israel* ("Time to Give Birth. Customs and Traditions of the Communities of Israel"), Tel Aviv, 2001.

Krauss, S., *Das Leben Jesu nach jüdischen Quellen*, Berlin, 1902.

Lauffer, J., *Beschreibung helvetischer Geschichte*, Zürich, Conrad Orell, 1706.

Leon da Modena, *Historia degli riti hebraici*, Paris, 1637.

– *Historia de' riti hebraici*, Venice, Gio. Calleoni, 1638.

Levi, Abraham, *Ghinnat veradim. Responsa* ("The Garden of the Roses"), Constantinopole Jonah b. Jaakov, 1715.

Lipschütz, Chaim, *Derekh ha-chaim* ("The Way of the Life"), Sulzbach, Aharon Lippman, 1703.

Machazor le-yamim noraim le-lì minhage' bene' Ashkenaz ("Formulario per le solennità secondo l'uso degli ebrei tedeschi"), by E.D. Goldshmidt, 2 vols., Jerusalem, 1970.

Machazor Vitry, by H Horovitz, Jerusalem, 1963.

Marcus, J.R., *The Jew in the Medieval World. A Source Book (315-1791)*, New York, 1974.

Meir of Rothenburg, *Responsa, Decisions and Customs*, by Y.Z. Kahana, Jerusalem, 1960 (in Hebrew).

Miranda, Chaim Abraham, *Yad neeman*, Salonicco, Nahman, 1804.

Modai, Nissim, *Sha' are' Zedeq* ("The Doors of Justice"), Salonicco, Nahman, 1792.

Morosini, Giulio (Shemuel Nahmias), *Derekh Emunah. Via della fede mostrata agli ebrei*, Rome, Propaganda Fide, 1683.

Mulin Segal, Jacob (Maharil), *Sefer ha-minhagim. The Book of Customs*, by Sh.J. Spitzer, Jerusalem, 1989 (in Hebrew).

Natan b. Yechiel, *Arukh*, Pesaro, G. Soncino, 1517.

Nissim D., Quaglioni, D. and Stock, O., *Simonino 1475. Trento e gli ebrei*, Trent, 2001, CD ROM.

Noiret, H., *Documents inédits pour servir à l'histoire de la domination vénitienne en Crète de 1380 à 1485*, Paris, 1892.

Ohana R., *Sefer mar'eh ha-yeladim* ("The Apparition of the Children"), Jerusalem, 1990.

Oldendorf, Mendele, *Autobiography*, in E. Kupfer, "Di goldene keyt. Periodical for Literature and Social Problems", LVIII (1967), pp. 212-223 (in Yiddish).

Palagi, Chaim, *Mo' ed le-chol chay* ("A Time Established for Every Living Thing"), Smyrna, 1861.

Pinton, P., *Codice Diplomatico Saccense*, Rome, 1894.

Plongiany, Simoner Sacharja, *Sefer Zechirah*, Hamburg, Thomas Rose, 1709.

Reinach, Th., *Textes d'auteurs grecs et romains relatifs au Judaïsme*, Paris, 1895.

Reischer, Jacob, *Shevut Ya'akov. Responsa* ("The Wickedness of Jacob"), Offenbach, Bonaventura de Lannoy, 1719.

Ristretto della vita e martirio di S. Simone fanciullo della città di Trento, Rome, Filippo Neri alle Muratte, 1594.

Roth, C., *The Ritual Murder Libel and the Jews. The Report by Cardinal Lorenzo Ganganelli (Pope Clement XIV)*, London, 1935.

Salfeld, S., *Das Martyrologium des Nuremberg Memorbuches*, Berlin, 1898.

Sanudo, Marin, *I diarii*, by R. Fulin et al., Venice, 1879-1903, vols. II-III.

– *Le vite dei dogi (1423-1474)*, by A. Caracciolo Aricò, 2 vols.; Venice, 1999-2004.

Scotton, I., *Compendio della vita, martirio e miracoli del Beato Lorenzino da Valrovina*, Venice, 1863.

Sefer Ha-Yashar, Fürth, 1768.

Sefer Nizzachon Yashan (Nizzahon Vetus). A Book of Jewish-Christian Polemic, by M. Breuer, Ramat Gan, 1978.

Segre, R., *The Jews in Piedmont*, 3 vols., Jerusalem, 1986-1988.

Shalom of Neustadt, *Decisions and Customs*, by Sh. Spitzer, Jerusalem, 1977 (in Hebrew).

Shanan, A., *Otò ha-ish. Jesus through Jewish Eyes*, Tel Aviv, 1999 (in Hebrew).

Shelomoh di Worms, *Siddur* ("Book of Prayers"), Jerusalem, 1972.

Shemesh, Yuspa, *Minhage' Warmaisa* ("The Customs of Worms"), 2 vols., Jerusalem, 1992.

Shoshanat ha-'amaqim. 'Emeq ha-Punm. Ozar minhagim wehanhagot lechag Purim ("Treasure of the Rituals and Customs of the Feast of *Purim*"), Jerusalem, 2000.

Shulvass, M.A., *Kippur ha-zarot she-'avern be-Italta* ("Compendium of the Tribulations in Italy"), in "Hebrew Union College Annual", XXII (1949), pp. 1-21.

Siddur mi-berakhah ("Order of Benedictions in the Customs of German Jews"), Venice, Pietro & Lorenzo Bragadin, 1618.

Simonsohn, Sh., *The Jews in the Duchy of Milan*, 4 vols., Jerusalem, 1982-1986.

– *The Apostolic See and the Jews. Documents: 1464-1521*, Toronto, 1990.

Sirena, Francesco, *L'arte dello spetiale*, Pavia, G. Ghidini, 1679.

Sonne, I., *Reshimat ghirushim* ("List of Expulsions"), in Id., *Mi-Paolo ha-revi'ì' ad Pius ha-chamishì* ("From Paul IV to Pious V"), Jerusalem, 1954, pp.183-203.

Sperber, D., *Minhage' Israel* ("The Customs of the Jewish People"), Jerusalem, 1991.

Spina, Alphonsus de, *Fortalitium fidei*, Nuremberg, Anton Koberger, 10 October 1485.

Steinschneider, M., *Catalogus librorum hebraeorum in Bibliotheca Bodleiana*, Berlin, 1852-1860.

Stem, M., *Urkundliche Beiträge über die Stellung der Päpste zu den Juden*, 2 vols., Kiel, 1893-1895.

Strack, H.L., *The Jew and Human Sacrifice. Human Blood and Jewish Ritual*, London, 1909.

Suriano, P., *Il trattato di Terra Santa e dell'Oriente*, by G. Golubovich, Milan, 1900.

Susanni, Marquardo, *Tractatus de Judaeis et aliis infidelibus*, Venice, Comin da Trino, 1558.

Talmud Bavli, Ketubot, Vilna, Menachem (Mendele) Man and Simcha Zimel, 1835.

Talmud Bavli, by A. Steinzaltz, Ketubot, Jerusalem, 1988, vol. II.

Talmud Bavli. III: Tractate Ketubos, New York, 2000.

Toaff, A., *The Jews in Umbria*, 3 vols., Leiden, 1993-1994.

Thomas de Cantimpré, *Bonum universale de apibus*, Douay, Baltazar Belleri, 1627.

Urbani, R. and Zazzu, G.N., *The Jews in Genoa*, 2 vols., Leiden, 1999.

Ultraquist Passional, Praga, Jan Camp, 1495.

Waldkirch, Johann Rudolf von, *Gründliche Einleitung zu der Eydgenossischen Bunds- und Staats-Historie*, Basel, Thurneysen, 1721.

Yoseph b. Moshè, Leqet yosher, by J. Freimann, Berlin, 1904.

Ytzhaky, Y., *Amulet and Charm. An Unknown Hebrew Manuscript*, Tel Aviv, 1976 (in Hebrew).

Zaviziano, G.A., *Un raggio di luce. La persecuzione degli ebrei nella storia. Riflessioni*, Corfu, 1891.

ESSAYS AND PAPERS

Abramsky, C., *Two Prague Haggadahs*, Verona, 1978.

Anderson, M.D., *A Saint at Stake. The Strange Death of William of Norwich, 1144*, London, 1964.

Andreolli, C., *Una ricognizione delle comunità ebraiche nel*

Trentino tra XVI e XVII secolo, in "Materiali di lavoro", 1988, nn. 1-4, pp. 151-181.

Antoniazzi Villa, A., *Fonti notarili per la storia degli ebrei nei domini sforzeschi*, in "Libri e documenti", VII (1981), n. 3, pp. 1-11.

– *Appunti sulla polemica antiebraica nel Ducato Sforzesco*, in "Studi di Storia Medioevale e Diplomatica", VII (1983), pp. 119-128.

– *Gli ebrei nel milanese dal Medioevo all'espulsione*, in P. Della Peruta, *Storia illustrata di Milano*, Milan, 1989, pp. 941-959.

Ashtor, E., *A History of the Jews in Moslem Spain*, 2 vols., Jerusalem, 1977 (in Hebrew.).

– *Gli inizi della comunità ebraica a Venezia*, in "La Rassegna Mensile di Israel", XLIV (1978), pp. 683-703.

Assaf, A., *Slavery and the Slave-Trade among the Jews during the Middle Ages (from the Jewish Sources)*, in "Zion", IV (1939), pp. 91-125 (in Hebrew).

Babinger, P., *Ja' aqub-Pascha, ein Leibarzt Mehmeds II, Leben und Schicksale des Maestro Jacopo aus Gaeta*, in "Rivista degli Studi Orientali", XXVI (1951), pp. 87-113.

Baer, Y., *A History of the Jews in Christian Spain*, 2 vols., Philadelphia (Pa.), 1966.

Bashan, E., *Yahadut Marocco 'avarah we-tarbutah* ("The Judaism of Marocco, its Past and its Culture"), Tel Aviv, 2000.

Bauer-Eberhardt, U., *Die Rothschild Miscellanea in Jerusalem: Hauptwerk des Leonardo Bellini*, in "Pantheon", XLII (1984), pp. 229-237.

Baumgarten, E., *Mothers and Children. Jewish Family Life in Medieval Europe*, Princeton (N.J.), 2004.

– *"Remember That Glorious Girl". Jephtaah's Daughter in Medieval Jewish Culture*, in "The Jewish Quarterly Review", XCVII (2007).

Beider, A., *A Dictionary of Ashkenazic Given Names*, Bergenfield (N.J.), 2001.

Ben Shalom, R., *Un'accusa di sangue ad Arles e la missione francescana ad Avignone nel 1453*, in "Zion", LXIII (1998), pp. 396-415 (in Hebrew).

Bergman, Y., *Ha-folklor ha-yehudì* ("Jewish Folklore"), Jerusalem, 1953.

Berman, J., *Medieval Monasticism and the Evolution of Jewish Interpretation to the Story of Jephtah's Daughter*, in "The Jewish Quarterly Review", XCV (2005), pp. 228-256.

Biale, D., *Counter-History and Jewish Polemics against Christianity. The "Sefer Toldot Jeshu" and the "Sefer Zerubavel"*, in

"Jewish Social Studies", VI (1999), pp. 130-150.

Bildhauer, B., *Medieval Blood*, Plymouth, 2006.

Billar, P., *View of Jews from Paris around 1300. Christian or Scientific?*, in D. Wood, *Christianity and Judaism*, Oxford, 1992, pp. 198-205.

Billiani, L., *Dei Toscani ed ebrei prestatori di denaro a Gemona*, Udine, 1895.

Blumenkranz, B., *Juifs et Chrétiens dans le monde occidental (430-1096)*, Paris, 1960.

– *Juden und Judentum in der mittelalterlichen Kunst*, Stuttgart, 1965.

Bonetti, C., *Gli ebrei a Cremona*, Cremona, 1917.

Bonfil, R., *Rabbis and Jewish Communities in Renaissance Italy*, Oxford, 1990.

Braunstein, Ph., *Le commerce du fer à Venise au XVe siècle*, in "Studi Veneziani", VIII (1966), pp. 267-302.

– *Le prêt sur gage à Padoue et dans le Padouan au milieu du XVe siècle*, in G. Cozzi, *Gli ebrei e Venezia (secoli XIV-XVIII)*, Milan, 1987, pp. 651-669.

– *L'événement et la mémoire: regards privés, rapports officiels sur le couronnement romain de Frédéric III*, in "La circulation de nouvelles au Moyen Âge", Société des Historiens Médiévistes de l'Ensegnement Supérieur Public, Publications de la Sorbonne, École Française, Rome, C (1994), pp. 219-229.

Burke, P., *Insulti e bestemmie*, in Id., *Scene di vita quotidiana nell'Italia moderna*, Bari, 1988, pp. 118-138.

– *L'art de l'insulte en Italie au XVIe et XVIIe siècle*, in J. Delumeau, *Injures et blasphèmes*, Paris, 1989, pp. 249-261.

Busi, G., *Il succo dei lavi. Studi sull'umanesimo ebraico*, Bologna, 1992.

Caliò, T., *Un omicidio rituale tra storia e leggenda. Il caso del beato Lorenzino da Marostica*, in "Studi e Materiali di Storia delle Religioni", n.s., 1(1995), n. 19, pp. 55-82.

– *Il "puer a Judaeis necatus". Il ruolo del racconto agiografico nella diffusione dello stereotipo dell'omicidio rituale*, in *Le inquisizioni cristiane e gli ebrei*, "Atti dei Convegni Lincei", CXCI (2003), pp. 471-501.

Cammarata, I. and Rozzo, U., *Il beato Giovannino patrono di Volpedo. Un fanciullo "martire" alla fine del secolo XV*, Volpedo, 1997.

Cammeo, G., *Studi dialettali*, in "Il Vessillo Israelitico", LVII (1909); LVIII (1910); LIX (1911).

Camporesi, P., *Il sugo della vita. Simbolismo e magia del sangue*, Milan, 1988.

Carlebach, E., *The Anti-Christian Element in Early Modern Yiddish Culture*, in "Braun Lectures in the History of the Jews in Prussia", Bar-Ilan University, Ramat Gan, X (2003).

Carpi, D., *The Jews of Padua During the Renaissance (1369-1509)*, doctoral thesis, Jerusalem, 1967 (in Hebrew).

– *Notes on the Life of R. Judah Messer Leon*, in E. Toaff, *Studi sull'ebraismo italiano in memoria di C. Roth*, Rome, 1974, pp. 37-62.

– *Alcune nuove considerazioni su Lazzaro di Raphael de Frigiis*, in "Quaderni per la storia dell'Università di Padova", XXX (1997), pp. 218-225.

– *L'individuo e la collettività. Saggi di storia degli ebrei a Padova e nel Veneto nell'età del Rinascimento*, Florence, 2002.

Castaldini, A., *Mondi paralleli. Ebrei e cristiani nell'Italia padana dal tardo Medioevo all'Età moderna*, Florence, 2004.

Castelli, E., *I banchi-feneratizi ebraici nel mantovano (1386-1808)*, Mantua, 1959.

Chazan, R., *The Blois Incident of 1171. A Study in Jewish Intercommunal Organization*, in "Proceedings of the American Academy for Jewish Research", XXXVI (1968), pp. 13-31.

Chiappa, F., *Una colonia ebraica in Palazzolo a metà del 1400*, Brescia, 1964.

Chiuppani, G., *Gli ebrei a Bassano*, Bassano, 1907.

Ciscato, A., *Gli ebrei in Padova (1300-1800)*, Padua, 1901.

Cluse, C., *Stories of Breaking and Taking the Cross. A Possible Context for the Oxford Incident of 1268*, in "Revue d'Histoire Ecclésiastique", XV (1995), pp. 215-228.

– *"Fabula ineptissima". Die Ritualmordlegende um Adam von Bristol*, in "Aschkenas Zeitschrift für Geschichte und Kultur der Juden", 5 (1995), pp. 293-330.

Cogo, F., *Vita e martirio del Beato Giovannino da Volpedo*, Tortona, 1920.

Cohen, J., *The Persecutions of 1096. From Martyrdom to Martyrology: The Sociocultural Context of the Hebrew Crusade Chronicles*, in "Zion", LIX (1994), pp. 185-195 (in Hebrew).

Colorni, V., *Note per la biografia di alcuni dotti ebrei vissuti a Mantova nel secolo XV*, in "Annuario di Studi Ebraici", I (1935), pp. 169-182.

– *Judaica Minora. Saggi sulla storia dell'ebraismo italiano dall'anttchità all'età moderna*, Milan, 1983.

Concina, E., Parva Jerusalem, in E. Concina, U. Camerino and D.

Calabi, *La città degli ebrei. Il ghetto di Venezia: architettura e urbanistica*, Venice, 1991, pp. 7-41.

Corazzol, G., *Sulla Cronaca dei Sovrani di Venezia ("Divre' hayamim le malke' Wenesiy'ah") di Rabbi Elia Capsali da Candia*, in "Studi Veneziani", XLVII (2004), pp. 313-330.

Cosmacini, G., *Medicina e mondo ebraico. Dalla Bibbia al secolo dei ghetti*, Bari, 2001.

Crosina, M.L., *La comunità ebraica di Riva del Garda (sec. XV-XVIII)*, Riva del Garda, 1991.

Dal Prà, I., *L'immagine di Simonino nell'arte trentina dal XV al XVIII secolo*, in I. Rogger and M. Bellabarba, *Il principe vescovo. Johannes Hinderbach (1465-1486) fra tardo Medioevo e Umanesimo*, Atti del Convegno promosso dalla Biblioteca Comunale di Trento, 2-6 October 1989, Bologna, 1992, pp. 445-481.

Damascelli, A., *Croce, maledizione e redenzione. Un' eco di Purim in Galati 3, 13*, in "Henoch", XXIII (2001), pp. 227-241.

Davide, M., *La comunità ebraica nella Venzone del Quattrocento*, in "Ce fastu?", LXXX (2004), pp. 167-186.

– *Il ruolo economico delle donne nelle comunità ebraiche di Trieste e di Treviso nei secoli XIV e XV*, in "Zakhor. Rivista di storia degli ebrei d'Italia", VII (2004), pp. 193-212.

De Benedetti, C., *Hatikwà: il cammino della speranza. Gli ebrei a Padova*, 2 vol., Padua, 1998.

Di Nola, A., *Antropologia religiosa*, Florence, 1971.

Di Segni, R., *Due nuove fonti sulle "Toledot Jeshu"*, in "La Rassegna Mensile di Israel", LV (1989), pp. 127-132.

Doniach, N.S., *Purim or the Feast of Esther. An Historical Study*, Philadelphia (Pa.), 1933.

Eckert, W.P., *Il beato Simonino negli "Atti" del processo di Trento contro gli ebrei*, in "Studi Trentini di Scienze Storiche", XLIV (1965), pp. 193-221.

– *Aus den Akten des Trienter Judenprozesses*, in P. Wilpert, *Judentum im Mittelalter*, Berlin, 1966, pp. 238-336.

– *Motivi superstiziosi nel processo agli ebrei di Trento*, in I. Rogger and M. Bellabarba, *Il principe vescovo Johannes Hinderbach (1465-1486) fra tardo Medioevo e Umanesimo*, Atti del Convegno promosso dalla Biblioteca Comunale di Trento, 2-6 October 1989, Bologna, 1992, pp. 383-394.

Einbinder, S.L., *Pucellina of Blois. Romantic Myths and Narrative Conventions*, in "Jewish History", XII (1998), pp. 29-46.

Esposito, M., *Un procès contre les Juifs de la Savoie en 1329*, in "Revue Historique", XXXIV (1938), pp. 785-801.

Fleischer, E., *Christian-Jewish Relations in the Middle Ages Distorted*, in "Zion", LIX (1994), pp. 267-316 (in Hebrew).

Flusser D., *The Blood Libel against the Jews According to the Intellectual Perspectives of the Hellenistic Age*, in Id., *Studies on Hellenistic Judaism in Memory of J. Levy*, Jerusalem, 1949, pp. 104-124 (in Hebrew).

– *Moza' 'alilot ha-dam* ("The Origins of the Blood Libel"), in "Mahanaim", CX (1967), pp. 18-21.

Franco, S., *Ricerche su Lazzaro ebreo de Frigeis, medico insigne ed amico di André Vésal*, in "La Rassegna Mensile di Israel", XV (1949), pp. 495-515.

Freimann, A., *Jewish Scribes in Medieval Italy*, in M. Marx, *Alexander Marx Jubilee Volume*, New York, 1950, pp. 231-341.

Fresacher, B., *Anderl von Rinn: Ritualmordkult und Neuorientierung in Judenstein 1945-1995*, Innsbruck, 1996.

Friedmann, A.B., *The Prioress' Tale and Chaucer's Anti-Semitism*, in "Chaucer Review", XIX (1974), pp. 46-54.

Fortis, U., *Venezia ebraica*, Rome, 1982.

Fox, E., *Storia delle osterie trentine*, Trent, 1975.

Fumi, L., *L'Inquisizione Romana e lo Stato di Milano*, in "Archivio Storico Lombardo", XXX (1903), pp. 300-310.

Gamba, A., *Gli ebrei a Brescia nei secoli XV-XVI*, Brescia, 1938.

Gardenal, G., *Ludovico Foscarini e la medicina*, in *Umanesimo e Rinascimento a Firenze e Venezia*, Florence, 1983, pp. 251-263.

Ghetta, F., *Fra Bernardino Tomitano da Feltre e gli ebrei di Trento nel 1475*, in "Civis", suppl. 2 (1986), pp. 129-177.

Ghinzoni, P., *Federico III imperatore a Venezta (dal 19 febbraio 1469)*, in "Archivio Veneto", n.s., XIX (1889), n. 37, pp. 133-144.

Glissenti, F., *Gli ebrei nel Bresciano al tempo della Dominazione Veneta. Saggio storico*, Brescia, 1890.

– *Gli ebrei nel Bresciano al tempo della Dominazione Veneta. Nuove ricerche e studi*, Brescia, 1891.

Ginzburg, C., *Storia notturna. Una decifrazione del sabba*, Turin, 1989.

Goldin, S., *The Ways of Jewish Martyrdom*, Lod, 2002 (in Hebrew).

Goldstein, M., *Jesus in the Jewish Tradition*, New York, 1950.

Grazioli, M., *L'arte della lana e dei panni nella Riva veneziana del sec. XV in due documenti dell'Archivio Rivano e Riva veneziano. Le uscite ordinarie*, in "Il Sommolago", III (1986), n. 1, pp. 109-120; IV (1987), n. 3, pp. 5-54.

Grèzes, H. de, *Saint Vernier (Verny, Werner, Garnier) patron des vignerons en Auvergne, en Bourgogne et en Franche-Comté*, Clermont-Ferrand, 1889.

Gross, A., *Struggling with Tradition. Reservation about Active Martyrdom in the Middle Ages*, Leyden, 2004.

Hattler, F.S., *Katholischer Kindergarten oder Legende für Kinder*, Freiburg, 1806.

Hind, A.M., *Early Italian Engraving*, 2 vols., New York-London, 1938.

Hoffman, L.A., *Covenant of Blood. Circumcision and Gender in Rabbinic Judaism*, Chicago (Ill.), 1996.

Hofmann-Wellenhof, V. von, *Leben und Schriften des Doctor Johannes Hinderbach, Bischofs von Trient (1465-1486)*, in "Zeitschrift des Ferdinandeums für Tirol und Vorarlberg", s. 3, XXXVII (1893), pp. 207-262.

Holmes, C., *The Ritual Murder Accusation in Britain*, in "Ethnic and Ritual Studies", IV (1981), pp. 265-288.

Horowitz, E., *And It Was Reversed. Jews and their Enemies in the Festivities of Purim*, in "Zion", LIX (1994), pp. 129-168 (in Hebrew).

– *The Rite to Be Reckless. On the Perpetation and Interpretation of Purim Violence*, in "Poetics Today", XV (1994), pp. 9-54.

– *Reckless Rites. Purim and the Legacy of Jewish Violence*, Princeton (N.J.), 2006.

Idel, M., *Golem. Jewish Magical and Mystical Traditions on the Artificial Anthropoid*, New York, 1990.

Introvigne, M., *Cattolici, antisemitismo e sangue. Il mito dell'omicidio rituale*, Milano, 2004.

Invernizzi, C., *Gli ebrei a Pavia*, in "Bollettino della Società Pavese di Storia Patria", V (1905), pp. 191-240, 281-319.

Jacob, W., *Christianity through Jewish Eyes*, Cincinnati (O.), 1974.

Jacobs, J., *St. William of Norwich*, in "The Jewish Quarterly Review", IX (1897), pp. 748-755.

Jacoby, D., *On the Status of Jews in the Venetian Colonies in the Middle Ages*, in "Zion", XXVIII (1963), pp. 57-69 (in Hebrew).

– *David Mavrogonato of Candia. Fifteenth Century Jewish Merchant, Intercessor and Spy*, in "Tarbiz", XXXII (1964), pp. 388-402 (in Hebrew).

– *Un agent juif au service de Venise. David Mavrogonato de Candie*, in "Thesaurismata. Bollettino dell'Istituto Ellenico di Studi Bizantini e Post-Bizantini", IX (1972), pp. 68-77.

– *Les juifs à Venise du XIVe au milieu du XVIe siècle*, in H-G. Beck, M. Manoussacas and A Pertusi, *Venezia centro di mediazione tra*

Oriente e Occidente (secoli XV-XVI). Aspetti e problemi, Florence, 1977, vol. II, pp. 163-216.

– *Recherches sur la Mediterranée orientale du XIIe au XVe siècle*, London, 1979.

– *New Evidence on Jewish Bankers in Venice and the Venetian Terraferma (c. 1450-1550)*, in A Toaff and Sh. Schwarzfuchs, *The Mediterranean and the Jews. Banking, Finance and International Trade (XVI-XVIII Centuries)*, Ramat Gan, 1989, pp. 151-178.

Jordan, William C., *The French Monarchy and the Jews. From Philip Augustus to the Last Capetians*, Philadelphia (Pa.), 1989.

– *Jews, Regalian Rights and the Constitution in Medieval France*, in "AJS Review", XXIII (1998), pp. 1-16.

Katz, J., *Hirhurim 'al ha-yachas ben dat le-kalkalah* ("Considerations on the Relation between Religion and Economics"), in M. Ben-Sasson, *Religion and Economy. Connection and Interaction*, Jerusalem, 1995, pp. 33-46 (in Hebrew).

Kedar, B.Z., *The Forcible Baptism of 1096. History and Historiography*, in K. Borchardt and E. Bünz, *Forschungen zur Reichs-, Papst- und Landesgeschichte: Peter Herde zum 65. Geburtstag*, Stuttgart, 1998.

Kofler, G., *La leggenda dell'omicidio rituale di Andrea Oxner di Rinn*, in "Materiali di lavoro", 1988, nos. 1-4, pp. 143-149.

Kracauer, L., *L'affaire des Juifs d'Endingen de 1470. Prétendu meurtre de Chrétiens par des Juifs*, in "La Revue des Études Juives", XVII (1888), pp. 236-245.

Krauss, S., *Imprecation against the Minim in the Synagogue*, in "The Jewish Quarterly Review", IX (1897), pp. 515-517.

– *Die Wiener Geserah vom Jahre 1421*, Vienna, 1920.

Lane, F.C. and Mueller, R.C., *Money and Banking in Medieval and Renaissance Venice. Coins and Moneys of Account*, Baltimore (Md.), 1985.

Langmuir, G.L., *The Knight's Tale of Young Hugh of Lincoln*, in "Speculum", XLVII (1972), pp. 459-482.

– *Thomas of Monmouth. Detector of Ritual Murder*, in "Speculum", LIX (1984), pp. 820-846.

– *Historiographic Crucifixion*, in G. Dehan, *Les Juifs en regard de l'histoire. Mélanges en honneur de Bernard Blumenkranz*, Paris, 1985, pp. 109-127.

– *Toward a Definition of Antisemitism*, Berkeley – Los Angeles (Calif.) Oxford, 1990.

Le Déaut, R., *La nuit pascale*, Rome, 1963.

Legè, V., *Il borgo di Volpedo e il Beato Giovannino Costa*,

Venice, 1921.

Lewis, B., *The Privilege Granted by Mehmed II to his Physician*, in "Bulletin of the School of Oriental and African Studies", XIV (1952), pp. 550-563.

Lowry, M.J.C., *Humanism and Anti-Semitism in Renaissance Venice. The Strange Story of "Decor Puellarum"*, in "La Bibliofilia", LXXXVII (1985), pp. 39-54.

Lucchetta, M., *Benedetto Jew of Ratisbona del fu maestro Josef banchiero pubblico di Venzone*, Udine, 1971.

Luzzati, M., *Ebrei, chiesa locale, principi e popolo. Due episodi di distruzione di immagini sacre alla fine del Quattrocento*, in "Quaderni Storici", XXII (1983), n. 54, pp. 847-877.

– *Dottorati in medicina conferiti a Firenze nel 1472 da Judah Messer Leon da Montecchio a Bonaventura da Terracina e ad Abramo da Montalcino*, in *Medicina e salute nelle Marche dal Rinascimento all'età napoleonica*, in "Atti e memorie", XCVII (1992), pp. 41-53.

Luzzi, S., *Stranieri in città. Presenza tedesca e società urbana a Trento (secoli XV-XVIII)*, Bologna, 2003.

Maffei, E., *Dal reato alla sentenza. Il processo criminale in età comunale*, Rome, 2005.

Malkiel, D.J., *Infanticide in Passover Iconography*, in "Journal of the Warburg and Courtauld Institutes", LVI (1993), pp. 85-99.

Manoussacas, M., *Le recueil de privilèges de la famille juive Mavrogonato de Crète (1464-1642)*, in "Byzantinische Forschungen", XII (1987), pp. 345-366.

Mantovani, G.A., *La comunità ebraica di Crema nel secolo XV e le origini del Monte di Pietà*, in "Nuova Rivista Storica", LIX (1975), pp. 378-406.

Manzini, V., *La superstizione omicida e i sacrifici umani*, Padua, 1930.

Marcus, I.G., *From Politics to Martyrdom. Shifting Paradigms in the Hebrew Narratives of the 1096 Crusade Riots*, in "Prooftexts", II (1982), pp. 40-52.

– *Tikse' yaldut. Chanichah we-limmud ba-chevrah ha-yehudit biyme' ha benaym* ("The Ceremonies of Girlhood. Initiation and Learning in Jewish Society of the Middle Ages"), Jerusalem, 1998.

McCullogh, M., *Jewish Ritual Murder. William of Norwich, Thomas of Monmouth and the Early Dissemination of the Myth*, in "Speculum", LXXII (1997), pp. 109-127.

Menestrina, M., *Gli ebrei a Trento*, in "Tridentum", VI (1903), pp. 304-316, 348-374, 384-411.

Melchiorre, M., *Gli ebrei a Feltre nel Quattrocento. Una storia rimossa*, in G.M. Varannini and RC. Mueller, *Ebrei nella Terraferma veneta del Quattrocento*, Florence, 2005, pp. 85-102.

Mentgen, G., *The Origins of the Blood Libel*, in "Zion", LIX (1994), pp. 341-349 (in Hebrew).

– *Uber den Ursprung der Ritualmordfabel*, in "Aschkenas. Zeitschrift fur Geschichte und Kultur der Juden", IV (1994), pp. 405-416.

Metzger, M., *La Haggadah enluminée*, Leiden, 1973.

Metzger, Th. and Metzger, M., *Jewish Life in the Middle Ages. Illuminated Hebrew Manuscripts of the XIIth to the XVIIIth Centuries*, Freiburg, 1982.

Milano, A., *Glossario dei vocaboli e delle espressioni di origine ebraica in uso nel dialetto giudaico-romanesco*, Florence, 1927.

Minty, M., *Kiddush Ha-Shem in German Christian Eyes in the Middle Ages*, in "Zion", LIX(1999), pp. 266-269 (in Hebrew).

Molinier, A., *Enquête sur un meurtre imputé aux Juifs de Valréas (1247)*, in "Le Cabinet Historique", n.s., II (1883), pp. 121-133.

Mortara Ottolenghi, I., *The Rothschild Miscellany MS 180/51 of the Israel Museum in Jerusalem. Jewish Patrons and Christian Artists*, in "Hebrew Studies", British Library Occasional Papers, 13, London 1991, pp. 149-161.

Mueller, RC., *Les prêteurs juifs de Venise au Moyen Age*, in "Annales Esc", XXX (1975), pp.1277-1302.

– *L'imperialismo monetario veneziano nel Quattrocento*, in "Società e Storia", VIII (1980), pp. 277-297.

– *Guerra monetaria fra Venezia e Milano nel Quattrocento*, in *La Zecca di Milano*, Atti del Convegno, Milan, May 1983, Milan, 1984, pp. 341-355.

– *The Jewish Moneylenders of Late Trecento Venice. A Revisitation*, in "Mediterranean Historical Review", X (1995), pp. 202-217.

Nardello, M., *Il presunto martirio del beato Lorenzino Sossio da Marostica*, in "Archivio Veneto", CIII (1972), pp. 25-45.

– *Il prestito ad usura a Vicenza e la vicenda degli ebrei nei secoli XIV e XV*, in "Odeo Olimpico", XIII-XIV (1977-1978), pp. 69-128.

Narkiss, B., *Medieval Illuminated Haggadot*, in "Ariel", XIV (1966), pp. 35-40.

– *The Passover Haggadah of Venice 1609*, Jerusalem, 1974.

Nirenberg, D., *Communities of Violence. Persecution of Minorities in the Middle Ages*, Princeton (N.J.), 1996.

Nissim, D., *Due viaggi in Palestina*, in "La Rassegna Mensile di Israel", XL (1974), pp. 256-259.

– *Nel quinto centenario delle prime stampe ebraiche (1475-1975)*, in "Atti e Memorie dell'Accademia Patavina di Scienze, Lettere ed Arti", LXXXVII (1975-1976), part III, pp. 43-52.

– *Spigolature di bibliografia ebraica*, in A. Toaff, *Studi sull'ebraismo italiano presentati ad Elio Toaff*, Rome, 1984, pp. 129-155.

– *Il legame tra i processi di Trento contro gli ebrei e la tipografia ebraica di Piove di Sacco del 1475*, in "Annali dell'Istituto Storico Italo-Germanico in Trento", XXV (1999), pp. 669-678.

– *La risposta di Isacco Vita Cantarini all'accusa di omicidio rituale di Trento (Padova 1670-1685)*, in "Studi Trentini di Scienze Storiche", LXXIX (2000), pp. 829-835.

– *Famiglie Rapa e Rapaport nell'Italia settentrionale (sec. XV-XVI). With an appendix from the Rothschild Miscellany*, in A. Piattelli and M. Silvera, *Minhat Yehudà. Saggi sull'ebraismo italiano in memoria di Yehudà Nello Pavoncello*, Rome, 2001, pp. 177-192.

– *I primordi della stampa ebraica nell'Italia settentrionale. Piove di Sacco-Soncino (1469-1496)*, Soncino, 2004.

– *Un "minian" di ebrei ashkenaziti a Venezia negli anni 1465-1480*, in "Italia", XVI (2004), pp. 41-47.

Norsa, P., *Una famiglia di banchieri: la famiglia Norsa (1350-1950)*, Napoli, 1953.

Occhiali da vedere. Arte, scienza e costume attraverso gli occhiali, Carl Zeiss Foundation, Istituto e Museo di Storia della Scienza, Cataloghi di mostre, II, Florence, 1985.

Offenberg, A.K., *How to Define Printing in Hebrew. A Fifteenth-Century List of Goods of a Jewish Traveller and His Wife*, in "The Library", VI s., XVI (1994), pp. 43-49.

Ottolenghi, A., *Per il IV centenario della Scuola Canton. Notizie storiche sui templi veneziani di rito tedesco e su alcuni templi privati con cenni della vita ebraica nei secoli XVI-XIX*, Venice, 1932.

Palme, R., *Sulla storia sociale e giuridica degli ebrei in Tirolo nel Tardo Medioevo e all'inizio dell'età moderna*, in "Materiali di lavoro", 1988, nn. 1-4, pp. 119-130.

Palmer, R., *The "Studio" of Venice and Its Graduates in the Sixteenth Century*, Trieste-Padua, 1983.

Parente, F., *Il confronto ideologico tra l'ebraismo e la Chiesa in Italia*, in "Italia Judaica", I (1983), pp. 303-381.

Parkes, J., *The Conflict of the Church and the Synagogue*, London, 1934.

Pauly, F., *Zur Vita des Werner von Oberwesel. Legende und Wirklichkeit*, in "Archiv für Mittelrheinische Kirchengeschichte", XVI

(1964), pp. 94-109.

Pfaff, F., *Die Kindermorde zu Benzhausen und Waldkirch im Breisgau. Ein Gedicht aus dem Anfang des 16. Jahrhunderts*, in "Alemannia", XXVII (1899), pp. 247-292.

Piovan, F., *Nuovi documenti sul medico ebreo Lazzaro "de Frigeis", collaboratore di Andrea Vesalio*, in "Quaderni per la storia dell'Università di Padova", XXI (1988), pp. 67-74.

Po-Chia Hsia, R., *The Myth of Ritual Murder. Jews and Magic in Reformation Germany*, New Haven (Conn.) – London, 1988.

– *Trent 1475. A Ritual Murder Trial*, New Haven (Conn.), 1992.

Porges, N., *Élie Capsali et sa Chronique de Venise*, in "La Revue des Études Juives", LXXVII (1923), pp. 20-40.

Pullan, B., *Rich and Poor in Renaissance Venice*, Oxford, 1971.

– *The Jews of Europe and the Inquisition of Venice (1550-1670)*, Oxford, 1983.

Quaglioni D., *Propaganda antiebraica e polemiche di Curia*, in M. Miglio, F. Niutta, C. Ranieri and D. Quaglioni, *Un pontificato e una città: Sisto IV (1471-1484)*, Città del Vaticano, 1988, pp. 243-266.

– *I processi contro gli ebrei di Trento (1475-1478)*, in "Materiali di lavoro", 1988, nn.1-4, pp. 131-142.

– *Il processo di Trento nel 1475*, in M. Luzzati, *L'Inquisizione e gli ebrei in Italia*, Bari, 1994, pp. 19-34.

– *Giustizia criminale e cultura giuridica. I giuristi trentini e i processi contro gli ebrei*, in I. Rogger and M. Bellabarba, *Il principe vescovo Johannes Hinderbach (1465-1486) fra tardo Medioevo e Umanesimo*, Bologna, 1992, pp. 395-406.

– *"Orta est disputatio super materia promotionis inter doctores". L'ammissione degli ebrei al dottorato*, in *Gli ebrei e le scienze*, "Micrologus. Natura, scienze e società medievali", IX (2001), pp. 249-267.

Rabinowitz, I., *The Book of the Honeycomb's Flow by Judah Messer Leon*, Ithaca (N.Y.) – London 1983.

Racine, P., *Dal Monte di Pietà alla Cassa di Risparmio: l'esempio piacentino*, in G. Boschiero and B. Molina, *Politiche del credito. Investimento consumo solidarietà*, Asti, 2004, pp. 345-361.

Radzik, S.G., *Portobuffolè*, Florence, 1984.

Ramirez, O., *Les Juifs et le crédit en Savoie au XIVe siècle*, in R Bordone, *Credito e società: le fonti, le tecniche e gli uomini. Secc. XIVXVI*, Asti, 2003, pp. 55-68.

Rando, D., *Dai margini la memoria. Johannes Hinderbach (1418-1486)*, Bologna, 2003.

Resnick, I.M., *On Roots of the Myth of Jewish Male Menses in*

Jacques de Vitry's History of Jerusalem, in "International Rennert Guest Lecture Series", Ramat Gan, Bar-Ilan University, III (1998), pp. 1-27.

Rogger, I. and Bellabarba, M., *Il principe vescovo Johannes Hinderbach (1465-1486) fra tardo Medioevo e Umanesimo*, Atti del Convegno promosso dalla Biblioteca Comunale di Trento (2-6 October 1989), Bologna, 1992.

Rohling, A., *Ein Talmudstelle für rituelle Schächten*, Münster, 1892.

Rohrbacher, F., *Ursula von Lienz: Ein von Juden gemartertes Christenkind*, Brixen, 1905.

Roth, C., *Feast of Purim and the Origins of the Blood Accusations*, in "Speculum", VIII (1933), pp. 520-526.

– *The Illustrated Haggadah*, in "Studies in Bibliography and Booklore", VII (1965), pp. 37-56.

Roth N., *Medieval Jewish Civilization*, New York – London, 2003.

Rubin, M., *Gentile Tales. The Narrative Assault on Late Medieval Jews*, New Haven (Conn.), 1999.

Rubin N., *The Beginning of Life. Rites of Birth, Circumcision and Redemption of the First-Born in the Talmud and Midrash*, Tel Aviv, 1995 (in Hebrew).

Safrai, Sh. and Safrai, Z., *Haggadah of the Sages. The Passover Haggadah*, Jerusalem, 1998 (in Hebrew).

Schreckenberg, H., *Die christlichen "Adversus Judaeos" Texte und ihr literarisches und historisches Umfeld*, Frankfurt a. M. – Bern, 1982.

– *The Jews in Christian Art*, Göttingen, 1996.

Schreiber, H., *Urkundenbuch der Stadt Freiburg im Breisgau*, 2 vols., Freiburg, 1829.

Schroubek, G.R., *Zur Frage der Historizität des Andreas von Rinn*, in "Fenster", XXXVIII (1985), pp. 3766-3774; XXXIX (1986), pp. 3845-3855.

– *The Question of the Historicity on Andrew of Rinn*, in S. Buttaroni and S. Musial, *Ritual Murder. Legend in European History*, Crakow – Nuremberg – Frankfurt, 2003.

Schwarzfuchs, Sh., *De Gênes à Trieste. Le commerce millénaire des cédrats*, in G. Todeschini and P.C. Ioly Zorattini, *Il mondo ebraico. Gli ebrei tra Italia nord-orientale e Impero asburgico dal Medioevo all'età contemporanea*, Pordenone, 1991, pp. 259-286.

– *A History of the Jews in Medieval France*, Tel Aviv, 2001 (in Hebrew).

Scuro, R., *Alcune notizie sulla presenza ebraica a Vicenza nel XV secolo*, in G.M. Varanini and RC. Mueller, *Ebrei nella Terraferma veneta del Quattrocento*, Florence, 2005, pp. 103-121.

Segre, R., *Testimonianze documentarie degli ebrei negli Stati Sabaudi (1297-1398)*, in "Michael", IV (1976), pp. 273-413.

– *Cristiani novelli e medici ebrei a Venezia: storie di Inquisizione tra Quattro e Cinquecento*, in M. Perani, *Una manna buona per Mantova. Man tov le-Man Tovah. Studi in onore di Vittore Colorni per il suo 92° compleanno*, Florence, 2004, pp. 381-400.

Sevenster, J.N., *The Roots of Pagan Antisemitism in the Ancient World*, Leiden, 1975.

Shatzmiller, J., *Did Nicholas Donin Promulgate the Blood Libel?*, in *Studies on the History of the People and Land of Israel Presented to Azriel Shochet*, Haifa, 1978, vol. IV, pp. 175-182 (in Hebrew).

Simon, M., Verus Israel, *Étude sur les relations entre chrétiens et Juifs dans l'Empire romain (135-425)*, Paris, 1964.

Simonsohn, Sh., *The Apostolic See and the Jews. History*, Toronto, 1991.

Sinnacher, A., *Beiträge zur Geschichte der bischöflichen Kirche Säben und Brixen in Tyrol*, Brixen, 1826.

Soloveitchik, H., Pawnbroking. *A Study in the Inter-Relationship between Halakhah, Economic Activity and Communal Self-Image*, Jerusalem, 1985 (in Hebrew).

– *Religious Law and Change. The Medieval Ashkenazic Example*, in "AJS Review", XII (1987), pp. 205-221.

– *Halakhah, Hermeneutics and Martyrdom in Medieval Ashkenaz*, in "The Jewish Quarterly Review", XCIV (2004), pp. 77-108, 278-299.

– *The Jewish Attitude in the High and Late Middle Ages (1000-1500)*, in D. Quaglioni, G. Todeschini and G.M. Varanini, *Credito e usura fra teologia, diritto e amministrazione. Linguaggi a confronto (sec. XII-XVI)*, Rome, 2005, pp. 115-127.

Sonne, I., *From Paul IV to Pius V*, Jerusalem, 1945 (in Hebrew).

Spiegel, Sh., *"In monte Dominus videbitur". The Martyrs of Blois and the Early Accusations of Ritual Murder*, in Mordecai M. Kaplan *Jubilee Volume*, by M. Davis, New York, 1953, pp. 267-287 (in Hebrew).

Me-haggadot ha-'akedah: piyut 'al shechitat Izchak we-techiyato' le-R. Efraim mi-Bonn ("Stories of the Sacrifice of Isaac: A Poetic Composition on the Immolation of Isaac and his Resurrection written by Rabbi Efraim di Bonn"), in M. Marx, *Alexander Marx Jubilee Volume*, New York, 1950, pp. 493-497 (in Hebrew).

– *The Last Trial*, New York, 1967.

Spitzer, Sh., *Das Wiener Judentum bis zur Vertreibung im Jahre*

1421, in "Kairos", II (1977), pp. 134-145.

Stacey, R.C., *From Ritual Crucifixion to Host Desecration. Jews and the Body of Christ*, in "Jewish History", XII (1998), pp. 11-28.

Stahl, A., *The Mint of Venice in the Middle Ages*, Baltimore (Md.), 2000.

Steinberg, I., *The Sexuality of Christ in Renaissance Art and in Modern Oblivion*, New York, 1983.

Stern, M., *Regensburg im Mittelalter. Die israelitische Bevölkerung der deutschen Städte*, Berlin, 1934.

Stow, K.R., *Catholic Thought and Papal Jewry Policy (1555-1593)*, New York, 1977.

– *Jewish Dogs. An Image and Its Interpreters*, Stanford (Calif.), 2006.

Stowasser, O.H., *Zur Geschichte der Wiener Geserah*, in "Vierteljahrschrift für Sozial- und Wirtschaftsgeschichte", XVI (1922), pp. 104118.

Straus, R., *Urkunden und Aktenstücke zur Geschichte der Juden in Regensburg, 1453-1738*, Munich, 1960.

Stuczynski, C.D., *A "Marrano Religion"? The Religious Behavior of the New Christians of Bragança Convicted by the Coimbra Inquisition in the Sixteenth Century (1541-1605)*, doctoral thesis, Ramat Gan, 2005.

Tabori, Y., *Pesach dorot*, Tel Aviv, 1996.

Tirosh-Rothschild, H., *Between Worlds. The Life and Thought of R. David b. Judah Messer Leon*, Albany (N.Y.), 1991.

The Life and Miracles of St. William of Norwich by Thomas of Monmouth, by A. Jessopp and R.M. James, Cambridge, 1896.

Thornton, T.C.G., *The Crucifixion of Haman and the Scandal of the Cross*, in "Journal of Theological Studies", XXXVII (1986), pp. 419-426.

Toaff, A., *Convergenza sul Veneto di banchieri ebrei romani e tedeschi nel tardo Medioevo*, in G. Cozzi, *Gli ebrei e Venezia (secoli XIVXVIII)*, Milan, 1987, pp. 595-613.

– *Il vino e la carne. Una comunità ebraica nel Medioevo*, Bologna, 1989.

– *Migrazioni di ebrei tedeschi attraverso i territori triestini e friulani fra XIV e XV secolo*, in G. Todeschini and P.C. Ioly Zorattini, *Il mondo ebraico. Gli ebrei tra Italia nord-orientale e Impero asburgico dal Medioevo all'Età contemporanea*, Pordenone, 1991, pp. 3-29.

– *Gli insediamenti ashkenaziti nell'Italia settentrionale*, in *Storia d'Italia. Annali*. XI: *Gli ebrei in Italia*, t. I: *Dall'Alto Medioevo all'età dei ghetti*, by C. Vivanti, Torino, 1996, pp. 153-171.

– *Mangiare alla giudia. La cucina ebraica in Italia dal Rinascimento all'età moderna*, Bologna, 2000.
– *Testi ebraici italiani relativi all'usura dalla fine del XV agli esordi del XVII secolo*, in D. Quaglioni, G. Todeschini and G.M. Varanini, *Credito e usura fra teologia, diritto e amministrazione. Linguaggi a confronto (sec. XII-XVI)*, École Française, Rome, 2005, pp. 103-113.

Toch, M., *The Formation of a Diaspora. The Settlement of Jews in the Medieval German Reich*, in "Aschkenas. Zeitschrift für Geschichte und Kultur der Juden", VII (1997), n. 1, pp. 55-78.

Trachtenberg, J., *Jewish Magic and Superstition. A Study in Folk Religion*, Philadelphia (Pa.), 1939.
– *The Devil and the Jews*, Philadelphia (Pa.), 1961.

Traniello, E., *Gli ebrei e le piccole città. Economia e società nel Polesine del Quattrocento*, Rovigo, 2004.

Treue, W., *Ritualmord und Hostienschändung. Untersuchungen zur Judenfeindschaft in Deutschland im Mittelalter und in der frühen Neuzeit*, Berlin, 1989.

Twersky, I., *The Contribution of Italian Sages to Rabbinic Literature*, in "Italia Judaica", I (1983), pp. 383-400.

Unna, A., *Mi-minhage' yahadut Ashkenaz* ("Among the Customs of the Jews of Germany"), in A. Wassertil, *Yalkut minhagim*, Jerusalem, 1976, vol. II, pp. 32-40.

Urbani, Re Zazzu, G., *Ebrei a Genova*, Genoa, 1984.

Varanini, G.M., *Appunti per la storia del prestito e dell'insediamento ebraico a Verona nel Quattrocento*, in G. Cozzi, *Gli ebrei e Venezia (secoli XIV-XVIII)*, Milan, 1987, pp. 615-628.
– *Il comune di Verona, Venezia e gli ebrei nel Quattrocento. Problemi e linee di ricerca*, in Id., *Comuni cittadini e stato regionale. Ricerche sulla Terraferma veneta nel Quattrocento*, Verona, 1992, pp. 279-293.

Varanini, G.M. and Mueller, R.C., *Ebrei nella Terraferma veneta del Quattrocento*, Florence, 2005.

Vauchez, A., *Antisemitismo e canonizzazione popolare: San Werner o Vernier (1287), bambino martire e patrono dei vignaioli*, in S. Boesch.

Gajano and L. Sebastiani, *Culto dei santi, istituzioni e classi sociali in età preindustriale*, L'Aquila, Rome, 1984, pp. 489-508.
– *La santità nel Medioevo*, Bologna, 1989.

Verlinden, Ch., *L'esclavage dans l'Europe médiévale*, 2 vols., Brugge, 1955.
– *A propos de la place des juifs dans l'économie de l'Europe*

occidentale au IXe et Xe siècles. Agobard de Lyon et l'historiographie arabe, in Storia e storiografia. Miscellanea di studi in onore di Dupré-Theseider, Rome, 1974, pp. 21-37.

Volli, G., *Il beato Lorenzino da Marostica, presunta vittima d'un omicidio rituale*, in "La Rassegna Mensile di Israel", XXXIV (1968), pp. 513, 526, 564-569.

Walker, T., *Jewish Views of Jesus*, London, 1974.

Wangrow, Ch., *Haggadah and Woodcut*, New York, 1967.

Weinstein, R., *Marriage Rituals Italtan Style. A Historical Anthropological Perspective on Early Italian Jews*, Leyden, 2004.

Weiss-Rosmarin, T., *Jewish Expressions on Jesus*, New York, 1997.

Wenninger, M.J., *Zur Promotion jüdischer Ärzte durch Kaiser Friedrich III*, in "Aschkenas. Zeitschrift für Geschichte und Kultur der Juden", V (1995), n. 2, pp. 413-424.

Yaari, A., *Hebrew Printers' Marks*, Jerusalem, 1943 (in Hebrew).

Yerushalmi, Y.H., *Haggadah and History*, Philadelphia (Pa.), 1975.

– *Zakhor. Storia ebraica e memoria ebraica*, Parma, 1983.

– *Dalla Corte di Spagna al Ghetto italiano*, Milan, 1991.

Yona, M., *Ha-ovedim be-erez Ashur: yehude' Kurdistan* ("Dispersed in the Land of Assyria: The Jews of Kurdistan"), Jerusalem, 1988.

Yuval, L.J., *Scholars in Their Time. The Religious Leadership of German Jewry in the Late Middle Ages*, Jerusalem, 1984 (in Hebrew).

– *Vengeance and Damnation, Blood and Defamation. From Jewish Martyrdom to Blood Libel Accusations*, in "Zion", LVIII (1993), pp. 33-90 (in Hebrew).

– *"The Lord Will Take Vengeance. Vengeance for His Temple". Historia Sine Ira et Studio*, in "Zion", LIX (1994), pp. 351-414 (in Hebrew).

– *"Two Nations in Your Womb". Perceptions of Jews and Christians*, Tel Aviv, 2000 (in Hebrew).

– *"They Tell Lies. You Ate the Man". Jewish Reactions to Ritual Murder Accusations*, in A. Sapir Abulafia, *Religious Violence Between Christians and Jews*.

Medieval Roots, *Modern Perspectives*, Basingstoke, 2002, pp. 86-106.

Zimmels, H.J., *Magicians, Theologians and Doctors*, London, 1952.

www.ingramcontent.com/pod-product-compliance
Lightning Source LLC
Chambersburg PA
CBHW052010070526
44584CB00016B/1698